KU-481-668

THE LOST DECADE
IRELAND IN THE 1950s

edited by
DERMOT KEOGH, FINBARR O'SHEA
CARMEL QUINLAN

MERCIER PRESS

MERCIER PRESS
Douglas Village, Cork
www.mercierpress.ie

Trade enquiries to COLUMBA MERCIER DISTRIBUTION,
55a Spruce Avenue, Stillorgan Industrial Park, Blackrock, Dublin

© The contributors, 2004

1 85635 418 0

10 9 8 7 6 5 4 3 2 1

Mercier Press receives financial assistance from
The Arts Council/An Chomhairle Ealaíon, Ireland

This book is sold subject to the condition that it shall not, by way of trade or otherwise, be lent, resold, hired out or otherwise circulated without the publisher's prior consent in any form of binding or cover other than that in which it is published and without a similar condition being imposed on the subsequent purchaser.

Printed in Ireland by ColourBooks Ltd

Contents

The Contributors   7

Acknowledgments   10

Introduction: The Vanishing Irish   11
Dermot Keogh

Memory and Forgetting: The Ireland of de Valera and Ó Faoláin   21
John Banville

Reflecting on Ireland in the 1950s   31
Brian Fallon

Leaving the Blaskets 1953: Willing or Enforced Departures?   48
Dermot Keogh

Population Change in the 1950s: A Statistical Review   72
Gerry O'Hanlon

The Vanishing Irish? The Exodus from Ireland in the 1950s   80
Enda Delaney

The Commission on Emigration, 1948–1954   87
Tracey Connolly

Changing the Rules: Why the Failures of the 1950s Forced a
       Transition in Economic Policy-making   105
John Bradley

Aspects of Local Health in Ireland in the 1950s   118
Andrew McCarthy

'Too Fond of Going': Female Emigration and Change for
       Women in Ireland, 1946–1961   135
Caitríona Clear

Before Cadden: Abortion in Mid-Twentieth-Century Ireland   147
Sandra McAvoy

Tourism and the Irish State in the 1950s   164
Irene Furlong

Ireland and the US in the Post-war Period   187
Maurice Fitzgerald

A Great Time to Be in America: The Irish in Post-Second   206
    World War New York City
Linda Dowling Almeida

Inadmissible Departures: Why Did the Emigrant Experience   221
    Feature so Infrequently in the Fiction of the
    Mid-Twentieth Century?
James Ryan

'You want to be a British Paddy?': The Anxiety of Identity in   233
    Post-war Irish Migrant Writing
Liam Harte

'Making Aliya': Irish Jews, the Irish State and Israel   252
Dermot Keogh

Notes   273

Index   298

The Contributors

Linda Dowling Almeida is an adjunct professor with the Ireland House program at New York University. Her most recent publication is *Irish Immigrants to New York City, 1945–1995* (2001) published by Indiana University Press.

John Banville's first book, *Long Lankin*, a collection of short stories and a novella, was published in 1970. His first novel, *Nightspawn*, came out in 1971. Subsequent novels are: *Birchwood* (1974), *Doctor Copernicus* (1976), *Kepler* (1980), *The Newton Letter* (1982), *Mefisto* (1986), *The Book of Evidence* (1989), *Ghosts* (1993), *Athena* (1995), *The Untouchable* (1997), *Eclipse* (2000), *Shroud* (2002). A non-fiction book, *Prague Pictures: Portraits of a City*, was published in 2003.

Dr John Bradley is a research professor at the ESRI in Dublin. His research explores the impact of the Single European Market, Structural Funds, and Economic and Monetary Union on the smaller, less developed peripheral states and regions of the European Union, as well as the transition of former Communist countries of Central and Eastern Europe to EU membership.

Caitríona Clear is a senior lecturer in University College Galway. Her recent book, *Women of the House*, was published by Irish Academic Press in 2000.

Tracey Connolly is a graduate of University College Cork where she completed her PhD on Irish emigration. She is a director of the 'Bridging the Gap' programme which helps disadvantaged students access higher education. She has published work on emigration nationally and internationally.

Enda Delaney is a lecturer in History at Queen's University Belfast. He is the author of *Demography, State and Society: Irish Migration to Britain, 1921–1971* (2000) and *Irish Emigration since 1921* (2002). He is currently working on a book, *The Irish in Postwar Britain*, to be published by Oxford University Press.

Brian Fallon worked for many years as a journalist for the *Irish Times* and served as its Literary Editor 1977–1988 and as Art Critic 1963–1998. He has written several books including *An Age of Innocence: Irish Culture 1930–1960*.

Maurice Fitzgerald is a lecturer in European and International Studies in the Department of Politics, International Relations and European

Studies at Loughborough University. A graduate of University College Cork (BA, 1990, & MPhil, 1997) and the European University Institute, Florence (PhD, 1999), his research interests and publications centre on Ireland's European integration, Irish neutrality, and Irish-American relations.

Irene Furlong graduated from NUI Maynooth as a mature student. In 1999 she was awarded a Government of Ireland scholarship to complete a PhD on the history of tourism in Ireland. Her article 'Frederick W. Crossley – Irish turn-of-the-century tourism pioneer' was published in *Irish History: Research Yearbook 2* (Irish Academic Press, 2003)

Liam Harte lectures in the Academy for Irish Cultural Heritages at the University of Ulster. He is editor, with Michael Parker, of *Contemporary Irish Fiction* (Macmillan, 2000) and, with Yvonne Whelan, of *Ireland Beyond Boundaries: Mapping Irish Studies in the Twenty-First Century* (forthcoming). His essay collection, *Modern Irish Autobiography: Self, Nation and Society*, will be published by Palgrave in 2005.

Dermot Keogh is Head of the Department of History at UCC. His book, *Jews in Twentieth Century Ireland: refugees, anti-semitism and the holocaust* (Cork University Press, 1998), was awarded the 1999 James S. Donnelly Snr Prize by the American Conference for Irish Studies in the history/social science category. His most recent publication is *De Valera's Irelands* (co-edited with Gabriel Doherty), published by Mercier Press, Cork, in 2003. He has also contributed to *A New History of Ireland* (ed. J. R. Hill), published by Oxford University Press in 2004.

Sandra McAvoy teaches on post-graduate and adult education Women's Studies programmes in University College Cork and coordinates the MA in Women's Studies. Her publications include: 'The Regulation of Sexuality in the Irish Free State, 1929–1935', in Elizabeth Malcolm and Greta Jones' 1999 book, *Medicine, Disease and the State in Ireland, 1650–1940* (Cork University Press).

Andrew McCarthy was educated at UCC and the University of Sussex. He completed his PhD thesis on Irish interwar financial history in 1996 and teaches in the History Department in Cork. He is currently working on a Historical Dictionary of Modern Ireland for the Scarecrow Press series.

Gerry O'Hanlon is Director of Social and Demographic Statistics in the Central Statistics Office where his responsibilities include the Census of Population, major household surveys, labour market statistics and consumer prices.

Finbarr O'Shea is a graduate of University College Cork. He was a Government of Ireland scholar and is currently completing his PhD on the Irish state, adoption and children in care in the 1950s.

Carmel Quinlan was a senior HEA Fellow in the Department of History at University College, Cork. She is the author of *Genteel Revolutionaries: Anna and Thomas Haslam, pioneers of Irish feminism* which was published by Cork University Press in 2002.

James Ryan's first novel *Home from England* was published by Phoenix House, London in 1995. *Dismantling Mr Doyle* followed in 1997 and his third novel, *Seeds of Doubt*, was published by Weidenfeld and Nicolson in 2001.

Acknowledgments

This book of essays is the outcome of work done under the University College Cork Department of History's HEA-funded project, PRTLI 1. Entitled 'Culture Contact – Nation and State', the programme of research reviewed aspects of Irish history from the Middle Ages to the Twentieth Century. The work has resulted in a number of articles, monographs, and collections of essays of which *The Lost Decade: Ireland in the 1950s* is the second in a series of five to be published by Mercier Press.

This book, *The Lost Decade*, began as a conference held at University College Cork on 2–3 February 2001. Dr Carmel Quinlan and myself planned the event. We worked very closely with the organisational team of Mr Gabriel Doherty, Ms Eileen Compagno, Dr Emma Cunningham and Dr Diarmuid Scully. The academic and administrative staff (particularly Mary Ring) of the History Department also provided assistance.

Following the conference, that attracted an attendance of over 200 people, papers were commissioned from a number of the speakers. Dr Quinlan and myself also asked a number of academics to write on areas that had not been covered by the speakers. The published volume has eighteen essays covering a range of different academic disciplines.

Mr Finbarr O'Shea, a former HEA scholarship holder, undertook to help prepare the volume for publication. He has earned the right to be an editor. Another former HEA scholarship holder, Ms Margaret Clayton, was of inestimable help at the different stages of editing, giving generously of her time and expertise. I would like to thank both of them very warmly for their help and support.

My thanks to Dr Robert McNamara who located the documents on the Blasket Islands in the National Archives reproduced in this book. The editors are grateful to the National Archives of Ireland for permission to reproduce these documents.

I am grateful to the HEA for providing resources to make the collection of scholarship of this kind possible. I am also grateful to the staff of the Boole Library at UCC for their help in tracking down a number of references and volumes. I am also thankful to Mary Feehan and the ever-helpful staff at Mercier Press, especially Aisling Lyons, for their patience and professionalism.

PROFESSOR DERMOT KEOGH,
Head, Department of History,
University College, Cork.
April, 2004

Introduction: The Vanishing Irish

Dermot Keogh

> You should go there, and don't forget on you way back in the port of Dublin to notice what's exported from Ireland: children and priests, nuns and biscuits, whisky and horses, beer and dogs.[1]

Heinrich Böll, visiting Ireland in the early 1950s, recorded that fragment from a conversation he overheard between a priest and a Connemara woman working in London as a waitress who also stated to him boldly and without remorse that she did not believe in God. Returning on the night mail boat after two years to visit her parents and grandmother, she told him that she would attend mass at home in order not to be so cruel to her father and mother. Her voice spoke from the shadows, only ever appearing in profile in the light of a glowing cigarette. The Connemara woman spoke more out of resigned defiance than as a penitent in the dark of the confessional. The priest called her 'my child' – a phrase she was used to from her home parish. Her grandmother had thirty-eight grandchildren. Two had died in the British forces during the Second World War – one shot down in the Battle of Britain and another going down in a submarine. Only twenty continued to live in Ireland, the rest scattered. She had a brother and two cousins priests – the only ones in the family with cars. She encouraged the priest to visit Connemara. He did not know that part of the country: '… notice what's exported from Ireland: children and priests, nuns and biscuits, whisky and horses, beer and dogs …'

The priest gently remonstrated with her. 'I don't believe in God,' said the light clear voice, 'no I don't believe in God – so why shouldn't I mention priests and whisky, nuns and biscuits, in the same breath? I don't believe in *Kathleen ní Houlihan* either, that fairy-tale Ireland'. She then recalled that the local priest used to cycle to her local parish church to say mass on Sundays.

But even he couldn't stop *Kathleen ní Houlihan* exporting her most precious possession: her children. 'Go to Connemara, Father – I'm sure you've never seen so much lovely scenery, with so few people in it, all at once. Perhaps you can read Mass to us one Sunday, then you'll see me kneeling devoutly in church.'

She went to sleep, still in the shadows.[2]

There were tens of thousands like her who traded the harshness and economic hopelessness of rural Ireland in the 1950s for a job in Britain. She did not appear to be particularly happy. Böll does not record if she was single or married. But the Connemara woman did note what

London had done to many daughters of *Kathleen ní Houlihan* forced to leave the 'Isle of Saints and Scholars'. She referred to them as 'loose' – a word to describe, perhaps, the trade of prostitution. It is not clear whether the Connemara woman herself had been forced through the hopelessness of her situation in London to take that route to survive.

That woman's personal history will probably never be written. Yet she was among the legions that emigrated in the 1950s from a young state that appeared to be unable – unlike all other states in democratic western Europe at the time – to provide work, education and economic security for its citizens.

Being of that generation, I can recall the enforced departures of aunts, uncles and cousins to Britain. They stayed for a few days in our family home in Dublin while arrangements were being made for accommodation in London, Leeds, Luton or Liverpool. Within a few years, cousins were back on holidays. We shared a common culture divided only by the by now strong local English accents.

That was the common experience of most of the poorer families in Ireland of the 1950s. It was a time of enforced departures. Böll again captures that atmosphere when he wrote about 'Mrs D's nine children'. The one certainty was, he wrote, that five or six would have to emigrate at a very early age – fourteen.

Carrying his cardboard suitcase, hung about with medallions, supplied with a package of extra-thick sandwiches, embraced by his sobbing mother, standing at the bus stop to begin the great journey to Cleveland, Ohio, to Manchester, Liverpool, London, or Sydney, to some uncle, a cousin, a brother perhaps, who has promised to look after him and do something for him.[3]

Böll records poignantly the departure of such a fourteen year old:

These farewells at Irish railway stations, at bus stops in the middle of the bog, when tears blend with raindrops and the Atlantic wind is blowing; Grandfather stands there too, he knows the canyons of Manhattan, he knows the New York waterfront, for thirty years he has been through the mill, and he quickly stuffs another pound note into the boy's pocket, the boy with the cropped hair, the runny nose, the boy who is being wept over as Jacob wept over Joseph; the bus driver cautiously sounds his horn, very cautiously – he has driven hundreds, perhaps thousands, of boys whom he has seen grow up to the station, and he knows the train does not wait and that a farewell that is over and done with is easier to bear than one which is still to come. He waves, the journey into the lonely countryside begins, the little white house in the bog, tears mixed with mucus, past the store, past the pub where Father used to drink his pint of an evening; past the school, the church, a sign of the cross, the bus driver makes one too – the bus stops, more tears, more farewells; Michael is leaving too, and Sheila, tears, tears – Irish, Polish, Armenian tears …

The journey by bus and train from here to Dublin takes eight hours, and what is picked up on the way, the ones standing in the corridors of overcrowded trains with cardboard boxes, battered suitcases, or duffel bags, girls with a rosary still wound around their hands, boys with marbles still clinking in their pockets – this freight is only a small part, only a few hundred of the more than forty thousand who leave this country every year: labourers and doctors, nurses, household help, and teachers – Irish tears that will blend with polish and Italian tears in London, Manhattan, Cleveland, Liverpool, or Sydney.[4]

Dónall MacAmhlaigh, in Valentin Iremonger's translation of *An Irish Navvy*, has left a portrait of one man's journey into emigration in Britain. This is the dominant narrative of the 1950s, tracking the departure of Irish male emigrants. Having left the Irish army in 1951, he returned to his family home in Kilkenny. [His family was from the west of Ireland and had been living in Kilkenny for ten years.] Having been idle for three months, he sought and secured work in the English midlands – as a stoker in a hospital in Northampton. 'You could give it a chance,' his mother told him, 'for surely God put it in your way'. But when news of the job was confirmed by letter, 'both of us got very melancholy, think how I'd be leaving home and going foreign'. But in order to celebrate the occasion, she bravely sent one of the children for sweet cake. As she made the tea, MacAmhlaigh saw that 'her eyes were brimming with tears.'

Immediately he set about the job of getting his documents in order. He had a passport photograph taken and then he went to 'fill up forms at the police station so that I could get an identity card'. With that done, he wrote to the matron and filled in his days waiting by digging the garden. But it was too early to plant. He had signed on at the 'Labour'. For the rest of the time he visited areas around his home, regretting that 'it was a pity, in a way, that I only got to like the place just as I was about to leave it'. He walked to nearby Callan with a veteran of the Connaught Rangers, named Mick Hogan. They could hear around them 'the rough voices of the crows ... raucously chattering to each other with, occasionally, the sweet music of the blackbird as it welcomed such a good day'. The 'mild country air was like a tonic'. But the evening ended in sadness. He was leaving his friend, Old Mick, 'thinking that maybe I'd never see him again now that I was off to England'. As the time for leaving drew nearer 'I could feel the talons of despair twining and untwining inside me'. MacAmhlaigh wrote:

> I knew that I'd miss the small ordinary things that I had been used to for so long: the company and the kind chat with the lads down at the corner every night; the good-fellowship and the gaiety of the poor people in the 'fourpennies' at the pictures on pay-night; and the excellence of the pints

in Larry's pub after closing time. I knew I'd be lonesome too for the sprees and the fun we used to have in our own house from time to time. My sister and two of my brothers were home at that time; my father and another brother were in the army – one in Cork, the other in Dublin. A garrulous family we were and whatever there was to eat on the table, you can be sure that was flavoured with memorable conversation.

As the day approached for him to leave, he made sure that all the jobs were completed, the garden planted and the house spruced up a bit on the outside. On 12 March 1951, he 'signed on' for the last time, carried a hundredweight of coal home for his mother, put his personal papers in order and went around saying goodbye to the neighbours. 'It would be hard to surpass them,' he wrote. His mother kept up her courage until it was time for him to set off: 'The tears came then. I didn't delay too long bidding her goodbye. I hugged her once, grabbed my bag and off with me. Indeed, you'd think that even the cat knew I was going for she followed me out mewing piteously'. Standing at the top of the boreen, he looked back at the house. MacAmhlaigh saw his mother 'with her hand to her mouth as was her habit whenever she was worried about something'.

He boarded the *Princess Maud* where he quickly found himself in the company of native speakers from his native Galway. But as the boat pulled out he moved to the stern to see the coast of Ireland receding into the darkness; 'and suddenly, I felt lonely all over again. I started thinking about the old house with the pots of tea that we'd drink before going to bed and my heart felt like a solid black mass inside my breast'. At Holyhead, he lost his travelling companions in the customs hall:

'And what a to-do there was about our bags! You'd think that we were carrying priceless jewels instead of the few old rags we had.' The man in front of him shoved onto the counter 'an old battered case that was tied with a bit of rope to keep it shut.' The following conversation ensued:
'What have you got here?' said the customs officer.
'Yerra, nothing at all,' said my lad with a grin.
'Open it up, all the same,' said your man.
'Sure, it's hardly worth my while,' said the lad.
'Look here, you're only wasting both our time. I can't let you through until you open up that bag.'
'Fair enough,' said my lad and drew out of his pocket a bloody big knife with which he cut the rope around the case. The lid jumped up just like a Jack-in-the-box and out leapt an old pair of Wellington boots that had been twisted up inside it. Devil the thing else was in the case – not even a change of socks.
A melancholy wintry little smile crossed the face of the customs officer as he motioned to your man to get along with himself.

MacAmhlaigh spent his working life in England, living in a multi-cultural world. But he lived much of the time in the Irish community with its cultural reference points, the church, the job, the dance-hall and public house. Soon after arriving, he concluded 'Damn this place, there's nothing in it. Bad and all as it might be, there's more in Kilkenny!'

Returning home to Kilkenny at Christmas one year, he found a warm welcome from his parents:

> The big Christmas candle was lighting in the window and there at the door the old lady herself to welcome me. Into the kitchen I went and there was huge fire there and the old man himself was delighted to see how well I was looking ... When I sat down at the table, I had a huge feed and the cleanliness of the house was in itself the best sauce I could have had with the food. The holly was already up with its little red berries showing plentifully and out in the scullery there hung an enormous goose ready to be cooked.
>
> The old man and I got up after a bit and moved off down to Larry's place where we had a nice cosy drink among all the old neighbours.[5]

The above is one narrative of the enforced departure of Irish men and women in the 1950s. They left because they had to do so. Many readers will identify with MacAmhlaigh and his trials and tribulations in the English Midlands.

Tony O'Malley, who died in 2003, wrote of his experiences as a bank clerk/painter. Born in Callan, Co. Kilkenny, he joined the bank – a safe job with a pension. A friend of his grandmother, on hearing the news, gave him a blessing and a copy of the *Imitation of Christ*, a book he began to read when he was committed to a sanatorium in the 1950s with TB – the fate of an entire generation. Two decades before that, he travelled around the country being posted from one bank branch to the other – Buttevant or Charleville in Cork, Arklow in Wicklow, New Ross in Wexford and Kenmare in Kerry. He travelled by bus, a bicycle on the top, with a cardboard suitcase which contained a single suit of clothes. On reaching the destination, O'Malley walked with his bicycle to a 'lodgings'. 'We were the post-treaty generation of Irishmen, who suffered from desperation and lust', he wrote:

> The culture then was respectable, decent, repressive. There was a tremendous suffocation. For courting we had the 'Ballroom of Romance' syndrome on a higher level. The great venue in Wexford was Adamstown Hall – the money went for parochial purposes, money generated by Guinness and lust! Irishmen of that generation did not fall in love – the average bankman of my generation was unmarried.[6]

O'Malley left his secure bank job in the 1950s and went to live in St Ives, Cornwall to pursue his career as a fulltime painter.

The title of this introduction is borrowed from a book of the same name, edited by John A. O'Brien, and first published in 1953. His pessimistic thesis, which received much criticism at the time the book first appeared, was laid out in his opening and concluding essays in the volume.[7] His research revealed an unbroken decline in the population since the mid-1840s. Coupled with an increasingly low marriage rate, particularly in the 1950s, the editor could well speak of the 'vanishing Irish'. He referred to a sermon delivered by Fr P. Fitzpatrick on 28 March 1953. The curate said that not a single farmer in the parish of Crookstown, Ballytore, south Kildare, had married in the previous five years. In the 1850s, the parish had 800 people and there were thirty-four couples married annually. Scarcely 200 lived in the parish in 1953, he said.[8] Economic depression may partially explain the lowness of the marriage rate.

The novelist, Bryan MacMahon, provides a contemporary argument for a low marriage-rate which captures the atmosphere of the 1950s in rural Ireland:[9]

> In the Ireland of today the conception of sin is everywhere ... True, in many dioceses the old catechism has latterly been replaced, and the change, long overdue, is undoubtedly for the better. However reading Question 256, page 62, of the *New Catechism*, 'What are the chief dangers to chastity?' and its answer, 'The chief dangers to chastity are: idleness, intemperance, bad companions, improper dances, immodest dress, company keeping and indecent conversation, books, plays and pictures', one is tempted to ask whether company keeping as such, with the use of a pejorative qualifying adjective, can be reckoned a danger to chastity ... For generations denied a catechism pervaded by the loveliness of God wherein euphony and accuracy united to form a picture of indelible beauty in an immature mind, we Irish have always been over-conscious of the thundercloud of sin above our heads. And since our priests are sprung from among us, their virtues and faults (which are ours, too) appear larger under the glass of holy orders. Time and again in my youth I have heard it thundered from country pulpits, 'It is a mortal sin to be in a lonely place with a girl' ... Never can I recall there being placed before me the possibility of connubial happiness, the essential incompleteness of single man, or the essential incompleteness of single woman.
>
> ... I can name a town where for a considerable number of years the pastor placed a complete ban upon dancing of every description; the result was that the young folk skulked out of their own parish after nightfall and sought dances farther and farther away from home and supervision.
>
> ... Despite the fact that mothers occasionally pay lip service to the desirability of the married state, at every opportunity they din into their sons' and daughters' ears that there is no life to equal the priestly or conventual one ... The end is glorious, but the motive would appear to be imperfect ...

Bryan MacMahon's dark profile of Irish life in the 1950s, very courageous for the times in which it was written, reveals a less flattering side to Irish society – sexually repressed and suffused in fears of the World, the Flesh and Devil.

John Banville writes in the opening essay in this volume about growing up in Wexford in the 1950s in the same de Valera's Ireland as had been so ably sketched above by Bryan MacMahon. Brian Fallon, is not much in agreement with Banville and MacMahon, as he relates his personal experience of growing up in the 1940s and 1950s in a Dublin of high culture, a vibrant artistic scene and progressive theatre. The latter provides a contrasting narrative of life in Ireland during the 'lost decade'. Ireland was a very good place to live in the 1950s if one had a permanent and a pensionable job. Being a teacher, a lower civil servant or a member of the other professions, provided quite a high standard of living.

That stands in contrast to the life of a small farmer or farm labourer. Based on a survey of official archives, I provide a snapshot of the hardship of living on the Blasket Islands in the post-war period and, by using files from the Department of the Taoiseach, set out the government's reasons to transfer the islanders permanently to the mainland. It was another form of involuntary leave-taking, a final act in what had been the slow attrition of emigration from the islands to the United States.

Tens of thousands left in the 1950s to find jobs abroad. The Ireland in which they were born and lived showed no signs of economic recovery. There was no 'economic miracle' in the last decade of Eamon de Valera's Ireland. In fact, de Valera was only in power until his retirement from politics in 1959 – and he had only been Taoiseach for five of those nine years. The Inter-Party Governments of 1948–51 and 1954–57 did not dramatically change the social and economic landscape. The ideology of protectionism had remained an Irish economic orthodoxy since de Valera came to power in 1932. Dr Gerry O'Hanlon provides an important essay on population change in the 1950s while Dr Enda Delaney analyses why so many Irish left. Dr Tracey Connolly sets this discussion in the context of an examination on the Commission on Emigration. Professor John Bradley evaluates the economic failure in that lost decade that forced a transition in policy-making. The march away from autarky had begun in the final two years of Dev's time in office. That significant change in policy was not really apparent until Seán Lemass, after de Valera's retirement in 1959, pressed for Ireland's full membership of the European Economic Community (EEC) in 1961.

However, throughout the 1950s, there was very little work at home for young men or women. The Irish economy was certainly the 'sick man' of western Europe. Britain's postwar Labour government had set in place free education, free dental and health care and many other social benefits necessary to make marriage and family life as stable as possible. De Valera did not bring Ireland through a welfare state revolution – so much a feature of continental Europe in the 1950s. About 400,000 souls left in ten years for Britain and, to a lesser extent, for Canada, the United States, Australia and New Zealand. Dr Andrew McCarthy provides a contribution on aspects of Local Health in Ireland in the 1950s. His findings stand in marked and depressing contrast to the strides taken in the welfare state societies of western Europe. Dr Irene Furlong's essay on the national tourist industry further reveals the backwardness of the country in the period.

The narratives quoted earlier in this introduction were exclusively the accounts of thee Irish males – Tony O'Malley, Bryan MacMahon and Dónall MacAmhlaigh. The voice of Heinrich Böll provided an insight into the world of female emigration and of the heartbreak of seeing a majority of children from the rural poor leave the country. What opportunity, in such a repressive and inhibited climate, had a woman of marrying? Across the channel in Britain lay career and work opportunities, freedom and hopes of a better life. Dr Caitríona Clear provides an innovative account in her essay: '"Too Fond of Going": Female Emigration and Change for Women in Ireland, 1946–61'. Dr Sandra McAvoy provides an important narrative on a neglected and secretive side of Irish history. She deals with the issue of abortion in 'Before Cadden: Abortion in Mid-Twentieth-Century Ireland'. Much work remains to be done to explore the worlds of the women emigrants and of the history of those women who remained at home.

Many young people left Ireland in the 1950s for reasons other than that they felt oppressed in a conservative, hierarchical society. There are other categories of emigrants whose journey abroad forms part of the 'hidden histories' of the Irish state. They are part of a 'covert', 'suppressed', or counter-culture. Their stories remain largely undocumented and untold. These were the young offenders who were given an ultimatum by the court to face a prison sentence or emigrate. There were the graduates of the reformatory and industrial school systems who felt compelled to leave. There were also those who had suffered sexual and/ or physical abuse in state-funded institutions who were too ashamed to remain. There were single mothers who had given their children up for adoption and felt compelled to go. There were also those expectant single mothers who left in order to have their children in anonymous surroundings or to have an abortion. It remains a matter of conjecture how many of those women were the victims of rape by their employers. How many were made pregnant through incest? Unfortunately the work has not yet been produced to include the proof in this volume. The findings of the Laffoy Commission in the early twenty-first century, investigating abuse in state-funded institutions for children in care, shows that many 'graduates' of such institutions left the shores of

941·70823

Ireland damaged human beings. This subject ought to form the focus for investigation in another volume.

Two further contributions evaluate literature as a source to explore the nature of Irish identity. Dr Liam Harte writes on '"You want to be a British Paddy": the anxiety of identity in postwar Irish migrant writing'. James Ryan refers to 'inadmissible departures' and asks why the Irish emigrant experience featured so infrequently in mid-twentieth-century fiction?

What of the Irish in America? Two essays in this volume take distinctive approaches to the question. Dr Maurice Fitzgerald reviews the diplomatic and economic relationship between Ireland and the United States. Dr Linda Dowling Almeida focuses on the Irish in postwar New York City in her essay, 'A Great Time to be in America'.

The final contribution in this book examines emigration of a different kind. Here there was not a question of enforced or inadmissible departures.

Many families of Irish Jews left voluntarily to 'make aliya' in the late 1940s and early 1950s to take up residence in Israel. My essay, the last in the collection, provides a diplomatic context in which such emigration took place.

In writing this introduction, I am conscious of the areas that remain to be covered in a comprehensive history of post-war Ireland. For example, the voluntary disability sector has largely developed over the past 50 years through lay voluntary organisations. The early emphasis was around vocational training (rehabilitation), understandable given the widespread incidence of TB and polio and their widespread social and economic impact within the community. The Rehabilitation Institute (founded in 1949), currently the Rehab Group, was set up by survivors of tuberculosis to help them to reintegrate into society and focused on training for employment. The Central Remedial Clinic (CRC) was established in 1951 to provide aftercare treatment to people with poliomyelitis following its outbreaks in Dublin in the 1940s and 1950s. In 1949 the Polio Fellowship of Ireland was established to represent and support post-polio adults and children. The Cork Polio and General Aftercare Association was also founded around that time in response to polio outbreaks in Cork and it now operates as COPE in the intellectual disability sector. The National Association for Cerebral Palsy, currently Enable Ireland, was established in 1948 and it pioneered the establishment of special schools for children with Cerebral Palsy. These organisations operated around education, training and employment for the most part, within a rehabilitation model, given the predominance of tuberculosis and poliomyelitis. 1960 saw the establishment of the Irish Wheelchair Association which was complementary in that its focus was broadly around community participation. The Cheshire Founda-

LIBRARY

19

400554 22

tion became active in Ireland in the 1960s having been established in the UK after the Second World War.[10]

Prior to the establishment of National Council for the Blind of Ireland (NCBI) and National Association for Deaf People (NAD) there existed a well-established service infrastructure operated by Catholic religious orders. In relation to deaf services, the Christian Brothers, the Vincentian and Dominican Orders had been active since the mid-nineteenth century.[11] The NCBI was founded in 1931 and it was modelled largely on the British experience. It is likely that its establishment 20 years ahead of other lay organisations owes much to its British influence and support. Prior to the establishment of NCBI, Catholic religious orders such as the Irish Sisters of Charity and the Carmelite Brothers were well established in the area.[12] The services of the religious orders were largely educational (schools) but they quickly, in many instances, became lifelong institutions with people coming in at an early age. These were effectively asylums where people who were deaf or blind found sanctuary from an unsupportive and hostile outside world. Similarly there was an institutional model for the mentally ill (lunatics) and mentally handicapped (imbeciles), with county mental hospitals which date back to the eighteenth century catering for the former while the latter were provided for primarily by religious orders or religiously motivated organisations.[13]

Religious orders and other organisations with a strong religious or philanthropic ethos, such as the Daughters of Charity of St Vincent de Paul, St John of God Order, Brothers of Charity and Stewarts Hospital, established institutions from the late nineteenth century to support people with intellectual disabilities (mentally handicapped). The latter half of the twentieth century saw a major development in the growth of community-based organisations responding to the needs of this group. By this time they were established and run by families and friends of people with disabilities and operated throughout the country. What we were witnessing were people forming organisations as the preferred way to respond to unmet needs at a community and family level and to advocate for the many changes needed.

This collection of essays is far from being comprehensive. But the writers pose many questions based on the use of new archival material. They open up debate and cast a spotlight on different aspects of Irish society. This volume reflects the complexities of the period under review and points to areas of historical research yet to be undertaken.

Memory and Forgetting:
The Ireland of de Valera and Ó Faoláin*

JOHN BANVILLE

When I was growing up in Wexford in the 1950s – I was five in 1950 – the town, or at least that lower-middle-class stratum of the town in which I lived, was dominated by Pierce's foundry, which at that time was one of the largest manufacturers of farm machinery in the country and the town's leading employer. None of my family worked for Pierce's, but my paternal grandfather claimed to have had an unhappy connection with the factory. My grandfather was a princely personage, with pretensions to grandeur which were inherited by his children, and, indeed, by some of his grandchildren. He was clever, genial, occasionally melancholic, and considered himself something of an inventor. The legend in the family was that he had designed a revolutionary type of plough, the blueprints for which he had unfortunately sold to a man in a pub for a fiver one day when he was drunk. This perfidious opportunist had promptly gone to the owners of Pierce's and presented the design as his own; Pierce's had recognised the value of the invention, and had bought the plans for a very great deal of money. Thus was a family fortune lost.

The day in our part of the town was punctuated by Pierce's siren, which went, if I remember correctly, at eight in the morning, at noon, and at five-thirty in the evening. Production at the factory was entirely dependent on demand, which of course fluctuated from season to season, and sometimes even from week to week, with a consequent fluctuation in the workforce. On Friday evenings, within minutes of the five-thirty sounding of the siren, word would spread as to how many workers had been laid off for the following week. Although, as I say, none of my family worked for Pierce's, this weekly oscillation in the balance of the town's fortunes affected me deeply, giving me a sense of great threat and instability. It was a local version of worldwide unrest. In my mind, the news from Pierce's was inextricably linked to the bad news coming in on the wireless, or in the pages of the *Irish Press* or via the bloodcurdling anti-Communist rhetoric of the *Irish Catholic* newspaper. The Korean War was grinding messily to a halt, the Cold War was steadily getting hotter. Before the decade was out we would have the Hungarian uprising and the Suez débâcle, both of which crises I remember with shivery vividness.

The weekly exodus of redundant workers from Pierce's foundry was echoed on a national scale in the waves of emigrants leaving for England and America. I recall very clearly a blustery spring in Rosslare Harbour, where I had gone with my parents to see off a relative who was going for a holiday to England. There they were, the crowds of awkward, lost young men with their cardboard suitcases, heading for the building sites of places with cruel-sounding names: Hackney, Wolverhampton, Liverpool, the Bronx. Many years later, at the very end of the 1960s when I was living in London, I would see them again, these same men, grown older and harder but still awkward, still lost, playing mournful two-man games of hurling in Hyde Park on summer Sunday mornings.

Other young men made other kinds of journeys as part of our seemingly endless internecine struggle in Northern Ireland. Wexford in the 1950s was a strong IRA centre. Wild types from the town would disappear for a week or two and the whisper would go round that they were 'up above'. Reports of border skirmishes, of customs posts blown up and Royal Ulster Constabulary patrols fired on, would be received with knowing looks, half in fear and half in pride. There was talk of blood oaths and punishment shootings, of arrests and excommunications. A young man from the town blew himself up when a bomb he was preparing went off prematurely in a shed somewhere in the Armagh countryside. No one of my acquaintance actually cared about Northern Ireland, or even knew about it. It was another country. I suspect the town elders were glad that there was a place, 'up above', where the rowdier elements of the town could vent their energies, thus sparing us from their depredations. The church fulminated against what the *Irish Press* referred to only as 'an illegal organisation' (but then, in those days the *Press* still referred to the 'Reformation' in quotation marks), but I suspect that the church's disapproval sprang not from an abhorrence of violence but from alarm at the thought of young men pledging spiritual allegiance to a worldly cause. The IRA campaign was exciting to us, menacing and faintly ridiculous. An air of madcap adventure attached to the doings of these young hotheads; they were our own Biggles and Bulldog Drummonds. In the early 1970s, grown older and wiser, they were among the ones who first spoke out against the new breed of Belfast- and Derry-based activists, with their car bombs and their armalites. Their protests had the peevish overtones of retired sportsmen deploring a change of tactics in the game. While they had been content to drill with wooden guns out on the windy boglands, the new lot were getting their training in the sands of Libya and the Lebanon.

My parents were Labour voters. It was less a political than a social commitment. Wexford was and still is, I imagine, a strong Labour town. My father was proud of his acquaintance with Brendan Corish, the Labour Party leader, and 'gave him his vote' as a gesture of solidarity with a good Wexford family. In spirit, my parents were quintessential Fianna Fáilers: small people, decent, pious, hardworking, suspicious, patriotic in a muted way, determined to 'get on', and fiercely ambitious, not for themselves but for their children. Both had left school early, for economic reasons, and consequently had an almost religious faith in education, especially university education. My father read de Valera's *Irish Press* every day, backwards: that is, he started with the back-page's sport and moved steadily in reverse order to the front page, largely ignoring, I suspect, whatever scraps of foreign news the paper saw fit to carry in those days. He was never an *Irish Independent* man; I heard an acquaintance of his one day referring to that paper with a contemptuous snort: 'The *Independent*? Ha! – full of horses and dead priests'. The *Irish Times*, of course, did not enter our field of vision. The *Times* was the choice of what my mother still referred to, with a sort of curtsey in her tone, as the 'Big House'. The *Irish Press* bored me; it was tame, staid, altogether too respectable, with none of the spice of the 'cross-channel' papers that were forever being denounced from the pulpit for their salacious reporting of scandalous matter: court cases involving vicars and choirboys, divorce suits among the titled, and, best of all, those grisly murders for which the English seemed to have a particular gift, involving heads in hat-boxes and bodies under floor-boards and limbless torsos being discovered in the mail coach of the night express to Edinburgh. The *Press*, on the other hand, was reticent to the point of primness: 'The woman's body was partially clothed, and there were multiple head wounds, and contusions to the chest, back and legs. She had not been interfered with'. My mother was not a great newspaper reader; the world of politics and public affairs she found faintly risible, and she was content to leave all that to the men. She was a devotee of the weekly *Irish Catholic*, with its accounts of the latest miracles at Lourdes, its blurred photographs of the Pope delivering a blessing from the balcony of his summer residence at Castelgandolfo, its horror stories of state schooling behind the Iron Curtain, and its simplified retellings of the lives of saints – martyrs, mostly, which gave the staff writers their chance to indulge in a bit of blood-and-guts storytelling just like their colleagues in Grub Street ('The saint's flesh had been pinched with red-hot tongs and her tongue had been torn out; she had not been interfered with'). My mother also read two weekly English magazines, *Woman* and *Woman's Own*. These harmless publications were the epitome of Home Counties respectability, carrying recipes and knitting patterns and a weekly feature on Queen Elizabeth and her corgis (though I did spend the odd instructive quarter of an hour poring over articles on period pains and the latest advances in obstetrics). In confession one Saturday morning, my poor mother, I suppose having nothing at all in the way of sins to tell the priest, made the mistake of admitting to her weakness for these mags. The priest gave her a stern lecture on the dangers of exposing herself to 'cross-channel filth' and made her swear to give up reading *Woman* and *Woman's Own*, which she did. It was a small piece of perfidy on that priest's part, but that this utterly pure-minded woman should be thus deprived of a couple of weekly splashes of colour in what was for the most part a monochrome life seemed to me then, and still seems to me, monstrous.

One loses one's religious faith not in moments of Dostoyevskian insight and despair, but by a gradual process of erosion. I did not give up the observances of religion until I was sixteen or seventeen, but I had stopped believing long before that. The Second Vatican Council brought a brief resurgence of religiosity into my life; I spent a couple of weeks on holiday in Rome when the council was opening, and saw Pasolini's great film *The Gospel According to St Matthew* in the tropical heat and gloom of a Roman cinema, weeping in secret when Jesus healed the leper to the strains of Lightnin' Hopkins singing the blues. John XXIII was said to be a friend of the Communist Pasolini. Surely anything was possible. What none of us realised, not even the cardinals themselves, was that the council marked not the first steps along the path to a new invigoration of the church, a new 'Reformation', but the beginning of what is proving to be its virtual dissolution.

My mother, who was far more devout than my father, deplored the changes brought about by the Second Vatican Council. She was one of the last of that breed of Irish Catholics who were more pagan than Christian. She treated priests with a mixture of deference and cloaked distaste; they were fine in their place, she said, but you wouldn't want to have them in the house. The translation of the liturgy into the vernacular struck her as little short of scandalous. I recall her account of finding herself at some sort of charismatic ceremony, at intervals during which her enthusiastic neighbour would turn and insist on embracing her, until my mother snapped at her, 'Ah, will you leave me alone, for Christ's sake!' But her trust in the church had already been badly shaken by a series of incidents in the late 1950s, when a mild form of witch-craze gripped Wexford. A couple of Jehovah's Witnesses, a man and his wife, arrived and settled in the town and set about proselytising. My mother was utterly without prejudice, and would receive a Jehovah's Witness at her door with the same tolerance and generosity that she would show to the priest collecting the Easter dues. The Jehovah's Witnesses were decent, dull people, though the husband proved himself to be unexpectedly pugnacious when things got rough – as they did. Two priests in particular in the town were very exercised about this invasion of their patch. One was a huntin', shootin', fishin' type, who threatened violence; the other was a vigorous, red-faced, usually amiable farmer's son, who did more than threaten. I no longer remember the details of the affair, but it culminated in what the papers in those days used to call 'an affray', when the farmer priest marched at the head of a mob to the house of the Jehovah's Witnesses, dragged out the husband and beat him up on the pavement, to the encouraging shouts of the mob, while the poor man's wife looked on. It was a disgraceful affair, and split the town between the witch-hunters on one side and, on the other, a mixed and troubled minority that included my mother and me. For me it marked the final stage of my apostasy, and the beginning of my determination to get out of Wexford and never return. When, years later, I heard that the same priest had been apprehended in England, stealing women's underwear from a Marks and Spencer store, I could not find it in my heart to pity him. Now, I suppose, I would be more sympathetic, seeing in the attack on the Jehovah's Witnesses evidence of forces deeper and more primitive in the human heart than belief in the tenets of this or that religion.

This, then, was the place, and the time, that I grew up in. An unremarkable place, in an unremarkable, mean-spirited time. I look back across the 40 years and more that have passed since then and I realise that my childhood is largely lost to me. Baudelaire said that the mark of the genius is that he can summon up childhood at will, but what he meant, I think, was the proustian *simulacrum* of childhood, not that grim incline of boredom and fear up which the child laboriously climbs on his way to the plateau of adulthood. In his wonderful, misanthropic poem 'I Remember, I Remember' (the title also, coincidentally, of a book by Seán Ó Faoláin), Philip Larkin finds himself brooding on his birthplace:

'You look as if you wished the place in Hell,'
My friend said, 'judging from your face'. 'Oh well,
I suppose it's not the place's fault,' I said.
'Nothing, like something, happens anywhere'.

What continues to surprise me, when I look back like this, is how docile we were, how grimly accepting of the status quo. Even in the fiercest years of my late adolescence, it never occurred to me that I could change anything. True, I knew I could change my personal circumstances, by getting out of Wexford certainly and, if possible, out of Ireland as well, and I intended to do both at the first opportunity, and did. But the society in which I grew up, and out of which I was striving to grow, seemed to me monolithic, impregnable, eternal. The structures of it appeared not man-made but the result of natural and inevitable forces before which the individual must bend, or break. This feeling of impotence was endemic, I think. It must have been, for otherwise, surely, change would have come.

Part of the reason for the stagnation of Irish life in the period from, say, the early 1930s to the end of the 1960s, was a failure of will among liberal intellectuals. This is a truism. Of far more interest, I think, is the triumph of will among reactionary intellectuals, led by the redoubtable corporatist politician and amateur mathematician, Eamon de Valera. From the start, de Valera set out to conduct a carefully prepared political experiment. I believe that de Valera, unlike Michael Collins, was not physically brave. There is no disgrace in that. Shocked by the violence of 1916 and the ferocity of the Civil War, he sought to impose controls on the country which would cure or at least curb the violence that for so long had been part of our heritage, without relinquishing the conditions which that violence had secured. The republic which he founded, with the aid and encouragement of John Charles McQuaid, was unique: a demilitarised totalitarian state in which the lives of the citizens were to be controlled not by a system of coercive force and secret policing, but by a kind of applied spiritual paralysis maintained by an unofficial federation between the Catholic clergy, the judiciary and the civil service. Essential to this enterprise in social engineering was the policy of intellectual isolationism which de Valera imposed on the country. And essential to that policy were the book and film censorship boards, which from 1930 onwards virtually sealed the country off from the rest of the world, as well as keeping a foot firmly on the necks of our native writers. In the 1960s, we used to laugh, despairingly, at the decisions made by the censors. There was virtually no Irish writer of any worth, with the exception of Corkery and his reactionary disciples, who was not banned at some time or other. The list of works by foreign authors banned in Ireland forms a worthy canon of international literature. Here is Julia Carson, in her introduction to her book *Banned in Ireland: Censorship and the Irish Writer*, published in 1989:

> Few major international authors have escaped the net of the Irish Censorship Board: to list all the books banned between 1929 and 1989 would be to list many of the major literary works of the twentieth century. For example Marcel Proust, William Faulkner, Ernest Hemingway, Saul Bellow, Vladimir Nabokov, Arthur Koestler, Heinrich Böll, Emile Zola, Jean Paul Sartre, Alberto Moravia, Sinclair Lewis, Dylan Thomas, Christina Stead, H. G. Wells, Mikhail Sholokov, Christopher Isherwood, Nadine Gordimer, and James Baldwin all have had their work banned.

Intellectually, says Carson:

> The most serious consequence of censorship for Irish writers has been to undermine their influence in the community. Censorship has created a rift in Irish society, fostering the ignorance and provincialism of the Irish people and the intellectual and moral alienation of Irish writers. Many writers have left the country in anger and in search of greater intellectual freedom. Those who have remained have found themselves isolated and unable to give significant shape to Ireland's social, political, and cultural life.

As recently as 1987, the Censorship Board banned Alex Comfort's *The Joy of Sex* and, a much more serious matter, Philip Rawson's *The Erotic Art of India*, a scholarly study published by the impeccable house of Thames & Hudson. At the time I was a member of the Arts Council, and we wrote to the Censorship Board to protest especially at the banning of Rawson's book. We received a reply which was remarkable for its arrogance and illuminating in its implications. Would we, the board asked, be willing for our children to read or see *The Joy of Sex* or *The Erotic Art of India*? (Shades of the prosecution in the *Lady Chatterley* trial asking the jury if they would allow their servants to read such a book.) Furthermore, the board's letter said, would we be content to see on open sale the books which were banned along with these two, which included works that were frankly pornographic? Here was de Valeran paternalism at its most candid. The duty of the state, and of state bodies, is to impose and maintain control. Parents will not be trusted to guide their children, adults will not be trusted to guide themselves. As far as the de Valeran state is concerned, there are no adults, except in the office of the Taoiseach and in the archbishop's palace in Drumcondra.

As I say, we used to laugh in the 1960s at the seemingly whimsical decisions of the Censorship of Publications Board and the Film Censorship Board. Small-minded ignoramuses, we believed, ran these institutions. We were wrong. Censorship in this country was administered by ideologues – reactionary ideologues, who knew exactly what they were doing. The country had to be protected from outside influences and from liberal tendencies within our own borders. Free thought is dangerous. I remember arguing in the 1960s with a priest – an intellectual and, according to his own lights, a progressive. The country, he said, was simply not ready yet to cope with influences from the world without the guidance of the Censorship Board. But, I replied, since education was in the hands of the religious – which it still was in those days – when would we be ready to stand on our own feet and think for ourselves? His reply was a faint smile accompanied by a gesture involving the turned-out palms of the hands. Many years later, in the early 1980s when I first went to eastern Europe, I had exactly the same kind of conversations with Communist ideologues: 'When would the people be ready to cope with freedom of thought and expression?' In reply, I received exactly the same wan smile, the same show of empty palms.

The artist is always in peril when he addresses public issues. Art, if it is any good, if it has any originality, is by its nature agonistic, is against received ideas, against the reigning pieties. This is not to say that art is active in a political sense, or that the artist has a view of himself as a social agitator (if he does, then heaven help him). Art is more responsible, in the moral sense, and this is a great part of its strength: it is

wholly necessary and wholly useless. Seán Ó Faoláin was a liberal intellectual, and he knew the risk he was running when in 1940 he founded
The Bell and embarked with great courage and tenacity on the task of
re-educating – or perhaps one should just say educating – the Irish public: not only that literate section of it that the magazine would reach
directly, but the large mass of people who might be influenced, however
subliminally, by the trickle-down effect of strongly expressed ideas. For
six years, from 1940 to 1946, Ó Faoláin waged a vigorous campaign against
what he referred to, with aptly respectful capitals, as 'the Literary Censorship'. He was perfectly well aware of the real nature of the dragon
against which he had unscabbarded his pen: '… the Literary Censorship is directed by those who would establish in place of thought a rigid
orthodoxy that no man must even discuss, let alone question or deny'.
Ó Faoláin was not against the principle of censorship – a matter on
which his contemporary, Frank O'Connor, criticised him – but he was
fervently and forcefully against the uses to which censorship had been
put since the foundation of the state by the puritan de Valera and his
civil service and judiciary. His editorials in *The Bell* might still be read
with profit by our latter-day moral watchdogs:

> … what an attitude, to want to cherish their ignorance! What it amounts
> to is 'Don't think about anything that does not concern you'. Combined
> with the implication that there is very little which does concern us. And
> although it is, indeed, very pleasant and easy to have such an obedient and
> innocent populace, surely if their obedience and innocence is automatic,
> i.e. based on indifference and not on an intelligent appreciation of what
> is involved, it will inevitably crack when they do come face to face with
> some difficult task which does concern them. And then it becomes futile,
> because it is too late for your man of action to argue and plead on reason-
> able grounds, since he has for years been deliberately nourishing what is
> tantamount to a contradiction in terms – a brainless morale, a moronic
> mass to which he can make no intelligent appeal whatever.
>
> If the reader hesitates to believe that this kind of populace is being
> created I would ask him how long it is since he has himself heard, or heard
> of, a frank, public discussion of any three of the following subjects – Birth
> Control, Freemasonry, The Knights of Columbanus, Unmarried Mothers,
> Illegitimacy, Divorce, Homosexuality, Rhythm, Lunacy, Libel, Eutha-
> nasia, Prostitution, Venereal Disease, or even Usury – to take only a few
> subjects which do concern us closely. Surely, it is the fact that we are not
> having enough public discussion of all sorts of things that breeds that 'not
> caring' attitude? Surely it is this indifferentism that made it possible for a
> pamphlet issued recently by one of the best-known organisations in the
> country, the Gaelic League, to say – with the amiable idiocy of a mental
> sleepwalker – 'But is there such a thing as Europe? It seems all very remote
> now except in terms of newspaper reports and air-raids'.[1]

It is tempting, and pleasingly symmetrical, to see Ó Faoláin and de Valera as the two opposing poles of Irish life from the 1930s up to the 1960s: Ó Faoláin as the intellectual, de Valera as 'your man of action'; Ó Faoláin as the cosmopolitan, de Valera as the 'Little Irelander'; Ó Faoláin as the aristocrat, de Valera as Paudeen with his greasy fingers in the till; Ó Faoláin as the healthy pagan, glorying in the Rome of the Caesars and of Michelangelo, de Valera as the scrofulous Catholic with his Legion-of-Mary pieties, poring over blurred photographs of the Pope at Castel-gandolfo; Ó Faoláin as the master of English prose, a 'lord of language', de Valera as the promoter of a dead tongue; Ó Faoláin as the lover of fair women, de Valera as the chaperone for comely maidens on their way to a céilí at the crossroads.

Some of these images are accurate of course, but incomplete: Ó Faoláin was an artist, but he had also fought with the IRA; de Valera was a devout Catholic, but his family background was as exotic as his name; Ó Faoláin's attitudes to Catholicism and Catholic organisations were complex, perhaps even a little sinister; de Valera had been a man of action, had fought in 1916, but he was also undeniably an intellectual; Ó Faoláin wrote in English, but he was Irish to the marrow; de Valera was an Irish patriot, but it was de Valera that de Gaulle liked to hobnob with. One could go on: life is complicated, history does not run to symmetry. It is not even possible to hazard a guess as to whose achievements will live longer. In most cases, if a comparison is made between an artist and a politician, one can say without hesitation that the art will endure and the politics be forgotten. But de Valera's legacy is strong – his influence not as obvious as it was in the 1950s, perhaps, but still, I would contend, all-pervasive. Ó Faoláin's reputation as a writer, on the other hand, has sunk very low – how many, among younger readers, not to mention younger writers, know his work now? Yet who is to say that intellectual life in this country would not be very much poorer had he not been there at a crucial time in our history? He stayed, holding on tenaciously with style and wit through the narrow years, when greater writers such as Joyce and Beckett, who took so much from this impoverished little bit of rock on the edge of Europe, had shaken the dust of Ireland from their heels and never looked back. He listened to the sound of the factory siren, he attended to the church's summoning bell and set his own warning bell clanging in opposition; had he been in Wexford that day in the 1950s when an ignorant priest with a mob behind him beat up a rival religionist Ó Faoláin would, I have no doubt, have stepped forward and defended the man with his fists if necessary. We need more Ó Faoláins, and now more than ever, to stand in opposition to the latter-day puritans and moral stick-wielders who are fighting a fierce rearguard action to keep Ireland holy and tight and right. In closing, I can do no better than to repeat a tribute paid to Ó Faoláin recently by his colleague Benedict Kiely:

> Ó Faoláin was the man that spoke out against censorship continually. He wasn't wild about it or anything; he spoke rationally about the nonsense of the thing … He loved the fight, I think. He was a monument in that he stayed. He was a good deal out of the country, but he was still permanently and, you might say, visibly and audibly here all the time, and in that way was, I think, a tremendous influence on everybody who came after him.[2]

Reflecting on Ireland in the 1950s

BRIAN FALLON

I must give warning in advance that what I have to say in this essay on Ireland in the 1950s will not be a learned discourse nor a piece of monumental research; to a large extent it will be personal, though not, I hope, over-subjective. I lived through the decade in question; its whole texture and 'feel' are still real to me, so much so that I am constantly struck by the contrast between those years as I experienced and witnessed them, and the stereotypes and distortions which have arisen around them and in some cases have passed into historical or literary textbooks. The usual spectres raise their heads – political isolationism, literary censorship, clericalism, cultural chauvinism and provincialism, sexual prudery or even sexual repression, large-scale emigration and so on. I will deal with some of these issues presently. However, to put some identity cards on the table first.

I left school in 1950, having sat and passed my Leaving Cert., as it was always called. I came from a literary household; my father was a distinguished poet, through whom I met most living Irish writers in person. In 1953, aged nineteen, I began work as a 'cub' journalist in the *Irish Times*, which was then edited by the famous R. M. Smyllie, a friend of my father's. A newspaper office is a reasonably good observation post for events political, cultural, social and general. Politicians were constantly on the telephone to us, various dignitaries and public figures were a familiar sight there as they passed down the corridor to the editor's office, literary types passed in and out (including older writers such as Pádraic Colum, whom I met several times, and of course Myles na Gopaleen – also known as Flann O'Brien and Brian O'Nolan – whose 'Cruiskeen Lawn' copy I often had to sub-edit). Events such as Patrick Kavanagh's long-drawn-out libel case against the *Leader* magazine were our daily bread. One might, on a day-to-day basis, have to cope with a drunken Brendan Behan who had arrived with a letter to the editor (sometimes printable, more often unprintable), or with some crank who believed we were all united in a Masonic conspiracy,[1] or with some stately, half-deaf Protestant cleric who had an article to sell.

Having established my credentials, let me look briefly at the so-called political isolationism of the period. Exactly in what area is this isolationism supposed to have operated, and how? The word is used almost automatically in any backward glance at the period, quite often without examining the factual basis for its application. Essentially, it is an allegation based on Ireland's wartime neutrality, an issue which had ceased to be current before my time but was still being fought over de-

31

cades later – and still is, at least in certain quarters. I have tried (as a non-historian, of course) to deal with this issue in my recent book *An Age of Innocence* and set it in the broad context of the times.[2] In the 1950s, the Second World War was safely in the past, but it was still the recent past, and various enmities and controversies from it were carried over, be they national, ideological or simply a matter of personal conviction.

I don't defend de Valera's wartime neutrality because, as I see it, he has no real case to answer and therefore needs no defence, least of all from me. Any small, endangered country has the right to stay out of a war not of its own making – a fact recognised at the time by the Spanish philosopher-statesman Salvador de Madariaga, among others.[3] So why should Ireland suffer obloquy on this issue when Switzerland and Sweden, also neutral nations, are widely seen as being free from blame?

Ireland joined the United Nations as soon as it was allowed to do so, just as previously it had joined the League of Nations. The country would have done so earlier except for opposition from the Communist bloc, which also opposed the entry of Spain – a poor return for de Valera's support of Russia's bid to enter the League back in the 1930s. As in the days of the League, Ireland played an honourable role in the UN, not least through the insistence by the Minister for External Affairs, Frank Aiken, that the issue of 'Red' China's entry to the Security Council should be debated and put to the vote. This was anathema to the United States, which still supported Chiang Kai-shek's highly dubious regime in Formosa (Taiwan) and wanted nothing to do with the Communists on the mainland. As a result, we cost ourselves some popularity across the Atlantic, though in retrospect Aiken's stand was not only courageous but also historically correct.[4] And in 1960, we sent troops as a UN contingent to the Belgian Congo, where Baluba tribesmen killed a number in an ambush. In 1956–7 we admitted a fairly large number of refugees from the Hungarian Rising, though in the end nobody quite knew what to do with them, and after an unhappy stay in a kind of improvised camp in Co. Limerick, most of them left for the United States.

These incidents, though chosen virtually at random, are surely enough in themselves to show that the Irish Republic was not a chauvinist stronghold. There was a reverse side, of course – attempts to boycott a soccer team from behind the Iron Curtain when it came to play in Dublin, and the campaign carried on when a number of Irish writers and journalists (including Anthony Cronin and James Plunkett) accepted an invitation to visit the Soviet Union. The *Catholic Standard*, a newspaper which folded years ago, was particularly vocal, probably more for the sake of its circulation figures than out of any real religious or ideological conviction. The matter died down eventually, but those involved – and their families – had a rather unpleasant time of it for several months. However, to my knowledge, ultimately nobody suffered in career or reputation, and certainly there were no official attempts to prevent them from going behind the Iron Curtain.

The issue of literary censorship in Ireland has been stressed so often and so heavily that it has got hopelessly out of focus. Censorship, after all, was still commonplace in many countries at the time, though Ireland was certainly an extreme case of it. Here, as so often in the 1950s, there was a collision between two generations, one of them ageing and reactionary, the other essentially modernising and libertarian. In the 1950s, the Catholic church in Ireland (never a liberal institution) was largely ruled by a number of despotic bishops who were essentially relics of another age – notably Archbishop John Charles McQuaid of Dublin, Bishop Michael Browne of Galway, and Bishop Cornelius Lucey of Cork. They were by no means isolated or untypical as senior clerics of that time went. They were the strongest personalities among the clergy and clung to certain authoritarian, almost Counter-Reformation attitudes. It is too easily forgotten today, however, that all were men of strong social conscience, with much solid work in public charities and other good causes behind them. Demonising them is rather pointless, since they were essentially men of their generation and background, men who were out of date, out of step with the times, and could not or would not admit it. However, the clergy alone cannot be blamed for the hysterias of the Censorship of Publications Board, which in fact was usually dominated by laymen and sometimes included Protestant members. 'Dirty books' were a virtual obsession for many perfectly ordinary people, who saw them as an insidious form of moral contamination and decadence.

Here too, however, the reactionaries were trying to stem an incoming tide, though it did not reach its peak until the following decade. An appeals board was already in force, which did something to mitigate the censors' folly, but Archbishop McQuaid, in particular, was active through the 1950s in applying pressure on the government to avoid any relaxation of censorship. He even tried to prevent Seán Ó Faoláin's appointment as chairman of the recently created Arts Council and was listened to more than he should have been by the Taoiseach, J. A. Costello, who was always something of a 'priest's man'. The attempt failed, but McQuaid had more success in stirring up various bodies and individuals to make a vocal stand against the state getting soft on 'dirty books'.[5] This led to absurdities such as the banning of Brendan Behan's *Borstal Boy*, which nonetheless became hugely popular and was soon recognised as a classic. Meanwhile, the Joyceanism of the younger writers grew steadily more pronounced and though Joyce's books had never been officially banned in Ireland, they became more and more a part of ordinary literature. (*Envoy* magazine, for instance, ran an entire edition on him in 1952.)

Censorship remained in force, then, but it was becoming increasingly porous and ineffectual, as well as subject to growing public ridicule. By the end of the decade, it was largely discredited and the state had quietly begun to weed out some of the more unbalanced personalities among the censors. But it was well into the 1960s before Brian Lenihan, as Minister for Justice, pushed through the Oireachtas the legislation which largely (though not entirely) gelded the censorship board. Though the long-term effects of literary censorship on Irish culture seem to have been greatly exaggerated, it was still a national blot, and most of Ireland's leading novelists suffered both financial loss and personal opprobrium through it. It remains one of the lunatic areas of the whole period, stretching back to 1929 when it was legally introduced. Behan, Frank O'Connor, Ó Faoláin, Benedict Kiely and Austin Clarke had all been sufferers under it and were placed in much the same bracket as mercenary pornographers and writers for trash magazines. It was not so much the triumph of puritanism as the apotheosis of philistinism and provincialism. And some of the worst offenders were the self-appointed lay-censors, who developed a nose for any 'sexy' passage in a book that could be compared to those police dogs who are trained and employed to track down drugs.[6]

Clericalism has been dealt with in the various contexts above to some extent, but one chapter of its history should be discussed entirely separately, because of its far-reaching effects. This is the controversy over the Mother-and-Child Scheme in 1951, which catapulted Dr Noël Browne, then Minister for Health, to national fame and eventual political martyrdom. The matter hinged on maternity benefits. The inter-party government of the time had inherited the bones of the scheme itself from its Fianna Fáil predecessor. McQuaid again played a central role, though the Catholic hierarchy backed him fully, presumably after considerable promptings and lobbying by upper-class, well-to-do Irish doctors who feared encroaching welfare statism, as in Britain. But the hierarchy would have needed relatively little prodding anyway, since creeping socialism was one of their nightmares, and they scarcely distinguished it from out-and-out Communism. 'Red' was a common, blanket term at the time for almost anybody to the left of centre.

A more seasoned and flexible politician than Browne might have pacified the bishops and piloted his legislation through the Oireachtas with only a few politic concessions or compromises. Browne, however, was idealistic, dogmatic and rigid, never a team player, and it sometimes seemed as if he was more intent on forcing a head-on fight with the hierarchy than gaining their agreement. A pragmatic, middle-of-the-road approach might have saved the situation and reconciled both factions, at least temporarily. But a fight it was to be, during which Taoiseach J. A. Costello acted cravenly – there is no other word for it – while Seán MacBride, the leader of Clann na Poblachta (to which party Browne belonged) played a highly ambivalent role.[7] The government backed down, Browne resigned, and not long afterwards the inter-party ministers fell from office. De Valera, once he was back in power, saw the original bill safely through with a few changes and compromises.

And that should have been that, by normal standards, but the djinn had been released from the bottle and would not be coaxed back. Even highly orthodox, conservative Catholics began to feel that the church had over-reached itself by dictating to the state on matters of public health, which was not its proper sphere, while, particularly in Dublin, a strong wave of working-class sympathy saw Browne as the people's friend who had been done down by the clergy and the well-off, conservative doctors. Controversy, both vocal and in print, raged for a long time, with Dr Alfred O'Rahilly, the champion of the Catholic right, being particularly outspoken and extreme. (He was taken on by Myles na Gopaleen in his Cruiskeen Lawn column in the *Irish Times*.) Yet even long after the dust-clouds had settled, and the issues had become blurred by time and verbiage, some of the bitterness remained and the scales fell from many eyes which previously would never have looked askance at a priest or bishop. Finally, all this hardened into an impersonal and historical verdict: the church had been wrong, or at least misguided. In the interests of some dogmatic or theological obsession, which made very little sense to anybody outside its ranks, it had acted against the interests of public health and the poorer classes. This change of attitude was slow and tentative, but it was fateful and ultimately irrevocable. From then on, the power and prestige of the Catholic hierarchy in Ireland began to wither slowly, though few observers recognised this for a long time. To this day, several historians have not fully admitted that this was the start of the decline. A haemorrhage had occurred and Maynooth continued to bleed, quietly but steadily, until it reached the nadir of today's generally unthinking (and often ignorant) anti-clericalism. When certain senior clergy complain so bitterly and so wistfully about growing public hostility and indifference towards traditional religion, or prevailing misconceptions about the subject, they should remember that their predecessors had industriously laid the foundations for that state of affairs.

In the late 1950s, I belonged to a fringe political party called the National Progressive Democrats, which had, in effect, only two Dáil members, Noël Browne and Jack McQuillan (an able parliamentarian, though forgotten today). Though a very minor cog in this body, which I left soon after, I frequently encountered Browne at the party offices in Harcourt Street, Dublin, and so could form some impression of his personality at first hand. In my experience, he was a man of little humour or pragmatism, capable of genuine self-sacrifice and devoted to labour for a chosen cause, but with an almost Robespierre-like conviction of his own rectitude, and suspicious of any disagreement with his own views. Political realities did not enter much into it: I rather suspect that Browne almost despised them, as something ultimately irrelevant to guiding principles. I also formed the impression that while he would throw himself utterly and unselfishly behind what he believed in, he was not a gifted organiser or administrator. And in fact, a number of older civil servants later told me, in private, that Browne's odd working methods and reluctance (or inability) to delegate had made him an awkward cabinet colleague as well as a difficult man to work under.[8]

Cultural isolationism is another social force regularly ascribed to the 1950s, though usually little proof is cited. As I see it, this is yet another of those catchall terms which have hardened into dogma. They are only rarely questioned or at least are rather poorly investigated. Once again, let me pose the question: in what particular area or areas, and in what manner, did this attitude manifest itself so powerfully and even over-bearingly? For the life of me, I cannot see quite where and how. There was, of course, literary censorship, but as I have attempted to prove already, by the 1950s censorship of foreign authors was increasingly ineffectual and most literate people read what they wanted to read. Resistance to modern art? Dublin was no Paris, but since the opening of the Irish Exhibition of Living Art in 1943 there had been a reasonably healthy modernist fringe in Ireland. I say 'fringe' deliberately because Paris-based Modernism – as represented by Picasso, Braque, Chagall and so on – was still very much a minority enthusiasm, even in France itself. It was not until the great Picasso exhibition of 1959–60 was mounted at the Tate Gallery in London that Modernism became officially accepted in these islands, and it was gradually to become the new academicism. Since then, people have grown to consider it the orthodox style for contemporary art and cannot remember the time when it was still considered a dangerous heresy.

Ireland in the 1950s had in fact some fine painters, even though Jack Yeats was at the end of his lengthy career and died early in 1957. Some eminent figures – the painters William Scott and Mary Swanzy, the sculptor F. E. McWilliam – were in voluntary exile in Britain; in any case, Scott and McWilliam were northerners and so counted as British citizens. Nevertheless, the Dublin art world included Patrick Collins, Louis le Brocquy, Nano Reid (who was actually based in Drogheda), Norah McGuinness, Gerard Dillon, George Campbell, Oisín Kelly, Patrick Scott, Patrick Swift, Maurice MacGonigal and Seán O'Sullivan. That, in retrospect, was probably as impressive a roll-call of talent as most European nations could supply at the time, France and Germany and perhaps Britain excepted. And they were aided and abetted by a dealer and art impresario of genius, Victor Waddington, whose gallery just off Grafton Street displayed not only the best Irish artists but various French and English ones as well. Waddington emigrated to London in 1957 and soon became a power in the art world there, but his work was at least partly carried on by the Dawson Gallery, run by Leo Smith, and the Ritchie Hendriks Gallery.[9] Another important factor was the criticism and lecturing of James White, who at the end of the 1950s took over the Dublin Municipal (now Hugh Lane) Gallery and revitalised it; some years later he moved to the National Gallery and became probably the most successful director in its history.

The Living Art group (composed of those artists represented at an exhibition of the same name in 1943) had always co-existed rather uneasily with the Royal Hibernian Academy (RHA), which represented the conservative wing of Irish art and relied heavily on portrait commissions for its bread and butter – these commissions were lucrative to individual members and provided the essential element of social *réclame* and snob appeal at the annual exhibitions. During the immediate post-war period, the academicians could treat the avant-garde with relative indifference – even with a degree of tolerant contempt. However, when the private galleries began to sell the products of Modernism reasonably successfully and it even began to infiltrate some public areas, it was time for the conservatives to think again and close ranks. A major controversy blew up in the mid-1950s when a bronze reclining figure by Henry Moore received much publicity in Dublin, as it seemed likely to be purchased by the state.

A noisy, blue-blooded eccentric named the Dowager Lady Dunalley denounced it in almost hysterical terms and was backed by various other people – some of whom should have known better. Others merely served their own ends, with the result that officialdom lost its nerve and it was decided to abandon the idea. However, a handful of dedicated people continued to campaign for it and eventually the sculpture was acquired by Dublin Corporation for the Municipal Gallery. It was a slap in the face for the reactionaries, who did not forgive their defeat and as a result grew increasingly embittered and paranoid. The president of the RHA, Seán Keating, was sometimes over-vocal concerning the 'apostolic succession of art' which, obviously, he and his fellow-RHAs saw themselves as continuing and preserving in the face of Modernist heresies. However, it was ultimately a losing cause, and throughout the remaining years of the decade, the RHA continued to decline in prestige.

Ironically, so did the Living Art movement, which had been at its most successful between 1945 and 1955; after that its arteries began to harden. Several of the artists who had been at its core were obviously losing their freshness and their energy. A new generation was coming up, many of whom were influenced by the contemporary American art (largely abstract) which was sweeping through Europe. New talents such as Camille Souter, Richard Kingston and Edward McGuire, a richly gifted painter of portraits and still life, did emerge to give the Living Art some further lease of life, but in effect it had passed its apex and was soon to be challenged by emerging groups such as the Independent Artists. It had based itself largely on French models, while the new generation was predominantly American-influenced; and Ireland was now yielding rapidly to transatlantic currents.[10]

This transatlantic influence, which inside another decade grew into virtual cultural imperialism, was already present in literature. The roots of such a development lie in pre-war times, but by the late 1940s it was already so strong that it threatened to become dominant and to push aside the more self-consciously 'native' writers. In the first place, English publishing had always dominated the Irish book market, and the house of Faber & Faber (of which T. S. Eliot was a director) always placed a strong emphasis on contemporary American poetry. Eliot himself, along with Ezra Pound, had been familiar to the Dublin literary world as leading Modernists since the 1930s, but after the war the poetry of Robert Frost (who was given an honorary degree in Dublin), Wallace Stevens (championed by the critic Denis Donoghue), and Marianne Moore became ultra-fashionable, though admittedly in rather limited circles. This trend extended to contemporary American novels, some of which were banned by the censor but were obtainable nonetheless for those who cared to make the effort. American short-story writers such as William Saroyan were also highly regarded, and the *New Yorker* magazine was almost required reading in the houses of cultivated people. James Thurber was always a favourite with the Irish middle-class, while Ernest Hemingway had been well known and read for some decades. Young, mildly rebellious readers – particularly university students – found a voice for their own frustrations and impulses in J. D. Salinger's novel *The Catcher in the Rye*, which had a strong underground readership in the middle and late 1950s. In due course, it became a kind of cult book for a whole generation, while the rather short-lived Beat movement reached Dublin near the end of the decade.

Above all, however, the younger poets (or at least a significant section of them) found their model in the poetry of W. H. Auden, who exercised a powerful influence on Irish writing for at least 20 years. In the past two decades the reputation of Louis MacNeice – overshadowed by Auden in his lifetime and regarded by some influential people as little better than his epigone – has risen rapidly and threatens to rise above that of his English contemporary. Yet MacNeice, curiously, made only a limited impression on the Dublin literary world and died (in 1963) before his proper status was appreciated – and even then the reappraisal was slow and gradual. It is true that there is now a flourishing critical industry which purports to show that MacNeice had a major shaping effect on younger poets in Northern Ireland, including Derek Mahon and Michael Longley. I cannot argue convincingly for or against this view, but as I remember, Belfast literary life did not make any great fuss of him at the time and in fact for most of Ireland, north and south, Mac-Neice remained essentially one of the so-called 'Thirties Poets' (sometimes colloquially known as the Auden Gang) which was almost exclusively identified with London and English literary circles. His 'Irishness' seemed patent to his contemporaries in the BBC, yet in Dublin – which he visited quite often and where he had many friends – he was generally seen as a half-foreigner.

In retrospect, MacNeice can be seen as very Irish, though in rather an 'Anglo' sense – indeed, some critics regard him as the greatest Anglo-Irish poet since Yeats.[11] He was also the epitome of what the younger Irish poets were seeking – a writer-intellectual in the new urban, cosmopolitan mode, with the insouciant tone which was then so admired: something of a globe-trotter, a lover of women, a man who combined the dual roles of classical scholar and journalistic commentator. He was also, however, sensitive and introspective, deeply divided psychologically and an exile by choice, even if London was much closer to the ordinary Irish consciousness than Paris or Berlin or even New York. All this should have commended him to the younger Irish poets, yet strangely enough it did not do so, or at least only to a very limited extent. Instead, it was Auden who became the glamour figure – the streetwise, clever, super-articulate, all-too-knowing poetic insider of his age. He represented what a large proportion of young writers would have liked to be – the 'international' poet equally at ease in London or Manhattan, or stretched out in the sun on a beach in Ischia. Hemmed in by an insular environment, they saw him as the cosmopolitan model to be studied and emulated. At this time Yeats, for many of them, had become a remote figure, loftily rhetorical and tainted by the arcane milieu of symbolism. Auden, and to a lesser extent Eliot and Pound, dealt in the currency of the topical present. And, of course, Auden was now virtually an Anglo-American, at a time when American reputations, American critics and the contents of American literary periodicals were at the forefront of people's minds. The swing against artistic and literary nationalism had grown almost to an obsession in certain quarters, and this reaction largely continues today.

In music, a field in which I have no expertise whatever apart from being (at this time at least) a devout concert-goer and record-listener, there was a good deal of activity, though again most of it was confined to Dublin, with a certain amount in Cork. I remember hearing recitals by the pianist Louis Kentner and the great oboist Leon Goossens, a performance of Beethoven's *Fidelio* by a visiting German opera company in the Theatre Royal, the anti-climax of a very disappointing concert by the Boston Symphony Orchestra under Charles Munch, various Spanish dance troupes in the Olympia and elsewhere and so on.[12] There were a number of excellent record shops, notably May's on St Stephen's Green, which also carried several shelves of recent musical literature, something virtually unobtainable today. And a landmark of a sort was the appearance of Bill Haley and his Comets at the Theatre Royal – not an event of inherent musical interest, but of socio-cultural importance nevertheless, because officially it brought rock and roll to Dublin. And in cinema, the long-vanished little Astor Cinema on the Dublin quays near O'Connell Bridge brought classic and recent French cinema to Irish viewers – films by Jean Renoir, René Clair, Clouzet, Jacques Tati and others. For decades, art-house cinema had largely gone unappreciated in Dublin, in spite of the efforts of a coterie of erudite and energetic aficionados such as Liam Ó Laoghaire. For the most part, Irish literary intellectuals, strangely, had tended to fight shy of it and saw cinema as strictly a mass-commercial medium – as of course nine-tenths of it was and still is. It was during the later 1950s that the great change of heart occurred. A core following of cultured Dublin students played a leading role in this; in general, they were far better informed about contemporary cinema than their elders.

Likewise, the media of the time, in spite of what is often stated today, were very much aware of international events and currents of opinion, in politics if not necessarily in the arts. When I was a youthful sub-editor at the *Irish Times* from 1953 to 1958, many of the news stories I handled nightly were 'foreign' rather than 'home' news. A glance back at the files of that newspaper, or indeed those of any daily Irish newspaper of the period, will show that front-page stories included a high percentage of foreign news and indeed the lead story was frequently a foreign one. The Suez crisis of 1956 which ended Eden's spell as prime minister of Great Britain, the long-drawn-out war in Korea, US presidential elections, UN debates, the Soviet invasion of Hungary, Khrushchev's famous speech condemning Stalinism, the various moves and counter-moves of the Cold War and the launch of the first Sputnik into space were all of absorbing interest to Irish newspaper readers. Radio Éireann, too, laid strong emphasis on what were called 'foreign affairs' and such eminent journalists as the late W. J. ('Jack') White and Erskine B. Childers were regular voices on radio. Post-war tension remained high: the Cold War continued long after the war of weapons had ceased and the mushroom cloud of atomic explosions was a nightmare image always present in the public's consciousness. This fear was renewed in the early 1960s when Khrushchev and Kennedy faced each other in a showdown over a shipload of nuclear weapons heading for

Cuba, ending in the Russian leader backing down and subsequently losing popularity at home. The nuclear terror was no respecter of small nations or even island ones; it dominated the great powers and the small ones equally.

At the *Irish Times*, the neo-Victorian figure of R. M. Smyllie still loomed like an Olympian god. He carried with him a prestige enhanced by his brushes with state censorship during the war years. Smyllie had become editor of the paper when it was still stuffily unionist, and with circumspection had moved it to a relatively liberal stance. He also patronised poets and men of letters, a number of whom gathered around him in the Pearl Bar or the Palace Bar, both Fleet Street pubs which became haunts of journalists and writers. Visiting intellectuals such as Cyril Connolly sought him out and cartoonists depicted him with his huge bulk and his everlasting pipe. He was one of the sights of Dublin as he emerged majestically from his office onto D'Olier Street or Westmoreland Street. Yet, he was really a crumbling monolith, nearing his end; this in fact came in September 1954 when he died suddenly of a heart attack. By the 1950s, Smyllie's great days were behind him; he was mentally and physically a tired man, going on more out of habit than with his old zest. (A friend of mine, now dead, who was a practising psychiatrist and knew Smyllie personally, told me that in his professional opinion the famous editor in his last years was a classic case of mental and physical depression resulting from years of overwork.) His successor, W. A. ('Alec') Newman, had been assistant editor for years and bore much the same relation to Smyllie as Eden bore to Churchill. Though a decent and cultured man, he lacked both the popular touch and the ponderous flair coupled with the massive personality of his predecessor. His editorship saw the newspaper slip further in prestige and readership, challenged increasingly by the *Irish Press* under an able and ambitious young editor, Jim McGuinness. It was not until the mid-1960s that the energy and radically new outlook of Douglas Gageby brought the *Irish Times* back on an even keel, though inevitably on a very different course.

Time was also running out for the great literary magazines, which had been at their peak in the previous decade. The *Dublin Magazine*, under the long-time editorship of the poet-scholar Seumas O'Sullivan, seemed in some ways a survivor from another age of gentlemanly belles-lettres, though many of the better poets still contributed to it. O'Sullivan remained a respected figure in literary Dublin and was a regular sight at the Pearl Bar with his Edwardian dignity and white moustache – and his quiet, efficient consumption of whiskey. The magazine had been his brainchild, and he had built it up (with very slight financial resources) into a publication read and respected throughout Ireland and the British Isles, had coaxed contributions from most of the distinguished writers of the time and had created a network of literary friendships and connections which was truly impressive. Yet the *Dublin Magazine* belonged essentially to the pre-war era, and the deliberately controversial tone which Seán Ó Faoláin cultivated in *The Bell* interested young or emerging writers more than the Edwardian courtliness of O'Sullivan. Ó Faoláin not only challenged censorship and the church; he addressed topical issues of all kinds and provided a forum for a younger generation increasingly at odds with the Ireland they had unwillingly inherited. Ó Faoláin was more than an outstanding man of letters; he was also a great journalist, something which O'Sullivan would have disdained even if he had been capable of it. *The Bell* ruffled politicians as well as churchmen; it was read by schoolmaster intellectuals and lonely dissidents in small towns as well as by the usual coterie of Dublin intellectuals. Ó Faoláin was not editor for very long but the magazine found an able successor in Peadar O'Donnell, who also was an *engagé* intellectual with a nose for controversy.

The third of the great literary journals was *Envoy*, edited by John Ryan. It was less politically conscious than *The Bell*, less 'public-spirited' but probably better adjusted to the tone and mentality of the Dublin literary cliques of the day. Patrick Kavanagh was a regular contributor, and Ryan managed to extract contributions from people as prestigious as Samuel Beckett. He adroitly mixed local appeal and local literary politics with a certain amount of 'international' interest. *Irish Writing*, published in Cork, was relatively short-lived but played an important role almost forgotten today. However, the vogue for the literary magazine was waning everywhere – exactly why it is hard to say, though it may have been connected with the rise of television and the increasing tendency of the visual arts to take over ground previously held by the written word. O'Sullivan died in 1958 and the *Dublin Magazine* died with him, though there were some attempts to refloat it. Its distinguished competitors died out too, victims of changing taste – or was it simply that literary Dublin, as it had been, was on the wane?

Certainly, it did not seem so at the time. Even with Yeats and the other leading figures of the Literary Revival long dead, Dublin retained a literary consciousness and a literary flavour which have virtually vanished from the city today. I say this quite deliberately, as one who experienced it at close quarters and in a variety of ways. It was not a matter of meeting literary geniuses at every street corner or inside every city-centre pub, since such figures were always rare; it was more an aura which had come down from the days of Yeats and Gogarty and George Moore, just as Vienna had inherited the musical aura created there by the great musicians of previous generations. But it was not this heritage alone, since there were outstanding talents to succeed the great writers, if not, perhaps, to equal them. Literature and the theatre were topics of conversation even among people who were quite unintellectual, and writers were often the subject of household chat and personal anecdotes in a way they are certainly not today. They were also, of course, familiar sights in the streets, in certain pubs and bookshops and cafés, on the racecourse, at theatrical first nights, or even – as in the case of Patrick Kavanagh's famous libel case against the *Leader* magazine[13] – in the law courts. Writers were, in fact, part of local mythology, and to be seen in their company was often a source of personal prestige and self-congratulation. (It could also, of course, be a source of personal embarrassment, as when a drunken Brendan Behan shouted raucous greetings across the street or Patrick Kavanagh ostentatiously attempted to borrow a few pounds from someone he had never met before – usually to back some racehorse which would inevitably lose.) The literary pubs, too, were at their peak, including the Pearl and the Palace as already mentioned, the Red Bank on D'Olier Street, and of course McDaid's, the haunt of Kavanagh and his coterie. Literary parties were almost nightly events, even though the majority of them were seedy affairs held in even seedier basements, with the party-goers usually going straight there from their favoured pub with a half-dozen bottles of stout under their arm and an argument or polemic on their lips.

It was true, of course, that personal legend frequently interested the layman more than literary merit, and it may well have been that many or even most of these writers were more talked about than read. Behan, for instance, was known mainly at this time for his column in the *Irish Press*, which was later collected in book form under the title *Hold Your Hour and Have Another*. At a time when Myles na Gopaleen was going through some bad, repetitive patches with his 'Cruiskeen Lawn' column, Behan's work was probably the most widely read and quoted contribution of its kind. Otherwise, Behan lived largely on the legend of his outsize personality, and it was not until the publication of *Borstal Boy* that the literary public began to admit to his solid literary merit as well as personal swagger and a way with words. *The Quare Fellow*, too, in spite of good notices from critics and full houses, was not appreciated for a long time as the masterpiece I believe it to be – a factor not helped by a particularly dismal production at the Abbey. Kavanagh had written relatively little for some years and his reputation did not take an upward turn again until the start of the 1960s; he was probably better known as a 'character' and wiseacre. I remember certain people who could quote long passages from *The Great Hunger* from memory, and some of his early lyrics had never gone out of currency, but certainly the virtual canonisation which occurred following his death was not predicted. His novel *Tarry Flynn* was slow to establish itself as the classic it surely is. He had his own devoted following, but for many people he was not so much a writer of stature as the rather aggressive oddity who talked to himself in the street, tried to 'touch' strangers for money, and was always liable to start an altercation at the bar counter.

All this was a considerable contrast to a quiet, austere-looking (though sharp-tongued) Austin Clarke, who came and went by bus from his house in Templeogue and usually confined his pub appearances to a few beers and a few dry *bons mots* in the Pearl Bar. Or to sensitive, charming Patrick MacDonogh, whose reputation sank into obscurity so unjustly after his death in 1961 – though it has recently been resurrected, with the overdue reissuing of his poems by the Gallery Press.[14] He, too, was essentially a private, fastidious personality, well able to take (and stand) his round with the others, but repelled by anything which savoured of exhibitionism or plain bad manners. Or Pádraic Fallon, who worked as an exciseman in Wexford and only visited Dublin occasionally to mingle with his friends and fellow-writers in the usual taverns or in the corridors of Radio Éireann, which produced his remarkable series of radio plays. Radio Éireann had a considerable part to play in the development of things cultural. To begin with, many writers worked on its staff, full or part-time – Roibeárd Ó Fearacháin, Francis MacManus, Mervyn Wall, Dan Treston and James Plunkett among others. Equally important, it offered a creative outlet for literary men, whether in the form of 'talks' or scripts or – as in the case of Fallon, Austin Clarke and various others – radio plays. The Sunday-night play, for instance, was a national institution, at a time when radio broadcasting was seen as a genuinely creative medium. In the BBC, poets as gifted as MacNeice and Dylan Thomas wrote for radio regularly. This area, too, hardly survived the coming of television, whose creative possibilities were exploited by film-makers more than writers. The definitive book has yet to be written about Irish writers and the radio (or the wireless, as it was popularly called), which is a remarkable omission; there were few important literary figures over several decades who did not either write for it or use it as a vehicle for opinions and criticism. (Frank O'Connor and James Stephens, for instance, were considerable performers on the radio.)

Culture apart, however, in defining the 1950s there remains the unavoidable area of political life, and here it should be said straight away that the decade does not show up very well. Essentially, Irish politics were bogged down in old enmities and outmoded attitudes and values, and though there was a growing ground swell of opinion against these, it was a long time before this took any coherent shape or trend – if indeed it ever did. There was a great deal of apathy among younger people, as well as a kind of unfocused resentment and disillusionment for which continuing emigration, for one thing, provided ready-made fuel. De Valera was still respected, but the old guard around him were often spoken of with derision – more out of simple desire for a change than

out of any objective judgement, since they included several men of outstanding calibre. One of them, Seán Lemass, was to lead Ireland into a
new era in economics and set its course firmly towards membership of
the Common Market. Nevertheless, to many young voters (and non-
voters too) these elder figures seemed to have been there far too long,
and their achievements were largely ignored or devalued, while their
failures stood out even more starkly. The queues for the emigrant boat
continued, much of the economy seemed stagnant, capital was in short
supply, the farmers were grumbling and it was not until the setting up
of An Foras Talúntais (the Agricultural Research Institute) late in the
decade that there was any concerted effort to tackle farming research
or to train a new generation of people living on the land in the economics of land management and the variety of new crops and methods available. Third-level education was the privilege of the well-off, though
many humble lower-middle-class families made considerable sacrifices
to see their children achieve the yearned-for target of university degrees. Even second-level education had obvious shortcomings, and it
was not until the 1960s that a major overhaul of it was achieved, mainly
by two successive Fianna Fáil ministers, Patrick Hillery and Donogh
O'Malley. The civil service was virtually a law unto itself and any
government minister who attempted to change or overhaul it was putting his head into a wasps' nest. (Not that many tried – the notable
exception being Charles Haughey a few years later.)

Though the monolithic rule of Fianna Fáil had been challenged by
two inter-party (i.e., coalition) governments, the various parties covered only a small radius of opinion and tended to cling without ideological focus to a right-of-centre base. There was a definite sense of stasis,
even of stagnation, though in many quarters this was sensed rather
than openly admitted. The Labour party was obsessed with not offend-
ing the church, while the staid clericalism and property-bound conservatism of Fine Gael remained inviolate until late in the 1960s. Maverick parties such as the National Progressive Democrats, already mentioned in connection with Dr Noël Browne, could only toss a few stones
into what seemed a large, stagnant pool. An epoch was obviously drawing to an end socially, economically and politically, but there was nothing like the emergence of the welfare state in Britain to enliven it, or
even a creative recrudescence from the right. For the most part, Irish
politics were mired, not in the past, as so many observers and analysts
claimed, but in a kind of muddy alley that led only to a large blank wall.
In 1959 de Valera was elected president and Lemass succeeded him as
Taoiseach; the previous year had produced *Economic Development* and
the five-year *Programme for Economic Expansion*, commonly known as
the Whitaker Plan after the secretary of the Department of Finance,
T. K. Whitaker, which was in effect the first shot fired on behalf of the

new economic pragmatism. However, its achievements belong to a later period than the one I am dealing with, and 'Lemassism' was essentially an affair of the 1960s, leading ultimately to the managerial Ireland of today. Meanwhile, personal loyalties and antagonisms, as so often in Irish life, tended to dominate at the expense of larger horizons and basic principles.

Nevertheless, it would be misleading and false to describe the public life of the decade as conservatism gradually winding down to very little, in the end. Underneath the surface apathy and even disillusionment, there was a new restless, modernising spirit, which was eventually to make itself felt in many spheres, public and private. Though the bastions of tradition – which included the political parties, the church, most of the civil service, even the universities and a great deal of the teaching profession – continued to stand immobile like stone walls, they were being steadily undermined. So when, inside a decade, they collapsed with a suddenness that surprised many people, the credit was rarely given to the submerged radicalism of the generation which had tunnelled through their rock-hard foundations.

Surprisingly, one cultural and national field which did gain a new lease of life was the Irish language, at a time when public apathy, poor teaching in many schools and political gobbledegook seemed to have killed off all popular feeling for it. Compulsory Irish in schools had for long been a sore point with many parents who saw no use for it, while the tribes of professional Gaelgeoirí, Irish-language lobbyists, opportunist schoolmasters and grants-for-the-Gaeltacht politicians were increasingly regarded – often unjustly – as an incubus on national life. The whole policy of reviving Irish as a spoken language, the language of everyday life, business and conversation, seemed to have failed, though no interested party was prepared to admit as much. Culturally, however, the language gained a remarkable and quite unexpected lease of life shortly after the Second World War, particularly in literature: Seán Ó Ríordáin and Máirtín Ó Direáin in poetry and Máirtín Ó Cadhain in fiction, among others, gave it a modernist energy which could also cope very well with tradition, and they showed that Irish could cope with contemporary life and contemporary terminology.[15]

Along with this went a whole new generation of talented journalists and broadcasters: Seán Mac Réamoinn, Dominic O'Riordan, Breandán Ó hEithir, Proinsias Mac Aonghusa, Aindrias Ó Gallchóir, to name only a few. Gael-Linn, the organisation founded by Dónall Ó Móráin, did much valuable work, including the sponsorship of recordings of Seán Ó Riada and the films of George Morrison and Louis Marcus. Folk and traditional music also enjoyed a huge renaissance, and in the early 1960s the fleadh cheoil became as essential a cultural rendezvous for Irish youth as the jazz festivals in America were for their contemporaries.[16] It should be added that many or most of these developments took place out of their own, autonomous energies, not from state subsidy or public approval. Some changes, indeed, genuinely shocked the old diehards of the 'official' language movement, who saw them as a sell-out to the Pop Age.

I have ranged widely in this brief survey; in doing so I have laid myself open to the charge of superficiality. So much of the spirit of an age lies in the eye of the beholder and in his own subjective experiences and impressions, even if he makes a show of historical objectivity and can back his arguments with a fair degree of fact. I know very well that a number of excellent and gifted people remember the 1950s as an era of frustration and even futility, financial difficulty and struggle, a period lacking genuine outlets for creativity and forward thinking, an age when the censor was still powerful if not omnipotent, when writers and artists had to make do without such institutions as Aosdána or the re-assurance of Arts Council grants, and when people of left-wing views felt marginalised and even under threat. All these criticisms and complaints are legitimate, but they form only part of the story. What is re-markable about the 1950s is the underlying creative force they showed without the financial and quasi-official props which are now considered essential for the survival of the arts in Ireland.

A reactionary church was challenged if not reformed, the shibbo-leths of officialdom were shown up for what they were (and Myles na Gopaleen was certainly not the only one active in this area), the visual arts were revitalised, journalism and broadcasting often reached a high level, a genuinely well-educated generation began to emerge, and Ire-land was able to engage politically and intellectually with other coun-tries again, after the enforced blackout of the Second World War. But above all, the 1950s was a decade rich in personalities – Behan, Kava-nagh, Ó Ríordáin, Myles/Flann O'Brien, Kate O'Brien, Seán Ó Faoláin and Benedict Kiely in literature (to name only a few among many); Patrick Collins, Louis le Brocquy, Gerard Dillon, Seán O'Sullivan and Seán Keating in painting; Evie Hone in stained glass; Oisín Kelly in sculpture; Seán Ó Riada, Brian Boydell, Frederick May and 'Archie' Potter in music; R. M. Smyllie, Séamus Kelly (Quidnunc), Peadar O'Don-nell, Anna Kelly and many others in journalism. I do not necessarily select these people as being the most creative of their time, or at least the sole creative personalities, but they gave it some of its diversity and liveliness. All in all, the 1950s was a very remarkable, even unique, period in Irish life and culture. A more balanced (and better informed) viewpoint than the present one is needed in order to see it in the round and give it its due. It was the era which led from the grimness of the 1940s to the more prosperous – if not necessarily more intellectual – Ireland of today.

Leaving the Blaskets 1953: Willing or Enforced Departures?

DERMOT KEOGH

John Banville's autobiographical view of growing up in de Valera's Ireland – the opening contribution to this volume – is a perspective on life in the 1940s and 1950s with which many people will empathise. It will approximate to their own experience of home life, of schooling and of the cultural limitations of living in a highly stratified society. Many tens of thousands of Irish people, in the 1940s and 1950s, had to leave annually for Britain in search of employment and a form of economic security. Leave-taking, however, took different forms in the Ireland of the 1950s. There was the drift from the land and the mass migration of people from rural to urban Ireland, particularly to Dublin. But there was also a singular episode, probably not unique, of leave-taking of a permanent and irreversible kind. The small population of the Blasket Islands abandoned their homes for accommodation and farmland on the Kerry mainland in sight of the islands.

It was a significant event in Irish history. The documents reproduced in this article will help to bring the event and the period to life. But it is the case that other small islands also lost their inhabitants during that decade. Unfortunately, their silent movement to the mainland or to take the train and boat for a life of emigration in Britain may have remained unacknowledged in works of contemporary history.

The distinguished English scholar Robin Flower published in 1944 a book with the title *The Western Island or the Great Blasket*.[1] It remains one of the most important works by an 'outsider' to capture the lives of the island people. Another Englishman, George Thomson, played an important role in encouraging local islanders to write.[2] A number told their own stories about life on the Blaskets.

Most prominent among those were Peig Sayers,[3] Muiris Ó Súilleabháin[4] and Tomás Ó Criomhthain.[5] More recently, Muiris Mac Conghail has produced an important TV documentary on the island, which was accompanied by a book titled *The Blaskets: A Kerry Island Library*.[6] In 2000, an English journalist, Cole Morton, produced a volume that successfully reconstructed the leaving of the island in 1953 and traced a number of the families who had emigrated to the United States.[7]

This article is an attempt to allow official documents to speak for themselves. In 1947, the Taoiseach, Eamon de Valera, made a visit to the Blasket Islands. He had been there 20 years before. There had also been a rumour that he might have spent a few weeks on the Blaskets during the Civil War of 1922–3. But his return visit after the ending of Second World War left him shocked and saddened by what he found.

The first document is the official minute of a meeting held in the Department of the Taoiseach on 6 August 1947.

CONDITIONS ON THE BLASKET ISLANDS

On 6 August 1947, the Taoiseach presided over a conference in his room in Leinster House which discussed the conditions on the Blasket Islands and the question of measures to improve those conditions. The following were present:

Mr E. Kissane, Parliamentary Secretary to the Taoiseach
M. Ó Muimhneacháin, Secretary to the Government
G. Mac an Bháird, Director of the Gaeltacht Services Division, Department of Lands
J. D. Rush, Principal Officer, Fisheries Branch, Department of Agriculture
P. Ó Cochláin, Principal Clerk, Technical Instruction Branch, Department of Education

The Taoiseach said that he had been deeply impressed by the deterioration in the conditions on the Great Blasket Island since his previous visit about 20 years ago. The islanders appeared to be in a state of despair and begged him to have some arrangements made without delay for their removal to the mainland. Having regard to the conditions under which they lived it was not surprising that they should have this desire, but, on the other hand, it would be regrettable if some solution could not be found which would enable them to remain on the Island in reasonable comfort. One of the most important aspects of the problem was that of transport and communications. Then there was the question of providing industries which would enable the islanders to earn a decent livelihood.

A general discussion of the conditions on the Island followed. Some of those present, particularly Mr Ó Cochláin, were inclined to the view that no satisfactory solution could be found other than that of removing the islanders to the mainland. The Parliamentary Secretary to the Taoiseach was also inclined to take this view. The Taoiseach agreed that this step might eventually prove to be unavoidable but felt that it should be taken only in the last resort. There should, he said, be a full examination of the position and an exhaustive effort to find ways of improving conditions without evacuating the Island. No doubt, any measures of improvement would be expensive but a considerable amount of expenditure would be well worthwhile if the desired objects were secured.

It was eventually agreed that Mr A. Gallagher, Outdoor Supervisor of Marine Products in the Gaeltacht Services Division of the Department of Lands, should be sent, within a week or so, to the Great Blasket Island and should be joined there by Mr Ó Cochláin, who said that he proposed to leave in a few days to spend a holiday at Ballyferriter. Mr Gallagher and Mr Ó Cochláin would not announce themselves as being government officials, but would spend some time on the Island as ordinary visitors. They would prepare a full comprehensive report, including particulars of the ages and circumstances of all the islanders and the existing resources of the Island, communications, etc. The government would be asked at its next meeting on Tuesday 12th instant, to give a direction for the setting up of an inter-departmental committee to consider the report to be furnished by Mr Gallagher and Mr Ó Cochláin, to examine fully the conditions on the Island and to make recommendations.

The Taoiseach made it clear that the functions of the proposed inter-departmental committee would, in the first instance, be limited to consideration of conditions on the Blasket Islands and would not extend to other Islands or other parts of the Gaeltacht. It was agreed that the experience which would be gained in dealing with the Blasket problem would be valuable in considering measures for the improvement of conditions in the Gaeltacht generally.

Mr Mac an Bháird was asked to make suggestions before the next government meeting as to the composition of the proposed committee. It was tentatively agreed that the following departments should be represented:

Department of Lands (Gaeltacht Services Division)
Dept of Agriculture (Fisheries Branch)
Special Employment Schemes Office
Department of Education (Technical Instruction Branch)
Department of Finance.

In the course of a further discussion which I had today with Mr Rush it was agreed that in view of the importance of transport and communications between the Island and the mainland the Department of Industry and Commerce should also be represented on the committee. The question of appointing a representative of the Dept of Posts and Telegraphs may also arise in this connection, but it is desired to keep the number of members as low as practicable.

7/8/47

*

The following document was appended to the file. The author is not known. A note at the end of the document reads as follows:

'NOTE: *The foregoing statement has been received from a correspondent whose name is not officially recorded.*
ROINN AN TOISIGH,
6ú Lúnasa, 1947'.

CONDITIONS ON THE GREAT BLASKET

The Blasket islanders are mostly housed in hovels as bad as anything in Gardiner Street or Gloucester Street in their worst days. They have no church, no priest, no doctor. There is not a single tree on the island and probably not more than half a dozen bushes. They have not a public house, a cinema or a dance-hall in which to find distraction from their woes. Their land is untillable. They have no cows that I saw, and apart from doles, their only means of livelihood are the grazing of mountain sheep and lobster fishing. They are dying out and perhaps it is better for them so.

I fear it is too late now, but I believe that they could have been saved at, relatively, a very small cost. Father Cussen, OP, almost single-handed and with a multitude of other preoccupations established a prosperous homespun industry in Knockadoon, near Youghal and a doll-making industry. It will not be easy to do anything like that for the ageing and despairing people of the Blaskets, but the government, with the resources under their control, should make the effort before the hopeless alternative of shifting the population is adopted.

The first step should be to send, *immediately, before this summer is out*, the Director of the Gaeltacht Services, the Head of the Fisheries Branch and the Staff Officer of the Technical Instruction Branch to spend a couple of weeks on the island and require them to report on what can be done to establish some little industries and to train the people to manage and operate them. (I understand that Father Cussen got people sent from Knockadoon to Donegal to be trained in spinning and doll-making.) They should also be required to consider means of improving communications with the mainland – for example, the provision of a motor ferry and the improvement of the landing stage.

A domestic economy teacher should be sent to the island for six or twelve months to show the people how to make the most of the food they can afford and to keep their houses decently, and a good handy-man to teach them how to do simple building and repairs and to induce them to knock down the loathsome ruins around their houses. There must surely be people with enough interest in Irish to undertake these jobs with enthusiasm for the sake of the language.

In anything that is done care should be taken not to weaken further any spirit of independence there is in the islanders. They will need it all to survive. There should be an effort to find or create leaders among them who will be able to keep going any industrial or social enterprise that is started in the place.

Also, the industry or industries should be based, if possible and so far as possible, on local resources. For example, it would be well worthwhile investigating the possibility of extracting vitamin oils from mackerel – perhaps the oiliest of fish – for which there is now no remunerative market owing to the deterioration, and rise in cost, of transport. The wool of the island sheep could, perhaps, be used in a local homespun industry. Lobsters could possibly be tinned on the island, if there is a sufficient supply to make tinning profitable – but this is doubtful.

Another thing worth thinking about is the establishment of a hostel for students of Irish and simple holiday-makers. In spite of the description I have given, the Blaskets would be a good place for a holiday for anyone who is satisfied with simple pleasures. There is an excellent bathing strand; boating and fishing are to be had cheaply and there is a good road, or broad pathway, for walking round the island.

The following document provides for the appointment of the interdepartmental committee on the Great Blasket Island and sets out its terms of reference.

MEAMRAM AN AIRE TAILTE AG CEAPADH

AN CHOISTE

I hereby appoint

Mr Gilbert Mac an Bháird,
Director,
Gaeltacht Services Division,
Department of Lands.

Mr P. Ó Cochláin,
Principal Clerk,
Department of Education (Technical Instruction Branch).

Mr T. K. M. Whitaker,
Assistant Principal Officer,
Department of Finance.

Mr Seán Ó Braonáin,
Assistant Principal Officer,
Department of Agriculture (Fisheries Branch).

Mr Richard O'Hegarty,
Assistant Superintendent,
Special Employment Schemes Office.

Mr Brendán Breathnach,
Higher Executive Officer,
Department of Industry and Commerce (Transport & Marine Branch).

to be an inter-departmental committee

a) to consider the report furnished by Messrs A. Gallagher, of the Department of Lands, and P. Ó Cochláin, of the Department of Education, following an inspection made by them of the Great Blasket Island;

b) to examine fully the conditions at present obtaining on the island, and

c) to make such recommendations as they think fit, with the object of improving living conditions on the Island.

I hereby appoint Mr Gilbert Mac an Bháird to be Chairman of the Committee and Mr Liam Mac Colla, Executive Officer, Gaeltacht Services Division, Department of Lands, to be Secretary of the Committee.

(Sd.) SEÁN MOYLAN.
Minister for Lands.
30, Deireadh Fómhair, 1947.

The following is an edited English version of the report of the interdepartmental committee.

REPORT OF THE INTER-DEPARTMENTAL COMMITTEE ON THE GREAT BLASKET ISLAND

The Minister for Lands:
We, the committee appointed by your warrant of the 30th October, 1947, wish to submit this report. As it was decided at the outset to carry on the work of the committee through the medium of Irish, the report has been written in that language.

1. Attached herewith (Appendix A) are the reports referred to in paragraph (a) of the terms of reference. Supplementary information was obtained from both authors of the reports and certain Officers of the Departments of Agriculture, Industry & Commerce (Transport and Marine Branch), and Posts and Telegraphs, who had particular knowledge of features of life on the island, were interviewed. Information on certain matters was requested from the following Departments of State: The Department of Industry & Commerce, the Department of Social Welfare, the Department of Lands, the Department of Posts and Telegraphs and the Department of Agriculture (Fisheries Branch). Much information and assistance was obtained from these officers and Departments for which we are most grateful to them. Sixteen meetings of the committee were convened.

THE ISLAND ITSELF
2. The Great Blasket is situated approximately three miles from the southwest coast of Kerry. Dunquin, near Slea Head, is the nearest point on the mainland and there the islanders usually land. Dingle, the nearest big town, is approximately sixteen miles from the island. The island stretches north-east and south-west. It is bare, high and unsheltered, except for the small portion directly facing the mainland. There are cliffs on all sides, and it is impossible to land, even in the curraghs or canoes of the islanders, except on the north-eastern side, where a rough pathway rises from the sea. The little arable land that is available is on this slope, on the north-east of the island, where there is shelter from the wind, and it is there that the entire population of the island resides. The island has an area of 1,132 acres, 2 roods and 36 perches, but the most of this consists of wild mountainous commonage useless for anything but sheep-grazing in summertime. The sea that surrounds the island is very frequently disturbed and the sound between the island and the mainland is very dangerous.

POPULATION OF THE ISLAND
3. The following was the population of the island since the year 1891 according to the official Census figures.

1891	-	132
1901	-	145
1911	-	160 (88 males, 72 females)
1926	-	143
1936	-	110 (64 males, 46 females)
1946	-	45 (32 males, 13 females)

51 people lived on the island in 1947 and the following table shows their sex and age.

Age	Males		Females		Infants	Total
	Married/Single		Married/Single			
Under 4			2	2		
Between 20–40	2	16	2	3	–	23
Between 40–60	–	4	–	2	–	6
Between 60–70	4	2	5	–	–	11
Over 70	4*	1	3*	1	–	9
TOTAL	10	23	10	6	2	51

* Among these were 3 Widowers and 3 Widows

REASONS FOR DECLINE IN POPULATION

4. The decline that has taken place in the island's population in this century is not peculiar as practically all rural districts in Western Ireland have been similarly affected. The decline in the number of islanders is due to the abandonment of the island by the young people and particularly by the girls and the absence of youthful couples taking up their lives there. It seems probable that the same fundamental reasons apply to emigration from the island as apply to emigration from rural Ireland generally, but there are certain features of life on the island which strengthen the inclination towards emigration, viz. – the remoteness of the island, loneliness in the winter, the dread of being without food, the danger of not being able to obtain the services of priest or doctor in time of need, the absence of teacher or nurse on the island and the hardness of life in general. As the number of islanders declines these matters affect them more. Loneliness is accentuated and there is a greater feeling of helplessness in times of emergency.

DWELLING HOUSES

5. There were 21 dwelling houses on the Blasket in 1891; 25 in 1901, and 29 in 1911. At present there are 20 dwelling houses on the island of which 15 are inhabited and 5 uninhabited. Five houses have slate roofs (four being uninhabited); nine have felt roofs, and six have galvanised iron roofs (one being uninhabited). The people, who formerly dwelt in the five uninhabited houses went to the mainland. Some of the houses are not in too good condition. 26 applications for assistance under the Housing (Gaeltacht) Acts 1929/1939 were received from the people of the island. Assistance was only given in three cases, and in these three cases grants and loans were allowed for the erection of new dwellings, these being built, however, on the mainland. In the remaining cases, the Gaeltacht

Services Division were not satisfied that loans could be repaid and, since it appeared that the applicants would not be able to carry out the work without both loan and grant, no assistance was sanctioned.

FISHING

6. Fishing is the most important means of livelihood to the islanders. The boats utilised are canoes which have the reputation of being the most suitable type of boat for the type of sea that surrounds the island. The canoe is a very light boat which can be carried on the shoulders. It is made of laths and tarred canvas. It is up to 25 feet long and has provision for eight crew. Three is the usual crew. A canoe costs approximately £30 at the present time.

7. The islanders pursue lobster fishing mainly and the canoe is quite suitable for this purpose. Some mackerel fishing is done, but since the United States government imposed a tariff on salted mackerel about 20 years ago, there has been little sale for mackerel until recently, when a demand arose in England for fresh mackerel. The islanders, however, cannot very well avail of this market due to the long journey they would have to make to Dingle, before the fish could be kept fresh for the market. We were informed that the islanders do some fishing with pocket nets and line. Haddock, cod and pollock are caught with these and in the main they are salted and stored for winter use.

8. In view of the high price obtaining for lobsters for some years past lobster fishing is very valuable to the islanders. It is pursued from spring to autumn each year, and it is understood that it is worth £500/£600 at least per season to the people of the island. The lobsters are sold to three individuals – one from Tralee, one from Dunquin and one from Dingle. Before the war a French boat used to come to the island to buy lobsters, but it has not come since then. The islanders have no difficulty, however, in obtaining a market for their lobsters.

TILLAGE

9. Only 60 acres of the total area of 1,132 acres of the island are arable. These 60 acres are situated in the north-eastern portion of the island and are divided in such a way that each household of the fifteen households on the island holds 2 to 4 acres. Only 10 acres approximately of this arable land are cultivated. The soil in the arable land is quite fertile. It is manured with seaweed, farmyard manure, and chemical manure. There is no limestone on the island, and it cannot be obtained nearer than Castlemaine on the mainland.

10. Each household plants about ½ acre of potatoes. The crop is as good as the crop obtained in many places on the mainland. In 1947, a crop of 6½ tons of ware potatoes per acre was obtained. In addition to potatoes some islanders grow a small patch of oats and some turnips. No hay is saved on the island and the oats are given to the cows in sheaves. Vegetables are not grown even for visitors. The islanders attend mainly to fish-

ing and are indifferent to improving their holdings. They have no desire to avail of any assistance obtainable under the Improvements Schemes of the Department of Agriculture, but they avail themselves of the scheme for obtaining a change of seeds. They would have nothing to do with any plot scheme of that Department or with bee keeping, although there is plenty of heather on the island. The same patches of land are cultivated year after year, the reason advanced by the islanders for this being that the crops must be grown in a place safe from storms. It is considered that the island would be unsuited to fruit growing.

Apart from the 60 acres of arable land the remainder of the island is a commonage which could not be cultivated.

CATTLE

11. The people of the island have 600 sheep, 6 milch cows, one bull, 15 hens and 15 donkeys (a donkey for each household). The sheep are kept on the island itself and on Beg-Inish island nearby. It is understood that one person owns 200 of the sheep, another person 100 and that nine other households own the remainder. Thus, there are four households who have no sheep … Some sheep are lost over the cliffs. The sheep are mainly kept for their wool, which is usually sold in Dingle. They thrive on the island and have never been known to have black scab though they are not dipped. The islanders rarely go to the mainland to sell sheep. A buyer comes from Dingle usually and the sheep are conveyed to the mainland in canoes – six or seven to each canoe.

12. A bull is now kept on the island which although unlicensed is well reputed. A bull is usually not kept for longer than a year. It is only for the past few years that a bull has been kept on the island. Until then, the cows had to be conveyed to the mainland in canoes, a difficult and dangerous task.

INDUSTRY

13. There is no industry on the island. The Gaeltacht Services Division attempted to establish a sock knitting industry there towards the end of 1937. Ten 120-needle hand-operated machines were sent in together with the necessary yarns, etc., and a manageress was appointed to control the industry. In addition, an organising manageress was sent to the island to assist in the training of the women of the island in the work. Premises were rented from one of the islanders, and in order to entice the women to work, wages were paid during the training period. This was the first occasion that this procedure was adopted, the usual practice being not to pay learners any wages. As soon as the women were trained, they were paid the usual piece-rates in operation in other sock knitting industries in the Gaeltacht at the time. At the outset, the industry had 9 women employed. Employment of a manageress was continued until the beginning of 1940. No proper progress was, however, being made and in February 1940, the manageress was withdrawn and one of the workers was put in charge of the industry. She was paid commission on the production and she could also earn money as a worker. This arrangement was continued

until the end of 1942, when it was decided to discontinue it as –

a) it was not possible to provide yarns for the manufacture of socks on 120 needle machines
b) there were at that time only three workers and there appeared to be no likelihood, due to emigration, of increasing that number; and
c) there seemed to be no likelihood of progress in the industry.

During the period that the industry functioned, viz. between 22nd November, 1937 and 31st December, 1942, the amount of wages paid to workers was £523.

FUEL
14. Bad turf or screws cut on the big commonage on the island is used as fuel.

FOOD
15. The islanders live principally on bread, tea, fish and potatoes. Meat is seldom eaten despite the fact that a large flock of sheep is kept. There are only six milch-cows and the islanders have to depend on tinned milk during the winter. The islanders obtain their supplies of flour, tea, sugar, etc., in Dunquin.

ASSOCIATION WITH THE MAINLAND
16. The only means of communication with the mainland are canoes and radio-telephone. The islanders utilise canoes for travelling to the mainland, for bringing visitors to the island and for carrying animals and all types of merchandise. A canoe is also used for the carriage of letters and parcels to and from the island ...

17. The post office on the island is connected with the post office at Dunquin by radio-telephone powered by batteries. Only 'morse' messages may be sent and these only when the post office at Dunquin is open, viz. between 9 a.m. and 7 p.m. Dunquin post office is closed on Sundays. 24-hour telephone connection between Dunquin and Dingle is not at present in operation. The radio-telephone has been on the Great Blasket Island since the 19th June 1941. In 1947 the apparatus broke down on the following occasions:

1. from 11.30 a.m. on 4th January and it was out of order until 2nd February;
2. from 9.30 a.m. until 6.30 p.m. on June 27th;
3. from 5.15 p.m. November 26th and it remained out of order until 6.30 p.m. November 27th.

This year the apparatus was out of order from January 15th until February 15th. Because of the stormy weather, it was not possible to send a mechanic to the island. It is not possible to communicate with Dingle or Bally-ferriter by radio-telephone, since the land-screen that lies between the island and those places reduces the power of the apparatus in such a way as to prevent messages reaching them. We understand from the Department of Posts and Telegraphs that it would not be worth while to provide a standby apparatus on the island since a competent person would be required to effect the change over from one apparatus to another when necessary. We understand that it would be impossible to substitute the ordinary telephone for the radio-telephone, because of the difficulty of laying a cable on the sea-floor between the island and the mainland.

18. The Department of Posts and Telegraphs has a contract with one of the islanders for the carriage of mails by canoe between the island and Dunquin. He is paid £80 per annum. The contract provides for a three-day service per week – on Tuesdays, Thursdays and Saturdays, subject to the weather being suitable. If the weather is not suitable, the service is carried out on the next suitable day. Some 15 letters and 3 parcels are usually posted per week on the island while deliveries amount to some 32 letters and 9 parcels. The progress of the mail service during the year ended 30th September, 1947, was examined. During the period of eight months from October, 1946 to May, 1947 seventy-two journeys were made and during the four months from May, 1947, to September, 1947, thirty-nine journeys were made. Only during one week – the week ended 17th September, 1947 – did the service fail to be carried out at all. There were eight weeks in which one journey only, in and out, was made, and twenty-six weeks in which two journeys only were made. Three journeys were made in each of the other seventeen weeks.

STATE ASSISTANCE
19. Nine of the islanders receive a sum of £292.10s.0d. by way of Old Age Pensions. Approximately £210 per annum between Unemployment Benefit and Unemployment Assistance is divided between 28 or 29 other persons. The Special Improvements Scheme Office has expended £1,200 on the maintenance of the bohreen on the island since 1933.

CONDITIONS OF THE ISLANDERS GENERALLY
20. In comparison with people in other districts in the West of Ireland it may be stated that the Blasket Islanders are reasonably well off. They do not and never have paid rates or annuities. A fair amount of money is made on fishing and on sheep and when regard is had to the produce of the arable land, the income from visitors and State assistance it appears that the majority of the households are comfortable.

ISLANDERS' DIFFICULTIES
21. It appears that the islanders' main grievance is the loneliness and remoteness of the island. They feel that they are entirely cut off from the life of the rest of the country and from association with other people. Besides this, they are apprehensive of their weakness in times of emergency since neither priest nor doctor nor nurse is available on the island. These difficulties have existed for a long time but they are felt more as the population decreases. The following complaints were specially mentioned:

a) the bad communication facilities with the mainland;

b) their fear of food shortage in times of bad weather;

c) the insufficiency of the amount of flour they get and

d) the insufficiency of their equipment for present day fishing.

They desire that they should be transferred from the island; that each household should be given a house and grazing for one cow; and that they should be allowed to retain their land on the island. These matters are considered hereinafter.

[Paragraphs 22–29 are not reproduced here.]

MIGRATION TO MAINLAND

30. The chief request made by the islanders was that they be transferred to the mainland. We do not see that it comes within our terms of reference to make any recommendation as regards such a policy and, accordingly, we refer here only to what would be involved in such a transfer as we understand the position. It appears that what the islanders desire is that they should be dealt with on the same basis as the islanders of Iniskea, County Mayo, viz., that the Land Commission should get land for them on the mainland near the island, should erect houses for them on that land and should undertake their migration thereto, subject to the proviso that they should be allowed to retain their land on the island for the purpose of sheep grazing. In their view, only a small amount of land would be required for each household as fishing would be their main pursuit and not tillage; and, accordingly, it would be essential that they should not be migrated to a place far removed from the island. We were informed that some of the original islanders have already settled on holdings on the mainland near the island, but we do not know how they obtained the land there, nor whether the remaining islanders, or some of them, could do likewise on their own without assistance from the State.

APPENDIX A

9th September, 1947

1. According to the Census Records the number of people living on the island in 1946 was as follows:

Total	Males	Females	Married	Single	Widows
					(men or women)
45	32	13	10	27	8

18 of these people were over 60 years of age, twenty-one others over 30 years of age, and six of the unmarried women were over 22 years of age. 15 houses were inhabited and eight houses and the School (which has been closed for 4 years) were empty. Two-thirds of the householders had small holdings (averaging 3 acres), the largest being 7 acres and the smallest ½ acre. All the people were Irish speakers and Catholics, the majority being without English.

59

2. Aindrias Ó Gallchobhair of the Gaeltacht Services Division and my-self [P. Ó Cochláin] visited the island on Wednesday the 20th August, 1947, as had been arranged in the Taoiseach's Room at Leinster House on the 12th August, to obtain some information with a view to seeing what best could be done to help the people of the Blasket. Attached herewith is a list of the people living on the island on that day as given to us by Seán Ó Dálaigh, Dunquin, who took us to the island in a canoe and by Pádraig T. Ó Cearnaigh of the island itself. The present population does not differ from that shown in the Census Records of 1946 except that there are two young couples there at present, one newly-married and the other waiting for a house on the mainland.

PEOPLE ON THE ISLAND – 20/8/1947
Pádraig T. Ó Cearnaigh
Eibhlín (his wife)
Tomás (his son)
Mairéad (his daughter)

Seán Ó Cearnaigh
Luise (his wife)) newly married

Seán T. Ó Cearnaigh
Tomás)
Pádraig) (his sons)
Máirtín)

Cáit (his daughter)   Looking for a house outside
Pádraig Ó Cearnaigh (Cáit's husband))   in order to leave the island
Their son (4 years old)

Luise Bean Uí Chearnaigh (widow) Post Office
Micheál Ó Cearnaigh (her son)
Seán Ó Cearnaigh (do)
Luise Ní Chearnaigh (her daughter)

Pádraig Ó Conchubhair
Seán Ó Cearnaigh (his nephew)
Cáit Ní Chearnaigh (his niece), a patient in Dingle Hospital

Pádraig Ó Dálaigh
Tomás)
Pádraig) (his sons)

Muiris Ó Catháin
Cáit (his wife)
Seán (his son)
Muiris (do)
Pádraig (do), a patient in hospital

Peats Ó Catháin (Caiste)

Siobhán (his wife)
Seán (his son)
Seán's wife
Their child (one month old)

Seán Ó Súilleabháin
Siobhán (his wife)
Pádraig)
Micheál) (sons)
Seán)

Eoin Ó Duinnshléibhe

Séamus Ó Duinnshléibhe

Máire Bean Uí Ghuithin
Micheál Ó Guithín (her son)

Pádraig Ó Guithín
His son (nicknamed 'Fine')

– Ní Chinnéide ('the weaver's daughter'), a patient in hospital

Máire Bean Uí Ghuithín
Seán)
Muiris) (her sons)
Máire (daughter)

Micheál Ó Seoghdha
Máirín (his sister)

*

The following report was submitted to the Department of Lands on 1 April 1953.

DEPARTMENT OF LANDS

Quarterly Progress Report – 1st April 1953 to 30th June 1953

Proposals for the transfer of the Blasket islanders to the mainland have been approved. Two farmers from the adjoining mainland (William Kavanagh and Ulick Moran) surrendered 111 acres and shares in commonage and were migrated in April to new holdings in Kildare and Dublin. The house surrendered by Moran has been allotted to the Keane family (4 persons) which includes the only child on the island and it is expected that they will transfer to it shortly. Four houses are to be erected on the surrendered lands for 4 other island families (15 persons). As regards the other islanders (6 in all) final proposals have not yet been sanctioned but the intention is to install 4 elderly unmarried men in Kavanagh's old home later in the year; it is expected that the local postman and his mother will take up residence in Dublin where employment is being provided for the former in the Post Office service. Accommodation land of 3 or 4 acres will be provided with the islanders' dwellings on the mainland, the islanders retaining ownership of their holdings on the Blaskets.

*

The following is the Cabinet minute authorising the transfer of the islanders to the mainland.

Extract from
CABINET MINUTES
G.C. 6/122   7/11/52   item 6.

GREAT BLASKET ISLAND: Migration of population to Dunquin, County Kerry

Following consideration of a memorandum dated the 5th November, 1952, submitted by the Minister for Education relative to the recommendations of an inter-departmental committee set up on the 30th October, 1947, to consider certain matters in connection with the Great Blasket Island, County Kerry, it was decided that the Minister for Lands should arrange for the migration of the inhabitants of the Island to Dunquin, County Kerry, where they are to be provided with alternative accommodation in accordance with the scheme outlined in the memorandum.

*

The following is the memorandum to government on which the government finally based its decision to arrange for the transfer of the islanders to the mainland.

AN ROINN OIDEACHAIS
MEMORANDUM FOR THE GOVERNMENT
MIGRATION OF THE POPULATION OF THE GREAT BLASKET
ISLAND TO THE MAINLAND

1. An inter-departmental committee was set up by the Minister for Lands in 1947 to consider certain matters in connection with the Great Blasket Island and to make such recommendations as they thought fit, with the object of improving living conditions on the Island.

2. In their report dated 21st December, 1948, the committee, having made recommendations as required, stated that the decline in the population of the island had been so great and life on the island had become so difficult that, in their opinion, the improvements recommended by them could not be expected to induce the inhabitants to remain on the island.

3. A translation of the summary of the committee's recommendations as embodied in their report is attached (Enclosure A).

4. The Minister for Lands, in September, 1949, submitted to the government the committee's report, together with a memorandum in which he requested a decision as to whether the Islanders should be migrated en bloc to the adjoining mainland where, free of the disadvantages of island life, they would have more incentive to keep their community intact. It was arranged at a meeting of the government held on 9th November, 1949 that the Ministers for Lands and Agriculture would communicate their views on the matter to the Minister for Education.

5. The Minister for Lands has had the question of migrating the population of the Great Blasket Island to the mainland examined from the viewpoint of providing houses and accommodation plots on the mainland and allowing the allottees to retain their island holdings for use in conjunction with the new allotments. It has been estimated that a migration scheme for the Islanders would cost about £23,000 (of which £2,250 would stand to be recovered from the migrants by way of repayable advances). This estimate includes provision of housing accommodation for nine households from the island at present living in temporary shelters on the mainland, as well as for the eleven families still remaining on the island, with a plot of, it is expected, at least 1 to 1½ acres for each household.

6. The Minister for Agriculture has expressed the view that the Blasket Island fishermen, if they decide to take up residence on the mainland, could arrange to continue with the type of fishing they practised from the Blaskets – mainly lobster fishing – but that there would be no hope of their being absorbed in the fishing industry at Dingle, where the fishing fleet consists almost entirely of motor boats, in the handling of which the islanders have no experience. The islanders could also, however, continue from their new homes to pursue their principal means of livelihood, which is the raising of sheep on the island.

7. The Parliamentary Secretary to the government is strongly in favour of the proposal. A copy of a memorandum furnished by the Administrator of his Office is attached (Enclosure B).

8. The Minister for Finance considers it extremely doubtful, in view of the islanders' past record as regards the payment of rates and annuities, that all or any substantial part of the £2,250 recoverable from the migrants would prove to be forthcoming and thus that virtually the total cost could fall to be borne by the Exchequer. He feels that the proposed accommodating of the migrants on the mainland is a responsibility which might more appropriately be borne by the Kerry County Council than by the Land Commission, as he considers that it is not a function of the latter to provide houses save in so far as they are needed in connection with the creation of economic agricultural holdings.

9. Other points made by the Minister for Finance are that the migrants might continue to reside on the island, at least during the April-September part of the year, and let the new houses to tourists or others; that there might even be the possibility of some of the islanders returning to permanent residence on the island and thus in a few years re-creating the whole problem; and that the migration at State expense of the Blasketers might give rise to demands for similar treatment for other islanders in the west and north, and that thus the present proposal, if implemented, might set in train a continuous and expanding outlay amounting ultimately to perhaps a £¼ million or more. The Minister for Finance has, therefore, expressed the view that 'from the financial standpoint, the proposal is most unattractive and he is definitely of the opinion that it should not be proceeded with at all in present circumstances. Economic or other conditions may change to the benefit of the Islanders. If such is not the case the natural drift to the mainland should be allowed to continue. Any mass migration would not only be expensive to the State or local authority but would intensify the congestion already existing on the mainland. Such migration would in any case destroy the distinctive Blasket tradition, and all the expense would have been incurred in vain'.

10. It is understood that the Blasketers themselves are very anxious to be migrated to the mainland. There were no children of school-going age on the island in March, 1950, nor were there any unmarried women. There were, however, at that time some ten men of marriageable age there, but it is understood that women are no longer prepared to marry into the island. The following shows the number of persons living on the island in the various years stated, since 1891:

Year	Number
1891	132
1901	145
1911	160 (88 male, 72 female)
1926	143
1936	110 (64 male, 46 female)
1946	45 (32 male, 13 female)
1947	51
1950 (March)	30 (23 men, 6 women, 1 child) (11 households)

11. The Minister for Education agrees with the view expressed by the Minister for Finance that it is possible that the £2,250 which would fall to be repaid by the islanders might not prove recoverable, and that, from the strictly financial viewpoint, the whole scheme is unattractive.

12. The Minister for Education has been informed by the Minister for Local Government that the matter does not fall within the province of Kerry County Council, since a County Council cannot allocate labourers' cottages under the Labourers Acts to farmers or other persons who do not come within the category of 'Agricultural Labourer' as the term is defined

in these Acts. In this connection, however, the Minister for Finance has stated that he is not convinced that the project, as it has emerged, would not be more appropriately undertaken by the Kerry County Council since it involves in effect the provision of houses with small plots for a number of rural people in humble circumstances and not the creation or improvement of agricultural holdings or relief of congestion – the normal and essential features of Land Commission re-settlement activity. With regard to this the Minister for Local Government has intimated that 'apart from the legal aspect – of which there is no doubt if the principal means of livelihood of the islanders is sheep farming, as indicated in paragraph 6 above – there is the practical difficulty that the Kerry County Council have a substantial programme to undertake for the re-housing of agricultural labourers at present in need of new accommodation. Cottages provided by the County Council must be let subject to the statutory priorities and it is most unlikely that the Council would be in a position to cater for a mass migration scheme within a measurable period. The State contribution in the form of housing subsidies towards a scheme of 20 labourers' cottages would amount to as much as £11,600 for cottages without water and sewerage services and to £13,400 for a scheme with services, on the basis of the present subsidies. The current rent for an unserviced cottage in Kerry is 6/8d per week plus rates'. The Minister for Local Government notes also that the migration of the Iniskea islanders in 1931 was carried out by the Land Commission.

13. With regard to the possibility of some of the islanders letting their new houses to tourists, the Minister for Education considers that it would not be feasible, nor, even if feasible, desirable, to prevent such a step on their part. He has no fear that any of the islanders would return to permanent residence on the island, as such has not occurred in the case of any previous migration.

14. The Minister for Education does not consider it likely that a Blasket migration would give rise to a general demand for like treatment. He is informed by the Minister for Lands that the only island in a similar plight is Inishark, where there remain only seven families, but that Inishark, unlike the Great Blasket, is seven miles from the coast, has no communal link therewith and is not Irish-speaking.

15. Having taken all the circumstances into account, and particularly the facts that the island is Irish-speaking, with close contacts and communal ties with the Irish-speaking mainland, thus rendering it likely that the migrants would fit without disturbance into the mainland community, the Minister for Education is of opinion that the problem is a national and a humanitarian one and that the best course would be that the Minister for Lands should arrange for the migration of the islanders to Dunquin.

16. He desires to mention also that if this course is not adopted very shortly it may not be possible at all to provide for the islanders on the Irish-speaking mainland, since the provision of the 52 acres which it is ex-

pected will be available shortly in Dunquin is contingent on the provision of an alternative holding in County Cork for the owner of the 52 acres, and the Minister for Education is informed by the Minister for Lands that the holding concerned in County Cork may soon be no longer available.

17. The Minister for Education therefore requests that a decision be taken as to whether, as a matter of government policy, the migration should be carried out as indicated in paragraph 15 above.

ENCLOSURE A
Translation of summary of recommendations of the Interdepartmental Committee, as embodied in their report dated 21st December, 1948, concerning the Great Blasket

1. That the Department of Posts and Telegraphs see to the improvement of the telephone service between the island and the mainland so that the islanders would have an opportunity of seeking assistance whenever they would require it;

2. that the Department of Local Government (since the care of all the islands in time of emergency was that Department's responsibility) arrange with the life-boat station at Valentia Island that the life-boat from Valentia would come to the assistance of the Blasket Islanders in time of need;

3. that the Office of Public Works improve the pathway from the sea on the north-east of the island;

4. that the Office of Public Works improve the boat slip and other facilities at Dunquin;

5. that the Department of Local Government see what arrangements could be made so that there would be a supply of food on the island as a reserve for emergencies;

6. that the Department of Industry and Commerce examine whether an increased ration of flour might be allowed to the islanders;

7. that the appropriate Departments consider whether the regulations under the respective Housing Acts should be modified so as to enable the islanders to obtain assistance towards improving their houses;

8. that the appropriate Departments examine the question of what action might usefully be taken to have instruction in agriculture, fishing, trades and domestic economy made available to the residents of the island.

*Comments on Draft Memorandum for the Government from
Department of Education with reference to migration of population
from Great Blasket Island*

I am in full agreement with terms of draft memo and I endorse in toto recommendation in last paragraph thereof.

As I inspected the Great Blasket and its inhabitants on behalf of the Land Commission in 1950 I still retain a vivid picture of the hopeless condition of the residents as then presented and make the following observations with reference thereto.

1. The Great Blasket community which was so vigorous up to the 1914–18 war can no longer survive in its island home. There is now absolutely no doubt about this. The men – young and old – want to be taken off and no woman will now marry and live on the island, as the hazards are too great. The land is being neglected and is reverting.

2. The Blasket community would merge naturally with its environment if migrated to adjoining mainland in the Dunquin vicinity. Irish is the spoken language used by all, and many of the Islanders are related by birth and marriage to the mainlanders, which would be conducive to swift assimilation.

3. If the Blasket Gaelic speaking community is to survive at all it can best survive on the adjoining mainland where Irish is the spoken language. The migration should strengthen the native language position in the Dunquin area.

4. If the islanders are left to their own resources they will in time – say 15 to 20 years – all have moved to the mainland and will do their best to provide themselves with whatever makeshift alternative homes they can. If this 'laissez faire' policy is adopted there is a great danger that the Blasket civilisation as it is now known will be permanently lost, as it is probable that the islanders will pick up isolated house sites on commonages over a wide area (some of them not in the Gaeltacht) if left to their own resources on the mainland and their distinctive community way of life will then quickly disappear.

5. The Land Commission have the facilities as well as the tradition for dealing with the problem. In 1931 the Iniskea islanders off Mayo coast were migrated to the Blacksod peninsula; the islanders were then – and still are – 100% Irish speaking.

(Sd.) J. F. Glynn,
Riarthóir.
26 Lúnasa, 1952.

The following is an article from the Cork Examiner, *18 November 1953,
on the efforts to evacuate the Blaskets.*

TURBULENT SEAS PREVENT EVACUATION OF BLASKETS

In a remote corner of County Kerry, where the huge Atlantic breakers
pound relentlessly on the rugged coastline around Slea Head and Dunquin, and where seldom a word of English is spoken by the hardy, weather-
tanned inhabitants, a drama of no little moment to its participants was
enacted yesterday.

It was the beginning of the final stage of the total evacuation of the
historic Blasket Islands, stronghold of an ancient and distinctive Gaelic
civilisation, home of peerless story-tellers and sages like Peig Sayers and
Tomás Ó Criomhthain, and a place of pilgrimage for generations of Irish
scholars and students.

Yesterday was the day fixed for the final exodus, but the weather de-
creed otherwise, and only six out of twenty-one were able to leave the
island owing to the huge swell in the rolling seas.

For years past, it had been regretfully realised that the Blaskets' days
of glory were no more. Not for the younger generation were the rigours of
life, on the dreary, winds-swept and often stormbound 'Oileán Mór' which
had been borne and overcome by their forbears. Emigration, death and
dwindling population all took their toll, and for a long time past, the
government, working especially through the Irish Land Commission,
have been arranging to transplant the remaining 30 or so residents of the
island to the mainland at Duncuin. In recent months quite a few had left.

When a *Cork Examiner* representative reached Dingle early yesterday
morning he found the sheltered bay as calm as a mill-pond. Arrangements
had been made that a 4-ton fishing smack, Mr M. Brosnan's *Naomh
Lorcan Ó Tuathail*, would sail from Dingle to the Great Blasket where the
islanders would transfer to it by means of their noamhóga (small rowing
currachs) and the boat would then bring them direct to Dunquin pier.

ANGRY SEAS

Our representative with Inspectors J. A. Goulding and D. O'Brien of the
Land Commission, with officials of the Department of Posts and Telegraphs
and other pressmen, was enabled to travel out from Dingle on board. As
soon as the almost landlocked harbour was left behind, however, the seas
rose and all along the rocky coast angry foam and huge showers of spray
could be discerned. The officials' hearts sank as they saw their destination
surrounded by a sea of white.

> As the Lorcan Ó Tuathail *neared the Great Blasket, groups of the is-
> landers gathered on the cliffs.*

It was obvious that the three women on the island would not attempt to
leave and that the task of transferring the islanders' belongings, including
bedding and furniture, could not be undertaken.

Eventually six men put out in their noamhóga and although their craft was tossed about perilously, they managed to bring some of their personal property with them. They brought blankets and suitcases, one had a folding armchair, another carried possessions in galvanised buckets. The noamhóga plied to and fro a few times. Mr O'Brien of the Land Commission spent some time on the island and after about an hour the *Lorcan Ó Tuathail* was ready to leave again, much to the relief of some of those on board who suffered extreme discomfiture as the vessel rolled up and down in the turbulent waters.

As there was not the slightest chance of landing at Dunquin pier, the boat faced again for Dingle. It arrived back about four hours after it had started on its journey. It had not fulfilled its mission in its entirety, but all arrangements were made for the completion of the transfer within the next few days, providing the seas calm down sufficiently.

During the proceedings on the island and the journey back, nothing but Irish was spoken.

Those who came ashore yesterday are Seán Ó Catháin, Seán P. Ó Cearna, Seán Ó Cearna, Seán Ó Súilleabháin, Seán Óg Guithín agus Pádraig Mistéal. The last-named, who was the eldest of them, was able to speak fluent English as well as Irish. He went to sea as a young man and also spent some years in the United States.

LIFE 'TOO PRECARIOUS'

Many of them spoke in Irish to our reporter and told of their last days on the island. Although they regretted leaving the homes of their ancestors they all agreed that life had become too precarious and hard, cut off from the supplies and other facilities of the mainland. They were all looking forward to their new life at Dunquin.

Although Gaelic scholars in all parts of Ireland will deplore the final evacuation of Robin Flower's 'Western Island' they have the consolation of knowing that the islanders will continue to dwell in a region every bit as Irish as the Blasket. More than many other Gaeltacht districts, Dunquin and its environs have preserved the ancient tongue. Irish is still the language of hearth and farmyard, church and school, shop and field. When our representative visited Dunquin School yesterday (a building in urgent need of care and attention from the Department of Education), nothing but Irish was to be heard from the twenty or so young children playing in the school yard.

One of the gayest of them all was young Gearóid Ó Cathair, the school's newest pupil, who up to a week or so age was the only child living on the Blaskets.

He played and laughed and shouted with the others, entirely unaware of the fact that in a language he does not understand he had won headlines in the newspapers as 'the loneliest boy in the world'.

Dotted around Dunquin, on land vacated by families who some months ago migrated to County Kildare, are four houses waiting to be occupied by the island families. They have been erected under the supervision of the Land Commission and are well-designed, well-built four-roomed structures. In all of them bright fires burned yesterday, and the Land Commission had left a ton of coal at each as a free gift. The occupants will hold the houses (and a few acres of land go with each) at a small rental.

LINK WITH ISLAND

Even when the last of the islanders have settled in on the mainland (in two or three days' time), their link with the Great Blasket will not be entirely severed. Not only do all their new homes look straight across the waves at their old, but it will be necessary for the menfolk at least to cross those waves quite frequently in their 'noamhóga' to tend to their flocks of sheep, which will be left to graze on the island. For a number of them the wool and mutton trades are quite profitable.

It is interesting to note that the islanders always buried their folk on the mainland, mostly at Dunquin. In former days, when there was a much larger Blasket population, those melancholy funerals across the sea were fairly frequent events. In future, when any members of their families die, the very obvious difficulties of such burial arrangements will not arise.

RUMOURS DENIED

There had been a number of rumours circulated in the last few weeks to the effect that a few of the older residents of the island (unmarried men) might refuse to leave. Yesterday some of those who landed at Dingle denied these, and said that all were ready to leave. Mr O'Brien, of the Land Commission, who, as has been stated, was the only official to go on to the island from the fishing smack, reported, too, that he had got the signatures to letting documents of those who it had been thought might prove to be difficult.

> *Temporary arrangements to house those unmarried men at Dunquin during the winter months have been made. They will live together for the present.*

The four new houses will be occupied by the Ó Catháin, Ó Súilleabháin, Guithín and Ó Dálaigh families. Seán P. Ó Cearna, who was the island's postmaster, has been offered employment in Dublin, while the postman, Seán P. Ó Cearna, will work in Dingle.

*

CONCLUSION

Did the Blasket islanders have an alternative in the early 1950s other than to leave the island for the mainland? The documents reproduced above demonstrate the harshness of their lives, the isolation and the precariousness of their very existence, living as they had to without a resident doctor or nurse. The new state had failed to produce a basic economic infrastructure. The pier and landing facilities were totally inadequate. There was no ferry or regular contact with the mainland. The presence of a doctor and a nurse was all the more necessary because of the age structure of the islanders. It would have required a heavy investment to keep the islanders on the Blaskets. On balance, the de Valera government in the early 1950s felt that it had no alternative other than to encourage the islanders to migrate to the mainland. In a sense, this was a form of emigration. Many of their fellow islanders had already left for the United States and settled in the Boston area. From their new farms near Dingle, the islanders could look out daily across the sea and remember life as it had been for their parents and ancestors.

Population Change in the 1950s: A Statistical Review

GERRY O'HANLON

INTRODUCTION

The 1950s stand out in the demographic history of the twentieth century in Ireland as approximately one in eight of the population emigrated over the decade. This rate of emigration, in both absolute and relative terms, was the highest recorded since the 1880s, and at the end of the period the population of the state had shrunk to an all-time low of just over 2.8 million.

The situation in the 1950s is examined here in the context of a longer perspective of population and labour-force changes in Ireland, in an attempt to identify the causes and effects of the large population exodus. The first section looks at demographic and labour-force trends over the 30-year period from independence to the start of the 1950s. The components of population change – births, deaths and migration – over this period provide an advance indicator of the likely population 'pressure' on the labour market in the 1950s, while the labour-force data provides some information on the capacity of the labour market to respond. The link between the labour market and migration is, of course, fundamental to understanding the emigration trends. The second section reviews what actually happened to the population and labour-force in the 1950s. The final sections present some information on the profile of the 1950s emigrants who went to Britain (estimated at approximately two-thirds of the total) and examine the evidence of return migration and the long-term impact on the population structure.

Most of the information presented in the paper has been derived from the results of successive censuses of population from 1926 onwards. Because of the absence of travel controls between Ireland and the UK, and because of the very nature of migration, it is not possible to measure it directly. However, by studying changes in the structure of the population over time, in conjunction with data on births and deaths, it is possible to assemble a reasonably accurate overall picture. The analysis of Irish emigrants in Britain is based on information collected on Irish-born persons in the 1971 census in Britain.

POPULATION AND LABOUR-FORCE TRENDS 1921–1950
Population

Table 1 summarises the components of population change for each decade between 1921 and 1950. It may be seen that the natural increase (the excess of births over deaths) varied greatly, from an annual average of 17,200 in the 1920s to 15,300 in the 1930s, rising to 23,600 in the 1940s. The variability in the average natural increase was due almost entirely to the changing birth rate, which fell from 20.2 per thousand population in the 1920s to 19.3 in the 1930s, before rising sharply to 21.9 in the 1940s. The latter increase can in turn be attributed to a corresponding rise in the marriage rate.

Table 1: Population Change 1921–1950

Annual Average	Population Change	Natural Increase	Net Migration
1921–1930	–16,300	17,200	–33,500
1931–1940	+6,000	15,300	–9,300
1941–1950	–3,200	23,600	–26,700

In the absence of migration over a period of years, an annual natural increase of these orders of magnitude would have required corresponding increases of between 10,000 to 15,000 per annum in the numbers employed in order to sustain labour-force participation rates. In the event, the 'no migration' scenario did not apply and the table shows that net emigration more than absorbed the natural increase over the entire period. It is interesting to note, however, that migration was quite volatile, ranging from an annual average of 33,500 in the 1920s to 9,300 in the 1930s. Much of the emigration in the 1920s would have been accounted for by the relatively large exodus that followed independence in 1921, while the lower figure for the 1930s reflected the difficult economic situation internationally during most of that period. In the 1940s, there was a net outflow of almost 270,000 and it is estimated that approximately 55% (150,000) of this occurred during the first half of the decade, which, of course, was dominated by the Second World War.

Due to the counter-balancing of natural increase and migration flows, the total population remained remarkably stable, at around 3 million over the entire period.

Labour-Force
Table 2 shows that the labour-force also remained very stable over the period. The 1936 census recorded a peak of 1.339 million, while a low point of 1.272 million was recorded in 1951.

Agriculture accounted for over 50% of the labour-force in 1926 and its size declined very slowly (at a rate of 0.5% per annum) over the following 20 years. This fall was broadly offset by small increases in the numbers employed in the industrial and services sectors. The decline in the agricultural labour-force accelerated sharply between 1946 and 1951 with approximately the same number leaving in these five years as in the previous 20 years. It is worth noting that the rate of decline,

Table 2: Labour-Force 1926–1951

	1926	1936	1946	1951
Agriculture	661,900	630,700	585,000	506,000
Industry	194,600	244,800	235,800	293,900
Services	448,400	463,600	477,600	472,100
Total	1,304,900	1,339,100	1,298,400	1,272,000

at 2.5% per annum, was the subject of much concern and debate in the context of the discussions that surrounded the preparation of the *Report of the Commission on Emigration and Other Population Problems*, which was published in 1954. Some argued that the solution to emigration was to enable more people to remain on the land through greater and more efficient agricultural production. However, the opposite viewpoint held that the new trend was more typical of what was already happening elsewhere and that it was driven by technological development, which was not reversible. In retrospect, we now know that the latter view proved to be correct in that the agricultural labour-force continued to decline consistently at over 2% per annum on average over the following 50 years or so! Indeed, it would now appear that the slow rate of decline in the agricultural labour-force before 1946 resulted in a large element of under-employment building up on Irish farms.

DEVELOPMENTS IN THE 1950S
Pressure on the Labour Market
The foregoing analyses show that the combined effect of the decline in the agricultural labour-force and the natural increase in population was the creation of an annual demand, in the absence of migration, for a net additional 30,000 jobs in the non-agricultural sectors. Satisfying such a demand would have required an annual employment growth-rate of approximately 4% in these sectors. With the exception of the recent 'Celtic Tiger' years, such a level of job creation has never been achieved on a sustained basis in Ireland over a prolonged period.

Unfortunately, the economic conditions in the 1950s were far from the Celtic Tiger experience. The available figures show that between 1947 and 1951 gross national product grew at 3% per annum, at just over 2% in the following four years, and at less than 0.5% per annum between 1955 and 1959. In short, for most of the decade the Irish economy was effectively stagnant. Table 3 shows that the resultant impact on employment levels was quite severe.

Agricultural employment fell by almost 120,000 between 1951 and 1961. Further analysis shows that while the number of farm holders fell by 25,000 (or just over 10%) there was a much greater decline of around a third in the numbers of farmers' relatives assisting and agricultural labourers over the decade. Employment in the industry and ser-

	1951–56	1956–61
Agriculture	–66,000	–51,000
Industry	–14,000	–11,000
Services	–13,000	–10,000
Total	–93,000	–72,000

vices sectors also fell by almost 50,000 over the 10-year period. Building workers (whose numbers fell by over 20,000) and domestic servants (down by over 17,000) contributed most to the decline in these sectors.

While the fall in the number of building workers could be directly attributed to the poor economic environment, the sharp decline in the numbers of farmers' relatives assisting on farms, agricultural labourers and domestic servants reflected more the start of major changes in the structure of employment and indeed society itself. These three occupational categories in total accounted for 328,000 workers in 1951, over a quarter of the labour-force. In contrast, their numbers had dwindled to less than 50,000 in 1991.

Accumulated over the decade, the surplus labour identified in the previous sections amounted in total to around 300,000, and this could only give rise to increased unemployment or emigration. Large-scale unemployment supported by the state, similar to that recorded in the 1980s and early 1990s, was not an option in the under-developed Ireland of the 1950s. Indeed, the official estimates show that unemployment increased slowly from 45,000 in 1951 to a peak of 78,000 in 1957 before falling back to 56,000 in 1961. The figures show that emigration was the chosen option in the vast majority of cases.

Surge in Emigration
The population balance for the 1951 to 1961 intercensal period was as follows:

Population change:	–142,200
Natural increase:	+264,500
Net migration:	–408,800

The net migration of over 400,000 was equivalent to an average rate of decline in population of 1.4% per annum. Not surprisingly, in view of their dependence on agriculture, Connacht and the three Ulster counties experienced the greatest annual rates of population decline due to migration (both within Ireland and abroad) at 1.8% and 2.0% respectively. However, the other provinces also experienced heavy emigration, and even Dublin, which traditionally would have benefited from inward migration from other parts of the country, registered an annual population decline due to migration of 1.0%.

Table 4 shows the impact of emigration in the 1950s on selected age cohorts. As is usual, emigration in the 1950s was dominated by the younger age cohorts: those aged 15 to 34 in 1961. Net migration of this cohort amounted to 287,000 or approximately 70% of the total outflow over the decade. More strikingly, it represented a loss of close to 30% of the cohort in only 10 years. However, there was also significant emigration amongst the older age groups on this occasion. Net emigration of the cohort aged 35 to 54 in 1961 amounted to 77,000, which was equivalent to a loss of close to 10% of the cohort. Such a high rate of emigration amongst older age groups was atypical and, as such, may have involved a degree of what might be termed 'deferred emigration', particularly amongst those in the farming community.

Table 4: Impact of Migration in 1951–1961 on Selected Age Cohorts

Age in 1961	Males	Females	Total
15–24	–73,500	–73,400	–146,900
25–34	–80,600	–59,400	–140,000
35–44	–25,200	–19,300	–44,500
45–54	–15,800	–16,500	–32,300

IRISH-BORN IN BRITAIN IN 1971

It is estimated that at least two-thirds of the emigrants in the 1950s went to Britain and, following some further outflows in the 1960s, the Irish-born population there peaked at over 700,000 in 1971. The following snapshot of their labour-force characteristics was obtained from the 1971 census of population in Britain. Ninety per cent of Irish-born males over the age of fifteen were in the labour-force, and of these, 9% were unemployed; one third of the males at work were in industry while a further 28% were in construction. Fifty per cent of females over the age of fifteen were in the labour-force and 5% of these were unemployed. Forty-seven per cent of married females were in the labour-force, compared with only 7% of married females in the Republic. Over 70% of working females were in the services sector, and professional services (e.g., nurses) accounted for 40% of these.

In short, this snapshot shows that a high proportion of the emigrants, particularly males, were in 'blue-collar' occupations, thus reflecting the unskilled background of many of them on emigration. The relatively high labour-force participation of married women is noteworthy in that it contrasted so sharply with those who remained at home. Indeed, it is only in recent years that married female labour-force participation in the Republic has reached the levels recorded by their emigrant counterparts in 1971.

Net outward migration continued throughout the 1960s, when there was a population loss due to migration of almost 133,000 over the decade. This was only one-third of the level in the 1950s and, with the exception of the 1930s, the emigration rate in the 1960s was also significantly below that recorded in earlier decades.

However, despite this improvement few, if any, anticipated the turnaround that occurred in the 1970s, when a net inflow of almost 104,000 was recorded. As can be seen from Table 5, those in the 35 to 44 age group (as measured in 1981) and children under the age of fifteen accounted between them for almost 85% of the inward flow. This pattern was consistent with the younger emigrants of the 1950s returning with their families. There is also evidence from the table of some of the older emigrants returning during this period.

Table 5: Net Migration 1971–1981

Age in 1981	Males	Females	Total
0–14	+24,400	+23,000	+47,400
15–34	–6,200	–5,100	–11,300
35–44	+22,700	+16,900	+39,600
45–64	+8,000	+1,800	+9,800
65+	+9,000	+9,200	+18,200
Total	+58,100	+45,800	+103,900

This pattern of return migration has also been in evidence to varying degrees in subsequent periods. In Table 6, the long-term impact of migration on 1946 population cohorts up to 30 years of age has been tracked over 50 years. This 50-year period can be split very conveniently into two equal sub-periods, namely pre- and post-1971. The migration impact has been calculated by tracking the cohorts over the 1946, 1971 and 1996 censuses and adjusting for mortality. This is not a true longitudinal study since we cannot identify individuals over time. However, since we do know that Irish-born persons were the dominant component of the relevant inflows in the latter period, the analysis gives a crude indication of the extent to which the cohorts were replenished through return migration.

Table 6: Impact of Migration 1946–1996

Age in 1946	Population in 1946	Net Migration 1946–1971	Net Migration 1971–1996
0–4	294,800	–113,100	+23,200
5–9	265,900	–108,200	+16,700
10–14	262,300	–104,400	+11,800
15–19	251,500	–87,300	+10,900
20–24	231,300	–56,700	+9,600
25–29	208,200	–30,500	+5,100

The table shows that the cohort aged 0–4 years in 1946 lost almost 40% through migration in the quarter of a century up to 1971 but over 20% of the outflow was replenished over the succeeding 25 years. Similarly, over 15% of the outflow from the cohort aged 5–9 was replenished. Comparing Tables 5 and 6, it may be deduced that almost all this 'early' return of the two younger age cohorts occurred in the 1970s – these were the young emigrants returning with their families, referred to above. The replenishment rate for those aged 10–19 in 1946 was about 12% and many of these were emigrants returning on retirement from the labour-force. The inward flows shown for the two oldest age cohorts would also have been largely composed of retirees (note, however, that a significant proportion of these inward flows, unlike those of the younger cohorts, would have involved emigrants who left before 1946).

CONCLUSION

Many commentators tend to lay almost all the blame for the huge surge in emigration that occurred in the 1950s on the poor economic conditions in Ireland over the decade. While these conditions and the increased demand for labour elsewhere were undoubtedly major catalysts behind the exodus, the analysis in this paper would suggest that long-term demographic factors and deferred labour market restructuring were the underlying reasons. The latter largely involved the onset of a more rapid rate of sustained decline in the agricultural labour-force that could not be absorbed by the relatively under-developed industrial and services sectors at the time.

Indeed, it is clear that, before the 1950s, the industrial and services sectors were able to meet only a fraction of the demand for more jobs stemming from the natural increase in population that was a permanent feature of Irish demography over the preceding decades. The unfavourable economic and political conditions over the preceding 25 years may also have served to dampen down the rate of emigration. Table 7, which tracks the rate of attrition in the 10–19 population cohorts as measured in successive censuses, would tend to support the view that there was a significant element of 'deferred emigration' in the 1950s.

Table 7: Persons Aged 10–19 at Selected Censuses: percentage remaining at 10-year intervals

Census	0 years	10 years	20 years	30 years
1926	100	81	68	61
1936	100	80	65	60
1946	100	68	59	59
1951	100	60	60	63
1961	100	74	81	79

Since mortality is not a significant factor for the cohorts over the 30-year interval, the attrition rates that may be deduced from the table can be attributed almost entirely to migration. After 10 years, the 1926 and 1936 cohorts had lost only 20% of their population, compared with 40% for the 1951 and, interestingly, 26% for the 1961 cohorts. After 30 years, on the other hand, we see that (with the exception of the 1961 cohort, for which significantly different conditions applied) the population loss had converged towards 40% in all cases.

A final comment that might be made in respect of the 1950s outflow is that it marked a turning point in the nature of Irish emigration – from one where the flow was essentially irreversible to one involving return migration for an increasing number of the migrants. The increased proportion of emigrants going to Britain, vastly improved transportation links and rapidly changing economic and social circumstances all contributed to this change, of course. However, it is also fair to contend that this was one further manifestation of the fact that the changes in the 1950s were all elements in a major turning point in Ireland's social and demographic history.

The Vanishing Irish? The Exodus from Ireland in the 1950s

ENDA DELANEY

The year 1958 was a watershed, according to the standard accounts of twentieth-century Irish history. This was the year that witnessed the publication of *Economic Development*, the seminal blueprint for Irish economic policy, which was for the most part formulated by T. K. Whitaker, the talented secretary of the Department of Finance. In that same year, the *Programme for Economic Expansion* – the white paper based on *Economic Development* – was published. With Whitaker as visionary and Seán Lemass as the pragmatic saviour, independent Ireland emerged phoenix-like from the economic morass to reap the benefits of international trade in the 1960s. Needless to say, this teleological yet influential characterisation requires qualification. For instance, it is an often-neglected fact that domestic policy initiatives coincided with external developments. Detailed assessments of economic performance illustrate how the international environment determined in a favourable way the destiny of the independent Ireland in the 1960s.[1]

Another event occurred in 1958 that understandably does not feature in the historical record, though it was by no means less momentous for the individuals involved. Eleanor (born in 1950) left Cork in April 1958 with her parents, to travel to London. She recounted her story with exceptionally vivid detail over 30 years later. Before departure, her parents lived on a local authority housing estate on the outskirts of Cork city, where 'they had a home but very little else'.[2] With her parents and siblings, she sailed from Cork to Fishguard and then onwards by train to Paddington Station in London, a well-trodden route for emigrants from the south of Ireland. Her first impressions of the metropolis were uncertain:

> I remember arriving at Paddington, and the noise and chaos of what seemed to me as a small child [to be] thousands and thousands of people all over the place, and feeling excited but apprehensive, quite frightened about the whole thing.[3]

Her testimony illustrates the ambivalent feelings she experienced on arrival – by no means a unique reaction for Irish emigrants travelling to Britain in the 1950s. This new, gigantic, strange and densely populated city differed greatly from 'home'. As with the offspring of many Irish emigrants in Britain, she spent her summer holidays with relatives in Cork. The time back in Ireland contrasted sharply with her new life in London. She remembered with affection and understandable nostalgia her halcyon days in Cork.

The other thing of my childhood I remember most clearly were long cold winters in London and long hot summers in Cork. We went home every summer for the full six weeks' holiday ... I can't tell anybody how appalling I used to feel coming back. My clearest memory was not just the first, but every time screaming and crying and being dragged into the boat to come back. I never wanted to leave Cork; I hated London, but in my earliest memories I wanted to be with my mum and dad. I hated school. I hated the lack of freedom because when I went home, for six weeks I was out on bikes cycling, playing with friends in the streets and then to come back and never be allowed out because there was nowhere to go.[4]

Why did Eleanor, her parents and thousands of other unnamed, unknown and unrecorded emigrants leave 'home' in the 1950s? Equally, why did Irish society allow this to happen and not do more – if indeed anything – to reduce the level of emigration? Before turning to these central questions, it would be useful to outline the extent of emigration from independent Ireland in the 1950s.

Between 1951 and 1961 over 400,000 people left independent Ireland – nearly a sixth of the total population recorded in 1951.[5] This was not a new development but the acceleration of a pattern of emigration to Britain evident since the mid-1930s, reinforced greatly during the Second World War, which continued thereafter. At least four-fifths of those who left in the post-war period, until the early 1970s, emigrated to Britain.[6] It was predominantly young people, both men and women, who left during the 1950s. One in three of those aged 30 years or under in 1946 had left the country by 1971.[7] Mass emigration had a far-reaching impact on post-war Irish economy and society, but in European terms, independent Ireland was by no means unique in this respect.[8] In addition to Portugal, Spain, Italy and Greece, in the 1950s one of Ireland's nearest neighbours, Scotland, also underwent a similar exodus, mainly to England and overseas destinations. Nevertheless, the movement of so many people from one country, relative to the size of the total population, within one decade was, in European terms, without equal.

Were the Irish people 'disappearing', as the Rev. John A. O'Brien and his fellow-contributors claimed in the well-known collection of essays *The Vanishing Irish*, first published in 1953? According to O'Brien, 'if the past century's rate of decline continues for another century, the Irish will virtually disappear as a nation and will be found only as an enervated remnant in a land occupied by foreigners'.[9] This volume, alarmist in tone and displaying some revealing misinterpretations of population statistics, captured the sense of malaise and despondency associated with emigration in the 1950s.[10] The deleterious effects of mass emigration in terms of population decline were demonstrated by the preliminary results of the 1956 census, which became available in June of that year. The 1956 census recorded a total population of 2.9 million people, the lowest figure since 1841.[11] Emigration and the economy dominated the general election of March 1957, with the level of population decline calling into question the very viability of the independent Irish state.[12] As Girvin has noted, this was probably the 'worst decade since the Famine, characterised by declining income, rising unemployment and accelerating emigration'.[13]

Most accounts of the exodus during the 1950s rightly stress two related explanations. In the first instance, emigration was a deeply ingrained stage in the life cycle of young Irish people from at least the immediate post-famine era. Emigration continued throughout the post-famine period, even in times of relative economic prosperity. Second, the decision to leave was shaped in part by the domestic economic environment, and many young Irish people in the 1950s faced a bleak future. Employment in agriculture was an unattractive choice of livelihood and there was little prospect of large-scale employment in the non-agricultural sectors. Unemployment increased in urban areas – prompting street protests in Dublin – from June 1953, stark evidence of the crisis in the Irish economy at the time.[14] The lack of sustained economic development was clearly the driving force underpinning the exodus. As the Commission on Emigration and Other Population Problems observed in 1954, the 'fundamental cause of emigration is economic', although the report continued, 'in most cases the decision to emigrate cannot be ascribed to any single motive but to the interplay of a number of motives'.[15]

The category of explanations that could be loosely categorised as 'economic' may be added to. An external factor facilitating the departure of thousands of young Irish people was the demand for unskilled labour in the post-war British economy. At first workers were required for the ambitious programme of post-war reconstruction initiated by the Labour government in the late 1940s. This demand for labour continued to exist throughout the 1950s. In addition, Irish citizens had unlimited access to the British labour market, one of the more neglected beneficial consequences of the political relationship between the two countries. Unlike immigrants to the United Kingdom from the 'New Commonwealth', Irish migrants could come and go as they wished and take up any form of employment. Therefore, both the demand for labour in the British economy and the absence of regulations on entry to this labour market determined the level of Irish emigration in the 1950s.

Expectations, aspirations and other elements of socio-cultural change also explain why so many people left independent Ireland in the 1950s. The first issue relates to standards of living, both real and expected, particularly in rural Ireland. Interviews with prospective emigrants demonstrate the importance of this consideration in the minds of many young people.[16] For those faced with a life in relative poverty, what was available in Ireland in terms of the levels of remuneration, types of employment, job security and associated status simply did not compare with the prospects on offer in Britain. The virtual absence of female employment in certain parts of rural Ireland resulted in the situation being more acute for young women. In other words, staying at home could rarely satisfy aspirations and expectations, and leaving home in many instances involved leaving Ireland. These expectations were fuelled by contact with emigrants already living in Britain. The mores, lifestyles and standard of living of the 'affluent worker' in Britain became a widespread aspiration in the 1950s.[17]

Central to the realisation of this aspiration was the nature of employment. One of the most frequently cited reasons for emigration in the 1950s was the sporadic and uncertain nature of employment: a few weeks here, a few weeks there, punctuated by long spells of under-employment or unemployment. As the Commission on Emigration noted in 1954, 'what he [sic] wants and needs is reasonable security and continuity so that he may have an opportunity of planning his future'.[18] For those who were categorised as 'relatives assisting', or family members working on the family holding, this was an especially precarious position to be in. The number of 'relatives assisting' declined by roughly a third in the 1950s and Walsh estimates that over 130,000 'relatives assisting' left farming in this decade, presumably with many emigrating to Britain.[19] Even for those not wholly dependent on the agricultural sector, local authority work or other forms of casual employment were uncertain and unpredictable. And it is in this respect that the principal contrast lay with the jobs available in Britain. In a situation where there was demand for unskilled employment, Irish emigrants in Britain could be reasonably confident of receiving rewards for their work each and every week. This was a subtle yet important change in attitudes. With expectations of regular remuneration and the associated impact on standards of living, from the point of view of prospective emigrants, staying at home in Ireland rarely offered a means to achieve these basic requirements. Emigrants who were interviewed in the late 1940s often cited the lack of secure employment as a reason for their departure and displayed a remarkable knowledge about the wage levels in Britain, usually through contact with migrant siblings and friends. This knowledge merely accentuated their own perception of relative poverty at home.

The exodus of so many people within a decade involved not only elements of socio-cultural change, but also the evolution of a structure that facilitated, aided and even accelerated emigration over time. The influential work of the distinguished sociologist Douglas Massey on contemporary migration from western Mexico to the southern United States is a revealing point of comparison. Massey and his colleagues argue that migration is a social process and that structures evolve over time which perpetuate the flow.[20] For independent Ireland in the 1950s, the main structures that facilitated emigration were social networks based on ties of kinship, friendship and membership of the same community that linked emigrants, returned migrants and non-migrants in both Ireland and Britain. Emigrant networks also allowed for the diffusion of information concerning wage levels and employment opportunities that were available to potential emigrants. This information lessened the inherent risks involved in leaving home for work in Britain.

What was the response from within Irish society to the haemorrhage of people during the 1950s? Perhaps the most obvious response was the Commission on Emigration and Other Population Problems, 1948–1954, the majority report of which remains the most complete and measured examination of emigration in the 1940s and early 1950s. Emigration was also a much-debated political issue, usually linked in contemporary political discourse to the related issues of unemployment, standards of living and poverty.[21] For Irish politicians in the 1950s the issue was not so much why so many people were leaving at a particular point in time or how these people fared, but rather a juvenile game of trying to embarrass political foes by highlighting an increase in emigration during the period of office of the other party in government.[22] This was a somewhat tedious practice, although judging from the volume of parliamentary questions asked in the Dáil on this matter, a pastime that some politicians clearly enjoyed. The policy on emigration followed by successive governments in the 1950s was not to have a stated policy on emigration. Ministers frequently outlined the putative successes or future benefits that would be derived from changes in economic policy, which would by implication result in a reduction in the numbers leaving. The reluctance to accept publicly that emigration was a central feature of Irish life might well have been politically expedient, and conveniently absolved the Irish state of the responsibility to care for its citizens living in Britain. This abdication of responsibility was rationalised on the dubious grounds that Irish emigrants in Britain would be returning home 'soon'.

In an illuminating discussion, J. J. Lee has explored the range of views on emigration held by the elite within Irish society at this time.[23] With the risk of greatly oversimplifying his arguments, two lines of thought may be discerned. First, there were those such as Eamon de Valera who believed that emigration was fuelled by unrealistic (and irrational) expectations on the part of the poorer sectors of Irish society. In a memorable comment uttered in the context of a public debate about the deplorable living conditions of Irish workers in Birmingham, de Valera observed in August 1951 that 'the saddest part of all this [emigration] is that work is available at home, and in conditions infinitely better from the point of view of health and morals … There is no doubt that many of those who emigrate could find employment at home at as good, or better, wages – and with living conditions far better than they find in Britain'.[24] Not only were the rural poor seeking to live at a level above subsistence by emigrating, but in the process they were exposing themselves to possibly harmful influences in Britain. For a politician whose ideal society was rural, simple and devoid of materialism, leaving rural Ireland simply to carve out a decent livelihood was out of the question. The other view, exemplified by Seán Lemass, centred on conventional logic: in order to reduce emigration, Irish living standards needed to be increased over time, rather than hoping that the populace would lower their expectations. In his famous Clery's speech in January 1957, Lemass declared that 'our standards must approximate to British standards, or our people will go'.[25] And he was quite right: those who were not prepared to subsist in poverty or near-poverty chose the exit option and left.

Another element of the discourse relating to emigration highlighted by Lee deserves further elaboration and this is the issue of class differences. Detailed reconstructions of the socio-economic profile of the emigrant flow demonstrate the preponderance of people who came, not from the affluent classes, but rather from the rural and urban working class.[26] However, in the context of discussions of emigration – both public and those behind closed doors – the image of the emigrant as somewhat feckless, easily led (especially in the case of women) and driven by a base and contemptible desire for higher income was a common one. But these were the desires, needs and aspirations of those who had relatively little in Ireland being viewed through the eyes and mindset of those who had a great deal more. Caution is therefore required when assessing much of the discourse from the 1950s emanating from official sources. A revealing example of the disparity between elite views and the harsh reality experienced by many people can be found in the discussions of whether emigration was the result of economic expectations or 'want' and whether the movement of people was a 'voluntary' or 'involuntary' process.[27] These distinctions are artificial constructions and, as Lee observes, they suited contemporary purposes: if emigrants left in order to improve their standard of living 'the blame accordingly lay with the emigrants themselves, not with the society they left'.[28] Of course, one obvious implication of the exodus during the 1950s was that people emigrated because they had lost confidence in the ability of their politicians, civil servants and other members of the ruling elite to create a society that might in the future allow them to enjoy a decent standard of living.

It has often been suggested that emigration acted as a safety valve in the 1950s. It served as an outlet for the release of class tensions by removing from the Irish landscape those who might become involved in class politics. There is much of value in this suggestion, notwithstanding its inherently counter-factual nature. For instance, if the British government had decided to restrict Irish immigration, as was mooted in the late 1950s, and Irish citizens had no longer been allowed to take up employment in Britain, the impact on Irish society would clearly have been far-reaching. With no possible outlet for the unemployed and under-employed, a reduction in the income of many households as a result of a lower level of emigrant remittances, and literally thousands of people back in Ireland without work, seeking welfare payments, the potential for social unrest would have greatly increased. This social unrest might well have resulted in the development of the politics of class and a more imaginative approach to economic and social policy on the part of politicians and civil servants.

Returning to Eleanor, her family and the thousands of others who constituted the 'vanishing Irish' in the 1950s, there is no doubt that the exodus during this decade was driven by a complex range of factors, against the backdrop of poverty, unemployment and the absence of sustained economic development. By the 1950s, the independent Irish state had failed to live up to the expectations of economic progress created by the nationalist elite in the first half of the twentieth century. The principal consequences of the mass emigration were threefold. First, Irish society retained its traditional complexion until the profound changes of the 1960s and 1970s. Second, the Irish-born population in Britain grew steadily, and by 1971 the Irish were the largest immigrant grouping in British society. Lastly, there is the impact on the hundreds of thousands of Irish people who were compelled to leave in order to obtain a decent standard of living, an aspect that has only begun to be explored in recent years. Using oral testimony, it is possible to reconstruct the experiences of Irish emigrants who left during the 1950s. It seems likely that *Economic Development*, the *Programme for Economic Expansion*, Seán Lemass and T. K. Whitaker will not feature prominently in any of these first-hand accounts of leaving Ireland and the process of adjustment to life in Britain.

The Commission on Emigration, 1948–1954

TRACEY CONNOLLY

The first 25 years of Irish independence witnessed poor economic performance coupled with minor social change and the failure of emigration to decline. The problems that high emigration posed were only officially investigated and acknowledged following the establishment of a commission set up by the first inter-party government to examine them.

Under the chairmanship of Dr J. P. Beddy, the Commission on Emigration and Other Population Problems commenced its investigations on 5 April 1948. This was the first and (to date) the only conscious effort made by any Irish administration to study population trends with particular emphasis on emigration. The members of the commission included four statisticians, two economists, a sociologist, two trade-union officials, two medical doctors, government officials, clergymen and writers. In total, there were twenty-four members. The terms of reference were as follows:

> To investigate the causes and consequences of the present level and trend in population; to examine, in particular, the social and economic effects of birth, death, migration and marriage rates at present and their probable course in the near future; to consider what measures, if any, should be taken in the national interest to influence the trend in population; generally, to consider the desirability of formulating a national population policy.[1]

It should be noted here that the main emphasis in the terms of reference was on 'population' as opposed to 'migration', although the commission primarily looked at emigration. The inclusion of 'other population problems' in the title of the commission reveals the negativity associated with the process of emigration from Ireland.

The main method of inquiry was to be surveys carried out throughout the country. Advertisements in the public press invited information on the subject from any persons or groups. Interviews were carried out with intending emigrants at local Department of Social Welfare offices. The commission also made a limited inquiry into the social and economic conditions of Irish emigrants in areas of Britain which were heavily populated with Irish emigrants. This involved interviews with emigrants and persons who were in contact with emigrants there, such as employers, foremen, welfare officers and clergymen. A vast array of statistical data was compiled pertaining to emigration. Analysis of economic and social developments in Ireland was made and assessed to correlate them with population trends. The study took six years to complete. The commission met 115 times and its report was released in March 1954.

The setting up of the commission in 1948 met with mixed opinions. Professor George O'Brien (of the Department of Economics, University College Dublin) welcomed the commission as it 'showed an end of the apparent indifference of the government on this central problem'.[2] The *Irish Independent* was also grateful that the commission would be 'getting down to essentials' by examining emigration, which the newspaper deemed to be 'a disease that grows stronger by feeding on itself'.[3] It felt that 'the new commission would perform a valuable service if it went no further than an objective examination of the effect of … urbanisation and changes in farming methods' on emigration.[4] The *Irish Times* felt:

> The very setting up of the commission was a brave departure. It was an admission that things are gravely wrong. It was a break with the ostrich-like behaviour of many patriots, who boast of their people's will to freedom, while ignoring the truth that their people's chief will, as revealed by the emigration statistics, is to clear out, bag and baggage, from the land for which their fathers strove.[5]

Speaking for the opposition party, Fianna Fáil, the *Irish Press* showed scepticism about the need for the commission: 'The causes of these trends in population are well known, and it is unlikely that the new commission can add much to our knowledge in that respect'.[6] In another issue, the paper pointed out that 'by setting up a commission of this sort, the government has done nothing about emigration, nor has the commission been given power to do anything'.[7] The *Irish Press* noted, of the members of the commission, that 'the majority of them have little direct knowledge of the problem to be solved'.[8] This was a fair point, as the commission for the most part consisted of academics. Furthermore, the joint secretaries of the Irish Housewives Association called attention to the fact that 'of its twenty-four members, only two are women'. They pointed out that 'the figures show that, since the end of the Emergency, the emigration of men is on the decrease, while that of women continues on a steady flow and is now much larger than the male exodus … the ways of remedying the situation are surely among the questions that women would be of help [in answering]'.[9] Certainly there were not enough female members, given the recent large emigration of females and the fact that in the past Irish female emigrants had outnumbered their male counterpart.

In examining the destinations that Irish migrants chose, the report noted that the Irish tended to choose destinations where they 'were not separated by any barrier of language or unfamiliar customs'.[10] Other considerations in choosing a destination were 'comparative cost of passage to different destinations, shipping facilities, and whether he was joining relatives'.[11] According to the report, this was an important reason for Britain's popularity with Irish emigrants.

The commission found that the majority of emigrants were from rural backgrounds. For the intercensal periods 1926–36, 1936–46 and 1946–51, Munster was 'the province of the greatest emigration, but the figures for Connacht were also high'.[12] The commission commented that 'in rural areas, generally, high density of population indicates poverty rather than wealth; it reflects a crowding of population on small holdings' and 'it is in the poor areas with high densities that recent population decline is most marked'.[13]

The report referred to the widespread drop in male workers engaged in Irish agriculture between 1946 and 1951 and the tumble in the number of non-family-member farm workers. It explained that these declines were created by advances in farm technology, which in many cases led to the emigration of workers who were displaced by new machinery. The decline in the number employed in agriculture also indicated that this was an area from which migration was high. The persistence of seasonal migration from rural regions was evident from the survey carried out in Dungloe, Co. Donegal: 'all going as seasonal migrants, nearly all to Scotland. Women save turf when men migrate'.[14] This suggests that there was not enough work at home to sustain the men in employment all year round. Another survey of Killarney and Tralee in Co. Kerry showed a similar trend: 'Emigrants mostly from rural parts. Few townsmen emigrating. More mature men would not leave if they had two weeks' work in the month. Many had experience in Britain during the war and wanted to go back'.[15] This implies that there was more employment in urban than rural areas, suggesting that opportunities in agriculture were declining. It is also evident that temporary migration was common from such districts.

Late marriage was a feature of rural Ireland. According to evidence submitted in the Congested District Summaries, the 'greatest enemy of Irish agriculture is the old bachelor. The flight of the girls is the greatest menace since Cromwell'.[16] This Co. Galway memorandum suggested the introduction of a 'resident agricultural instructor in every parish or barrack area' to make agriculture more productive.[17] It recommended decentralising the Departments of Lands, Agriculture and Fisheries. In order to prevent female migration from rural areas, it put forward the idea of prohibiting the 'emigration of girls for one year, and have marriage dowries'.[18] However, the commission disagreed with prohibiting emigration as it viewed it as 'drastic interference of the State with the liberty of its citizens' other than at times of war when 'such restrictions could take the form of regulating the movement of individuals'.[19] Already the prohibiting of emigration had been discussed in political circles and dismissed for the same reason. The report explained that late marriage was 'because farmers succeed to their holdings at a relatively late age', which the Central Statistics Office had estimated at 38 to 40 years of age.[20]

It has also been suggested that late marriage was the reason for much female emigration. One member of the commission stated in the press that females were 'primarily activated in going abroad by a desire to get married'.[21] The low marriage-rate in Ireland was also a cause of emigration and the commission pointed out that it 'has had an unfavourable effect on the outlook of young people, and has contributed to discontent, unsettlement and emigration'.[22] In rural areas, the system of inheritance was somewhat responsible for the low marriage-rate. The chief executive officer of the County Galway Vocational Education Committee emphasised in his submission that the 'cost and difficulty of transfer of property prevent parents from transferring it. This results in late marriage'.[23] The commission showed that unemployment and low income hindered marriage, and stated that 'until men can find employment which can support homes, even those girls who could find employment locally will continue to emigrate'.[24] It was also shown that the low marriage-rate 'contributes to emigration and the intention to emigrate tends to keep the marriage-rate low'.[25] Decline in employment in agriculture, low rate of marriage, late ages at marriage and emigration were the primary causes of rural decay, which was a major concern for the commission and it later suggested how this could be halted.

The report found that 'the fundamental cause of emigration is economic' but 'in most cases the decision to emigrate cannot be ascribed to any single motive but to the interplay of a number of motives'.[26] The motives, it suggested, were 'social, political, cultural and psychological'.[27] In assessing economic reasons for emigration, the commission examined the case of Co. Mayo, which experienced a net emigration of 52,200 between 1926 and 1951.[28] The report concluded, 'conditions in County Mayo failed to provide that economic expansion which would absorb the natural increase of the county'.[29]

The report confirmed that not only in Co. Mayo but also 'throughout the country, lack of opportunities for employment to absorb the natural increase in population' was a cause of emigration.[30] The commission also believed that much emigration was due to 'the failure of the economy to provide the rising living standards which are increasingly sought, particularly in the rural areas'.[31] According to a memorandum submitted to the commission by the Irish Tourist Board, 'a proportion of those who leave rural areas do so because of the casual nature of the employment available in or near their own houses and hold-

ings'.[32] The board believed 'numbers of people … would probably remain at home if they could be assured of regularity of earnings, even for
a period of the year, during which they could save money to carry them
through the slack months'.[33] To create such employment, it recommended that apart from facilitating and encouraging visitors from abroad, Irish
people should be promoted to spend their holidays in their own country.[34] Other obvious remedies to economic emigration put forward by
the commission were development of natural resources such as forestry
and fisheries and investment in industry. Economic improvements would
create employment, increase the standard of living and counter-act emigration. Besides the lack of funds to carry this out, the other problem of
such a policy was that while people in rural areas were emigrating for
economic reasons, social motives were also involved, thereby increasing
the difficulty of halting emigration. Intending emigrants often considered emigration due to their 'dissatisfaction with life on the land, whether
in its economic or in its social aspects' and this was a reason for much
emigration.[35]

Labour demands in Britain, America and Australia, where the Irish
emigrant had no language barriers and few cultural differences, were
important factors in the decision to go there. The disparity between
agricultural wages in Ireland and Britain, for example, was quite substantial. In addition, numerous British companies advanced fares to emigrants. According to one submission to the commission 'return tickets
for 7s 6d [were paid] when coming home on holidays and the payment
of 24s 6d a week extra to men with dependants directed to employment
in the priority industries'.[36] There is little doubt that even if employment
were increased in rural areas, if wages remained unchanged, then emigration for higher wages would continue.

Another influencing factor for rural dwellers in the decision to
migrate was 'the attraction of urban life'.[37] In particular 'social amenities' were important and included 'standards and availability of housing
as well as … services such as electricity, water supplies and transport'.[38]
The advent of the welfare state in Britain and the failure of the Mother
and Child Scheme in Ireland became decisive factors later for some.
According to the commission, those most influenced by the glamour of
urban life were the young, to whom 'rural areas appear dull, drab, mono-
tonous, backward and lonely'.[39] 'Opportunities abroad and a realisation
of differences between conditions at home and in other countries' was
seen as another factor.[40] 'This was confirmed and encouraged by the reports of emigrants who return well dressed and with an air of prosperity,
by glowing accounts in letters of high incomes and easy conditions and
by practical demonstrations in the remittances which were sent home'.[41]
However, Dr Cornelius Lucey, Bishop of Cork (who was a commissioner), later warned that the emigrant home on holidays was 'usually typi-

cal only of those who made good'.[42] Other social motives for emigrating, according to the findings of the commission, were 'a natural desire for adventure or change, an eagerness to travel, to see the world … to secure financial independence by having pocket money … to obtain freedom from parental control … and to be free to choose one's own way of life'.[43] The role of 'tradition and example' was viewed as a 'very powerful influence' in the decision to emigrate.[44] In parts of Ireland, emigration had become 'the established custom of the people' and 'a part of the generally accepted pattern of life' because many emigrants had 'a traditional path from the known to the known, that is to say, from areas where they lived to places where their friends and relations awaited them'.[45] Naturally, these contacts made the emigration experience appear less traumatic. All of these social reasons for emigration were practically impossible to prevent.

Various reasons for emigration were suggested in the multiple submissions and surveys conducted for the commission. The influence of the media was emphasised by a submission from Connemara, Co. Galway, which claimed: 'Films make the young emigrant more at home when he goes abroad than he used to be. He already knows Bing Crosby and Mickey Mouse. Dublin is less known than Boston. Dáil Éireann is only something in the papers'.[46] 'Young men reluctant to take up farming on small farms' as they 'see them as no profit' was identified as the essential economic reason for emigration from Co. Leitrim.[47] The extent of this problem in the county was explained by the fact that over 3,000 farms were under fifteen acres and therefore not profitable.[48] Amongst the social reasons, 'the lack of village centres at which young people could meet during their free time is a factor that is adding to the desire to leave the land'.[49] One psychological reason for emigration from Co. Leitrim was put forward: 'it is in the nature of most young people to see life away from home'.[50] A memorandum from Co. Louth noted that 'the emigrant believes that he or she will do better abroad and will have opportunities which do not offer at home'.[51] 'These beliefs', the memorandum observed, 'are fostered by the coloured reports of emigrants who write home and by the display of the occasional one who returns for a visit or to stay'.[52] As regards the role of tradition in emigration, the memorandum postulated that 'there is some persistence of an aftermath of the panic which accompanied the great exodus in the last century, which has helped to foster a tradition of emigration'.[53]

It appears that amongst the vast array of motives for emigrating, economic reasons were the most dominant in all areas. The findings of the Irish Housewives Association concluded that 'the fundamental reason why so many Irish men and women export themselves, even if only temporarily, is an economic one: the search for a higher wage and better living conditions than at home. The fact that Britain can supply these, in spite of great rationing and housing difficulties, must be faced'.[54] From the Kilkenny rural survey, it was found that 'those who do emigrate evince a strong desire to return. This was markedly noticeable when the aluminium-ware factory was opened. As many could find work there, they returned and many more expected to return as the plant expands'.[55] This suggested that economic reasons were important in the decision to return home as well as to leave. The commission concluded in turn that economic factors were the central cause of emigration – not simply economic necessity, but the desire for economic advancement through greater variety of employment, higher wages and better promotional prospects.

Although the greatest number of emigrants before and after the Second World War were female, the report devoted little attention to this. Female emigration was found to be 'the result of a variety of causes, the purely economic cause is not always so dominant'.[56] The quest for 'higher wages and better conditions of employment' was important, as were greater opportunities of 'obtaining factory or office work' than at home, and in the case of domestic work, girls went to Britain as 'they consider that the wages, conditions of work and also the status of domestic service in this country are unsatisfactory'.[57] Evidence from the Irish Housewives Association highlighted the disparity between Britain and Ireland in wages for trained Irish maids; in Ireland in 1948, wages were £1 5s, whereas in Britain wages were £1 17s 6d.[58] Conditions for nurses in Ireland influenced many to emigrate because 'the remuneration, facilities for training, pension schemes and hours of work in this country are considered to be unattractive'.[59] Only two social reasons were cited which pertained specifically to female emigration. One was the 'prospect of better marriage opportunities' abroad.[60] The *Irish Times* quoted one commissioner who believed that the main reason for female emigration was because 'they were mostly attractive country girls who are striving to get away from the late marriage prospect in this country and also, perhaps, from the prevalent mother-in-law difficulties'.[61] One Connemara commentator in his submission to the commission also claimed that females emigrated to improve their marriage prospects: 'Girls want husbands. Therefore if men emigrate, girls must also'.[62]

The other cause, according to the report, was created by 'the problem of illegitimacy', which often resulted in 'the loss by emigration of many unmarried mothers who find it preferable, for one reason or another, to emigrate rather than to face all the circumstances of an illegitimate pregnancy and confinement in this country'.[63] It is impossible to estimate how many unmarried mothers left Ireland or how many babies were put up for adoption abroad. The report suggested that 'the welfare and care of unmarried mothers and their children should be fully examined ... so that the problems relating to illegitimacy in the twenty-six counties might be dealt with fully in our own country, instead of partly in Great Britain as at present'.[64] This was only one example of the many social problems which were exported.

The evidence submitted to the commission on the causes of female emigration was more elaborate than the reasons stated in the final report. The fear that 'the emigration of the girls as soon as they come to emigration age means that the countryside will be reduced to a wilderness of derelict bachelor farms' was expressed in one submission to the commission.[65] According to the Department of Social Welfare, the economic situation was an important motive since 'the greater part by far of the present movement of female workers to Britain is actuated by the attraction of seemingly better conditions of employment and of life as well as by the spur of economic necessity'.[66] Lack of marriage dowry was also seen as a reason for female emigration, as one commentator explained: 'Money spent on marriage dowries would enable girls to remain at home and, at the same time, make the farmers less slow about marrying ... a scheme of marriage dowries is long overdue and essential. Most of the girls who emigrate and drift to the towns have no dowries and so cannot hope to marry in the country'.[67] It was generally felt that rural females asserted their autonomy and social status by migrating. According to one submission, 'A girl reared on a small farm, having no dowry, feels that she is improving her social position, and consequently her prospects of marrying, by taking up a position in a town, where she is no longer known as Johnny So-and-so's daughter'.[68] The Irish Housewives Association claimed that 'mass emigration of women, low marriage-rate of women [and] high marriage age' was a 'symptom' of the 'condition' which created 'the inferior status of women in several aspects of the social and economic life, in spite of their recognised political equality in the form of the vote'.[69] The association listed the areas where 'the inferior status of women' was evident, such as 'refusal to admit to the principle of equal pay for equal work; automatic dismissal of women from many positions on marriage; inheritance laws permitting the favouring of the sons to the detriment of the daughters'.[70] In addition, the social standing of females in the 1937 Constitution annoyed most female associations. This was in direct contrast to the British government's stance on females, where women were seen as an essential part of the paid workforce rather than simply essential to the family and community units. The Galway City rural survey confirmed that females felt that there was a better social and economic life for them elsewhere. The survey's 'principal conclusions' drawn from the girls interviewed was that 'these girls have lost confidence in Ireland's ability to provide them with what they consider is necessary for a proper life. The propaganda about the advantages of England is still very strong. The smart appearance of girls home on holidays and the letters from girls in England have a tremendous effect upon young girls'.[71]

The dangers, which confronted female emigrants particularly, were dealt with in many of the submissions. This fear echoed a fear in public circles throughout the late 1940s and early 1950s, especially felt by the Catholic church, for the moral well-being of emigrants. Of the problems which confronted emigrants, the Department of Social Welfare cited 'boredom in surroundings often remote and friendless, the lack of the restraints of home environment and the possession of more money than experience would enable them to apply to their advantage' as some of the 'factors which usually operate to the moral detriment of immature girls who emigrate to Britain'.[72] According to the memorandum, 'ample proof is furnished by clergy in contact with emigrants and by Protection and Welfare Societies of the distressing consequences of the impact of a largely materialistic and alien way of life on girls from Irish rural districts'.[73] This view that urban society was corrupt reverberated in Bishop Lucey's minority report to the commission. Lucey clearly shared de Valera's belief that people should return to the land.

Although the commission reported much of the information it acquired from interviews and research, it is remarkable that so little was written on female emigration. It seems probable that this was a result of the focus of those on the commission, who considered the issue of female migration to be somewhat less significant than that of their male counterparts, reflecting the ethos of the wider society. In society as a whole, females were perceived as homemakers rather than for their contribution to the country in other ways. The dowry system still existed in many parts of Ireland and the system of farm inheritance excluded females from making any advances in finance or status. The priority placed on female marriage over employment is best illustrated by the fact that female civil servants were required to leave the service once they married. In other countries, females had greater status, which prompted some female emigration from Ireland. Naturally, much information was probably not revealed in the interviews and research undertaken by the commission, which perhaps explains in part the neglect of other social reasons for female emigration in the report.

It is also surprising that the report glided so quickly over the question of young emigrants considering that the majority of Irish emigrants were young. The age distribution of emigrants from 1841 and 1946 was tabulated in the report but there was little commentary on the data. It simply stated that 'the age-structure of the population is distorted by having a very high proportion over the age of sixty-five and a low proportion aged between fifteen and forty-five. This distortion is due mainly to the heavy emigration of young persons ...'[74]

In dealing with the occupational profile of emigrants, the commission found that female emigrants were more likely to be skilled than males. A commentator from South Kerry showed that females went to factories and domestic work in Dublin and Britain and that few returned, while 'men go all over Britain [to] factories, farms [and] building'.[75] According to a Sligo employment-exchange manager, the situation was similar: 'From Sligo to Ballyshannon migrants do not go to farm work, but to building and industry. Women to domestic service and nursing … Emigration tends to be permanent …'[76]

Information provided through a survey of returned female emigrants in 1948 showed that female emigrants in Britain were becoming conscious of their social standing. According to the findings, 'girls dislike domestic service; dislike is based on pre-war memories, real or imaginary, of long hours and very, very small wages, e.g. 5/– per week indoor' whereas 'employment as factory hands, hotel and café waitresses is very much sought after. A certain social distinction (or, better, perhaps, lack of social stigma) attaches to these occupations …'[77] On the whole, it appears that middle-class emigration for the period examined (namely 1948 to the early 1950s) was slight and that the majority of emigrants were semi-skilled or unskilled.

The report showed that the consequences of emigration were both negative and positive, but as two commissioners in an addendum to the report concluded, 'it is not possible to decide whether emigration is good or bad'.[78] They felt 'such terms are almost meaningless in their application to emigration from Ireland' and instead they saw emigration as 'a fact'.[79] One of the negative consequences of emigration cited in the report was that 'it prevents a healthy increase in population' and it 'depopulates the countryside'.[80] Rural decay had been a visible feature in Ireland since the late 1930s and was deemed a result of emigration. The fact that 'the degree of internal mobility of labour was slight'[81] meant that declines in rural population were not counteracted by rises in urban population; therefore rural depopulation greatly contributed to the overall depopulation. In his survey of counties Mayo and Sligo, Dr Beddy took Lahardane Parish as an example of rural decay. He wrote that the parish had the 'outward appearance of comfort, but population declining, forty families disappeared in 10 years, others declined substantially. Farms too small to expand employment. Emigrants will not return even to inherit the farms. Son may renounce title when he cannot get wife to share the drudgery … marriage problem solved by going abroad. Remittances keep a good appearance at home. Dependence on outside resources takes from people's willingness to do anything for themselves'.[82] The commissioners believed that 'there is no evidence to support the contention of some witnesses that emigration deprives the country of the best of its people; it does, of course, deprive the country of large numbers of its young people, resulting in an undesirable age-distribution of the population. Nor is there any evidence to suggest that the quality of the home population has improved or deteriorated as a result of emigration, or that, as a direct result of a selective policy of emigration, there is a tendency to physical or mental stagnation in the country'.[83] The report expressed concern over the potential of 'emigration [to remove] from a country a proportion of its potentially productive manpower'.[84] However, its findings showed that this was not a problem in Ireland, as the report stated: 'We have received no evidence that there is any serious shortage of labour. On the contrary, the figure of unemployment, and particularly the existence of under-employment on a wide scale, shows that development is not impeded by emigration'.[85]

However, one adverse consequence of emigration noted by the commission was the negative outlook that it created for those people who remained in Ireland. According to the report, 'the failure of the economy to support and retain a larger population' resulted in emigration, which in turn 'weakens national pride and confidence, which of itself retards the efforts required for national progress'.[86] In other words, emigration for economic reasons was not the long-term solution to the country's lack of economic progress. Emigration debilitated morale in Ireland and engendered pessimism towards future prospects. The report claimed that while 'the intrinsic quality of those who in each generation remain in this country is at least as high as those who emigrate, it may be that the effects of heavy emigration produce an environment, both social and economic, which is unfavourable to the latent potentialities of the population'.[87] The Rev. Luce, in his reservation to the report, stated that 'emigration has come to be taken as a matter of course by the public' as 'people have grown up into it, are hardened to it, acquiesce in it, and hardly notice it'.[88] By 1954, emigration had become inevitable for many people throughout Ireland. Luce noted that the knowledge of this fate 'is a dead weight upon the spirit of the whole country, a dead hand upon her economy'.[89] In addition, the commissioners wrestled with the issue of 'whether an emigrant is an economic loss or gain to the community'.[90] The report simply sized up the two sides to this question rather than reaching a conclusion: 'on the one hand, there is a view that when a person emigrates, the community in which he was reared suffers an economic loss which may be measured, say, by the cost of his upbringing (including education), less the value of any output or services rendered by him. On the other hand, there is the view that the emigration of an individual who, while drawing on the available goods and services for his sustenance, is unemployed and rendering no service to the community, results in an economic gain to the country'.[91]

The report recognised the negative aspects of emigration for the individual. It was considered 'bad' when 'it is forced … when the emigrant would prefer to remain at home but cannot obtain a livelihood and is accordingly compelled to emigrate'.[92] Another example where emigration was 'bad' was when emigrants are 'worse off materially and morally in the land of their adoption than those of their generation remaining at home'.[93] The final example of 'bad' emigration presented was 'when it entails the breaking up of a home, where, for example, the father of a family emigrates without his wife and children'.[94] These scenarios were very real for numerous Irish emigrants. The report also briefly acknowledged the 'dangers' to young emigrants, 'the majority' of whom 'lived comparatively sheltered lives before emigrating' but after emigrating 'may succumb to the temptations of city life'.[95]

In the short term, emigration avoided 'that sense of urgent necessity to develop resources rapidly and resolutely which would have arisen if the pressure of an increasing population were operating to force the pace of development'.[96] The report held the view that emigration was 'a safety valve' which 'reduced the pressure of population on resources, as they are now developed, and has thus helped to maintain and even to increase our income per head …'[97] This appears to be somewhat callous, but in a period of limited economic development, it seems to have been a realistic appraisal. However, migration also undoubtedly reduced the potential for development, creating a more conservative society which was less amenable to change. One commissioner, A. Fitzgerald, held that emigration 'releases social tensions which would otherwise explode and makes possible a stability of manners and customs which would otherwise be the subject of radical change'.[98] It was possible that 'social tensions' would result from a higher unemployed population. Previous social revolutions in the world had been in part mobilised by unemployment and poverty created by the order of the day and over-population. With high levels of migration, the risk of a social revolution in Ireland by 1954 was slight.

Emigrant remittances were one of the few benefits for Ireland to be cited in the report. Remittances increased the 'incomes' of 'many of the families of those who emigrated'.[99] The commission found that 'in some cases, this increase in income has made it unnecessary for other members of the family to emigrate, but, in other cases, it has been the means of enabling them to do so'.[100] Such diverse findings highlight the complexity of emigration. The report also acknowledged the importance of remittances 'in the national economy' as 'they partly redress the adverse balance of trade, they may stimulate production, or in certain circumstances they may have a limited inflationary effect'.[101] Such uses emphasised the magnitude of Irish emigration. The 'social effect' of remittances made 'greater equality in the distribution of wealth' more possible.[102]

It is apparent from the report that the disadvantages of emigration out-numbered the positive consequences. The advantages of emigration benefited the population at home in the short term, such as the maintenance of the status quo and the bonus of remittances. In the long term, emigration would upset the country's demography and in particular disrupt the age distribution of the remaining population. Such unevenness would hinder any development – economic, social or otherwise. In addition, the amount of revenue collected would be slight, as the population would be too young or too old to contribute, increasing the dependency ratio. Although the report gave balanced views throughout, it is nevertheless clear that there was a large degree of concern over the continuation of large-scale emigration and its adverse consequences.

The recommendations put forward by the commissioners attempted to show how such problems could be tackled. In order to improve the measurement of emigration, the report recommended that the censuses of population be taken 'more frequently and thereby discover the extent of net emigration at shorter intervals'.[103] This possibly would alter people's apathy towards the issue of mass emigration and could result in greater enthusiasm to prevent further loss of population.

Most of the recommendations made by the commission pertained to the economy, indicating that the economy was held to be the prime reason for emigration. The commissioners showed that lack of economic development created emigration, and emigration hindered economic development. Consequently, the report emphasised the necessity of economic development. In dealing with rural migration, the commissioners recognised that 'there is a tendency in developed countries for the agriculturally occupied population to decline in number' as a result of agricultural development. Putting a brave face on this trend, it suggested rather over-optimistically, in the face of all the evidence, that this 'is unlikely to bring about a substantial increase in the size of the agricultural community'.[104] The report conveyed the belief that 'expansion in industry and services ... will provide the additional employment without a reduction in living standards'.[105] The commissioners were aware that 'development – agricultural and industrial – and the rising standard of living which the population seeks, call for a programme of large-scale and long-term investment which far exceeds the present volume of domestic savings'.[106]

The report termed the Gaeltacht, and other regions of heavy emigration on the western seaboard, as 'special areas', and resolved that 'it is unlikely that the measures recommended ... for developing agriculture and industry and for raising production and productivity will benefit them as much as other areas'.[107] Although efforts were made to improve these regions, 'the population continues to decline and the commission is particularly concerned at the comparatively recent tendency in these areas for families to abandon their holdings'.[108] Rural decay was the inevitable result of such a practice. As the root problem was economic, the report advised 'providing supplementary earnings locally which, when added to the produce of the farm, will afford to families a reasonable comfort on their holdings'.[109] In order to test the viability of this proposal, it recommended a pilot scheme whereby 'the men concerned could be profitably employed and the nation would benefit from their labour, as large-scale schemes of afforestation, reclamation of hill-land, farm improvements to permit the use of agricultural machinery and construction of tourist roads would become immediately practicable'.[110] This was certainly a farsighted idea, but would only be feasible if economic need was the sole reason for emigration. In order to keep the Irish language alive, it was vital that the Gaeltacht population was maintained, therefore emigration from such areas was a vexing issue which needed to be addressed with some sort of preventative measure. In the past, the government had introduced various schemes to improve conditions in these areas, such as the establishment of small-scale industries, land improvements, housing grants and, under the 1952 Unemployment Areas Act, assistance in the creation of industrial enterprise. The crux of the problem of unemployment was that it was mostly seasonal, as was much emigration, and earnings were not enough to sustain the population. For that reason, the scheme suggested by the commission was exceptionally functional. Taking a pessimistic view, the report indicated that further development in fisheries might increase employment, but, it suggested, 'a loss of interest in that way of life'[111] could have been a deterrent and concluded that the subject was 'far too complex for any commission other than a special one'.[112]

In addition to the creation of employment through development, the report showed that the emigration flow could be diminished by 'narrowing the gap between wage-levels' in Ireland and in Britain, which constituted a major pull-factor.[113] However, the report acknowledged 'that substantial improvements in wage-levels on a wide scale cannot be achieved without increased production and increased national income'.[114] Increases in employment, improvements in the standard of living and the cessation of emigration all hinged on economic development and were well identified in the report.

Various proposals were made in the report to prevent rural outflow. It was suggested that improvements in living conditions in rural regions might influence the population to stay. The commission found that 'much drudgery is caused by outmoded methods of day-to-day working and living' and the people subjected to this life 'are gradually becoming less willing to accept the relatively frugal standards of previous generations'.[115] Hardship was created by the 'inadequacy of such amenities for houses and farms as power, light, water and sanitation'.[116] It was felt that in time the rural electrification scheme would solve all these problems. There were, however, additional difficulties associated with rural life. 'The contrast between rural and modern housing' was another cause of strife, and the report postulated that the differences 'must have a considerable effect on the decision of a person in a rural area whether to emigrate or to marry and settle down in his locality'.[117] 'Availability of housing' was seen as 'a first requirement' and 'other such requirements of a rural community as church, school, hall and shops' were other necessary amenities.[118] It was blandly recommended that 'a higher standard of efficiency in all branches of public and social services should be aimed at, particularly ... transport, postal and telephone services and health services'.[119] Such developments not only would improve the quality of rural life but would also 'contribute directly or indirectly to production' and possibly 'promote and increase employment'.[120] Much evidence of 'relative loneliness, dullness and [the] generally unattractive nature of life in many parts of rural Ireland' was presented to the commission.[121] The report was expressive of a general shift among the general public, politicians and public servants towards the idea that material conditions had to be improved. It recognised the social and cultural poverty resulting from the severe lack of resources in rural areas.

The report paid tribute to rural groups like Muintir na Tíre, the Irish Countrywomen's Association and Macra na Feirme for their work in providing a social outlet for people in the countryside. Lack of funds hindered their development and the report requested that 'applications from such bodies for financial help' from the government 'should be sympathetically considered'.[122] Ideas for additional betterment in rural social life were put forward. These improvements involved 'an extensive provision of community, village or parish halls for use as centres for recreation and entertainment, such as billiards, dancing, concerts and card-playing, for more serious activities of an educational or cultural kind (lectures, study groups, debates, library services, local history studies and musical and dramatic clubs), as foci around which the social life of the parish might be built'.[123] The effects of improving rural life could have been far-reaching; they might have appeased the desire for social activity, hindered emigration created by this need and could even have boosted the marriage rate as the community could have become more integrated.

The report made some recommendations to improve conditions and benefit intending emigrants and those who had already emigrated. It was ascertained from the evidence submitted to the commission that a central committee in Britain would greatly benefit Irish emigrants there and would 'give more continuous attention' to any problems they encountered.[124] The commissioners obviously believed that the establishment of such a committee was important, as they recommended that 'it should be provided out of State funds'.[125] It is therefore evident that those who provided the commission with information were deeply concerned over the welfare of the emigrant. From the research carried out in Britain for the commissioners, the reality of the problems experienced by emigrants was starkly revealed.

According to the report, the advancement of emigrants in the workplace would be made possible if 'the educational standard of those who emigrate' was 'raised so that they are not confined to the more arduous and menial forms of employment through lack of adequate education'.[126] One of the commissioners asked, 'is it not a good thing that our young emigrants should be equipped with some skill as they board the ship?'[127] It is plausible that the emigrant's lot would be better according to the qualifications he could offer. However, it seems that in the context of employment in Britain during the 1940s and 1950s, labour shortages were primarily in the skilled, semi-skilled and unskilled sectors. Perhaps if education had been evenly distributed at that time in Ireland, people would not have emigrated, as they would not have accepted jobs lower than those for which they were qualified. But, with unemployment as high as it was in Ireland, such qualified people probably either would have been forced into emigration, taking on work considered below them, or would have remained unemployed at home. For Ireland, the disadvantage of universal education was that if the individual was educated specifically for export, the cost of their education would be a loss to Ireland, plus the country would lose out on talent that could be used to its advantage.

Despite the numerous recommendations put forward by the commission, it failed to fulfil its aim 'to consider the desirability of formulating a national population policy'.[128] Chapter 9 of the report dealt extensively with population, but no policy on population was formulated. The report explained that it was inappropriate for the state to deter people from emigrating:

> The individual exercising his free will is in normal circumstances free to live where he wishes. Consequently, we believe that those who wish to and can emigrate have the right to do so, and that the State should not consider interfering with the exercise of this right, except in the case of a national emergency or where the survival of the nation is in jeopardy.[129]

It therefore claimed that 'in present circumstances, direct government action in the demographic field, such as the banning or limitation of emigration, the imposition of a tax on bachelors or the provision of marriage loans and grants' was unnecessary.[130] This stance was in line with that of contemporary political thinking.

The Report of the Commission on Emigration and Other Population Problems was released in May 1954, a month after the second inter-party government came to power. It had taken six years to complete the work, and because of this delay, public interest had waned somewhat in the commission's progress. The publication was primarily delayed because of the commissioners' request for a special census in 1951 to compile better data. It appears that many were fed up waiting for the commission to release its findings; in 1952 a member of the opposition sarcastically asked the Minister for Social Welfare, Dr James Ryan, 'if the commission had since emigrated?'[131] There were numerous other references made to the delay in publication on various occasions in the Dáil. Obviously some remarks were propelled by political ploy. The report was not available in book form until 1956, which limited the readership somewhat. Many of the recommendations made in the report were feasible, but could not guarantee the desired end of checking emigration. In essence, the commission was not a means to an end – its significance lay in the manner in which it highlighted issues pertaining to both emigration and the need for economic development. Its analysis of the reasons for emigration showed that it was no longer valid to blame Ireland's colonial experience for the high rate of emigration. Dr R. C. Geary, director of the Central Statistics Office, stated that 'the present attitude was an inheritance from the long period of the independence struggle, when it was an effective argument'. He affirmed that 'it is high time that the Irish people examined the validity of their traditional attitude towards emigration'.[132] The findings of the commission confirmed that Britain could no longer be blamed for Irish emigration.

The likelihood of the report being read widely was slim; therefore it had to rely heavily on media coverage to promote it. Newspapers primarily referred to the commission's findings once the report became available in July 1954. However, little else was written in the newspapers and in letters to the newspapers on the commission. It appears that the public was generally apathetic about the report and its findings, despite the extensive coverage and practical recommendations contained within it. The commission was the brainchild of the first inter-party government; this partially explains its critical appraisal of the realities of life in rural Ireland, which was very different from the utopian representations of rural Ireland made by de Valera.

The Fianna Fáil government that held power between 1932 and 1948 spoke of emigration in terms of tradition as well as social and psychological causes – all of which were conveniently difficult for any administration to tackle. In contrast, the first inter-party government was more realistic, and saw emigration principally as a product of lack of economic thought and progress. In this regard, the first inter-party government marked a new departure, and the establishment of a commission to examine emigration was a manifestation of this change.

The importance of the commission in the 1950s was overshadowed by the publication of *Economic Development* in 1958, spearheaded by Fianna Fáil, which was to guide economic progress in Ireland up to the early 1970s. It was the first of a series of plans which outlined the main thrust of government development policy. It appears that the significance of emigration, the sluggish economy and unemployment was heightened according to the increase in numbers that were affected, and as the situation worsened, the likelihood rose of some new policy being adopted. While the commission did not formulate a programme, its findings certainly provided a greater insight into the subject. Its stark appraisal of circumstances in rural Ireland, and the causes of emigration, created a greater urgency in the quest to improve Irish economic development. Its recommendations had little impact on government, yet it marked a more realistic appraisal of the wider implications of emigration for Irish society at an official level. This was probably its most significant feature. It baldly recognised the lack of social and economic development in much of Ireland, and the impact that this had on a large section of the population. The commission was working during a period of recession, when it was recognised that the state needed to play a more proactive role in economic development. The report and its conclusions reflected this transition. The report marked the end of the utopian idealisation of life in rural Ireland, by starkly revealing the realities of people's circumstances. This led to a more measured, pragmatic response to the Republic's need for sustained economic development.

Changing the Rules: Why the Failures of the 1950s Forced a Transition in Economic Policy-making

JOHN BRADLEY

INTRODUCTION

The dismal facts of the economic failures of the 1950s are well known and do not have to be rehearsed here in any great detail. The policy of the incoming Fianna Fáil government in 1932 of attempting to build an Irish industrial base behind protective tariff barriers was continued well beyond its sell-by date into the post-Second World War era. While industrial output grew fairly rapidly in the early years of protection, demand for labour fell well short of what would have been needed to keep pace with the high natural increase in the population and growth in the labour-force.

The rapid recovery and growth of the main economies of western Europe – after an initial period of post-war reconstruction – cruelly exposed the poor performance of the Irish economy. Policy-makers in Ireland recognised and acknowledged these failures and attempted to address them to the best of their ability. Dramatic new policy initiatives were implemented. That these initiatives eventually led to a sea-change in performance during the 1960s is also well known. By 1970, net outward migration had ceased and for the first time since the Famine, reversed in direction for the following eight years (Figure 1). However, it was to resume again in 1980, and in 1989 outward migration peaked at about 45,000. Today, birth rates have largely converged to lower European norms, annual net inward migration is running at over 20,000,

Figure 1: Half a century of migration in Ireland: net migration 1950–2000

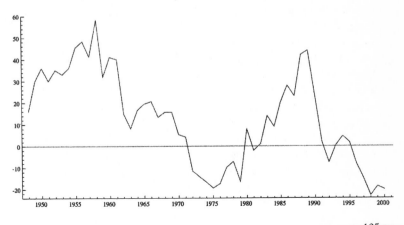

and Irish agencies and firms spend their time scouring the world for workers willing to relocate here to service our economy.

When economists revisit and re-examine the failures of the 1950s, their perspective is rather different from that of historians, writers, psychologists and others who seek to understand how individuals and groups experience drastic times. We must tread carefully here, for even if economists regard the 1950s as merely a transitional period – a time when Ireland's external economic environment changed and adaptation to that change was very slow in coming – nevertheless the difficulties of the time have left semi-permanent scars on the lives of individuals and on society itself. I well recall the game we used to play as young children, passing the time counting the cottages through Roscommon and Mayo that were boarded up and abandoned, as my father drove down to Westport to visit his elderly parents. Coming back – usually at night when the depressing countryside was hidden from view – we delighted in greeting the first double-decker bus near Maynooth as we returned to civilisation and security.

Why should the 1950s continue to be of relevance to economists? Do we not now inhabit a brave new world characterised by globalisation and high technology? Have we not carved out a prosperous niche by dint of our homespun cunning and intelligence? The reason for the continuing relevance of the 1950s goes deep into how policy-makers plan and implement long-term strategies. In the hurly-burly of daily life, one can live with a certain amount of lack of coordination; one can switch direction many times and experiment; one can even be inconsistent. Tactical policy mistakes and errors can usually be detected before too much damage is done, and revised policies implemented in a game of trial and error. However, this is only the case when the strategic thrust of policy has been set correctly. Getting the medium-term strategy right is vital mainly because change is difficult and errors are costly. When strategy is wrong, retribution usually follows. This is as important today as it was in the 1950s, for Ireland as for any other country or region.

Here, we first examine the strategic setting for Irish economic policy that was implemented in the early 1930s. The simple, unqualified and dogged embrace of protection by Irish policy-makers had appeared to offer exactly what the country needed at that time, and was in tune with an unfolding political and economic drama being played out in the rest of the world. We are uniquely privileged to have an evaluation of that policy, written at the very time of its design and implementation, by the greatest economist of the twentieth century – John Maynard Keynes. We know from Robert Skidelsky's magnificent biography that when Keynes spoke, the world listened, even if – as in the case of post-war America – it did not always obey. But why were Keynes' nuanced insights of 1933 neglected by his Irish policy-making contemporaries, who woke up too late in the 1950s to the peril of their position?

During the 1950s, economic failure forced a rethink of policy fundamentals and eventually appeared to produce a well-thought-out alternative: trade liberalisation and access to foreign capital. The central document in this period was *Economic Development*, a report composed by Dr T. K. Whitaker that motivated and justified a complete change in policy direction. With the benefit of hindsight, it is of interest to examine the extent to which the policy programmes that derived from *Economic Development* foresaw correctly the shape of the new and improved performance that would emerge during the 1960s.

We conclude by examining what we can learn from the process that led to the seismic shift in policy that took place during the 1950s. J. J. Lee, in his magisterial *Ireland 1912–1985*, has brooded on the causes of failure and reached fairly damning verdicts concerning the role played by contemporary economists and policy-makers. Could such errors be repeated today?

BEFORE THE STORM

The seeds of the 'Lost Decade' were sown in 1932. The Cumann na nGaedheal governments of 1922 to 1932 had largely followed UK policy norms: a fixed link with sterling and free trade. Given the dominance of the UK as a destination for Ireland's mainly agricultural exports, few seriously challenged the link with sterling at that time. However, the efforts to restore the certainties of the pre-First World War economy – based on free trade and the gold standard – had collapsed by the early 1930s, and the world moved into depression and fragmentation.

As countries were confronted by depression, there was an aversion to international economic interdependence. Nations turned inward, fell back on their own resources, and there was a proliferation of exchange controls, tariffs, import quotas and the like. Even in the UK – the spiritual home of free trade – the Import Duties Act of 1932 imposed tariffs on a wide range of non-empire goods. That the incoming Fianna Fáil government was committed to a policy of protection was hardly surprising. One might speculate that if the world trading system had not been having a nervous breakdown, even the avowedly Sinn Féin policies of the new government might have not been given such a free rein.

The driving motivation for the new policies of protection was the need to create an Irish manufacturing sector from almost a zero base. The partition of the island in 1922 had split off the one heavily industrialised region that was centred on Belfast, leaving the Free State with the modest remainder. The lurch to protection must have appalled the pro free-trade politicians of the previous administration. It is said that the invitation to Keynes to deliver the first Finlay lecture in University College Dublin on 19 April 1933 had been on the expectation that the speaker – a well-known advocate of the benefits of free trade – might bring an end to the madness. We can imagine the horror of the ranks of conservative politicians and academics when Keynes declared – in the most often-quoted extract from his lecture:

> Ideas, knowledge, science, hospitality, travel – these are the things which should by their nature be international. But let goods be homespun when-ever it is reasonably and conveniently possible, and, above all, let finance be primarily national.

and concluded:

> If I were an Irishman, I should find much to attract me in the economic outlook of your present government towards greater self-sufficiency.

What is seldom quoted is what immediately followed these remarks, and heavily qualified them:

> But as a practical man and as one who considers poverty and insecurity to be great evils, I should wish to be first satisfied on (some) matters ... I should ask if Ireland is a large enough unit geographically, with sufficiently diversified natural resources, for more than a very modest measure of national self-sufficiency to be feasible without a disastrous reduction in a standard of life which is already none too high.

Keynes went on to suggest an economic arrangement with 'England' that resembled nothing so much as the Anglo-Irish Free Trade Agreement that was concluded over 30 years later in 1965. But even more interesting are the reasons why Keynes had become disillusioned with free trade and international interdependence. Remember, this was the author of *The Economic Consequences of the Peace*, a man who foresaw exactly where the vindictive treatment of a fallen Germany would lead. The Finlay lecture was given one month after Adolf Hitler was ap-pointed German chancellor and one month before the burning of books in the square of Unter den Linden in Berlin on 10 May. It is little wonder that Keynes declared:

> It does not today seem obvious that a great concentration of national effort on the capture of foreign trade, that the penetration of a country's economic structure by the resources and the influence of foreign capita-lists, that a close dependence of our own economic life on the fluctuating economic policies of foreign countries are safeguards and assurances of in-ternational peace.

So, while the Fianna Fáil government had domestic objectives of in-dustrialisation and wanted to erect protective barriers to shield the in-fant industries, Keynes' was the wider vision that may not have struck much resonance in a country preoccupied with its own internal prob-lems. The policy of tariff protection put in place in 1933 endured through the Second World War (a time when access to vital imports was a more pressing problem than protection) and continued through the period of post-war recovery that lasted until 1949. The relative successes of the immediate post-war period – when Ireland had captive British markets for its agricultural and food products – served to conceal the problems that the resumption of more normal conditions brought during the 1950s.

More fundamentally, the political incorporation of Ireland into the United Kingdom between 1801 and 1922 generated forces that led to comprehensive economic and trade integration as well. The full extent of this integration after more than 100 years of union is illust-rated in Figure 2, which shows the UK–Irish trade position from just after independence in 1922 to 1950. The proportion of southern ex-ports going to the UK showed only a very small reduction from 99% in 1924 to 93% by 1950.

In addition to other problems, the failure of Ireland to diversify its economy away from an almost total dependence on the UK had serious consequences for its economic performance when compared to a range of other small European countries. The reluctance of the new Irish public administration to deviate too much from British policy norms has been well documented. It was hardly surprising. While policies and policy-makers in Ireland may have been less assertive and innovative than might have been desired, in the absence of a competitive and ex-port-oriented industrial sector there was probably very little that could have been achieved to accelerate an earlier economic decoupling from the UK. The consequences followed inexorably. In the words of Lars Mjøset:

Figure 2: Destination of Irish exports 1924–1950

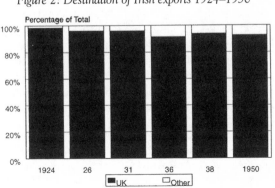

Ireland became a free rider on Britain's decline, while Austria and Switzerland were free riders on Germany's economic miracle.

Ireland's relationship with Britain, which had involved a strong and enduring web of dependency before 1960, weakened considerably thereafter for very specific reasons.

DURING THE STORM

Even while the war was in progress, and before it was clear that the allies would be the victors, Keynes and others worked to ensure that post-war barriers to trade and currency exchange would not disrupt the proper functioning of the international economy as it had after the First World War. Robert Skidelsky notes that Keynes used to say, ironically, that he used the calm of war to reflect on the turmoil of the coming peace! The international institutions that emerged from the Anglo-American negotiations – the International Monetary Fund, the International Bank for Reconstruction and Development (or World Bank) and the General Agreement on Tariffs and Trade – were heavily influenced by Keynes, even if the detailed implementations carried the imprint of the immensely powerful USA. The European scene was further transformed by the European Recovery Programme (Marshall Aid) from April 1948 and the major devaluations against the dollar of September 1949. In addition, the Schuman Plan of 1950 set up the European Coal and Steel Community, and led eventually to the signing of the Treaty of Rome in March 1957. This international context was to test the robustness of the inward-looking Irish policies and cruelly expose their weaknesses.

The early part of the 1950s was characterised by a series of balance-of-payments crises that were handled in the conventional way by imposing higher taxes and cuts in expenditure to drastically reduce demand. Tentative efforts were made to run an independent lower interest-rate policy, but this was soon abandoned. These problems were simply the consequences of the uncompetitiveness of the manufacturing sector, and not the primary causes. Not only had protection failed to produce self-sufficiency – since the protected industries still needed to import materials and capital goods – but any increase in consumption also quickly ran into the sands of the balance-of-payments constraint. In other words, this was exactly what Keynes had warned about back in 1933! Ireland was simply too small to be a producer of goods where it had no comparative advantage. In his book *Planning in Ireland*, Garret FitzGerald summarised the dilemma as follows:

> [Ireland] thus drifted into the 1950s unconscious of the difficulties it was creating for itself, or of the urgency of tackling them if stagnation of output and a decline in population were to be avoided. [By 1955] the basic dis-

equilibrium between competitive Irish exports, and the imports demanded by an Irish public increasingly conscious of the disparity between its living standards and those of the British public, was dangerously exposed.

The Control of Manufactures Act – which had been used to prevent foreign ownership of Irish industry – was relaxed, but was not to be formally abolished until the 1960s. By 1956, the second inter-party government had started to use industrial grants to attract foreign activity into Ireland, rather than merely to divert it to particularly deserving locations. Also, an export-tax relief scheme – exempting profits earned from new or increased exports – was put in place.

The disparate policy changes that evolved during the 1950s were consolidated in *Economic Development* and codified in the *First Programme for Economic Expansion*. An extraordinary and diverse range of ideas and proposals were advanced, mainly in the areas of agriculture and the agri-food sector. But with the benefit of hindsight, we can now recognise *Economic Development* as a transition between old and new perspectives, and not a whole-hearted embrace of a modern view of the economy. For example, we now know that the zero rate of corporation profits tax, along with the liberalisation of trade and foreign investment as well as the freedom to repatriate profits, were absolutely central factors in a process that would inexorably lead to the decline of the indigenous manufacturing sector and the rise and eventual dominance of a new foreign-owned sector. Yet, the tax initiative lies buried in Appendix 2 of *Economic Development* (Measures Designed to Encourage Investment in Irish Enterprises) on page 232 and is not mentioned in the main text.

We also now recognise that when a mainly agricultural country attempts to modernise, the primary requirement is for the farming sector to shrink in size as a proportion of the overall economy, and for the manufacturing sector to expand and develop in a way that drives export growth through improvement in cost competitiveness. In the post-war period, this involved attracting direct investment from America. Yet, the vision of *Economic Development* was one of agriculture-led export growth, with a continuing indigenous base.

The crucial policy changes made in the 1950s, brought together in the strategy of *Economic Development* in 1958, were a heady and novel mix of a commitment to trade liberalisation, a range of direct and indirect grant aid to private firms, and a singular incentive of zero corporation profits tax on exports. This policy mix was precisely what was needed to ride the future wave of American foreign direct investment, contradicting the declared policy aim of growing on the back of an expanding indigenous agri-industrial base. The right policies, but the wrong outcome!

The Irish economy that emerged from the 1950s was still in a weak state, but at least was now equipped with a policy strategy that happened to be uniquely in tune with the changed times. Furthermore, Ireland was no longer alone in having difficulty in coping in a new European and international environment. American investment into Europe at that time was so dynamic and threatening that it presented the major European economies with what Jean-Jacques Servan-Schreiber characterised as the 'American Challenge'. In his book *The American Challenge*, Servan-Schreiber wrote:

> While French, German, or Italian firms are still groping around in the new open spaces provided by the Treaty of Rome, afraid to emerge from the dilapidated shelter of their old habits, American industry has gauged the terrain and is now rolling from Naples to Amsterdam with the ease and speed of Israeli tanks in the Sinai desert.

The best explanation for the rise of American inward investment into Europe, and eventually into Ireland, was provided by the late Raymond Vernon. Vernon's main insight was to link the product life-cycle with international trade and foreign direct investment. At a time when US foreign direct investment had come to dominate the post-war European economy, standard trade theory offered little by way of explanation. Vernon's theory acknowledged that the US home market played a dual role: it was the source of stimulus for the innovating firm as well as the preferred location for the actual development of the innovation. At the early stage of the product life-cycle, producers need great freedom and flexibility to modify, improve and test new processes, before the preferred production technology has stabilised. Also, demand for innovative products tends to be relatively insensitive to price, so there is less pressure to seek lowest cost production locations. Finally, communications between producers, suppliers and final customers must be facilitated, which argues for a home location.

As the product matures, a certain degree of standardisation takes place, and this has locational implications. The need for production flexibility declines and there is now a greater concern for lower costs. Also, demand from abroad increases. However, as long as the marginal production cost plus the transport costs of shipping from the US to the foreign market is lower than the average cost of prospective production in the market of import, there will be no pressure to invest in foreign production capacity. Markets will be served by exports from the US. But as economic and political pressures build up, eventually some production moves abroad, initially into the larger more developed economies like the UK, France and Germany, but soon even to smaller and less developed economies like Ireland. Eventually, as the product fully matures and perhaps enters a declining phase, low-cost considerations become paramount: production ceases in the US, declines in other developed economies, and concentrates in low-cost developing economies.

The strong web of dependency between Ireland and the UK that had endured relatively unchanged until the late 1950s only began to weaken after the shift to foreign direct investment and export-led growth that followed the various French-style Programmes for Economic Expansion in the late 1950s and during the 1960s. Figure 3 shows the behaviour of the shares of Irish exports going to the UK and of Irish imports originating in the UK for the period 1960–95, after which shares tended to stabilise.

Figure 3: Southern trade with the UK: export and import shares 1960–95

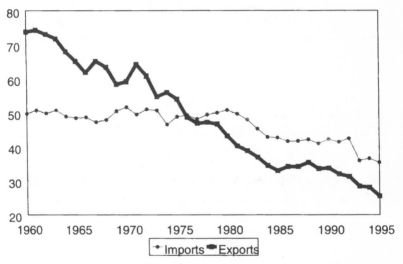

REFLECTING ON THE EXPERIENCE
We have come a long way from the failures of the 1950s. For example, in a remarkable comment on the state of the Irish economy today, Intel president Craig Barrett recently reflected on why his firm had come to Ireland. Speaking to Thomas Friedman, author of *The Lexus and the Olive Tree*, Barrett said:

> We are there because Ireland is very pro-business, they have a very strong educational infrastructure, it is incredibly easy to move things in and out of the country, and it is incredibly easy to work with the government. I would invest in Ireland before Germany or France.

The modern economic age dawned for Ireland in the late 1950s. The successes and challenges that we face today are an extraordinary reversal of the failures and problems faced by policy-makers at that time. In the words of Dr Whitaker, in the late 1950s we had 'plumbed the depths of hopelessness'; today we bask in the world's admiration of our success. Then we began to take our first tentative steps out from behind stultifying barriers of tariff protection and economic and political isolation; today we have embraced the global economy to an extent that few other states have, and we are cosmopolitan citizens of the world. Then we were predominantly an agricultural economy; now, while agriculture remains important, we are a major supplier of Europe's computers, software and pharmaceuticals and our concerns are with maintaining a leading position at the cutting edge of new technology-based manufacturing and quality services.

The 1950s represented a watershed for the Irish economy. Policy actions initiated then launched the economy on a development path that differed radically from that pursued before and after independence. The core policy dilemma was not about whether the Irish economy should be open to trade and investment flows with the wider world economy, since Ireland – in spite of almost three decades of protection – already had a relatively open economy when compared to the other small European states in the late 1950s. Rather, the issue was the nature of this involvement and whether there was to be a break with an almost total dependence on the British market as the destination for exports of a very restricted variety of mainly agricultural products.

The opening of the economy and the removal of tariff barriers were necessary policy changes to kick-start from stagnation. Free trade with the UK – our main trading partner – happened in the mid-1960s. This initiative – the brainchild of Taoiseach Seán Lemass – provided a very useful opportunity to test the water of outward orientation. Free trade with Europe came later, when Ireland joined the then EEC in 1973. The strategic orientation of Irish economic policy-making since the 1950s has always emphasised the need to face the consequences of extreme openness, to encourage export orientation towards fast-growing markets and products, and to be aligned with all European initiatives. Thus, we joined the European Monetary System in 1979, breaking a long link with sterling and its deep economic and psychological dependency. We embraced the Single Market of 1992, the Social Chapter of the Maastricht Treaty, and most recently, Economic and Monetary Union from January 1999. Perhaps this is the main legacy bequeathed to us by the prescient policy-makers of the time of Seán Lemass. The enthusiastic embrace of openness provided the strong and enduring strategic backbone of our economic planning.

But Ireland was still not a very attractive place in which to invest in the early 1960s. It was remote and unknown, had little by way of natural resources, and had no industrial heritage. The main inducement provided to inward investors was initially a zero rate of corporation tax on exports of manufactured goods. Under pressure from the European Community, this was later replaced by a low rate of 10% on all manufacturing profits. This tax policy, combined with aggressive and sophisticated initiatives designed by the IDA to attract and aid inward investors, provided the main driving force for the modernisation of the economy through export-led growth.

However, an attractive corporation tax rate and the absence of tariffs were only a start. They would not in themselves have made Ireland a major host for high-quality foreign direct investment. Other factors came together to reinforce Ireland's success and interacted to create a virtuous circle of superior performance that replaced the previous vicious circle of decades of under-performance that had culminated in the failures of the 1950s. Educational standards in the Irish workforce had lagged behind the world. Policies were urgently needed to bring about a steady improvement in the quality, quantity and relevance of education and training, and this had been initiated by farseeing educational reforms starting in the 1960s. These reforms were extended by the emphasis given to scientific and technical skill formation through the use of generous European Community Structural Funds from the late 1980s. Although issues of social inequality are still of concern, the general level of educational attainment in Ireland is higher than in other, wealthier European states.

On the global economic map, the lines that now matter are those defining 'natural economic zones', where the defining issue is that each such zone possesses, in one or other combination, the key ingredients for successful participation in the international economy. With falling transportation and telecommunication costs, national economies were destined to become increasingly interdependent, and in the words of former US Labour Secretary Robert Reich:

> The real economic challenge ... [of the nation] ... is to increase the potential value of what its citizens can add to the global economy, by enhancing their skills and capacities and by improving their means of linking those skills and capacities to the world market.

This process of global competition is organised today mainly by multinational firms and not by governments. Production tends to be modularised, with individual modules spread across the globe to exploit the comparative advantages of different regions. Hence, individual small nations and regions have less power to influence their destinies than in previous periods of industrialisation, other than by refocusing their economic policies on location factors, especially those which are relatively immobile between regions: the quality of labour, infrastructure and economic governance, and the efficient functioning of labour markets.

The Irish path of economic development followed since the 1950s is not without its risks. The most dynamic part of manufacturing is almost completely foreign-owned and is concentrated in a narrow range of technologies that are fast moving towards maturity. The policy initiatives that ensured Ireland had an advantageous head start in the early 1960s may not be sufficient to facilitate the inevitable switches to newer technologies, since other countries and regions have been learning by watching what Ireland was doing! Until recently, we could rely on an abundant supply of highly trained Irish workers. But birth rates fell rapidly in the 1980s, and if growth is to continue, we may have to rely on inward migration to supply the labour.

At various times in the life of a country or region, often when the economy is facing major new challenges or performing particularly poorly, state and regional governments and agencies carry out in-depth reviews and re-evaluations of economic and business strategy. To the extent that the focus is on problems and challenges that are regarded as 'strategic' rather than 'tactical' in nature, such policy reviews are only carried out infrequently, and have a medium- or long-term orientation. The ability of such reviews to improve economic and business performance depends both on the extent and quality of the review of past policies and future options as well as on the extent to which any policy prescriptions are systematically implemented.

Major socio-economic and business reviews of public policy draw from – and depend crucially upon – the existing pool of academic and applied research, and seldom if ever contribute to that pool. If a country or region faces major policy challenges, but either has an inadequate stock of research-based knowledge or fails to draw comprehensively from its available research, then policy prescriptions are very unlikely to be soundly based. A singular exception that proves this rule was the case of *Economic Development*, a policy review that heralded major changes in the strategic orientation of policy and led eventually to a sea-change in economic performance. The stock of research and knowledge about the functioning of the economy was woefully inadequate, and the analysis and research contained in *Economic Development*, which initiated a subsequent series of three Programmes for Economic Expansion running into the early 1970s, actually came from within the civil service. However, initiatives were quickly put in place that led eventually to a significant expansion of the capacity for academic research, including the founding of the Economic and Social Research Institute in 1960 and the expansion of university and other institution-based research.

A capacity for academic applied socio-economic and business research is a necessary condition for good policy-making, but is certainly not sufficient. One must also try to ensure that the research community directs its efforts and investigations towards the problems and challenges that are actually facing local policy makers. Perhaps sovereign states have an advantage over regions in this aspect of research, since small states like Denmark and Ireland tend to face the same set of policy challenges that confront much larger states, and their policy-makers now have to function in international forums (such as the European Union, the Organisation for Economic Cooperation and Development and the United Nations) on their own account rather than – as in the case of regions like Northern Ireland, Scotland and Wales – as part of a larger national entity.

Perhaps the most striking consequence of foreign investment inflows was that it hastened the de-coupling of the Irish economy from its almost total dependence on the United Kingdom. Ireland's development dilemma had always been that it could stick closely to UK economic policy and institutional norms and be constrained by the erratic UK growth performance, with little prospect of rapid convergence to a higher standard of living. The alternative was to implement a politically acceptable degree of local policy innovation that offered hope of a faster rate of growth than its dominant trading partner. The Irish economic policy-making environment during this period can be characterised as having shifted from that appropriate to a dependent state on the periphery of the UK to that of a region more fully integrated into an encompassing European economy. Foreign direct investment renovated and boosted Irish productive capacity. The Single Market provided the primary source of demand. All that remained was a big push on improvement in physical infrastructure, education and training, and this arrived in the form of a dramatic innovation in regional policy at the EU level. It had taken about 30 years for the policy of protection to fail miserably. It took slightly more than 30 years for the policy of openness to succeed beyond our wildest dreams. I remain to be convinced that we could have shortened these periods to any significant extent.

Aspects of Local Health in Ireland in the 1950s*

ANDREW MCCARTHY

Despite the controversy attendant on its evolution from the 1945 Health Bill, and subsequent passage, the 1947 Health Act was a landmark in progressive legislation. This act attempted a revolutionary restructuring of health service delivery in Ireland. Not only did it consolidate some twenty-six previous statutes and codify infectious diseases, but it also mapped out a new role in local public health with a distinctly preventive focus. In doing so, it appeared to usher in an exciting new era for local health services, particularly in the trail of the proposed mother and child services. This essay will attempt to examine some of the issues, looking particularly at the west of Ireland, encompassing aspects of health infrastructure and how services such as BCG vaccination operated at local level.

It is instructive firstly to recall certain details of what the Mother and Child Health Service Scheme would entail, as this proposal was central and fundamental to the local health services. Rather than review the controversy, of which much has already been written,[1] it is more useful to reflect on the views of James Deeny, the originator of the scheme and chief medical adviser of the Department of Health from 1944 to 1962. Addressing a medical audience in Cork shortly after the passage of the 1947 Health Act, Deeny outlined the scheme as the first part of the reorganisation of the health services, a reorganisation that would be based on integrating existing services and concentrating on maternal and child health. Simply put, the proposals envisaged a medical service for mothers in relation to child-birth and for children from birth to 16 years. The service would be based on the existing dispensary doctors and be supervised by the county medical officers of health. To provide the service, the dispensary districts would be surveyed and additional medical staff would be provided, including the absorption of a certain number of general practitioners. In some cases, whole-time assistants would be provided, and each doctor would be assisted by a nurse and midwife. New or improved clinic accommodation would be provided. The maternal service would consist of ante-natal examination, attendance if required at the confinement and post-natal care to include examination. In the obstetrical care of such women, the doctor would have the services of a specialist located at the county centre and available to visit other centres in the county and to handle emergency referrals.

The service for infants in their first year would involve the doctor providing a supervisory service, assisted by nurse or midwife, the latter carrying out domiciliary visits and the former seeing the infant at the clinic and, if requested, at the infant's home. Regular examination of pre-school children would take place under the district nurse. A sliding scale of attendance would be arranged so that as the child grew, the number of visits to the clinic would decrease. The doctor would be responsible for diet, correcting posture, immunisation, general physical examination and other areas during the school years, followed up by more frequent school visits by the nurses. In addition, each county would have access to specialist services in the fields of dentistry, orthopaedics, ear nose and throat, ophthalmology and psychiatry, although not necessarily exclusively so, as specialists might serve a range of counties. In practice, counties would have several clinics running weekly sessions at which referred cases would receive advice and treatment, and arrangement for admissions would be made if necessary. Parallel with these specialist services, participant doctors would also provide instruction to the parents in the rearing and care of their families and general practitioner treatment to those under their care.[2]

The basic unit envisaged for this scheme, then, was the dispensary service. In the 1940s, as Whyte pointed out, this service ensured that there was a qualified doctor living in every part of the country, even the most remote.[3] This situation obtained especially in the poorer western counties, as a 1960 internal departmental survey of all doctors (private and dispensary) resident in dispensary districts tended to confirm an urban–rural imbalance in numbers of resident general practitioners. In Clare, 17 out of 25 dispensary districts had no resident doctor other than the dispensary doctor. In Donegal the ratio was 21:38, in Galway 17:38, in Kerry 17:30, in Leitrim 10:13, Roscommon 14:19, Sligo 11:16, and West Cork saw 12 of its 15 districts without an effective choice of doctor. Mayo fared better than most western counties, with only 11 of its 31 districts so deprived.[4]

Responsibility for delivery of local public health services rested with the county medical officer (CMO) and district medical officer (DMO). However, the DMO – usually the local dispensary doctor – was only responsible to the CMO in preventive health areas, such as immunisation, and answered to the county manager in respect of dispensary service rendered. The role of the CMO was essentially administrative, an advisory function to the local health authorities relating to provision of health and sanitary services, housing, and direct operation of maternity and child health services as well as implementing food hygiene regulations and implementing infectious diseases services.[5] For the historian of local health, however, the CMO has an outstanding role arising from his function. The County Medical Officers Order, 1926, outlined ten main headings of a general nature for presentation of their annual report. An additional twelve categories, dealing with the operation of approved schemes, were added by circular in 1942. Finally, the Health (Duties of Officers) Order, 1949, required the CMOs to:

> ... prepare as soon as possible after the close of each calendar year and in such form and dealing with such subjects as the Minister may ... direct, in addition to any other matters relating to his duties on which it may be considered desirable that he should report, an annual report ... and furnish to the Corporation/County Council and to the Minister such copies of such report as they may require.[6]

By the early 1950s, the utility of these reports was being questioned within the administrative side of the Department of Health. John Darby expressed reservations in a wide-ranging minute:

> It would be interesting to know the origin of these reports and the idea behind them. Why should a CMO submit an annual report more than a County Manager, a County Engineer ... etc? Certainly it is the duty of a CMO to submit proposals and to make criticisms but surely not in a public report! It may be argued that the annual report is principally a report to the local authority, but it is not generally regarded as such.
>
> I haven't studied many reports but some I have seen have been critical of the local authority while others are merely a collection of statistics. In the former case it seems extraordinary to me that a CMO is not only allowed to criticise his employer publicly but that he can do it at the public expense.
>
> ... I do not think these reports are necessary or justified.[7]

To be fair, Darby further recommended that if the reports were to be continued, they should be standardised and that the views of the CMOs would be desirable on statistical content. This view in turn generated a debate within central health on the future of the reports. It is fascinating for what it reveals about the working of the official mind and a brief review of contributions is instructive. Patrick Fanning, medical inspector and later deputy chief medical adviser in the department, who felt much of this information in reports could be compiled centrally, outlined his views on the role of the report:

> What should properly be reported in the CMOs Annual Report turns surely on the purpose of such report. As I see it, the CMO in this report should account for his stewardship to the Local Authority and the people of the county. They have a right to know how their money was spent, to what purpose, and with what results; and the CMO should, as simply and succinctly as possible, tell them just this. Statistics, except in the simplest form, repel the ordinary reader; and too much information in a report of this kind is almost worse than too little, for if the report is very comprehensive it will not be read at all by the general public, and a valuable opportunity for local health propaganda will be missed.[8]

That last point was essentially shared by most of the medical inspectors who, when presented with the question whether the reports should be continued, argued in favour. Harry O'Flanagan, later registrar at the Royal College of Surgeons, felt the reports had good potential for shaping public health and would be of interest to students of social conditions and medical postgraduates. Tom Murphy, later president of University College Dublin, felt it was good for CMOs to have an annual critical review and keep local health records. The balance of opinion in other sections – while interspersed with observations such as 'little or no value', 'not worth continuing' and continuance unnecessary and unjustified – generally favoured retention. There was a general consensus that if the reports were retained they should be standardised for comparative purposes. Yet no generally agreed format presented itself – probably the major stumbling block to any progress emerging from these consultations. One aspect did, however, find almost unanimous – with the exception of Darby – approval: that the department should not attempt to censor reports. But even here motives differed, ranging from genuine concern for freedom of expression for CMOs to realisation of the practical limits, as acknowledged in one administrator's comment: 'after all, we cannot control the adverse comment by CMOs at local council meetings, etc.'[9]

This review process is instructive for what it reveals about decision-making in the Department of Health and the time span involved in rolling out change at national level. It might first be remembered that the 1947 Health Act envisaged considerable changes in the functions of CMOs – an expanded administrative role in the co-ordination of the local health services. What is surprising is that no review of the scope of the CMO's annual report took place before this legislation was enacted, given the broader functions over which the CMO would now comment on from a front-line position. If central health was anxious to muzzle potential criticisms one might expect new guidelines or the elimination of the reports altogether. Neither happened although both options were contemplated. Instead, central health initiated lengthy internal consultations – from 1951 to 1960 – which appeared to lack any urgency.[10] This process revealed a wide variety of opinions on the utility of the reports, ranging from 'useless' to 'valuable'. No section within central health had a unanimous opinion and sharp differences suggest the department was not a combine of monolithic views. Nevertheless, this process generated perceptive suggestions for standardisation of reports, consultation with the CMOs on desirable content, but ultimately yielded no changes, no consultation and no further action.

The lack of clear direction for a future role for the CMOs was matched by the inadequacy of the resources devoted to local health needs. The basic infrastructure of the dispensary system was in various stages of decay by the 1950s. The Dublin network of forty-four dispensary districts was, literally, crumbling by the 1940s. In 1947 Deeny particularly acknowledged this problem in Dublin, noting that buildings, 'except in the possible case of three … would be unsuitable for a modern medical service'. The throughput of patients among the forty-four doctors administering the service averaged out at less than one minute's consultation each – just enough time to sign a certificate! In the country, in contrast, Deeny maintained that the dispensary service 'has a long record of useful work and has been regarded in the past as the best rural medical service in Europe'.[11] By the 1950s, that record appeared to be well in the past. During the Emergency, no formal inspection of dispensaries was undertaken and premises consequently fell into varying states of disrepair. The situation in Mayo in 1950, as reflected in the summary document then written up at the Customs House, illustrates clearly the difficulties facing this sector:

> County Manager states that he finds that remedying the defects will cost a considerable amount. All dispensaries where residences are not attached are merely rented at somewhat low rents from private individuals and these people are not prepared to undertake the repair work at their own expense. If the Council undertake the work, the possibility arises that the landlords may in a short time determine the tenancies, and the Council will have been put to considerable expense in respect of property over which they have no control. County Manager states that he is rather at a loss to know how to deal with the problem [19 September 1950].[12]

> Department says that in regard to difficulties met in rented dispensary premises this is common throughout the country and frankly speaking no ideal solution can be seen. The minister has very strong views on the question of improving dispensary accommodation and it is a sphere where improvement is urgently needed. In the first place, would it be possible to draw up a written agreement with the landlords concerned that would enable you to proceed with the repairs and yet protect the Council's tenancy? If this is not feasible, I would suggest that you examine the question of securing alternative rented premises which would be suitable for dispensary purposes, or better still, proceed with the erection of your own dispensary premises [30 October 1950].[13]

> County Manager states that in regard to rented premises, he has considered the possibility of leasing the dispensary premises from the landlords for a period of years so as to safeguard the council in respect of any expenditure they might incur, but the problem which existed in certain cases was that even after repair a number of them would not be considered entirely suitable, and alternative premises might have to be obtained, which I may say is a remote possibility or that new premises would have to be built. The Council have committed themselves rather heavily in regard to certain capital works in respect of which assistance from Central Funds will not be forthcoming (such as the extension to the Nurses' Home at the County Hospital, estimated to cost £21,000) and you can realise there is

a natural reluctance on the Council's part to embark on any further extensive schemes requiring capital expenditure. The County Manager will have the matter further investigated on the lines suggested by the Department and ascertain what can be done [31 October 1950].[14]

While the administrators appeared baffled as to what could be done, Michael Daly, who conducted the 1949 inspections in Mayo, on which the above reports were based, was clear on what needed to be done. Overall, he deemed five dispensaries unsuitable. The range of faults found with an additional twenty-four premises was wide: lack of water, sanitary facilities, light, heat, consulting couches (and rooms large enough to accommodate the couches), waiting-rooms and basic equipment, while several required remedial work on plaster and leaks. All of this prompted Daly's general observation that buildings were 'on the whole poor enough and in some cases very bad'.[15] Despite abysmal conditions endured by those already humiliated through the issuing of 'tickets' to use this service, Daly noted some vestiges of dignity. The small number of cases attended to by dispensary midwives arose from the fact that 'most people prefer to pay the midwife something, however small, and hence the number of tickets is small'.[16]

The position in Leitrim was that following the 1949 inspection, seven out of twelve dispensaries required remedial work, of which four were regarded as unsuitable. These views were conveyed to Leitrim County Council on 21 July 1949, and by 1 May 1950 repairs had been carried out at two dispensaries while two were rented and it was not possible to effect repairs or find alternative accommodation. Leitrim, then, appeared likely to benefit from the department's grant-aided programme of dispensary reconstruction. However, a note in departmental files dated 12 February 1960 almost casually observed:

> A query was received from the Minister's Office on 12/2/1960 regarding the condition of dispensaries in County Leitrim. It was ascertained that the last inspection of dispensaries by a Medical Inspector had been on 17/11/1954. In 1953/54 there were 9 dispensaries and 2 dispensary depots in the County, which required replacement. Included in the 9 unsatisfactory dispensaries were those at Ballinamore and Mohill, where new dispensaries were being built. These two new dispensaries were completed in 1956.
>
> The local authority wrote to the Department on 16/8/1956 in connection with the provision of grants for dispensaries, referring to Circular 52/56. Since grants were not forthcoming for dispensaries, the dispensary replacement programme in County Leitrim did not proceed.[17]

The Leitrim situation was not typical of general conditions. In fact in the period 1952–6 progress was made. In 1952, after the survey of dispensary districts was completed, a general plan was drawn up to improve buildings, whereby the department would contribute £600 towards each building. At that time, there were 621 dispensaries and 392 depots. Local authorities proposed replacing 400 of them; of these, 33 had already been completed, progress was reported on 120 and an additional 96 sites had been acquired.[18] Approximately 219 dispensaries were constructed before reductions in the state capital programme curtailed this initiative.[19] However, a review of progress in Mayo at the end of the 1950s suggests much work still remained to be done. At this stage there is quite a contrast in the local and central health approaches. Mayo County Council had requested sanction for a loan of £28,000 'to defray the cost of a programme for the erection or reconstruction of dispensaries and dispensary residences'. But Malachy Powell had conducted his inspection in June 1958 and reported 'in the light of the present need for stringent economy'. Translated into prioritisation, it meant that three dispensaries and three dispensary residences would proceed while seven projects were turned down and a further four deferred.[20] At this stage, it should be noted that the department's guidelines – albeit 1947 guidelines – for residences recommended they consist of four bedrooms (plus a maid's bedroom), with ample living space – sufficient for use as a private practice.[21]

The Galway CMO, C. F. McCon, presents a good example in his 1954 report of the type of criticism Darby found objectionable. In reviewing the schools in the county, he generally classed the convent schools in the main towns as exemplary, but he continued:

> There are also many badly kept schools, some of them structurally sound and some not. There is a general dreary similarity about most of them, dingy unpainted interiors, rickety desks, damp patches on walls, missing slates or gutters, badly kept out-offices, cloakrooms without hooks and often acting as a turfhouse as well; these bespeak a disinterested attitude on the part of those responsible for their care and maintenance. Such defects are, to say the least of it, a bad object lesson to the pupils and in time they will contribute to the general deterioration of the whole school building.[22]

Not surprisingly such comment raised eyebrows in central health where, despite some deliberation, no attempt was made to censor it. Undoubtedly, it was not the language the department's own annual report would use to describe any deficiencies in services. In contrast, for example, the 1959 drafting of the department's commentary on the child welfare clinics employed highly refined generalisations:

> In most areas these clinics are conducted by whole-time medical officers on the staff ... Due to other demands on the services of those officers, particularly for immunisation and school health work, child welfare clinics have not been provided, so far, on a wide scale. The services made avail-

able at the clinics are mainly diagnostic and advisory. Treatment is not provided.[23]

Many of the CMOs in the west of Ireland had already outlined deficiencies in much stronger language. The two clinics in Donegal were deemed unsatisfactory since inception, with attendance 'pathetic' and decreasing. Dr MacParland summed it up thus: 'It is patently impossible, within the framework of the present arrangement, to provide sufficient preventative advisory or health educational facilities. Lack of services makes clinics "farcical"'. Co. Sligo's solitary clinic was located in the county hospital, making it difficult to maintain a good attendance. Distance was also a problem for the county's sole clinic in Roscommon town, which was a 'complete failure'. The three Mayo clinics were attended only when treatment was needed, with the conclusion that domiciliary visiting was the best way to boost attendance. A similar conclusion arose from the operation of Galway's two clinics, where 'parents regard all clinics as a centre for diagnosis and treatment of the sick'. In Kerry, it was suggested that services at the three clinics be expanded to improve attendance. In Clare, it was deemed worthwhile persisting with the scheme despite the very poor attendance.[24] This picture of the service is quite different from that etched in the department's draft report which suggested that medical officers were distracted from clinic work 'due to other demands on the services'. This was not the case and was far from it. The reality was that child welfare clinics were an addendum to existing services – services already stretched to the point where targets for school medical inspections and immunisation drives could not be met. Grafting on new functions without additional staff allocations simply diluted resources further, thereby reducing prospects for success in any sphere.

Measuring success in public preventive health is, of course, fraught with difficulty. Quantitative statistics are useful indicators of achievements and work-in-progress, but if there is an underlying shortage of resources then the key question is how intelligently those resources are applied. The responses to a Department of Health circular on the prevention and control of tuberculosis of 9 December 1953 are instructive. The Clare CMO, G. P. McCarthy, later promoted to Cork City, welcomed the circular as 'opportune' and 'progressive'. He felt the 'prevention of the spread of Tuberculosis from active cases to their contacts is the kernel of the whole problem, and to achieve this desirable result there is but one remedy, viz. rigid segregation'. However, certain preconditions were not yet realisable: institution beds for every case, annual universal adult mass-radiography, public awareness that TB was an infectious disease contracted from 'open' cases, prompt notification of all proven and suspected cases of TB, and an enlightened outlook from the general public. This was crucial, he felt, because although 'all the services essential to the stamping out of tuberculosis are in existence here', without the cooperation of the public 'we cannot hope for any appreciable reduction ... for some time to come'. McCarthy's area had completed a two-year intensive scheme of tuberculin testing, visiting all 'schools, factories, institutions and communities' and vaccinating selected cases with BCG. There was 'in general a big response to this scheme', and he looked forward to the appointment of an assistant CMO so that this aspect of preventive medicine would become a permanent routine feature of public health. Well might McCarthy welcome it as a preventive feature, given the difficulties encountered in the curative aspects of TB:

> As soon as possible after the detection of a proved case of pulmonary tuberculosis the public health nurse visits the patient's house and records all relevant particulars – the number of contacts, the age, sex, and present occupation of each, number of rooms in house, economic circumstances etc. This visit takes place within a month – sometimes within a week – of the date of the notification of the case. All advice and information concerning the facilities available under the County Tuberculosis Scheme are then given to the relatives of the case; they are encouraged to attend for clinical examination, and chest x-ray tickets are issued to all contacts. But despite this exhaustive investigation and painstaking exhortation it is disconcerting to find how very few of the contacts act on this medical advice. Time after time we encounter the same pathetic attitude on the part of the public – an unwillingness to face facts or to discharge their obligations towards themselves or the general community. They will not admit even that the stricken person has tuberculosis and is, while at home, a menace to all contacts. They will, in fact, go so far as to forbid the public health medical and nursing staff from coming near the house.[25]

The Mayo CMO, P. B. O'Meara, summarised the factors influencing morbidity rates under a number of categories, some deductive, others speculative. He felt over-crowding and poor housing conditions were a primary cause, with many Mayo people existing on a low economic standard. Difficulties were encountered persuading sputum-positive patients to avail of sanatorium treatment 'even though plenty of beds' were available, as the 'Celtic temperament is responsible for a certain amount of concealment and disregard of disease, with the result that there is a greater chance of dissemination'. Migratory workers were sent back from England to '"Recuperate". This really means that the English authorities get rid of their Irish workers as soon as possible when they contract disease'. And finally, facilities for diagnosis were not sufficiently available – an instance of an individual having to travel eighty miles from Blacksod to Castlebar illustrating the point. O'Meara's action plan for Mayo County included an assistant CMO (to be trained in BCG) and nurse stationed in Belmullet hospital, which also required in-house and mobile x-ray facilities, and National Mass Radiography would be invited to tour again in the current year.[26] Both CMOs faced a formidable battle both in fighting for resources and in fighting public perceptions of TB, conditions no doubt replicated across the other counties and city boroughs. It is virtually impossible, then, to measure progress and prospects on the basis of statistics alone. Also, in referring to the return of migratory workers, O'Meara had in fact touched on aspects of a highly contentious issue that had controversial local, national and Anglo-Irish dimensions. This issue therefore merits some attention.

Systemic repatriation from Britain of Irish workers suffering from TB began towards the end of the Second World War. In August 1944, the Department of External Affairs alerted the Department of Health to inquiries the British were making as to procedures for tuberculosis sufferers returning to Ireland. Then, in December 1944, a British Ministry of Health circular proposed reimbursement of tuberculosis authorities in England and Wales of the cost of treatment of workers from Ireland brought into Britain under government auspices since 1 January 1942. But, it continued, 'In certain cases, particularly in those arising in the future, the most suitable course will be that the worker will return to Ireland if he is fit to undertake the journey'.[27] In January 1945 the newly appointed chief medical adviser at the Department of Health, James Deeny, raised a 'larger issue':

> What responsibility will the British accept for persons who leave this country in good health to work in England and as a result of war conditions, of food, employment in hardship, fall victim to tuberculosis? These are returning to Ireland in fairly large numbers and we are forced to maintain, accommodate and treat them. I think the responsibility of the British should be pointed out to them.[28]

In response, Dr Con Ward, the parliamentary secretary with responsibility for public health, authorised External Affairs to request similar status in reimbursement for Irish authorities. Despite representations to London, the British did not accept financial responsibilities other than those relating to ex-servicemen who contracted TB while serving in British forces. Irish negotiations then centred on whether an adequate notification system could be established which, despite initial confusion, was in place by the end of 1945 when the British liaison officer for labour in Dublin was authorised to inform Irish officials of case details.[29]

The implications for the Irish were not immediately obvious but repatriation subsequently became a significant feature of Ireland's TB problem, as indicated in Table 1. Despite Deeny's assertion that 'fairly large numbers' were involved, it was not until 1952 that central health began analysing the problem.[30] The reason presumably arose from the fact that until 1952 repatriated tuberculosis cases were not perceived as a major problem in relation to the total number of TB cases. However, as Ireland moved comparatively slowly but systemically to address TB in the 1940s – initially in the curative sense through provision of institutional treatment and then on the preventive front – this problem was acknowledged, though its solution was by no means certain. The impetus for BCG immunisation appears to have arisen from the dilemma posed by repatriated tuberculosis. On 19 August 1946, Deeny advanced the case for BCG vaccination, not as a panacea for all ills but one that 'offered greater possibilities in relation to our tuberculosis problem than practically any other approach'. This was quickly followed by a balanced critique from Tom Brady outlining the risks and limitations of a vaccination programme but nevertheless supporting Deeny's proposal. Arising from this, on 31 August the Minister for Health, Seán Mac-Entee, requested that the Medical Research Council investigate the issue.[31] The council's findings led to the establishment of the National BCG Committee under Dr Cowell and employing the expertise of Dr Dorothy Price, who had been engaged since 1937 in pioneering work at St Ultan's Hospital.

Table 1: Irish TB Cases Repatriated from Britain, 1950–7

| Year | British Services/Ex-services | | Other TB Patients | | Total |
	Accepted Liability	Not Accepted Liability	By Arrangement	Not by Arrangement	
1950	38	13	127	118	296
1951	28	11	174	117	330
1952	14	9	60	172	255
1953	14	6	57	165	242
1954	11	7	73	106	197
1955	6	3	48	114	171
1956	9	1	65	147	222
1957	n/a	n/a	n/a	n/a	208

Sources: Memoranda and Tabulated Statements in Department of Health Files D119/19 and D119/21, NAI

The early findings of the National BCG Committee suggested a clear focus for their work:

... almost fifty per cent of young rural dwelling adults, people of likely emigrant age, are, in fact, tuberculin-negative, proving that, far from suffering from tuberculosis disease, they have never even met with tubercle bacillus. The older they grow, and thus the more their sphere of contact widens, the greater are the risks of such people meeting with an infection which may take hold and later develop into a progressive form of phthisis. These are the people who must be given the protection against tuberculosis which, at the present time, only BCG can provide.[32]

In their 1953 report, the National BCG Committee acknowledged the limitations of its programme, arguing that 'the public should realise that one vaccination with BCG cannot be taken as a guarantee of absolute freedom from the threat of contracting tuberculosis at any time afterwards'. But they were also clear where the focus should be. Pointing out that about 20,000 young people, coming mainly from 'the more impoverished districts on the western seaboard', migrated to work in England each year, they argued that people from these areas were less resistant to TB than people from elsewhere in the country.

The potential for conflict was of course enormous. In March 1953, the British health minister, Iain MacLeod, faced a parliamentary question on whether the British Standing Tuberculosis Advisory Committee had been considering the issue of tuberculosis among persons immigrating to Britain. However, he had at that stage no information to offer. Then, on 7 May, the Conservative MP, Sam Storey, stated in the House of Commons that Irish people entering Britain should have a certificate of medical fitness. In response, MacLeod finessed and denied that medical officers had information as to the nationality of tuberculosis sufferers. However, when Storey pointed out the higher rate of notifications in Ireland, and linked the areas with high emigration, MacLeod then conceded that 'A certain amount of difficulty has been caused by people coming here from Ireland'. Without accepting Storey's request for radiological screening, he felt it would merit further investigation.[33] The Irish health authorities, responding to *Irish Press* queries on the Commons allegations, maintained that it was unlikely that many tuberculosis sufferers left Ireland to work in Britain, and stated that most of the 300 cases returning annually originally left Ireland completely free from the disease. However, due to living in over-crowded conditions in Britain without prior primary infection, they were highly exposed. The Department of Health maintained that these cases required institutional treatment and were a drain on Irish sanatoria resources. In addition, the department reinforced the advice of precautionary immunisation for all intending emigrants, as advocated by the National BCG Committee.[34] This drew a response from James McPolin: 'Such statements will convince these emigrants that vaccination by BCG will guarantee them protection against tuberculosis. This is not true, and leading world experts on this question are sharply divided'.[35] In this, he was essentially correct and, it might be added, medical opinion is still divided on the subject some 50 years later.

On the British end, MacLeod received sufficiently conflicting advice to take no action. While the Central Health Services Council (CHSC) advised appropriate action to ensure immigrants were tuberculosis-free, his Standing Tuberculosis Advisory Committee (a subcommittee of the CHSC) held that the situation did not indicate a serious menace to the health of Britain. Special inquiries in May 1954 suggested that the numbers entering with active tuberculosis were very small.[36] It appeared in fact from a *Lancet* article two months later that British medical opinion was coming round to the view of the Irish Department of Health: that the vaccination of all tuberculin-negative Irish immigrants before they leave home receive serious consideration. A study, conducted by Evelyn Hess and Norman MacDonald, found that such tuberculin-negative immigrants were more susceptible to tuberculosis not due to any racial weakness, but because Ireland was at a stage of resistance to tuberculosis which England passed a long time before. In the course of their inquiry, Hess and MacDonald found serious misunderstanding of the problem amongst medical personnel in Britain. Doctors who were interviewed had said of Irish immigrants: 'They bring it over with them; you will find whole families over in Ireland who are rotten with it'. Indeed, one tuberculosis officer remarked: 'It's the Irish who are our biggest problem; if it weren't for them things would be much easier'. At the same time, many of the Irish sufferers, often with no family history of TB, wondered how they contracted it. Commenting on the study, Noël Browne felt that universal BCG vaccination on leaving Ireland would be impossible to execute. The real solution would lie in the British ceasing to employ open infectious cases in their factories as the Irish 'virgin soil' were exposed to a 'massive dose' and fell immediate victims.[37]

The following year, MacLeod was under pressure again, this time to take action to protect the Irish. On 25 July 1955, a Labour MP, Dr Barnett Stross, raised the high incidence of pleural effusion and progressive primary tuberculosis lesions in young Irish immigrant girls in Britain, and the high incidence of pulmonary TB amongst Irish-born people in British cities who mainly became infected in Britain. MacLeod indicated an awareness of certain studies, but nothing sufficient to warrant action.[38] At the same time, the Irish health authorities, obviously aware of the pending parliamentary question for MacLeod, took the opportunity to issue a press release coinciding with coverage of the issue. It stated:

> Certain reports of meetings, discussions, etc., which have appeared in the public press in recent months may have conveyed the impression that racially the Irish people are more susceptible to tuberculosis than other races, that the emigration of Irish people to Great Britain since the war has aggravated seriously the tuberculosis problem in that country, and the

Irish health authorities are doing nothing to protect the health of Irish emigrants.[39]

The statement denied this was the case, and indeed any racial slur. It explained that TB was 'primarily a disease of urban communities' and maintained that Irish emigrants were largely tuberculosis-free when departing. The problem, then, seemed to centre on preparation in Ireland for emigration and remedial action in Britain. These were the precise issues addressed by two Irish CMOs in a paper entitled 'Migration and Tuberculosis – the Irish Aspect' and delivered at Cambridge in the summer of 1955. The authors were Dr Michael P. Flynn, Westmeath CMO and future president of the Medical Association, and Dr Joyce, assistant CMO in Roscommon. They focused on addressing the problem in the uncontrolled emigration to the UK, such as tuberculin tests as part of the pre-employment medical, and vaccination of tuberculin-negative school-leavers in emigration areas.[40]

Consultations duly took place between the Irish health authorities and their British colleagues who visited Dublin to discuss the incidence of TB amongst Irish emigrants.[41] In November 1957, however, the British chief medical officer, J. A. Charles, advised his opposite number in Dublin, James Deeny, that 'In recent months there has been renewed concern in this country as to the occurrence of tuberculosis amongst immigrants, particularly Indians, Pakistanis and West Indians. As a result ... a census [was] carried out of the number of immigrants ... who were in hospital suffering from pulmonary tuberculosis or who were attending chest clinics'.[42] Although Irish cases figured prominently in the findings, Charles was not sufficiently worried to recommend any action, as his conclusion noted: 'Apparently, some 40,000 to 50,000 people come from Éire to work in this country each year and so the pulmonary tuberculosis problem revealed is a relatively small one. Also, it is appreciated that your department is well aware of the matter and is making all efforts to deal with it'.

Some progress was made in efforts to deal with the problem on the Irish side. In 1959, a health analysis of the trends noted:

> ... the general tendency is towards a slight decrease in the total. The size of the total is, of course, affected not alone by the extent of the prevalence of TB in Great Britain and in this country, but also by the extent of the annual emigration from this country. This last mentioned factor is illustrated by the relatively high numbers for 1957 relating to such counties as Clare (9), Donegal (17), Galway (13), Mayo (31), and Roscommon (12), which, relative to populations, have high rates of emigration.
>
> A special study made in respect of the 1955 figures for the counties Donegal, Clare, Cork, Mayo, Kerry and Galway showed that of a total of 84 persons who returned in that year to these counties, 12 were people

who had suffered from tuberculosis before they emigrated and 14 had contact with tuberculosis before leaving this country. This would appear to indicate that about one-third of those who return in any year for treatment did not necessarily contract the disease abroad.

Further analysis of the 1955 study found that twenty-four had been diagnosed within twelve months, five in their second year, and thirty-four after two years or more, while no information was available on twenty-one of these eighty-four cases. While the department intended examining the 1958 figures with a view to following up on aspects, it ended on an abysmal note: 'we are continuing our efforts, relatively ineffective up to the present, to protect with BCG vaccination those going abroad, particularly young adults'.[43] This approach made sense. In 1958, 107 men and 59 women returned from Britain; 76% were aged under 35 years. Based on the small numbers involved, conclusions are necessarily tentative, but the departmental analysis suggested about 20% of these people 'did not necessarily contract the disease abroad'. The implications were clear:

> Whilst there is, therefore, in a relatively small number of cases a connection between the shortness of period in Britain and a previous history of TB or contact with TB before leaving this country, there is in the majority of cases of early return to this country no close link with a previous history of TB or contact with TB. The majority of those who became victims of TB within three years of leaving this country might have escaped the disease if they had the protection of BCG vaccination.

The key, then, was vaccination before emigration. Policy in this respect was not successful, partly because the 'vaccination process, including the tuberculin test, is tedious and time consuming, necessitating four visits to the vaccinating doctor to complete the process'.[44] Deeny had already surmised that something needed to be done to improve the effectiveness of the vaccination programme. In 1958, he advocated reducing the number of pre-tests from two to one, and the inclusion in the vaccination programme, on a sessional or capitation basis, of general practitioners throughout the country. The CMOs and their assistants should be directing the work, he insisted, not doing it.[45]

At this stage it is instructive to return to Mayo and Clare to review progress since the 1953 departmental circular on TB. In January 1959, as the department queried all CMOs on progress, it was pointed out that in Mayo only 8% of new TB cases were found by mass radiography, and 1% through examination of contacts, compared to national averages of 14% and 5% respectively. Further, since the inception of the programme, only 33% in Mayo had availed of mass x-ray, while in 1957 only 7% had, against a national average of 11% for that year. The department questioned the sufficiency of effort in following up contacts and general use of mass radiography. Dr Joyce took exception to some of the criticism, questioning the overall county returns and suggesting there was 'no uniformity in the registration of cases'. In the west of Ireland, he continued, returning immigrants were added to the register, increasing it by 15–20% and thus reducing the average. 'Every effort is made to keep attendance as high as possible', including advertising, announcements, local publicity and other measures. While he argued that 'There is little more that can be done', he did suggest that the temporary assistant CMO be re-appointed for BCG work, that an x-ray unit be sited in Ballina and that those in Castlerea and Galway be deployed to a limited extent. The department also criticised the sufficiency of effort in Clare when pointing out that its returns were below the national averages. The new CMO there, Dr Hanrahan, pleaded that rural areas involved special difficulties and argued that if the Dublin figures were excluded from the returns, Clare would be nearer the average. In conclusion he raised the spectre of the 1945 Health Bill, arguing:

> For some years this department has worked very hard in the prevention and treatment of tuberculosis. The conservatism of the Irish people is one of our major difficulties. I feel that in this County as much is being achieved as is possible unless compulsory measures are introduced. The advisability of introducing compulsory measures would be very questionable.[46]

Any conclusions arising from this article are necessarily tentative. Until a clearer picture emerges of how the health services actually operated at local level, our scope for interpretation of this period remains limited. Nevertheless, the contours of the emerging picture indicate one constant theme: a chronic lack of resources to execute policy. While a gradual improvement is discernible, there is little evidence that as the 1950s progressed, social needs in the health sphere were virtually satisfied. Much remained to be done in transforming a dilapidated dispensary model into a modern community health apparatus, as originally envisaged under the mother and child proposals. Yet, tempting though it may be to assume that even if a fraction of the capital resources pumped into the hospitals programme had been channelled into local infrastructure, a difference might have been made, this is by no means certain. For in the aftermath of the mother and child debacle, the county medical officer model appeared to lack central direction, as evidenced by the failure to co-ordinate the annual reports. It seems almost as if there was an expectation of change, but the changes did not materialise until successor structures were put in place in the 1970s. This raises questions as to whether the county structures failed or were allowed to fail. Further research may address these issues. Even a cursory examination of BCG vaccination raises further questions, apart from the controversial issue of whether BCG functioned as a prophylactic. Given the slow rate of progress in rolling out BCG nationally in the 1950s, there was, apparently, major scope for recrudescence of TB. Why did it not materialise? Another intriguing question concerns the rationale behind the creation of the National BCG Committee. Since prophylactic immunisation emerged as a permanent feature of preventive public health, it might have made more sense to concentrate on building up the local capacity to conduct campaigns. The expertise of the National BCG Committee might have been deployed at higher level research, aimed at streamlining the inoculation process. Further research will doubtless shed light on these and other issues as the lost years continue to be rediscovered.

'Too Fond of Going': Female Emigration and Change for Women in Ireland, 1946–1961

CAITRÍONA CLEAR

Each morning, before I went to school, I had two chores: I would go down to the
train to collect the Dublin papers for Henry's and the container of ice cream for
Delia Sweeney. This was the up train to Dublin, the emigrant train. Morning after
morning in the 1940s ... [t]he train would pull into Charlestown to a crowded
platform. It had travelled about thirty miles from Sligo through Collooney,
Coolaney, Tubbercurry and Curry, and the young girls who had left these towns
and villages were still crying as the train came to a stop. The mothers who had come
down to see a son and daughter off or two sons and one daughter off, bit their lips
when they saw the still-crying strangers from down the line. Eyes, red from having
wept at leaving the home, tried to look away so that there would not be a scene ...
The Guard's door slamming shut was the breaking point: like the first clatter of
stones and sand on a coffin, it signalled the finality of the old life ...

John Healy[1]

Last Sunday at church, just as the priest was about to come to the altar, a young
girl, faultlessly dressed, minced up the passageway seeking a place, her young, well-
dressed husband close behind her. With a start I recognised her. She was a maid who
had left our town for England some years before, then being gawkish and shy. To all
intents she was now a lady! As she passed the pews the young girls of our town
became brilliantly alert. The incident was a sermon without words.

Bryan MacMahon[2]

The 1940s and 1950s saw what was almost an epidemic of emigration
among Irish girls and women, as they fled to the plentiful work and
training available in Britain. Historians, sociologists and others agree
that they went because they could not find a satisfactory way of life in
Ireland. Many also speculate that low marriage rates in Ireland made
women socially as well as economically redundant. Some commentators go farther and theorise that not only economics but ideology drove
women out – the combined effects of the 1937 Constitution, marriage
bars in teaching and the public service, the exclusion of women from
some kinds of industrial work, the unavailability of divorce and contraception, the lack of a universal health-care system and a vaguely defined 'ideology of domesticity' upheld by the state and the church of
the majority. The emigrants, it is implied, were the lucky ones; emigration was a happy ending, a blessed release from dependence and spinster-
hood. (Even in feminist accounts, marriage is seen as part of the release.)
The Ireland left behind is depicted as a virtual prison for women whose
lives continued unchanged and sunk in darkness, until they emerged,
blinking, into the light of the 1970s.[3] This essay argues that the mass emi-

gration of girls and women was one of a number of social changes in Ireland in this decade and a half, and that the decision to emigrate can only be understood in the context of the coming of age of a generation of women who wanted to change their lives whether they emigrated or not.

First of all, though, it should be pointed out that female emigration from Ireland was not new. In the years after the Famine, more single girls and women emigrated from Ireland to North America and Australia than from any other European country. The females from other European nations usually travelled in family groups, or under the 'protection' of older relatives. Because of the peculiar nature of Irish emigration – where it was the surplus offspring from farms rather than entire families who left – girls and women travelled with their peer groups: sometimes siblings, sometimes cousins and friends.[4] Once in the New World, they tended (with some important exceptions) to work away from their family, in domestic service where they lived in, in contrast to, say, Italian female emigrants who worked in factories and sweatshops and returned to their family each evening.[5] This does not mean that Irish female emigrants lived lives of blissful independence – far from it. The disadvantages of domestic service as a way of life are well-known, and very often money was being sent home regularly to bring out another family member, or simply to support the old people and the heir and his family on the holding. The Irish domestic servant in America or Australia could have been more tied to the home place than ever, under these circumstances. What this does mean, however, is that the idea of a teenaged girl or young woman emigrating on her own and making a life for herself in a foreign land was acceptable and familiar to Irish people.

What gives the emigration of the 1940s its peculiar character is the fact that it was part of a wider economic change in Irish women's lives, one which was happening from the 1920s. Drawn from the census occupational tables of the years 1926, 1936, 1946 and 1961, Table 1 presents a wealth of data on female employment patterns during this period.

This table shows that women had begun to leave agriculture in large numbers from 1926 onwards, and that they began to leave domestic service after 1936.[6]

The censuses also show a rise in the numbers of women working in secretarial, white-collar work and professional work despite marriage bars, in industry and to a lesser extent, in shop service. The newspapers in the 1920s and 1930s were full of advice to the 'business girl' about how to dress, furnish her bedsitting-room and even eat. To a certain extent, this was a 'media trend' which, like most media trends then and now, reflected an urban, even a metropolitan reality, and amplified it out of all proportion.[7]

*Table 1: The main female occupations and areas of work,
according to the censuses of 1926, 1936, 1946 and 1961*

	1926	1936	1946	1961
Total no. of adult women	1,127,077	1,072,204	1,081,362	1,001,095
Total no. of women in gainful employment	343,894	351,367	334,862	286,579
Women in gainful employment as % of total no. of adult women	30.5	32.7	30.9	28.6
Agriculture				
Total no. of women employed in agriculture	121,957	106,723	81,526	42,111
Women employed in agriculture as % of women gainfully employed	35.0	30.0	24.3	14.6
Women employed in agriculture as % of total no. of adult women	10.8	9.9	7.5	4.2
Domestic Service				
Total no. of women employed in domestic service	87,553	86,102	78,522	39,971
Women employed in domestic service as % of women gainfully employed	25.4	24.4	23.4	13.9
Women employed in domestic service as % of total no. of adult women	7.7	7.6	7.2	1.3
Shop Service				
Total no. of women employed in shop service	17,382	19,879	21,450	24,670
Women employed in shop service as % of women gainfully employed	5.0	5.6	6.4	8.6
Women employed in shop service as % of total no. of adult women	1.5	1.8	1.9	2.4
Industry				
Total no. of women employed in industry	32,601	36, 532	35,252	43,496
Women employed in industry as % of women gainfully employed	9.4	10.3	10.2	15.1
Women employed in industry as % of total no. of adult women	2.8	3.4	3.2	4.3

	1926	1936	1946	1961
White-collar/ Secretarial Work *(including post office and telephonists)*				
Total no. of women employed in white-collar/secretarial work	17,679	25,425	32,602	48,442
Women employed in white-collar/secretarial work as % of women gainfully employed	5.1	7.2	9.7	16.9
Women employed in white-collar/ secretarial work as % of total no. of adult women	1.5	2.3	3.0	4.8
Professions				
Total no. of women employed in the professions	29,505	32,937	36,806	41,176
Women employed in the professions as % of women gainfully employed	8.5	9.2	10.9	14.3
Women employed in the professions as % of total no. of adult women	2.6	3.0	3.4	4.1
Home Duties				
Total no. of women engaged in home duties	550,147	552,176	589,461	601,392
Women engaged in home duties as % of total no. of adult women	48.8	51.4	54.5	60.0

Still, there was a rise between 1926 and 1936 of 7,473 women in gainful occupations. This does not look very dramatic, but when we see that there was also a substantial decline of 15,234 women in the occupational category of agriculture between these two dates, this leads us to count up the areas of work which saw an increase of women; the result is that overall there were 17,596 more women in paid work in 1936 than there had been 10 years earlier. A fairly negligible rise of 2,029 women 'engaged in home duties' in the same decade completes the picture of a rising visibility of women in the paid workforce. The biggest increase (proportionately) happened in the white-collar/secretarial/clerical area, but industry was also significant.

Feminists were immensely cheered by the census figures of 1936; Dorothy Macardle referred to the female occupational tables she acquired in 1931 as 'a story of infinite romance and adventure'.[8] One reason why the Conditions of Employment Act of 1936 – which barred women (regardless of marital status) from certain kinds of industrial work and night work – aroused such angry opposition from women's trade unions and women's organisations was because at this stage they expected better.[9]

Girls and women on the land also expected better, which is why they were leaving it. Only a small and fairly stable percentage of women in agriculture were farmers in their own right. Most of these were widows, as might be expected, but there were also single women who inherited farms, and married women who had inherited from their parents and whose husbands worked at other jobs locally or abroad. The latter category was large in Mayo and Roscommon compared to other parts of the country, though even here it was in the minority of women working in agriculture.[10] The vast majority of women 'gainfully occupied' in agriculture were 'assisting relatives', sisters, daughters or daughters-in-law of farmers. Farmers' wives were never counted as assisting relatives, and were included under the non-gainfully occupied category of 'engaged in home duties'. Except in rare cases, the assisting relative (male or female) got his or her keep, pocket money and, if lucky, the promise of either the farm or a dowry. Many were dissatisfied with this; Bryan MacMahon told of how two young men from his native north Kerry in the 1940s gave up working for their fathers for pocket money to work on the bogs in the midlands. Later, they emigrated.[11] Oral and other evidence suggests that women who were working as assisting relatives up to the 1950s felt themselves to be unusually disadvantaged, especially if the dowry they received was not big enough by their standards.[12]

Where the assisting relatives led, the domestic servants followed. The decline in the number of domestic servants between 1926 and 1936 was negligible, but a sign of things to come. By 1946, although they still represented 23.4% of the female workforce, the numbers of domestic servants had declined significantly, and the big change came between 1946 and 1961. At the latter date there were 49% fewer women working as servants than there had been in 1946. Domestic service in Ireland seems to have been a particularly hard job. John D. Sheridan, writing in 1958, placed the 'general' maid firmly in the past, or 'the day before yesterday', as he called it. He wondered how they had ever worked for such low wages and under such conditions: 'any undue pampering of the domestic was looked upon as treason to one's own class', and remarked that 'discussing the general servant position with our neighbours … was a popular pastime in the suburbs in the grim days before television'.[13] There is no retrospective irony in Pauline Bracken's memoir; she tells comical stories about the maids her family and other neighbouring families employed, confessing unabashedly that when they read the maid the letter from home, '(w)e would omit the summons home if there was one, for the mothers of these girls often called them back once they had received a good training in someone else's house'. Bracken's father was Charles E. Kelly, editor of the *Dublin Opinion*, which carried many comic reflections on the servant shortage from the early 1940s.[14] The big houses, where the servant could hope to train and to better herself and where conditions were often quite good, were comparatively few, but even here there were aspects of domestic service which were unattractive.[15] Although she had few complaints about her time in service in a number of 'big houses' in Co. Tipperary in the 1930s, Mary Healy so fiercely resented the able-bodied men of the house summoning her from her well-earned rest in the kitchen after a long day, to close the curtains in the room they were sitting in, that she handed in her notice. (They subsequently agreed to close the curtains themselves.)[16] The warning notes about the difficulty in getting 'girls' for domestic service were sounded as early as 1936 in some quarters, and once opportunities for work opened up in Britain when the war began, more and more of them began to go. In vain might middle-class women's organisations like the Irish Housewives Association, in 1946, recommend that the servant be given a uniform and strictly adhered-to time off – though at least their publication insisted upon the responsibility of the mistress for the maid, unlike some others. In vain would veteran feminist Louie Bennett urge that domestic service and home-making be seen as 'a vocation and a social service', and argue for the more regulated training and working conditions of the servant. Girls and women in the west, Peter Moser tells us, were leaving even 'good places' where they were well-treated, to attain a higher standard of living.[17]

Far from being, as some commentators have suggested,[18] a period when Irish women were ushered back into the home, the first four decades of independence show that the most depleted workplaces were those associated with the home – one's family's farm or somebody else's house. Being 'engaged in home duties', moreover, could often represent a considerable improvement in one's authority and standing, if one's previous work had been in either of these areas.[19] As mentioned before, the census recorded a farmer's wife as 'engaged in home duties'. A designation which was sometimes interpreted by women in the late twentieth century as representing economic powerlessness and social surbordination[20] – as it undoubtedly sometimes did and does – in the case of farmers' wives, it obscured a reality which was much more authoritative and less confining than the 'gainfully occupied' status of assisting relative. Nor did the farmer's wife from the mid-1940s want other assisting relatives, particularly female ones, to be on the farm with her, and she tended to object far more strongly to someone of her own generation than to a mother-in-law or aunt-in-law.[21] If some of the female emigration of the late 1940s and the 1950s was 'push' emigration, it was non-emigrating women in Ireland who were doing the pushing. The same cannot be said for domestic service, because in this sector demand remained high, and none of the laments or promises of higher wages, better training, higher status or any other blandishments could lure women back into this hated occupation. Domestic servants were not being pushed out by women, but they fiercely resisted being pulled back by them.

The women who emigrated left in the face of stern disapproval from some authorities and deep regret from others. There were even suggestions from some quarters in the 1940s that women be prevented from emigrating, suggestions which Eamon de Valera rejected.[22] Religious publications, articles in journals and women's organisations all deplored emigration, not necessarily because of the hardships imposed upon the women who went, but because of the bachelors left behind, the faith in danger, the home life destroyed and the potential domestic servants beyond reach. Life was changing beyond recognition for women in Ireland, however. The impulse to emigrate was part of a bigger change and a broadening of female expectations after the 1920s, and one which also expressed itself in the rising numbers of women in non-service, white-collar and industrial occupations in the same period, in the rising numbers of girls staying on at secondary school, in the falling number of single women 'engaged in home duties' and in the rising number of women delaying or refusing marriage altogether.[23]

Late marriage and permanent celibacy had been features of Irish life since the nineteenth century. Several reasons have been advanced by historians for Irish people's failure to marry, and many conclusions about gender and power have been offered.[24] It has been assumed by some historians and others that women were victims rather than perpetrators of this late marrying/non-marrying system, which made them socially as well as economically redundant.[25] Looking at the 1940s and 1950s, however, it seems that the low marriage rates and high rates of permanent celibacy were almost entirely because of women's choices. Women were rejecting men – not the other way around. Some contemporaries did not see it that way:

> Ninety-five per cent of Ireland's eligible women would marry tomorrow were the eligible men of the nation to transfer their affections from horses and dogs and football matches and 'pubs' to the nobler activities of courtship and marriage.[26]

This was the opinion of Irish-American theologian Edmund Murray, and some of his co-contributors to John A. O'Brien's *The Vanishing Irish* agreed. Some saw the villains of the piece as being the parents of potential husbands – Irish priest Patrick Noonan, for example:

> Hence it often happens that a happy union is prevented or postponed, simply because an excellent young girl cannot satisfy all the exaggerated

demands of two old grave-dodgers whose days would be better spent at prayer than at domestic administration.[27]

John D. Sheridan placed the blame on the girls' parents rather than the boys':

> This habit of tying a girl to the house is far too common in Ireland, and it has the sad effect of crossing one girl in every three or four from our list of potential wives and mothers. The country is full of spinsters who are little better than drudges ...[28]

According to Irish writer Mary Frances Keating, however, mothers were discouraging their daughters from marriage because it was a life of drudgery and hardship. She quoted a mother of her acquaintance:

> Oh, don't sigh, Mary ... Is it like your sister above in the village you'd be, with your small children driving you crazy wailing and crying, and your husband always at the dogs or horses and you scarcely knowing where the next meal is to come from? Aren't you the foolish girl, Mary, scorning your good home and your ease and plenty and the knowledge that you'll have a tidy bit to come when your father and myself are laid to rest?[29]

Keating deplored this attitude, which she saw as life-denying and dreary, yet in reproducing the mother's warnings she gives us very real reasons why women might have chosen not to marry – inability to control the behaviour of a spouse, and the prospect of money and independence when her parents die. One wonders where Edmund Murray got his figure of 95% of women who would marry if they could. An Irish nun working in America, Sister Una, tells Irish-American psychologist and mother of five Miriam Rooney what marriage means in Ireland, by way of explaining why her sister, at home, never married:

> I'll tell you why not. Marriage means a lot of children, and a lot of hunger, and a lot of work. There's no food to feed them. There's no vacuum cleaners and washing machines. There's not even any water except what we went down to the well to get and carried home in a bucket. Sure when they're young and in love marriage looks all right, but when they get older they count the cost.[30]

A young woman who spoke to Seán Ó Faoláin put it more succinctly: 'I saw what my mother went through. Not for me, thank you'.[31] He, along with Fr John Hayes, suggested that economic considerations were the primary factor in discouraging men and women from marriage.[32] Arnold Marsh and Robert Collis' addendum to the Report of the Commission on Emigration and Other Population Problems suggested quite starkly that the inevitability of a large family was putting women off marriage: 'The women themselves have made their views plain by their actions', they commented, the actions, of course, being avoidance of marriage.

Nearly 20 years earlier, Dr Michael Browne, Bishop of Galway, had noted women's reluctance to marry, as Peter Moser tells us: 'if they [the women of Ireland] will not bear the duties of marriage and motherhood and strive to give to God and to Ireland good sons and daughters, then no legislation or constitution can save us'.[33] In oral testimony for my own research, one woman from Mayo explained why a good friend of hers had never married, in the 1950s:

> She was in the Civil Service in Dublin, now she was getting on, about thirty-five or thirty-six and she wasn't married, and her parents ... would have liked if she was married. And she said, she'd go to a girl who had worked with her, going back five or six years, of an evening, and this girl would be maybe living in a flat, two or three children with her, and maybe waiting for her husband to come in with two or three pounds [in] wages to get something to eat. She said, I couldn't do that. She said, if I don't get married to somebody that [...] we'd have a better life, she couldn't do it ... And she'd rather stay the way she was.[34]

Were mothers discouraging daughters from marriage, not necessarily out of selfishness, but out of a desire that the daughters would have a 'better life', and were the women who came of age from the second half of the 1940s particularly receptive to such suggestions? If the single 'girl', keeping house for her parents, was a drudge, was not the mother of a growing family also a drudge, particularly in a house without water or electricity, and in a social environment where she had very little control over the number of children she would have? The single 'girl', 'kept at home', was in any case a fading phenomenon; in 1926, 24% of women described by the census as 'engaged in home duties' (i.e. whose sole occupation was care and maintenance of their own homes) were single; in 1946, it was down to 21.2%, but the major decline happened in the crucial 15-year period under scrutiny. By 1961, only 13.5% of women engaged in home duties were single. It is, of course, quite likely that single women in the paid workforce were living with their parents, but the very fact of earning gave them an independence they might not have otherwise had and, arguably, more independence than the married woman who did not work for wages. Besides, many of these single women engaged in home duties, at the earlier as at the later date, were living with unmarried brothers or sisters in the sibling households which were such a feature of Irish rural life – and indeed urban life – at this time. If we believe that an unmarried woman keeping house for a parent, sister or brother was at more of a disadvantage than a married mother of a family, we are acquiescing without question in the view of late-nineteenth-century sexologists and mid-twentieth-century psychologists, that women find personal fulfilment only through marriage and motherhood.

The low marriage rate of women in Ireland, when taken alongside the high emigration of women, has been taken by many to indicate that women were emigrating 'to get married'. There are also indications, however, that the women who stayed and married in Ireland were starting to insist on whatever changes they could, admittedly within a very limited field. Several observers noted women's reluctance to marry into unserviced farms; their distaste for sharing living space with in-laws of their own age, and older, has already been noted. Others noticed a rise in the ideal (at least) of companionship, and a certain equality in the sharing of the burdens. Several contributors to *The Vanishing Irish* referred to Eamon de Valera's proposal (in 1943) to erect dower houses on farms for the older couple, so as to give the younger couple some privacy.[35] The proposal was not realised in the way that de Valera had hoped it would be, but the fact that it was raised in the first place and referred to some years later shows that the modern Irish ideal of marriage saw an extended family as an obstacle or, at the very least, a burden to be borne. There is also evidence that women were making more demands of men, or that men were prepared to invest more time and work in the house. My own research showed that in settings as different from each other as farms, small towns and cities, and in jobs as different as farmer, factory worker, railway worker, bus driver and bank official, some men who married from the late 1940s on saw themselves as partners rather than as patriarchs, comparing themselves with the generation of men who went before them.[36] The man who was deplored, in the 1950s, as 'single and selfish' might have been quite willing to marry, but rejected by some girls and women as too selfish for the kind of marriage they had in mind. Moser makes a very convincing case for the women as the rejecters, in Connacht at least.[37] In 1942, Anna Kelly, writing in the *Irish Press*, had asked 'What's Wrong With Marriage?' She claimed, like Fr Murray 12 years later, that:

> The average woman is a realist who wants a real home. She wants this or that man to go with it. She is prepared to work as unpaid housekeeper, cook, charwoman, laundress …

She went on to say that, having spoken to what she obviously thought of as a representative sample of young women (showing the natural urban bias of national print media) – a shorthand typist, a 'shopgirl' and a 'girl clerk' – she believed that it was men, and not women, who had unrealistically high standards of material comfort, and refused to marry. What is significant about the evidence she presents, however, is that these women, as well as their potential husbands, cannot find a good economic reason to get married – as the author herself points out, four girls earning three pounds a week each, and sharing a flat, can have a better time than each one would have if she gave up her job to marry 'a four-pound-a-week husband'. Besides, the women were quick to point out, men were too dilatory in their courtship, and expected women to do all the running, something also noted by the women who spoke to several of the contributors to *The Vanishing Irish*.[38]

Kelly's mention of a 'better time', however, is telling; many contemporary commentators concurred that all women were interested in was a good time. Eldon O'Brien, for example, in the same year, offered his opinion that Ulster women feared marriage:

> They are afraid that to settle down as a faithful wife means the end of fun and freedom for them … Ulster girls are ready to meet men as often as possible, but only for the purposes of having a good time. When the question of marriage arises, they are afraid to face the prospect, and retire to flirt with somebody else.[39]

The belief that girls and women were only interested in 'a good time' caused many bishops to thunder in the 1930s, prompted John D. Sheridan to remark with mild concern in 1954 that young people of both sexes were too fond of pleasure, and made Bishop Cornelius Lucey comment, in 1956, that family size in the cities and towns was declining because women were availing themselves of the social and other amenities and did not want large families.[40] We are accustomed to treating all such pronouncements as paranoid over-reactions to the spectacle of young women with money in their pockets, in public space – over-reactions which were, to some extent, common all over the western world ever since the rise of the female office and commercial employee in the 1890s.[41] Suppose, however, that they were at least partly true. Is it so unlikely that a woman with a modicum of spare cash but, crucially, independence of movement, would have refused to give up her control over money and her freedom? As one woman, talking about a friend, a teacher born in 1939 who hadn't married, commented:

> … she said, 'I'm too fond of going'. Now she's into the Legion [of Mary] work, and she's into a lot of these things, she smokes and she plays cards, she plays Bingo …

The Legion of Mary, smoking, card-playing and Bingo might not seem like very exciting uses of women's freedom to many modern feminists, but to women of the time, membership of organisations and spending money on themselves – and there were twenty times more hairdressers (as distinct from barbers) in Ireland in 1961 than there had been in 1926 – represented a release from family duty and gave them a sense of self-worth.[42]

It is true that girls and women left Ireland in these years because, as one of Pauric Travers' informants so simply and poignantly put it: 'There was nothing for me there'.[43] Peter Moser, however, suggests that women in Connacht in the 1930s and 1940s 'saw their economic displacement as an opportunity rather than as a loss'.[44] They felt privileged, in other words, to be able to up sticks and go, while their brothers were tied to the land. For the women who stayed in Ireland, however, this was a time of opportunity and change also, and very often it was their changing values and raised expectations – in the case of farming women in particular – which made emigration the only possible choice for other women. John Healy's comparison of shutting the door of the guard's van with sand on a coffin is a powerful one. The old life was dead. But it was dead not only for those who emigrated. Girls might have cried their eyes out on boat trains; they also did so in lonely beds in boarding schools, and maybe sometimes in bedsitters in Irish cities. But the same women were turning their faces away from a lifelong commitment which might have made them cry the more bitter tears of material and emotional privation, while those who got married were starting to insist upon change.

Emigration was one of a number of strategies employed by Irish girls and women to better their lives in Ireland and abroad. Use of the word 'strategies' might imply that women were free agents, calmly and freely selecting the best options for themselves. We know that this is not true, and that whatever way of life they chose – emigration, staying single, marrying a spouse who shared the work and the authority – the costs were heavy. But whether they left or they stayed, from the mid-1940s Irish girls and women were intent upon 'going', one way or another.

Before Cadden: Abortion in Mid-Twentieth-Century Ireland

SANDRA MCAVOY

The Irish ban on the importing and sale of contraceptives, introduced under Section 17 of the 1935 Criminal Law Amendment Act, had been in place for almost 21 years when, in April 1956, the body of five-months-pregnant Helen O'Reilly was found on the footpath in Hume Street, Dublin. She was 33 years old and a mother of six. A post-mortem showed that she had died of an air embolism arising from an abortion attempt which involved pumping a mixture of water and disinfectant into her womb. The subsequent investigation established that her visit to a Dublin abortionist was a last resort. She had already travelled to England in an effort to 'have something done about her condition' and had bought quinine tablets there in the hope that they could be used to induce a miscarriage.[1]

Mary Anne (Mamie) Cadden, a 62-year-old disqualified midwife, who lived in Hume Street, was charged with Helen O'Reilly's murder.[2] 'Nurse' Cadden's reputation, as much as her proximity to the spot where the body was found, made her the chief suspect. She had already served prison sentences for child abandonment and abortion, imposed in 1939 and 1945 respectively. Although the evidence against her was largely circumstantial, she was found guilty and sentenced to death. It was the first time that the death sentence had been imposed in an abortion death case in the history of the Irish state. The death of the client, the sensational nature of the case and, in particular, the murder charge and gravity of the sentence (though it was commuted to one of penal servitude for life) might have played an important part in identifying 'backstreet' abortion with death in the Irish public consciousness in the second half of the twentieth century. It might also have driven home – more forcefully than any previously reported abortion prosecution – that the Irish state regarded abortion, not as a fertility-control option, but as a criminal act. That said, however, it is interesting that former High Court judge Kenneth Deale concluded his account of the trial by questioning whether such a prosecution would have succeeded if Cadden had been a 'respectable midwife of good reputation'.[3]

Many of the elements of the Irish abortion story are contained in the Cadden case: a woman's desperation to control her fertility; her trip to England; her use of abortifacient drugs; her final resort to a backstreet abortionist. This essay uses a number of contemporary sources, including court files and newspaper accounts of trials, to examine some of the reasons why Irish women chose abortion, and the methods they used, in the 25 years before the Cadden case. It begins, however, by examining aspects of the legal, ethical, and political context within which the attitudes of legislators and medical professionals to abortion were shaped in the mid-twentieth century.

Under Section 58 of the 1861 Offences Against the Person Act, all parties to abortion, including the woman seeking the operation, faced penalties up to life imprisonment. There was an ambiguity in the legislation in that it referred to those 'unlawfully' administering drugs or using instruments to procure abortion, implying, perhaps, that there were circumstances in which abortion might be lawful.[4] What was the implication of this legislation for medical professionals? As no charges were brought against doctors or midwives for performing abortions for medical reasons, the application of the 1861 legislation in such cases was never tested in the Irish courts. Their position, even in regard to cases in which the life of a woman might depend on the termination of her pregnancy, was never clarified.

The issue was raised in 1931, however, in a period of crisis in relations between the Irish Catholic hierarchy and the Cumann na nGaedheal government. The context was a controversy regarding local government appointments, during which the Roman Catholic hierarchy seized the opportunity to focus on medical ethics and object to the appointment of Protestant doctors to dispensary posts.[5] One matter of concern to the Catholic bishops was the Anglican church's acceptance, in August 1930, that, in some circumstances, the use of contraception was morally justifiable. (The Protestant Church of Ireland was part of the Anglican community.) This decision broke the previously united front of the main Christian churches on fertility control. In December 1930, Pope Pius XI issued an encyclical letter, *Casti Conubii*, restating Catholic opposition to contraception, abortion and sterilisation. The bishops' focus on Protestant doctors was one aspect of a campaign to ensure that the Irish medical profession adhered to Catholic teaching on fertility control. The primary concern was that they might provide Catholic women with information on contraception. In February 1931, however, when a government minister met Archbishop John Harty of Cashel to discuss where the hierarchy stood on aspects of the appointments controversy, the archbishop raised the abortion issue. He quoted the requirements in the 1927 Maynooth decrees that the clergy should not only 'prevent that impious crime by which, through the aid of surgical instruments or other means, the infant is killed in the womb ...' but also 'use their best efforts' to ensure that only doctors trained in Roman Catholic medical ethics were appointed to 'public positions'.[6] A memorandum for government ministers, prepared at this time, set out the legal position as currently understood. In a crude reference to termination for the purpose of fertility control, it stated that an abortion intended to 'relieve' a woman 'who is not ailing physically ... of an incumbrance' [*sic*] was illegal, but that a 'medical abortion' to save the life of a 'mother' was permissible in Irish law. The memo raised the option of criminalising abortion to save the life of a woman.[7] That such a possibility could even be pencilled in may reflect the low status accorded to women in Irish society – despite the 1922 constitution's guarantee of equal citizenship.

What was the Roman Catholic church's teaching on abortion? A 1922 article on medical ethics by Rev. David Barry set it out in stark terms. He dismissed abortion to save a woman's life as 'an excuse in law'. He did admit that, in cases in which, without medical intervention, there was a likelihood that both the woman and the foetus would die, Irish women and their doctors might not have fully understood or taken account of Catholic medical ethics:

> … Mothers and their medical advisers may easily be in good faith, and may not regard embryotomy or abortion as murder, when it offers the only avenue of escape from certain death. So, if there is little likelihood that he will be obeyed, a priest should not attempt to disturb their conviction.[8]

The Barry article set out the distinction between 'direct' and 'indirect' abortion, important concepts in Roman Catholic medical ethics. Direct abortion – the deliberate termination of a pregnancy – was considered illicit even if the aim was to save the life of a woman. The church did, however, permit procedures in which medical treatments intended to save her life also had the effect of terminating her pregnancy – that is, caused abortion indirectly. For example, if she was suffering from uterine cancer, the cancer treatment might involve the removal of her womb. If it contained a pregnancy, the result would be an abortion; however, as this was not the primary intention of the treatment, it could be considered an indirect abortion. Barry, however, argued that the church condemned even indirect abortion in cases in which it would not be possible to baptise the foetus.[9]

A question may arise about the extent to which this teaching was understood by the Catholic laity. In 1929, for example, a year of growing concern about infanticide rates, the Catholic Bishop of Ossory referred to both infanticide and abortion in his Lenten pastoral. First asserting the 'inalienable right' to life of the newly born infant, he then stated his church's position on abortion and added: 'These principles should be made known to our people and our legislators'.[10] The bishops might have seized the opportunity offered by the 1931 controversy to ensure that Catholic teaching on abortion was better understood, at least by the legislators and medical profession.

Were there grounds for the Catholic bishops' concern that non-Catholic doctors might perform abortions? The Church of Ireland's position, for example, was clear. The Anglican church's 1930 Lambeth

Conference report, though accepting the use of contraception in some circumstances, condemned abortion as 'the destruction of life which has already come into being'. The fact that the words appeared in the section on birth control, and were followed by a reference to the widespread 'sale of drugs designed to procure abortion', placed the condemnation in the context of abortion for the purpose of fertility control.[11] It is possible that the Catholic bishops were alarmed by a further statement in the same section of the report which set out the moral circumstances in which a woman might not be expected to undertake parenthood – though they referred to conditions in which conception should be avoided, not grounds for abortion:

> ... where a birth would involve grave danger to the health, even to the life, of the mother, or would inflict upon the child to be born a life of suffering; or where the mother would be prematurely exhausted, and additional children would render her incapable of carrying out her duties to the existing family.[12]

While recommending abstinence from intercourse in such cases, the report also accepted the use of contraception: 'scientific methods which are thoughtfully and conscientiously adopted'. It is possible that the Roman Catholic bishops, who viewed contraception and abortion in the same light, as infanticide, were alarmed at the prospect that Protestant doctors, using similar, woman-focused criteria in making decisions on when abortion was morally justifiable, might terminate pregnancies in circumstances unacceptable in Catholic teaching.

A further concern of the Catholic hierarchy was craniotomy. An obstetrical practice, used in cases of foetal death (it involved perforating and breaking up the skull in order to extract the remains from the womb), this was also used as a method of emergency abortion to save the life of a woman when a crisis arose during childbirth. In sterile hospital conditions some childbirth emergencies might be dealt with by a caesarean section, or by symphysectomy (also referred to as symphyseotomy) – the breaking of the mother's pelvis to extract the infant.[13] During a home-birth emergency attended by a general practitioner with limited obstetrical training, perhaps called in by the midwife at a late stage – the circumstances a dispensary doctor might find himself facing – a botched caesarean could result in the death of the woman without saving the child. In such a tragic case, craniotomy was an alternative which might ensure her survival and physical recovery.

During the 1931 local-government appointments crisis the Roman Catholic Archbishop of Tuam, Thomas Gilmartin, made clear his objections to the practice. He suggested that candidates for dispensary posts should be required either to take a course in Roman Catholic medical ethics or to give an undertaking that they would comply with that church's teaching on contraception and craniotomy.[14] Clearly the anxiety was that, in cases in which the life of a woman was threatened during child-birth, non-Catholic doctors might intervene at an earlier stage than was permissible in Roman Catholic teaching – that is, before the foetal heartbeat ceased. The memorandum for the government written by Gilmartin suggested making craniotomy a criminal offence, but admitted that it was not easy to prove whether a foetus was alive before an operation was performed.

In the event W. T. Cosgrave's government negotiated a settlement of other aspects of the 1931 crisis without being forced to take legislative action on the abortion issue – though it did reassure the bishops that it would examine the possibility of banning contraceptives.[15] It received legal advice that the employment position of non-Catholic doctors was constitutionally protected, and that there was little possibility of excluding them from dispensary posts. During 1931, however, the essentials of Catholic medical ethics on reproduction were spelled out in pastorals, sermons, and articles in religious journals, some of which attacked the professional standards of the (Protestant) Trinity College medical school. The message that career prospects might be damaged by failure to comply with Catholic ethical standards was further driven home in August of that year when the Catholic Archbishop of Dublin, Dr Edward Byrne, rejected the candidacy of Andrew Horne for the mastership of the Holles Street maternity hospital. A former assistant master of the hospital and the son of a past master, Horne was a Roman Catholic Trinity College medical graduate. In a letter to the hospital board, the archbishop declared that to accept a candidate trained at Trinity would 'nullify my own Episcopal monition'.[16]

What was the impact of such teaching on women? The making of a distinction between direct and indirect abortion may have allowed Irish medical professionals some room for manoeuvre in dealing with life-threatening pregnancies, though it must have been difficult for a conscientious Catholic doctor to gauge the moment at which a medical condition constituted so immediate a threat to the life of a woman that abortion was permissible. As demonstrated by the experiences of two women who were forced to give evidence in Dublin abortion prosecutions in the mid-1940s, the fact that a pregnancy constituted a potential, rather than an immediate threat to a woman's life was not considered an ethical or legal ground for contraception or abortion. For these women, 'backstreet' abortion was an option.

Both Mrs W. and Mrs A. had histories of haemorrhaging in childbirth. Both chose to have illegal abortions in preference to continuing what they knew from experience might be life- or health-threatening pregnancies. Both were clients of Dublin abortionists Mary Moloney and Christopher Williams. Mrs W. was a mother of four, who stated in evidence that her doctor had advised her to avoid conceiving again. She acted quickly when she found that she was pregnant early in 1942. She twice accompanied her husband on business trips from Limerick to Dublin to search for an abortionist. Her initial attempt was unsuccessful. Although a Fownes Street medical hall proprietor, Charles Brocklebank (who had previously been prosecuted for supplying contraceptives), told her that he could organise an abortion, the fee quoted was fifty pounds; this was more than she could pay. Growing desperate, she returned to the shop a few weeks later and found that Brocklebank's contacts were willing to accept twenty pounds. There were no complications after her abortion, which involved inserting a tent to open her cervix, but the police traced her when they found a letter she subsequently wrote to Mary Moloney, asking if she could forward her some quinine contraceptive pessaries.[17]

The second woman, Mrs A. of Aungier Street, Dublin, was a middle-aged mother of seven children ranging between 8 and 22 years of age. Her doctor, James Ashe, initially suggested that she was not pregnant but menopausal and prescribed a sedative. She was distressed when her pregnancy was confirmed, anxious about her health and afraid for her children because her husband (who died before the case involving his wife came to court) suffered from a serious heart condition. Dr Ashe was a highly respected Protestant physician in his late sixties. Though he initially rejected pleas for assistance in terminating the pregnancy from Mrs A. and her husband, and stated that to do such a thing was 'against his profession', he ultimately referred her to a friend, Cecil Flynn, a businessman whom he knew would put her in touch with Mary Moloney and Christopher Williams.

Mrs A. haemorrhaged during the abortion. James Ashe was called in and succeeded in treating the complication, but he paid a heavy price for his association with Flynn, Moloney and Williams. Police investigating their activities were told that when Flynn took his 'cut' of the money paid to the abortionist, he also took a five-pound referral fee for the doctor. Though he denied such involvement, Dr Ashe was tried for his part in this case. The jury, possibly influenced by the tragic circumstances and the medical nature of Mrs A.'s problem, found him not guilty. He was, however, found guilty in a second case in which he referred a young, unmarried woman from the Italian Legation, based in Luttrelstown Castle, to Flynn. Her period was only a few days overdue and Mary Moloney, suspecting that she was not pregnant, merely gave her laxative chocolate. The Italian woman gave evidence that menstruation recommenced within days. James Ashe was sentenced to eighteen months' imprisonment for his involvement in this case, with a recommendation that, given his age and health, he should be permitted to serve it in the prison hospital.[18] His conviction in such circumstances was a reminder that under Section 58 of the Offences Against the Person Act, whether the woman was actually pregnant when an attempt to procure an abortion was made was immaterial. Those involved could still be prosecuted.

James Ashe denied criminal involvement in the above cases, though in a statement in state files he did admit that 'over the past four years [since the outbreak of the war] at least thirty women, married and single, from all parts of Ireland, have called on me to see if they were pregnant and if anything could be done for them'.[19] Why did these women believe that James Ashe would be sympathetic to their position? As a Protestant and former honorary president of the British Legion in Ireland, he may have been perceived as influenced by a British – rather than an Irish Catholic – medical culture. In Britain during the 1930s and 1940s, it was increasingly accepted that abortion was an ethical procedure in cases in which pregnancy threatened the health of a woman. While abortion for the purpose of fertility control remained illegal there, it was also increasingly argued that it might be an ethical option, particularly when women faced social and economic distress.[20] Dr Ashe's associate, Cecil Flynn, gave evidence about a 1941 conversation with Ashe in which they discussed a patient, married for 17 years and facing a first and unwanted pregnancy. Flynn said that he asked James Ashe whether he had many patients 'who did not want to have children' and that Ashe confided that he had 'several' and that before the outbreak of war it had been possible to refer them to a doctor in London. When Flynn asked him whether an Irish doctor would perform an abortion Dr Ashe allegedly replied that 'it was very difficult as the church was very much against it, and like himself they were not keen on it'.[21]

Was abortion in Britain an option for Irish women? Sociologist R. S. Rose has suggested that the English 1938 Bourne case – which established that abortion to protect the health of a woman was permissible – opened the Irish 'abortion trail to England', but that wartime travel restrictions may have temporarily closed this option.[22] Given the secrecy and anonymity attaching to abortion, it is impossible to do more than speculate on the extent to which Irish women may have used British abortion facilities. It would be wrong to suggest that the Bourne case made it easy to access medical abortion there, although, as Barbara Brookes points out, it did provide some protection for English doctors by putting 'the onus on the Crown to prove that a medical abortion had not been performed in good faith'.[23] The 1939 Birkett committee report on abortion in Britain did, however, suggest that during the late 1930s an average of between 300 and 400 terminations were performed daily in England and Wales and that some 40% of these were criminal abortions.[24] Given the scale of emigration of women from Ireland to Britain and the movement of both males and females between the two

islands in search of work, it is likely that there was a high level of awareness of the possibility of obtaining 'backstreet' abortions in England.
For those with that knowledge and sufficient funds, or contacts they
could visit in Britain, it was an option.

If women were denied safe medical terminations, is there evidence
of attempts at self-abortion or using the services of backstreet abortionists in Ireland? As might be expected, given the intimacy of the
issue, the evidence on self-abortion is fragmented. It does, however, indicate that drugs, alcohol, and 'physical exertions' were used in the hope
of inducing miscarriage. For example, in a 1932 Donegal abortion case,
in which the accused woman received an eighteen-month suspended
sentence, the charge was that she had taken 'six pills the nature of which
is unknown, two Beecham's pills and a bottle of castor oil'. In a 1935
Monaghan case a woman was accused of taking ferrous sulphate, oil of
pennyroyal and aloes.[25]

Statements in state files relating to one 1944 Dublin Circuit Court
case described the failed attempts of a disqualified (because of her previous involvement in an abortion case) maternity nurse to cause the miscarriage of a young girl who was under the age of consent and pregnant
by a relative's husband. Initially advised by a married neighbour, the
young woman had already tried taking gin and doing skipping exercises
before the 'nurse' began a three-week 'treatment' which involved a variety of potions and tablets, including Epsom salts and black draught, castor
oil, and cascara. The deposition of the state pathologist, Dr John Mc-
Grath, explained the purpose of such concoctions:

> Drastic purgatives – including Epsom Salts, Black Draught, Cascara – may
> tend to provoke abortion by causing congestion of the pelvic organs, in-
> cluding the womb. In a pregnant woman, therefore, such doses of purga-
> tives as would produce severe purgings on many occasions over a period of
> about three weeks, would especially be hurtful and injurious to health and
> therefore noxious.[26]

It seems unlikely that these 'purgings' would cause a miscarriage in a
healthy woman, but if she was malnourished or in poor health they may
have been more effective.

The evidence of the use of abortifacient drugs, or drugs which were
advertised as abortifacients, is not only found in court files. The earliest
reference to this practice among state papers may be in the February
1926 submission to the Evil Literature committee from a Clones chemist and druggist, James J. Kerr. He expressed concern about the advertising of 'Female Pills' as 'menstrual regulators' and described them as
'only camouflaged abortifacients'.[27] Copies of an advertisement for 'Dr
Patterson's Famous Pills' among Evil Literature committee papers indicate that the manufacturers promised that the 'pink pills' would remedy

'irregularities of every description', and could be used in cases in which '… Pennyroyal and steel, Pil Cochiac, Bitter Apple …', drugs used as abortifacients, failed.[28]

The Evil Literature committee's 1927 report referred to Kerr's submission and suggested that advertisements relating to 'the prevention or removal of irregularities in menstruation, or to drugs, medicines, appliances, treatment, or methods for procuring abortion or miscarriage or preventing conception' should be defined as 'indecent'.[29] Section 17 of the 1929 Censorship of Publications Act gave effect to this recommendation, while Section 16 banned books and periodicals advocating the procurement of abortion or miscarriage and of appliances used in procuring abortions.

The question of access to abortifacients and contraceptives was raised at Pharmaceutical Society of Ireland meetings during 1931 – the year when the medical ethics issue was raised by the bishops – in a period when a strong Catholic social-movement lobby within the society pressed for the sale of both to be defined as 'unprofessional conduct'.[30] It was pointed out that banning sales of abortifacients might have extreme results: a prohibition on supplying enema syringes, for example, or the striking off of stockists of ergot of rye.[31] Fitted with narrow tubing, enema syringes, like douching cans, could be used to introduce noxious liquids into the uterus. Ergot of rye was legitimately used in childbirth. Taken by mouth or injected in the final stage of labour, it caused powerful uterine contractions, which speeded the delivery of the afterbirth. It also appears to have been the abortionists' drug of first preference because, taken after the fourth month of pregnancy, there was a possibility that it would induce contractions and miscarriage.[32] A number of other commonly used drugs or preparations were also regarded as potential abortifacients. Quinine was used to induce labour, or abortion, and as a spermicide, but was widely used to treat heart disorders, varicose veins, fevers and menstrual problems. Homemade infusions of pennyroyal were used to induce sweating and bring fevers to a head. The drug was also used to increase or restore menstruation and was considered an abortifacient. During a 1948 abortion trial, the state pathologist described its use to make a pregnant woman 'ill so that abortion might ensue', though he added that its efficacy would depend on the strength of the dose and the state of health of the woman.[33] Apiol was sold as a diuretic. Common household cleaners and disinfectants, when injected into the womb, could make effective abortifacients – though, as the Cadden case demonstrated, this method carried particular risks.[34]

The evidence in abortion prosecutions suggests that all of these methods were known in Ireland, though despite the concerns expressed within the pharmaceutical profession in the early 1930s, there is little reliable information on how easily accessible such drugs were to the general public (particularly after 1935, when the enforcement of the Poisons and Pharmacy Acts became a police matter) or the extent to which women knew how to use them as abortifacients. In the post-war period, however, a note in a 1947 edition of the *Irish Ecclesiastical Record* indicated that the question of 'female pills' and other possible methods of self-abortion continued to cause concern. It suggested that some priests might welcome guidance in dealing with women who disclosed in the confessional that they had attempted self-abortion by taking drugs, including menstrual regulators, or a combination of drugs and 'abnormal exertion'. It advised confessors to give the penitent who attempted self-abortion during the first trimester 'the benefit of the doubt' even if she 'insists that menstruation was interrupted and recommenced only after abortifacient medicines had been taken': a view which took account of the difficulty of confirming at this stage that the cessation of menstruation resulted from pregnancy. The item explained that the censure of excommunication for self-abortion could only be incurred if the woman was actually pregnant, not merely because she believed she was pregnant. It also expressed doubt as to whether readily accessible drugs, taken orally, could cause abortion unless consumed in toxic doses and suggested that the 'abortifacient effectiveness' of a combination of drugs and exercise was 'not clearly established'.[35]

That it was considered necessary to address this issue in a journal directed at members of the clergy implied that, regardless of their effectiveness, in the late 1940s 'menstrual regulators' may still have been considered a remedy when unwanted pregnancy was first suspected. It is also possible that some women may have perceived attempts to restore or 'regulate' menstruation in a period before pregnancy was confirmed, or before 'quickening', in a different light from termination at a later stage. In a 1948 statement a client of a Laois abortionist noted:

> She asked me how long I was pregnant and if there was life because if there was life she did not wish to have anything to do with me.[36]

For comparative purposes, it is interesting to note that the 1939 British Birkett committee report found that in England and Wales 'many women take drugs as a precautionary measure whenever menstruation is delayed and pregnancy is feared'.[37]

There are numerous references to the use of ergot of rye and quinine, drugs which were considered the more effective abortifacients, in state files relating to abortion prosecutions. In a Cork case tried in 1940, for example, a maternity nurse, Ellen Anthony, and a local bookmaker, John Daly, a married father of six, were accused of murder following the death of B. K., a 25-year-old woman, allegedly from ergot and quinine poisoning. The case is of particular interest because Nurse Anthony fitted Kenneth Deale's description, quoted above, of a 'midwife of good reputation'. Married with one child, she was described as 'a hardworking, conscientious nurse with a large practice' who, in the view of local doctors, had 'carried on that practice blamelessly for many years'.[38] The two accused were tried separately, something which may have benefited the nurse as it was possible to state during her trial that Daly, who was responsible for the pregnancy, had already been found guilty of manslaughter and sentenced to five years' imprisonment in connection with the case, and that he had a previous conviction for supplying 'poison or other noxious drugs with intent to procure abortion'.

The case highlighted an issue central to Deale's comment on convicting a respectable midwife. If a patient died during an abortion attempt and a nurse swore that she was called in to treat what she believed was either a natural miscarriage or an abortion induced by another party, it was difficult to prove beyond reasonable doubt that she was the abortionist. The case also demonstrated that maternity nurses had ready access to ergot. Nurse Anthony admitted giving B. K. the drug but insisted that this was the routine treatment in a case of miscarriage and that she had given the correct dose.

There were incriminating factors in Nurse Anthony's case. She, and not B. K. or Daly, had booked the boarding-house room in which the abortion took place. At the time of booking she had also insisted on inspecting the bathroom. She had met and dined with the couple on their arrival, after which they spent the night in a local hotel rather than the room the nurse had arranged. B. K. did return to the room the next morning and spent time there alone with the nurse. She appears to have begun miscarrying that night. If the nurse was called in at that stage to treat a natural abortion, she had already spent a surprising amount of time with her patient in the previous twenty-four hours. A further question arose regarding why a nurse of Ellen Anthony's experience failed to call a doctor until her patient was close to death. Was it because she knew that she would be implicated in a criminal abortion?

During her trial Nurse Anthony did admit that, a month before her death, B. K. had confided to her both that she was pregnant and that she was taking pills in an attempt to do something about it, but she insisted that she had advised her to discontinue doing so. (A 30 May 1940 Irish Times report stated that she got the pills from 'a traveller in Midleton', while the same day's Cork Examiner said that she got them from England.) When questioned about her access to quinine, the nurse stated that she always carried it as she took it herself 'on doctor's orders'. With regard to her booking the room in the boarding-house, she claimed that she had done this at Daly's request, and on the understanding that it would be occupied by B. K. and her mother. Was Ellen Anthony guilty only of extraordinary naivety or, in a society in which pregnancy outside marriage was severely punished, did she use her medical knowledge in an attempt to procure an early, safe abortion, perhaps unaware that her patient was also taking quinine? Did she supply B. K. with both quinine and ergot? There were unanswered questions about the nurse's behaviour, but comparing the prosecution's conduct of the Anthony and Daly trials it seems likely that the state prosecutors had little stomach for winning a case in which a maternity nurse might face the death penalty. The case against her was not pursued with the same vigour as the Daly case. The jury returned with a 'not guilty' verdict within forty-five minutes of retiring.[39]

Another case, involving a 30-year-old, three-months-pregnant, un-married Cork woman illustrated a range of methods used by abortion-ists. K. O'C. travelled to Dublin in 1943, confident that she would find an abortionist there. Directed to the chemist's shop run by Mary Moloney and Christopher Williams, she bargained over the fee, agreeing to pay thirty-five pounds. (She was initially asked for eighty pounds. Since in the case of a domestic servant, MD, Moloney and Williams accepted a fee of four pounds, paid in instalments, fees appear to have been fitted to clients' estimated means.) As was the case with most of the Moloney and Williams clients whose evidence is in state files, it took several at-tempts to procure the abortion. The first two attempts involved using a dilator to open K. O'C.'s cervix and a curette to probe and disturb, rather than scrape out, the contents of her womb. No anaesthetic was used and she described the process as having 'hurt terribly'. It was an amateurish method of procuring abortion: less effective than curetting. The latter method required considerable skill, however, given the pos-sibility of puncturing the uterus.

When these attempts failed, the young woman was given an oral dose of ergot and a small plug-like device, a sea-tangle tent, was in-serted in her cervix. This did induce a miscarriage.[40] Giving evidence in this case, the state pathologist, Dr John McGrath, described the legi-timate use of such tents and their likely abortifacient effect:

> These tents are used for insertion into the mouth of the womb. This is normally a tightly closed channel. After insertion the material of the tent slowly swells and this forces open the mouth of the womb. The tent is then pulled out and leaves a space through which instruments can be introduced into the womb. Insertion of the tent and subsequent swelling would alone be likely to cause abortion in a pregnant woman.[41]

A 1948 Co. Laois case provided an example of the use of more pri-mitive methods and an insight into a rarely documented rural, work-ing-class women's culture in which women assisted each other in preg-nancy and childbirth without reference to the medical profession and in which the knowledge that it was possible to terminate pregnancies passed by word of mouth. Kathleen Gilbourne was a 47-year-old mother of four who had some nursing experience. The information in state files indicates that she performed abortions for fees ranging between ten shillings and three pounds, sometimes paid in instalments, and that her abortion methods were crude. She used a teaspoon handle to open the cervix and probe the uterus. She was arrested following the death of a client, Mrs B., a 40-year-old farmer's wife and mother of five children aged between four and eleven years old. Mrs B. had suffered poor health since her last confinement and her doctor admitted in evidence that childbearing had left her 'anaemic and debilitated'. She chose abortion because she understood from experience the likely effect on her health of a further pregnancy, but her case also illustrates the consequences of dependence on an amateur abortionist. Her death, within a week of the operation, resulted from the retention of parts of the afterbirth – a complication which Mrs Gilbourne may not have had sufficient experience to recognise, but which her client had suffered in a previous confinement. Mrs B. developed toxaemia and haemorrhaged. Tragically, medical attention at an early stage could have saved Mrs B.'s life but she and her husband delayed calling in their doctor because she had had an illegal operation.

Kathleen Gilbourne was prosecuted on eight counts of 'using an instrument or other means' to procure the abortions of eight women, four married and four unmarried, one of whom had had two terminations; one count of supplying pennyroyal (obtained from a daughter in England) knowing that it was to be used as an abortifacient; and one count of infanticide.[42] Mrs Gilbourne pleaded guilty to eight abortion charges and received eight concurrent seven-year prison sentences. On the infanticide charge she entered a plea of guilty of manslaughter rather than murder and was sentenced to a further concurrent seven-year term.[43]

Why did women choose abortion in a state in which to do so was a criminal offence punishable with sentences up to life imprisonment? Even in the limited sample of cases examined in this essay it is clear that the reasons were varied. In some of the cases quoted, experience of previous confinements made women aware that they faced life- or health-threatening complications. They considered illegal abortion a safer option than continuing with their pregnancies. These were women who already had a number of children (Mrs W. was a mother of four; Mrs A. of seven; Mrs B. of five) for whose sake they desperately wanted to survive. The material in state files also shows that in each case the woman's choice was supported by her husband. Some women, like Helen O'Reilly or B. K., chose abortion because they lived in a society in which pregnancy outside marriage – or, as in Helen's case, by a man other than her husband – could be punished by loss of employment and 'reputation', ostracism and poverty, or the loss of freedom involved in confinement in a convent. An unmarried woman's fear of the reaction of her own family was a further factor. A doctor who attended B. K. reported that, even when close to death, she kept repeating: 'Don't tell my mother! Don't tell my mother!'[44] Similar concerns presumably motivated the under-age girl, pregnant by a relative's husband, and the women who tried to help her. For the man responsible, organising an abortion in that case was an attempt to hide an alleged crime. Other women, like Dr Ashe's patient, married for 17 years, or Mrs F., one of Kathleen Gilbourne's married clients, did not want children or did not want them at that time. Two of Mary Moloney's clients (whose cases I have not examined here), a married hotel employee and a married traveller for a textile firm – a mother of two young children – were also in this category.[45]

What evidence is there on the incidence of illegal abortion in Ireland? Asked about the 'prevalence' of backstreet abortion, when giving evidence in the 1943 Moloney and Williams trial, a Dublin detective replied, 'We know very little about it but we understand that it is fairly prevalent. It is done in secrecy'.[46] The following year, defence counsel in the trial of three Nigerian final-year medical students on abortion charges, T. C. Kingsmill-Moore, suggested that 'Dublin was always humming and buzzing with stories about abortion ...'[47]

Did abortion rates rise after the introduction of the 1935 ban on contraceptives? An attempt to answer this question would require accurate statistical information on rates before and after 1935, which is not available.[48] As illegal abortions were carried out in secret, successful operations went undetected and left no traces for historians. R. S. Rose speculated that an increase in numbers of crimes known to police in the years 1942 to 1944 – seventeen cases – suggested a rise in the incidence of backstreet abortion in a period when wartime travel restrictions made it difficult to get an abortion in Britain.[49] An examination of information in state files relating to these cases, however, makes it clear that a number of those prosecuted were not abortionists and that the rise in absolute numbers of prosecutions resulted from a number of factors. The first was the strict application of Section 58 of the 1861 Offences Against the Person Act, which resulted in the prosecution not only of abortionists, but of third parties. This meant that a number of individuals who helped women to make contact with abortionists – including, in some cases, the men responsible for the pregnancies – were charged with 'using an instrument' to procure abortion although they did not literally do so. In one 1943 case, for example, a young garda who helped a woman he had made pregnant to contact Mary Moloney and Christopher Williams, and paid one pound towards the cost of her abortion, was charged with both conspiracy and using an instrument.[50]

Another reason for a rise in known cases in that year was that the police managed to trace a number of women who had had abortions. (In some instances, they found their addresses when searching abortionists' property.) These women were persuaded to give evidence, presumably having been advised that by doing so they might avoid prosecution. A further factor was that, following their conviction, Mary Moloney and Christopher Williams gave evidence against their former associates in an attempt to reduce their own sentences of ten years and seven years respectively.

During the 1940s heavy sentences were imposed on others who fitted the professional abortionist stereotype – those who used medical instruments as well as drugs. For example, in 1944 William Coleman, who operated from Merrion Square, Dublin, received a fifteen-year sentence, reduced to seven years on appeal.[51] Mamie Cadden received a five-year sentence in 1945 when a client developed peritonitis following douching and the insertion of a tent.[52] These cases, like the 1940 Daly and Anthony case, received considerable publicity. The severity of the sentences may have inhibited other practitioners and perhaps made Irish women more aware that in a state dominated by the Roman Catholic church, abortion was unacceptable and harshly punished. There were only three abortion prosecutions between the 1948 Gilbourne and 1956 Cadden cases. Two involved procuring abortions in England – one of these also involving the use of drugs – while the third arose from a clumsy attempt to obtain ergot, in order to end a pregnancy resulting from sexual crime.[53] This might imply that there was a decline in the rate of 'backstreet' abortions performed in Ireland in the postwar period, even before the death sentence was imposed in the Cadden case. The medical, social and economic reasons for choosing abortion did not disappear, however, and it is interesting to note that as late as April 1974, in an address to a Catholic Women's Federation conference, obstetrician Professor Alan Browne suggested that some Irish women continued to choose illegal abortion:

> Nobody has died in Dublin in recent years as a result of criminal abortion operations. But patients do arrive in Irish hospitals from time to time with septic abortions, and this is a good pointer that they have been operated on by illegal abortionists.[54]

By then the English 1967 Abortion Act had been in place for half a dozen years, theoretically making it easier for Irish women who could afford to travel – and who had the knowledge and confidence to use the British system – to use safe, legal abortion facilities in England and Wales. The fact that Dublin hospitals still saw evidence of criminal abortions suggests that the British abortion statistics of the period, which provided the first evidence that large numbers of Irish women chose abortion, do not fully represent the numbers of Irish women obtaining abortions. The 1973 figures, announced in June 1974, suggested that, in that year, 1,193 women giving Irish addresses had abortions in Britain under the 1967 Act.[55] We can only guess how many thousands in previous decades had taken the mailboat, used menstrual regulators and abortifacient drugs when they missed periods, tried purgatives and excessive exercise, or sought the assistance of sympathetic maternity nurses, handywomen or backstreet abortionists.

This essay has reviewed some of the material in state files and other sources dealing with abortion in mid-twentieth-century Ireland. The evidence on the Catholic bishops' lobbying on abortion and contraception in the early 1930s brings home the extent to which fertility control was a gendered and sectarian issue in that period. Attitudes adopted then by male hierarchies in the church, the political arena and the medical profession shaped the ethical, legal and professional approaches to women's reproductive health in Ireland for the remainder of the twentieth century. There is little evidence that, in establishing the principles guiding legal or medical practice, consideration was given to either women's health needs or the fact that women were capable of making rational decisions on fertility control. Irish legislators unquestioningly accepted Roman Catholic teaching that abortion was never justifiable. They failed to review or clarify the 1861 legislation – even to the extent of establishing the legality of intervention to save the life of a woman. Within the medical profession, decisions about women's rights to life and health were made in the context of Catholic medical ethics. Caitríona Clear has highlighted a chilling statement in a 1956 Irish medical article on the management of pregnancy in patients suffering heart disease, which perhaps sums up attitudes in the period:

> Advice as to the spacing of pregnancies and the use of the safe period should be tendered if thought necessary, but no matter how severe the lesion or disastrous the pregnancy, no woman should ever be told that if she has another baby it will kill her.[56]

This was an Ireland in which doctors, clergy and politicians controlled information and services and in which women could be denied both effective contraception and knowledge of the possibly damaging effects of pregnancy on their health and lives. Women in what today we recognise as crisis pregnancies were expected to carry the pregnancy to term. Yet the evidence in abortion prosecution files and other sources provides poignant glimpses of women struggling to control their fertility, seeking or providing abortions and supporting others in doing so, despite the hostility of the church and legal authorities. The files record the use of drugs – from menstrual regulators to pennyroyal, aloes, quinine and the more effective ergot of rye – in attempts at self-abortion. They indicate that, for those with the knowledge of how to contact them, backstreet abortionists in Ireland and England were an option. They raise questions about the passing on of knowledge by word of mouth. Was it only Dublin that buzzed with rumours of abortion? They provide an insight into aspects of a mid-twentieth-century women's culture in Ireland which is at variance with the stereotype of prayerful, passive obedience to strict social and religious rules – the image so familiar in traditional representations of the period.

Tourism and the Irish State in the 1950s

IRENE FURLONG

In Ireland there is always time to talk, time to think, time to live. In the last analysis, it is this free-and-easy atmosphere, this joyous equilibrium of the spirit, which constitutes the intangible magic of Ireland. During the past 30 years the country has made rapid strides in the political, economic and social spheres. But in Ireland, as we have already suggested, you can live in two worlds, for progress has not robbed the Irish of their fundamental belief that tomorrow is another day, that time is a bottomless well, that the hustler is always too late (or too early) for the only appointment that matters – the rendezvous with contentment and peace of mind.[1]

Seduced by the rhetoric of tourism advertisements and promotional literature, the English writer of the above paean to the Emerald Isle was living in cloud-cuckoo-land. Ireland in the early 1950s was not a place of magic contentment and peace of mind. Rather, it was a country which offered many of its children nothing but the mailboat and a one-way ticket as their way of becoming people on the move, with emigration levels soaring while the economy staggered along under the weight of stagnant policies and desperate measures. By 1950, a realisation of the importance of the tourism industry was growing in Ireland. It had replaced emigrants' remittances as the country's largest source of dollars, and an increasing number of people were finding employment in the sector. However, there was a serious lack of recognition of this fact by many politicians and by the general public, and a severe shortage of accommodation and other facilities for visitors, due to a lack of investment in the post-war period. An official guide to Ireland published in 1950 conceded this reality: 'Ireland has not great and long traditions of catering for foreign visitors as a highly specialised industry ... she does not boast palatial hotels, fashionable spas and casinos or elaborately-equipped resorts'.[2] Seán Lemass, Minister for Industry and Commerce in the Fianna Fáil government from 1932, had not always been a strong supporter of tourism as an important cog in the state's economic machine. However, the secretary of the Irish Tourist Association, which was established in 1925 as an organisation to promote Ireland as a tourist destination, was John P. O'Brien, a former fellow-traveller from Civil War days who later became honorary treasurer of Fianna Fáil. C. S. (Todd) Andrews, who worked with O'Brien in the Irish Tourist Association in the 1920s, maintained a close relationship with him and wrote in his autobiography that O'Brien's dedication to the cause of tourist development impressed both Lemass and John Leydon, secretary of the Department of Industry and Commerce.[3]

The various administrations in power during the 1950s took a three-pronged approach to the industry: legislation, which mainly sought to improve the provision of accommodation; promotion in the form of a cultural festival; and the development of Irish civil aviation. However, no coherent strategy was applied to the development of the industry, as there were still many within the country who saw tourism only in negative terms, and opposed the provision of central funding on principle. In addition, the lack of an entrepreneur culture in Ireland at this time, when applied to an industry which depended so much on the individual efforts and commitment of accommodation providers, was to prove an obstacle to progress.

LEGISLATION

In July 1939 An Bord Cuartaíochta (the Irish Tourist Board) was established as a statutory body by the Tourist Traffic Act, 1939, with J. P. O'Brien as its chairman, and was given powers to register and grade hotels, guesthouses, hostels and holiday camps. To enable the tourist board to exercise its functions fully, it was also empowered to engage directly in these activities and provide financial assistance to others to do so, and to acquire land compulsorily for these purposes. A non-repayable grant of up to £45,000 per annum was conferred on the tourist board, and it was entitled to provide repayable advances up to an aggregate of £600,000 for works of a profit-earning nature. It can fairly be argued that the bestowing of such wide-ranging powers on the new body was not anticipated by the industry, and the establishment of the Irish Hotels Federation in 1939 was a direct and defensive response. However, the outbreak of the Second World War in September of that year compelled the tourist board to suspend its programme of rapid expansion, and during the conflict tourist accommodation and facilities became run down due to lack of investment. In addition, the development of commercial transatlantic passenger traffic – which began with Pan-American Airlines' Yankee Clipper flight to Foynes in July 1939 – all but ceased. Nevertheless, preliminary plans were made during the early 1940s by the tourist board for the development of existing holiday resorts in the post-war period and they acquired several properties for this purpose. The question of the provision of adequate accommodation and facilities also preoccupied the government and their concern was demonstrated by the 1946 Tourism Development Programme, which amended the 1939 Tourist Traffic Act, increasing the limit on advances for acquiring and refurbishing suitable premises from £600,000 to £1,250,000. Unfortunately, it retained the stipulation that advances would be made only for schemes certified by the tourist board as being of a profit-earning character.

Irish tourism experienced a short-term boom in the immediate post-war period, generated by an influx of British visitors in search of plentiful food and entertainment. International currency restrictions and the poor state of the transport infrastructure discouraged travel to a war-devastated Europe, and Ireland reaped a huge benefit from this situation. As the new decade approached, the invasion of British visitors began to taper off, as currency restrictions were lifted and food rationing was phased out in the United Kingdom. Continental countries ravaged by the Second World War were investing heavily in tourist development, and it was obvious that Ireland would have to keep up with the competition or lose the advantage gained in the late 1940s. Post-war developments in aviation, combined with the desire of Seán Lemass to see the Irish state represented on the transatlantic route, led to the decision to set up an Irish transatlantic airline, Aerlínte Teoranta, and to inaugurate its services on 17 March 1948. It was not to be; the inter-party government, which took power in February of that year under John A. Costello, cancelled the service and sold off the aircraft, much to the chagrin of Lemass. J. P. O'Brien's services as chairman of the tourist board were also dispensed with on the change of government, and he was succeeded by William F. Quinlan, county manager for Kerry.

Having been approved in April 1948 for a loan of ten million dollars for the first three months of the European Recovery Programme under the terms of the Marshall Plan, Ireland, in common with most other European countries, found itself in the position of needing to increase its dollar-earning capacity.[4] The first loan agreement was signed on 28 October 1948, and as tourism seemed set to supersede emigrants' remittances as the primary source of dollar income, it was crucial that the government throw its weight behind efforts to develop the industry to its fullest potential. To this end an inter-departmental working party on dollar earnings was set up by the Minister for Finance in November 1948, with representatives of the Departments of Finance, Agriculture, External Affairs and Industry and Commerce and of the Revenue Commissioners and the Central Statistics Office.[5] Its first Interim Report was devoted to tourism and submitted to the government in November 1949. Tourism was chosen because it was the largest single dollar-earning source, offering the greatest possibilities of rapid expansion, and because 1950, being a Holy Year, presented an opportunity to Ireland of attracting pilgrims who had been visiting Rome.[6] At the same time, John A. Costello, head of the inter-party government, wrote to the minister of each department in June 1948 expressing his disappointment at the level of economies achieved in the public service.[7] The Minister for Finance, Patrick McGilligan, had already announced that the tourist board's allocation was to be reduced in his budget speech, while lamenting the fact that the substantial saving resulting from the abandonment of the transatlantic air service would only meet the losses incurred on services in 1947.[8] Speaking at the annual general meeting of the Irish Tourist Association at the end of October 1948, Daniel Morrissey, Minister for Industry and Commerce, pointed out that in 1947 the nation's total earnings from tourism were estimated at £28 million, at a time when cattle exports were worth just over £15.5 million. Referring to the difficulties inherent in establishing accurate tourism figures, Morrissey promised to examine the question of reorganising the statistical services of the country in order to overcome the dearth of economic information on tourism.[9] On the question of accommodation, the tourist board expressed itself pleased with progress up to March 1949 on structural improvements in hotels and guesthouses, with the installation of running water in bedrooms, an increase in the number of bathrooms available and improved standards of furnishing equipment, but bemoaned the lack of trained personnel, especially in smaller residential and commercial hotels.[10] However, the provisions of the Control of Buildings Order, which required the obtaining of a building licence before work could commence on repair and reconstruction of hotels, were a continuing obstacle to the improvement of the hotel stock in the country for many years after the Second World War, as shortage of materials persisted. The question of adequate tourist accommodation was one which would continue to bedevil the industry throughout the 1950s, despite the various efforts to provide financial aid to the hotel sector.

During the autumn of 1949, the Irish Tourist Board submitted proposals to the Minister for Industry and Commerce, Daniel Morrissey, for the reorganisation of the national tourist service. Morrissey considered the reorganisation proposals, presenting his conclusions on them to the government in February 1950; as a result a committee on tourism was established, consisting of the Taoiseach and the Ministers for External Affairs, Agriculture and Finance, as well as the parliamentary secretary to the Minister for Industry and Commerce. The need for such a committee was doubtless prompted by the reaction of the Minister for Finance, Patrick McGilligan, who opposed Morrissey's plans for development in no uncertain terms: 'The remedying of existing defects is primarily a matter for those engaged in the industry ... they have ample resources to finance improvements which would serve to maintain the greatly increased prosperity they have enjoyed in recent years'.[11] Castigating the board for submitting a reorganisation scheme based on the premise that higher salaries and more staff were a condition of the formulation of general policy, he continued: 'The Board's proposals are not a basis on which the minister would consider it justifiable to agree to place £3 million at its free disposal, as is recommended by the Minister for Industry and Commerce, even if no problem of financing grants of such magnitude existed'.[12] McGilligan also pointed out that although dollar earnings from tourism were important, they constituted only a tenth of total tourism income, and were likely to remain of secondary importance in relation to revenue derived from British visitors. The Tánaiste and the Minister for Defence also took part in the deliberations of the committee on tourism, and its report was presented to the government in June 1950.[13] The committee made thirty-four recommendations ranging over subjects as diverse as the improvement of landing facilities at Cobh and the avoiding of the 'caubeen-and-pipe' type of advertisement, in addition to the usual one of the urgent need for provision of better accommodation for tourists. They also reported on matters pertaining to the membership and staffing of the tourist board, and the desirability of unifying the functions of that body and those of the Irish Tourist Association, but concluded that a merging of the two bodies would not be feasible in the near future. A meeting of the cabinet on 23 June 1950 considered the report and two appendices, one a memorandum entitled 'The Irish Tourist Board and Tourist Publicity' drawn up by M. K. O'Doherty, general manager of the tourist board, and the other a document on 'The Irish Hotelier' by T. J. Sheehy. They approved the immediate putting into effect of recommendations regarding provisions for sale of Irish goods at airports, including a permanent display of Irish-made goods at Shannon; the production of a leaflet explaining customs procedures for visitors, a source of much irritation at the time; and the production of sets of Irish stamps and books on fishing in Ireland. As these were but minor details in the tourism field, it is evident that no serious attempt was being made to address immediately the basic problems besetting the industry.

Theodore J. Pozzy, chief of the Travel Development Section of the Economic Co-operation Administration (ECA) office in Europe, visited Ireland in 1949 and as a result a proposal was made by the ECA that the Hilton International hotel group should set up and operate a hotel in Dublin.[14] Writing to Joseph Carrigan, the head of the ECA Mission to Ireland, in January 1950, Pozzy informed him that he had been advised by Washington that the Hilton people offered two suggestions for such a project, neither of which would involve them in any capital investment and under which they would seek a guaranteed percentage of profits before tax as well as recoupment of all out-of-pocket expenses. However, Pozzy also mentioned the possibility of a technical survey to resolve difficulties facing the Irish government in the matter, and Daniel Morrissey readily availed of this offer, although both he and McGilligan were opposed to the Hilton proposal.[15] Accordingly, under the Technical Assistance Programme in Travel, Hotel and Allied Activities operated by the ECA, various groups involved in Irish tourism participated in a joint tourism mission to the United States sponsored by the Organisation for European Economic Cooperation with four other European nations during the first three months of 1950. They submitted reports with recommendations for improvements in the administration and development of the industry in Ireland. Members of the Irish delegation included M. K. O'Doherty and Kevin Barry from the Irish Tourist Board; Brendan O'Regan, catering comptroller at Shannon Airport; and Patrick F. Dornan, manager of the Great Southern Hotel, Parknasilla, Co. Kerry. However, O'Regan and Dornan did not agree with the group's conclusions and submitted a separate report.[16]

Interestingly, despite the acknowledged shortage of suitable tourist accommodation in the country, representatives of the Irish Hotels Federation and the Hotel and Restaurant Association were not initially supportive of the suggestion that a party of practical hoteliers visit the United States to study American tourist ideas.[17] At a meeting with Industry and Commerce officials in February 1950, hotel representatives agreed that the project was a desirable one, but emphasised that it was required by the national interest rather than the hotel trade, and stated that they were not prepared to contribute to the cost of a three-week visit, which was estimated to be in the region of £5,000.[18] Furthermore, it was stated that hotelkeepers were satisfied with the current state of affairs, were interested only in the profits in the business and were unconcerned whether these profits came from American or British visitors. They expressed a preference for British visitors, with many of whom they had built up connections of long standing, and who were better spenders and less critical than Americans, who would probably never return to Ireland in any case.[19] Nevertheless, an Irish Hotels Federation delegation did visit the United States later in the year and presented its findings to the government, while a Tourism Survey Group from the United States, led by Robert K. Christenberry, visited Ireland in July and August 1950 and did likewise. The collection of six reports, to be known as 'The Christenberry Report' for reasons of convenience of presentation, was published by the government in July 1951 under the title *Synthesis of Reports on Tourism 1950–1951*, and established what were seen as the main areas of concern. These were: 1. official organisation; 2. Ireland's tourist areas; 3. accommodation; 4. hotel operation; 5. publicity and advertising; 6. transport facilities; and 7. miscellaneous.[20]

The reports generally agreed that the existing situation whereby two separate bodies administered the development and promotion of Irish tourism was most unsatisfactory, asserting that they were 'completely inadequate to handle the important mission to which they are assigned, that of actively promoting tourism to Ireland from abroad'.[21] They recommended the integration of the two bodies, with a new board consisting of members with practical experience of the industry, which was not permitted under existing legislation, and they also proposed a name change to improve the image of the organisation in the public mind. The augmentation of the range of activities of the tourist board, with a consequent increase in financial aid from the government, was considered essential if the industry was to realise its full potential. The section dealing with Ireland's tourist areas divided the country into seven regions, with an emphasis on the concentration of promotion on the perimeter – almost the entire midland area, from Cashel to the Northern Ireland border area, was excluded. The report dismissed most of the east coast, except for Dublin, as unattractive, and regarded the southern and western parts of the country as being most suitable for promotion at that time. Although Donegal's rugged and magnificent scenery was commented on, it was not deemed a realistic proposition for development because of the poor provision of basic necessities such as electricity and water. On the question of tourist accommodation, the report cited the figure of 20,000 American visitors to Ireland in 1949, and estimated that this number could be increased to 40,000 in 1951, 55,000 in 1952 and 70,000 by 1953 if definite steps were taken to put a planned publicity and promotion campaign into effect in the United States without further delay. It also referred to the fact that 99,679 North Americans visited Great Britain in 1949, and that efforts should be made to divert such traffic to Ireland. On accommodation, it was pointed out that most of the recommendations were intended to promote tourism generally, not merely from the United States, and Christenberry recommended the expansion of hotel and guesthouse accommodation, with the construction of new hotels and the modernisation and rehabilitation of existing ones in strategically important areas. However, his report also referred to the placing of guesthouses and small hotels, and commented:

> Our survey showed that there are a number of homes which have been converted into guesthouses ... which in our opinion will provide the best answer for tourists with the least amount of expenditure involved ... An American tourist living in the atmosphere of a home would not consider private baths of the utmost importance, providing there prevailed in such homes cleanliness, cheerfulness and decoration and good food ... one of the wonderful things we found in Ireland was the warmth and hospitality of its people and this can best be extended to tourists in the small guesthouse operation where the owner can extend his hand of welcome and personalise the entire visit of his guests ... This is a procedure that is almost impossible in large hotels and in overlooking this great Irish characteristic you would be overlooking one of the finest things you have to offer.[22]

In addition, the report spoke of the need to overhaul the registration and grading systems already operated by the tourist board.

On hotel operation, sanitation and hygiene were singled out as being deficient on a countrywide scale, and staff training schemes for both management and lower grades of workers, in order to improve standards of service in all types of accommodation, were recommended. The need for development of accountancy skills was also highlighted, and this section ended with a summary of suggestions on 'what American travellers want'. Mooting a budget of $200,000 for tourism promotion in the United States alone, the section dealing with publicity and advertising stressed the need for educating the Irish public on the economic value of tourism and suggested that factors of appeal to the Irish-American market should be investigated and that promotion by individual hotels was an option to be considered. The Irish Hotels Commission report pointed out that while £33 million was earned in 1948 from tourism, only £31,761, representing less than one-tenth of 1% of that figure, was spent by the Irish Tourist Association under all headings, while the British Travel Association spent £297,663 in that year on overseas publicity alone. Quoting *The Wimble Report on European Recovery and the Tourist Industry*, they gave a figure of £350,000 as the amount of grant aid received by the British Tourist and Holidays Board from the British government for 1947–48, while Italy made an appropriation of 60 million lira for tourist promotion, Norway expended $27,000 on its New York office alone, and Denmark spent $21,000 in the United States, exclusive of the cost of tourist literature, which was printed in Denmark.[23] The report submitted by O'Regan and Dornan made the point that as 90% of overseas travel by Americans was estimated to be purchased through travel agents, they would need to be constantly briefed and cooperated with fully by Irish promotional agencies.[24] The necessity for expansion in off-season traffic, particularly by Irish-Americans, was also emphasised. The section on transport facilities alluded to the unsatisfactory landing conditions at Cobh and Dun Laoghaire and to the possibility of persuading more of the American tourists passing through Shannon airport to spend some time in Ireland before journeying on. It also suggested a need for car-hiring facilities, deeming Irish roads satisfactory apart from their signposting. The final section consisted of comments on subjects such as places of historic interest; evening entertainment; problems with tipping, water shortages, postal and telephone services; hotel signs and food, all of which were considered to be important in the overall provision of a satisfactory tourist package for the American visitor.

The initial government response to the reports was cautious, with Morrissey recommending that they should not be published, as government policy on the tourism question had not yet been established, and proposing instead that information should be disseminated by way of lectures to meetings of hoteliers and other interested parties: 'Appropriate steps will be taken to ensure that … no matter affecting government policy on tourism is discussed or published'.[25] At the same time, Seán MacBride, who as Minister for External Affairs took an active interest in tourism matters, suggested that interest-free loans for the building of hotels by private individuals and low-rate loans for substantial extensions of existing hotels should be made available. He further proposed the construction of 500 ten-bedroom units of the type utilised at Shannon airport for overnight transit visitors:

> These units, to contain adequate bathrooms, showers and to be fully furnished and decorated … could then be sold, hire purchased or leased to existing hotels as extensions … could also be used for the purpose of enabling country houses to accommodate tourists.[26]

The cabinet kicked this suggestion into touch at a meeting held on 9 May 1950, but decided instead that a committee to be called 'The Dollar Exports Advisory Committee' should be established to advise on the promotion of commodity exports to the dollar area.[27] On a note of comparison, it is interesting to observe that tourist interests in Great Britain, despite the much higher profile of their country and its attractions in the United States, were also bemoaning the lack of adequate and suitable accommodation for American visitors at this time, with Arthur Bottomley, Secretary for Overseas Trade, suggesting to the House of Commons that floating hotels on the Thames might be a solution to the problem![28] Back in Ireland, Dr Paul Miller, chief of the ECA Mission in Dublin, advocated the development of a unified programme by the Irish Tourist Association and the tourist board 'so that they could be mutually helpful to each other' at the Irish Tourist Association's annual general meeting in October, reinforcing the view of the Christenberry Report that having two organisations was a waste of time and effort and led to duplication and overlapping of work.[29] The holding of the Sixteenth General Assembly of the International Union of Official Travel Organisations, representing thirty-eight countries, in Dublin in October 1950 focused public attention on the potential of the industry, and Liam Cosgrave, deputising for Morrissey, made the point that tourism was now the state's biggest dollar-earner.[30] The submission of a detailed memorandum from the tourist board on policy proposals, and a reorganisation scheme, with estimates, on 12 December 1950, spurred Morrissey into action. This took the form of the Tourist Traffic (Amendment) Bill which was introduced in the Dáil on 14 February 1951, but following the return to power of Fianna Fáil in May 1951, this bill was not proceeded with.

In December 1951, Lemass introduced another Tourist Traffic Bill to legislate for changes that he had already made. In October 1951 he had announced the establishment of a new organisation, Fógra Fáilte, to combine the publicity functions of the Irish Tourist Board and the Irish Tourist Association, and in July 1952 An Bord Fáilte came into being as the new statutory body with responsibility for development of accommodation, amenities and facilities for tourists.[31] Speaking on the second stage of the bill, Lemass stressed the importance of the industry to the national economy; overall earnings from tourism were second only to earnings from agricultural exports and represented the largest single item in dollar earnings. During 1950, gross receipts from tourism were estimated at just under £33 million, exceeding by about £3 million the gross receipts from all livestock exports, and falling short of receipts from all agricultural exports by only £12 million: 'It would be no exaggeration to describe it as a cornerstone of the national economy ... Certainly on the success or failure of our efforts to expand tourist revenue will depend whether we can maintain, much less improve, the present standard of living of our people'.[32] With a balance of payments deficit of £66 million in 1951, Lemass saw the only solution to the nation's economic problems as being an increase in both production and exports and believed that tourism 'offers an opportunity of expansion and the prospect of a quicker return than any other trade'.[33] Referring to the fact that only 260 copies of the Christenberry Report had been sold out of a total print run of 2,500, Lemass expressed his disappointment at the failure of the accommodation sector of the industry to take advantage of the expert opinions contained therein, seeing this as a sign that the government had not yet succeeded in arousing sufficient interest in the potential of the tourist trade.[34] In fact, the number of hotels registered in the country had decreased from 875 in 1950 to 872 in 1952,[35] and the grading of hotels and guesthouses had been suspended for 1952, pending preparation of a revised registration and grading scheme,[36] a lapse which can only have led to a deterioration in the quality of accommodation during that time. While broadly maintaining the functions given to it in the 1939 Act, the new tourist board was given two more – the power to protect and maintain historic buildings, and responsibility for the provision of signposting. As Fógra Fáilte was to have responsibility for publicity, An Bord Fáilte would relinquish its power in that regard, and also that of building and operating hotels.[37]

Many deputies agreed that radical action was needed to galvanise the industry, as the contribution of Dominick Cafferky, Clann na Talmhan deputy for South Mayo, illustrates:

> I would like to welcome this Bill and to say that I remember a time when it was anathema to this House to recommend the development of tourism and the invitation of tourists to this country. A big change in outlook has taken place during the past five or six years. When I was a member of this House during 1945, 1946 and 1947, quite a number of Deputies who have contributed to the debate and who have welcomed this Bill were very much opposed to the number of tourists coming to this country.[38]

Nevertheless, concerns were expressed about some aspects of the proposed legislation, such as the future of the Irish Tourist Association, which henceforth would be reduced to being an agent of Fógra Fáilte, providing tourist bureaux in Ireland. As the proposals ran contrary to the recommendations of the Christenberry Report, in that there would now be three bodies engaged in tourism work instead of a single cohesive unit, some deputies were bold enough to imply that Lemass was engineering a post for his old friend, J. P. O'Brien, with Independent deputy Jack McQuillan accusing him of acting with his heart and not his head.[39] However, the main provisions of the bill allowed for a programme of government-guaranteed loans up to a limit of £3 million for the improvement of hotels and guesthouses, with grants from the tourist board to cover the interest charges for the first three years (later extended to five years), and this move was almost unanimously welcomed.

As expected, J. P. O'Brien became chairman of Fógra Fáilte and a member of the board of An Bord Fáilte, as despite the best efforts of Lemass, it had not been possible to find him a job within that organisation.[40] The inter-party government, which came to power in May 1954, wasted no time in dealing with the administrative inefficiency and conflict that arose from the existence of two tourism bodies. The new Minister for Industry and Commerce, William Norton, reported that the relationship between the two bodies was 'distinctly unsatisfactory, if not openly hostile', and that Fógra Fáilte was failing to consult An Bord Fáilte on policy matters.[41] The 1955 Tourist Traffic Act provided for the dissolution of the former body and the transfer of its functions and funding to the latter. Norton decided on this course of action after consultation with the boards of the two bodies, during the course of which a member of one board informed him that the existing arrangement was wasteful of funds in that there was a duplication of board members, staffs, premises and transport arrangements.[42] At this time, the two boards had seven different premises spread over Dublin. Seán Lemass did not agree that Fógra Fáilte should be dissolved, and he continued to advocate the separation of development and publicity functions, as he felt that the imposition of publicity functions on An Bord Fáilte would dilute the attention that body could devote to its development role. Speaking on the second stage of the bill, Norton answered Lemass' query on the tourism policy of the inter-party administration by declaring:

I hope that whatever differences there may be between one party and another on other issues, there will at least be unanimity among all parties and governments that it is highly desirable, from the national point of view, that we should endeavour to exploit our tourist potential to the fullest. So far as I am concerned, and as long as I am Minister for Industry and Commerce, I will do my best to ensure that the policy of developing the tourist trade will be pushed as far as possible, and that every possible assistance will be given to any organisation or group which is concerned with promoting the immense possibilities which this country has from a tourist point of view.[43]

Lemass and many other deputies disagreed with Norton's intention of adding 'Irish Tourist Board' to the statutory nomenclature of the new body, arguing that giving it an official title in English would spell the death of its Irish one, while Norton contended that this change was to help the organisation in its many dealings with English-speaking people overseas, wherein lay the greatest market for Irish tourism promotion. A compromise was reached by agreement on the title Bord Fáilte Éireann, although it is difficult to see how that would help to identify the organisation any more than its original title did! Some deputies pushed for the bestowing of statutory standing on the Irish Tourist Association, but Lemass and Norton were in agreement on this question, both insisting that it should retain its voluntary and independent status. Henceforth it would have three directors on the board of the new body, although Lemass demurred on this point, asserting that it had always been a body concerned only with tourism promotion, and that dealing with issues of development of facilities and amenities would force those directors into a situation where they might not have had any expertise. The association would continue to operate tourist bureaux inside the country as it had done as an agent of Fógra Fáilte, relying on contributions from the local authorities – which at this stage were running at around £16,000 a year – to finance its activities. The point was made that from 1925 to 1951 the association had carried out all tourism promotion for the country at a cost of just £300,000, while the new state body would now receive £500,000 in one year, with half of that amount earmarked for publicity purposes alone.[44] The act became law on 21 March 1955 and Bord Fáilte Éireann became the sole statutory body dealing with tourism matters in the Republic of Ireland. J. F. Dempsey, director general of Aer Lingus, took over the same function in the new body on a *pro tem* basis; he was succeeded in 1956 by T. J. O'Driscoll, Irish ambassador to the Netherlands and a former civil servant with a long record of service in the Aviation and Marine Division of the Department of Industry and Commerce. However, his close relationship with Dempsey dating from his work in the development of the airline companies appeared to some to mean that the main thrust of tourist development at this time was predicated on the potential of air travel, at a time when the overwhelming majority of tourists to Ireland were still arriving by sea.[45]

The merged tourist bodies were reorganised structurally into three main groups dealing with advertising and publicity activities; promotional and development activities, including accommodation registration and grading, staff training schemes, provision of amenities and facilities at tourist centres and holiday resorts; and general administration departments.[46] Surveys had been undertaken in 1955 to obtain the data crucial to future development of the industry on aspects such as place of origin of visitors, purpose of their visit and what pleased and displeased them during their stay.[47] This information was needed to help redress the decline in tourism receipts which had taken place since the decade began. Garret FitzGerald, in a series of articles on tourism in the *Irish Times* in December 1954, pointed out that gross tourist revenue had decreased from 30% of external revenue in 1948 to 15% in 1953, when total earnings stood at £29.9 million.[48] He put the decrease down to a drop in the rate of visitor spending, which naturally followed the increase of visitors drawn from lower-income groups, but also to a drop in the number of British tourists, as opposed to those travelling to Ireland to visit relatives or do business there. While he hailed the dramatic increase in American traffic due to the extensive Fógra Fáilte campaign there, he voiced the need for a similar campaign in Britain to capitalise on the emigrant population there. On Northern Ireland, he commented: 'One of the most appalling features of partition is the mutual ignorance on both sides of the border – [tourism] could help the development of mutual understanding'.[49]

He went on to state that the Irish tourist industry was facing intense competition from every other west European country, as well as Communist Yugoslavia, and that Ireland was losing the battle as far as the vital British market was concerned. A number of deterrents existed in relation to that market. High on the list were the atrocious travelling conditions between Holyhead and Dun Laoghaire for those who could not afford air travel. Despite repeated requests by the Irish government, very few improvements had been effected by British Rail in facilities at Holyhead and aboard their ships for the comfort of those travelling by sea. William Norton was reduced to threatening to take the matter up with the British Minister of Transport in 1955.[50] Nor was Coras Iompair Éireann (CIÉ) blameless in this respect; the condition of the railway carriages transporting visitors to Dublin from Dun Laoghaire was a matter of concern to succeeding administrations. Another problem was the refusal of the Irish government to allow British coach companies to organise tours in Ireland using their own vehicles, in an effort to safeguard the interests of CIÉ. This regulation was finally rescinded in 1957, and coach tours of Ireland by British companies proved to be one of the biggest planks in the success of the tourist industry in Ireland in the 1960s.

Discussing the adverse trend in tourist travel to Ireland in 1957, Garret FitzGerald alluded to the IRA border raids, which were undoubtedly playing a major role in discouraging visitors, but also blamed a shortage of hotel accommodation and high hotel prices, costly coach tours and a lack of adequate publicity in Britain.[51] It would seem that not much had changed in three years and this certainly applied to the problem of the improvement of facilities and amenities at tourist resorts, which had not materialised, despite the existence of guarantees and grants since 1953. The stipulation that only profit-earning schemes could qualify for these incentives naturally minimised the benefit to be had from them.

In the meantime, efforts to expand the accommodation available in the country were not meeting with much success, with the number of bedrooms in hotels and guesthouses decreasing from just over 17,000 in 1952 to 16,000 in 1957.[52] To halt the decline, Lemass introduced another Tourist Traffic Act in December 1957, which extended for five years the guaranteed loan scheme for hotels and resorts. It also made provision for grants towards the payment of interest on loans other than under the scheme.[53] By the end of March 1958, twenty-nine loans totalling £184,000 had been guaranteed but the Department of Industry and Commerce was not pleased with the lack of take-up on the scheme, and introduced modifications to speed up the loans procedure in an effort to have it more widely used.[54] Fuelled by demands from fishing visitors, a list of private accommodation for anglers was also published, a new development in the range of accommodation available. However, results for the 1957 tourist season were disappointing, and reflected precisely the vicious circle of malaise described in *Economic Development*, a study of national development problems and opportunities published in 1958:

> increasing emigration, resulting in a smaller domestic market depleted of initiative and skill, and a reduced incentive … to undertake and organise the productive enterprises which alone can provide increased employment opportunities and higher living standards.[55]

The 1959 Tourism Traffic Act was an effort to change things for the better by utilising a provision of the First *Programme for Economic Expansion*, based on *Economic Development*, to provide Bord Fáilte with additional grants of £1 million for a 10-year programme of major resort development, and a maximum sum of £500,000 for the development of holiday accommodation. The board would continue to receive its annual grant of £500,000 for general development and publicity for the tourist industry.[56] Presented to the Oireachtas in November 1958, the First Programme was a five-year plan which contemplated capital expenditure of £220.5 million, of which £2.5 million was projected for tourism development. In the event, the actual amount expended on the total programme amounted to £297 million, while the expenditure on tourism at £1.21 million was less than 50% of the target.[57] The failure to expand and improve the accommodation sector adequately during the 1950s was acknowledged by Lemass in 1960 when he addressed the Congress of International Hotel Associations:

> While we are new to, and somewhat inexperienced in, the organised international tourism business, the Irish people have a reputation going back a long way for hospitality, and a flair for hospitality is not a bad foundation on which to build a tourist industry ... We keep reminding ourselves that even the wealthiest tourist may seek other things beside luxury. A few kind words to one far from home may sometimes compensate for a lack of chromium; and a guest who is made to feel that he is a personal friend of the owner may be prepared to overlook the hardship involved in having to walk up a flight of stairs to his bedroom.[58]

AN TÓSTAL

In the area of tourism promotion, one of the primary objectives of Fógra Fáilte was to encourage increased traffic from the dollar area, with a view to easing the burden of dollar repayments under the Marshall Plan. To this end, and to some degree inspired by the Festival of Britain, which took place in 1950, a campaign to extend the tourist season by attracting American tourists to Ireland in the springtime was inaugurated in 1953. In 1951, the president of Pan American Airlines, Juan Trippe, had suggested to Lemass that a 'Come Back to Erin' festival, aimed mainly at Irish-Americans, could prove a solution to the dollar problem and presented him with a lengthy memorandum on the subject.[59] The idea appealed to Lemass and he entered into discussions with the tourist board regarding the possibility. In February 1952, the *Irish Times* reported that a good deal of progress had been made for the preliminary organisation of a civic festival to be held in Dublin in 1953, and that a committee appointed by Dublin City Council had held meetings with people representing cultural, athletic and economic bodies in the city, with a view to considering financial backing.[60] However, Lemass effectively pulled the rug from under the city council's feet by announcing just ten days later that a national festival would be held in 1953, into which the Dublin event would be subsumed.[61] The Irish Tourist Board would sponsor the festival, but no state funds would be forthcoming, and commercial and other interests would be called upon to raise the necessary finance. It was decided that the festival would be called An Tóstal, meaning a pageant, muster or array, but that its English rendering would be 'Ireland at Home'.[62] The tourist board explained that it was meant as an expression of Ireland's national life, presenting an opportunity to project widely 'our spiritual and cultural place in the modern world', and stressed that while it would be mainly based in Dublin, it was hoped that all parts of the country would participate. Despite a recommendation to Eamon de Valera for cautious action from Patrick Little, director of

the Arts Council established the previous year,[63] Lemass planned to inaugurate the festival in 1952, but was stymied by the lack of time. Major
General Hugh MacNeill, a retired army officer who had previously organised a military tattoo, was appointed organiser, and tourist board staff
travelled the country advising local and church authorities as well as
sporting, cultural and social organisations. Outside Dublin, 172 centres
distributed over the thirty-two counties organised programmes designed to attract overseas visitors.[64] An Tóstal was officially launched
by President Seán T. O'Kelly on Easter Sunday, 5 April 1953, outside
the General Post Office in O'Connell Street, Dublin, while simul-
taneous opening ceremonies took place in many other centres around
the country, many of them performed by government ministers, deputies
and senators. Opposition from temperance and church bodies persuaded Gerard Boland, Minister for Justice, that there was no public support for the extension of licensing hours, a suggestion mooted by the
Dublin Tóstal committee.[65]

Despite the enthusiasm of official and voluntary bodies, the event
could not be deemed a success. A rowdy beginning in Dublin and sustained aesthetic criticism of the festival's artistic endeavour, the 'Bowl
of Light', which was labelled 'a tawdry contraption' by the Royal Hibernian Academy,[66] were extensively reported upon by British newspapers.[67]
Bord Fáilte lamented the shortage of events of national and international standard, but stressed that the successful organisation and promotion of the festival was to be regarded as a long-term project, and
saw it as benefiting the Irish people in a non-material manner, in that
it would develop a better sense of civic spirit and would stimulate an
increase in public interest in cultural affairs and Gaelic activities.[68] However, Eamon de Valera, speaking at the concluding ceremonies organised by Ennis Tóstal Council, typically professed himself pleased with
the festival's achievements in the area of cooperation:

> The thing … which pleases me most is not so much the advertising of the
> good things we can offer visitors here, but the effect it has upon ourselves
> … It has thrown us back very largely upon ourselves, making us think of
> the things of the past and realising the treasures we really possess.[69]

These were not words designed to gladden the heart of Lemass, who
was striving to wrench the Irish people out of their obsession with the
past and make them confront the harsh economic realities of the mid-
twentieth century. It was decided to continue with the festival, and that
material assistance by way of grants and guarantees against financial
loss was necessary to encourage the organisation of major events, a process which continued up to 1958, when the faltering festival was more
or less abandoned. In 1957 an international theatre festival was inaugurated in Dublin during An Tóstal, which proved a success with the

public, but ended with the effective suppression of a production of Tennessee Williams' *The Rose Tattoo* by the police. For 1958, the theatre festival director, Brendan Smith, had commissioned Seán O'Casey to write a new play, *The Drums of Father Ned*, to be performed by Dublin's Globe Theatre Company, while the Edwards–Mac Liammóir company would present an adaptation by Alan MacClelland of *Ulysses*, by James Joyce. Controversy arose in January 1958 when it became known that the Archbishop of Dublin, John Charles McQuaid, had refused permission for a mass to be celebrated in the Pro-Cathedral to mark the opening of the festival, as had occurred in previous years, on learning of plans to present these plays. On 12 February, O'Casey withdrew his play from the festival[70] and the Dublin Tóstal Council then announced that the production of *Ulysses* would not proceed, due to the contention it had aroused.[71] Samuel Beckett, a close friend of Joyce, weighed in by withdrawing three new plays of his, which were to be performed, as a mark of protest,[72] and in the end a decision to cancel the 1958 theatre festival was taken at a Bord Fáilte board meeting on 10 April.[73] The *Irish Times*, in a leading article, was scathing in its condemnation of these events:

> No evidence has been adduced that either of these productions contains a hint of obscenity or of blasphemy; yet pressure has been brought to bear against both of them from high places, and the [Tóstal] Council has kissed the rod … The primary function of An Tóstal has been to attract visitors to Ireland. It has not been a conspicuous success in that regard but the introduction of a theatre festival last season commanded international attention … Next year's Tóstal Council will be well advised to submit its programme to the Archbishop of Dublin in advance of publicity if it is to avoid a similar wastage of money and effort. Perhaps, however, the necessity will not arise. It will be hard to find men of sufficiently stern fibre to constitute a Tóstal Council next year after the embarrassments entailed upon their predecessors! Will there, for that matter, be a Tóstal?[74]

The writer was not too far out in his analysis of the situation. Although the 1958 Tóstal did go ahead, a board meeting of Bord Fáilte in May of that year concluded that the level of public support over its six years of existence was not sufficient to justify its continued financial scaffolding of the event.[75] As local contributions declined progressively, the tourist board had spent £305,000 on An Tóstal in that period, and they estimated that a mere five thousand visitors had come to Ireland specifically for the festival in 1957, a year in which they had spent £32,000 and which had seen only thirty-three centres in the country organise events.[76] At a meeting organised by Bord Fáilte in the Mansion House, Dublin, on 24 July 1958 and attended by over a hundred members of Tóstal councils as well as national and cultural organisations, it was overwhelmingly agreed that the timescale of the festival should be extended to cover the entire period from April to September in future.[77]

The tourist board would promote, stimulate and sponsor events, as distinct from organising them, and the main events would take place between June and September, with April and May being devoted to a campaign of spring-cleaning and preparation to improve the appearance of urban centres, the countryside and seaside resorts, and an extension of the Tidy Town, Village and Garden competition. Announcing the changes officially in September 1958, Bord Fáilte chairman Brendan O'Regan listed a Dublin theatre festival among the proposed events for future years. Again, the *Irish Times* had its finger on the pulse:

> Tóstal is dead; long live Tóstal!! Thus oversimply and perhaps unkindly, one might summarise last Saturday's announcement by Bord Fáilte ... The concept of Tóstal was a noble one, but in its translation to reality it fell foul of adverse forces, some of them – such as our inability to fuse private gaiety and public pageant – inherent in the Irish character ... No one can quarrel with Bord Fáilte's desire to clean up our cities, towns and villages ... The danger is that by sticking a Tóstal label on this laudable work – and on any 'major tourist attraction' – the odour of failure may cling.[78]

Although the festival did continue in many centres over the years, it was no longer a coherent national effort enjoying committed government support, and it never achieved its primary aim of attracting hordes of Americans to Ireland in the off-peak season. However, it certainly achieved its secondary aim: the education of Irish people as regards the importance of tourism in the national economy. It stimulated a tradition of community co-operation which bore fruit in the results of the Tidy Towns competition. These in turn transformed the appearance of many drab and depressed Irish towns and villages. In urban centres, the festival brought about some legislative change in the amounts that local authorities were permitted to expend on the decoration of their areas, and encouraged the government in its own willingness to decorate and floodlight public buildings. Angling competitions organised for the festival had the effect of generating a demand for cheap accommodation in private homes, a phenomenon which led to the establishment of the Irish 'bed and breakfast', a reasonably priced, high-quality facility providing a satisfactory alternative to hotel accommodation. These things are taken for granted today, but taken together, constituted a major step forward in the appreciation of tourism in the 1950s. In addition, many of the particular festivals which sprang from An Tóstal have survived for almost 50 years, including the Dublin theatre festival, the Cork film festival, the Waterford light opera festival and the Cork choral festival, and none of these (and the multitude of other festivals which now attract thousands every year to these shores) could exist without the continued support of tourism bodies. There was also an opening up of cultural awareness, such as that which extended from the appreciation of the Gaelic tradition into the commercial success of folk singers in the 1960s, and a realisation that external influences, in the shape of foreign tourists, could assist the Irish people in both enjoying and exploiting the uniqueness of their own culture. For decades, visitors to Ireland, when asked for their favourite constituent of our tourism 'product', have replied simply 'the people', and An Tóstal generated the awareness of the value of that ingredient of the Irish package.

CIVIL AVIATION

In the post-war period, social, cultural and political links with the United States at a time when Irish-Americans were emerging into affluence and influence in that country had convinced J. F. Dempsey, general manager of Aer Lingus, that the time was ripe for an Irish transatlantic service. Lemass concurred, and an order for five Lockheed Constellations was placed in 1946, while a new company, Aerlínte Éireann Teoranta, was formed to operate the service. The inauguration of the service was fixed for St Patrick's Day, 17 March 1948, and the Taoiseach, Eamon de Valera, stated his intention of travelling on the first flight. However, his decision to call a general election in February of that year resulted in the first inter-party government replacing Fianna Fáil in power. To the great dismay of the outgoing administration, the inauguration of the transatlantic service was abandoned, as the new government decided that they were not justified in continuing with it, due to the financial commitments involved.[79] The following year, Transocean Airlines, an American charter company, proposed to Aerlínte that the two companies should jointly operate a transatlantic service to Shannon during the summer of 1950. Industry and Commerce felt that an arrangement might be made which would operate to the financial benefit of Aerlínte, and that it might be possible to conclude a long-term agreement with Transocean which would provide the basis of a regular transatlantic service. At this time they were resisting efforts by the Department of Finance to have Aerlínte wound up in the Air Navigation and Transport Bill, which was being planned at the time. In the end, this project did not get off the ground, but the Department of Finance's efforts to wind up the company were successfully stymied.

Fianna Fáil came back into power in 1951 and Lemass, once again at the helm in Industry and Commerce and eager to recommence activity on the transatlantic scene, entered into negotiations in 1952 with Seaboard and Western, an American freight airline which had been using Shannon Airport since 1947, to lease DC4s to Aerlínte, for the operation of a transatlantic route. Despite the sustained criticism of opposition deputies in the Dáil, he proposed to utilise the proceeds of the sale of Aerlínte assets in 1948 to cover initial costs and possible losses. There were also complaints from the British members of the board of

Aer Lingus, who feared that the proposed service might endanger the British Overseas Airways Corporation service from Shannon to North America. In the end, the new venture did not go ahead. The American Civil Aeronautics Board decided that they would only issue a permit for a two-year leasing period, after which Aerlínte would have to provide its own aircraft. Given the capital expenditure necessary for such an eventuality, there was no point in proceeding with the project. However, it is worth considering that there were ulterior motives for the American decision. Ireland had concluded a bilateral agreement with the United States in 1945, which provided for full commercial rights for American airlines at Shannon airport on routes between the United States, Ireland and countries beyond. In view of the long transoceanic flight and considering the still limited development of aeronautical science, all aircraft on these routes, both eastbound and westbound, were required to stop at Shannon.[80] Irish airlines were accorded full reciprocal rights at US airports to be specified subsequently, but when the Irish government requested that landing rights at New York, Boston and Chicago should be granted to Aerlínte Éireann in October 1946 in connection with the proposed transatlantic service, the Americans replied that it was their understanding that this would involve a revision of the agreement, and indicated that they also wished to effect other changes. What they had in mind was the elimination of the mandatory stop at Shannon, and the right of their airlines to choose to land at either Dublin or Shannon. Lemass feared that the granting of landing rights at Dublin would result in its substitution for Shannon as the main transatlantic terminal, and talks in Washington in January 1948 with the US State Department and the Civil Aeronautics Commission, which were attended by John Leydon, secretary of the Department of Industry and Commerce, and other departmental officials, ended in a refusal by the Irish delegation to accede to the American demands.[81] Later that year an American delegation arrived in Ireland to confront representatives of the Departments of Finance, Industry and Commerce and External Affairs[82] but the Irish team was obdurate, despite the intervention of the American minister who handed in two notes to External Affairs pressing the American case.[83] The Minister for Industry and Commerce, Daniel Morrissey, informed the government that with a capital investment of over £2 million and an operating loss of £30,000 at Shannon airport, his department could not afford a further drop in revenue if the stop there were abandoned: 'The airport at present gives employment to over 1,000 people and any reduction of activity there would have the most serious repercussions for the area'.[84] Furthermore, he felt that Dublin airport could not be used by transatlantic aircraft without incurring further expenditure there, and that if rights were given to the US, other states would feel entitled to apply for them, providing further competition for Aer Lingus on its British and European routes. However, the Americans did appear to have found an ally in Seán MacBride, who intervened in July 1950 to propose to the government, on the suggestion of George Garrett, the American ambassador, that it would go a considerable way towards allaying American feelings if permission were given for one service daily by an American airline to Dublin airport for the period during which night flights were being operated between Dublin and London.[85] Both Finance and Industry and Commerce were quick to oppose this suggestion.[86]

With a change of government in 1951, it was Lemass who had to deal with the problem in 1952 when the US once again renewed their request, but although he did consider removing the mandatory stop at Shannon, he was not going soft on the principle of denying them access to Dublin airport, 'even at the risk of the United States government refusing to allow the operation of the proposed Irish transatlantic service under the terms of the permit issued by them in 1948'.[87] As regards the mandatory stop, he told the American chargé d'affaires that 'if the development of traffic at Shannon continued and the Irish line got started, the government would reconsider its attitude'.[88] However, William Norton, Minister for Industry and Commerce in the inter-party government which came to power in 1954, doubted whether the compulsory stop could be retained indefinitely.[89] In the event, it was done away with in April 1957, at the same time as the government was approving expenditure on the construction of new runways to cater for the jet aircraft which were anticipated to come on stream in the 1960s, and which would certainly result in the general bypassing of Shannon. However, over 15 years was to pass before a revision of the bilateral treaty in June 1973 allowed one American airline to serve Dublin airport. The snag was that it had to touch down at Shannon first!

Nevertheless, there is no doubt that Lemass saw the development of civil aviation in the state as being crucial, not only in commercial terms, in the development of the tourism industry, but also as a symbol of the emergence of Ireland as a modern and independent political entity. Speaking just before his election as Taoiseach, he told the Irish Airline Pilots' Association that the aeroplane was 'the real instrument of liberation for this country, and from that aspect ... perhaps the single most important development of this century'.[90] However, the financial results from Aer Lingus in the early 1950s were not promising, with small surpluses of £14,646 and £72,405 for 1950/51 and 1951/52 respectively giving way to a deficit of £83,313 for 1952/53.[91] In January 1954 the Department of Industry and Commerce informed Aer Lingus that it was not prepared to make provision in the Estimates to cover the Aer Rianta share of Aer Lingus losses in that financial year. There was a loss of £62,663 in 1953/54, but the following year showed a profit of

£25,428, and by 1956–57 an operating surplus of £158,548 had been achieved. In addition, a new method of financing capital expenditure by means of bank loans conditional upon a government guarantee was put in place which relieved the Minister for Finance of the onus of advancing capital to the airline free of interest. Lemass was circumspect in his appraisal of the company's future prospects on its twenty-first birthday:

> For the company, challenge accompanies the congratulations ... it seems to me that the choice of occasion is peculiarly appropriate as it marks the emergence of the company as a strong, self-reliant, self-supporting body after those groping years which succeeded the long period of State foster-age.[92]

The most dramatic development in 1957 was the decision to finally launch an Irish transatlantic air service. Lemass, back in Industry and Commerce yet again, was determined to achieve this target third time around: 'no intelligent plan of national development can fail to make provision for the growth of air transport'.[93] In February 1958 he announced that arrangements were being made for Aerlínte services to be operated with Seaboard and Western, based on the 1952 agreements, which entailed the leasing of aircraft and operating crews from that company pending the purchase by Aerlínte of Boeing 720s. It took only three months for his dream to come true. On 28 April 1958 the inaugural flight left Dublin with a large official party, which included Lemass, John Leydon and T. J. O'Driscoll, director general of Bord Fáilte. At Shannon, they were joined by Brendan O'Regan, chairman of Bord Fáilte and chief executive of the Shannon Free Airport Development Company.[94] Figures for the first eleven months in service showed that the company had carried 14,781 passengers, slightly up on the figure of 13,000 which had formed the basis for the decision to take the plunge, and its first six months' operating loss was £180,000, considerably less than forecast.[95] Despite the pessimism of James Dillon on the opposition benches, who described the project as 'misconceived, reckless and ... a wholly improvident gamble with the resources of this country' during the debate on the Air Transport and Navigation Bill 1959,[96] the enterprise did not fail. On 18 November 1960 the Boeing 720 St Patrick broke the existing record for the New York-Shannon route by covering it in four hours fifty-seven minutes, heralding a new era in Irish air travel, which was to become the means of transport for the majority of American visitors who helped to make the 1960s a golden age for Irish tourism.

It can be seen therefore that there was an uneasy relationship between the state and tourism interests in Ireland in the 1950s. Despite the fact that four pieces of tourism legislation were passed in the decade, it would seem that there was a lack of commitment on the part of the various administrations to the forceful development of the industry. The debates on the tourism acts reveal a residual opposition to the industry *per se*, with many deputies still convinced that the hotel and accommodation sector should be capable of generating the capital and the promotional efforts to sustain and develop tourism in Ireland. The inability of those concerned to do so made the creation of a single statutory body financed by the exchequer almost inevitable. Seán Lemass, while undoubtedly the politician who was most committed to the industry, did it no favours with his hamfisted creation of two new bodies in 1952, and the positioning of political appointees on the various boards who had little interest or expertise in the industry was certainly of limited use to it. On the other hand, the establishment of An Tóstal, while short-lived, resulted in the general brightening-up of the country and stimulated public awareness of the industry as a significant contributor to the economy. In civil aviation, the airline companies ended the decade in a more settled state, although Lemass' protectionist policies in favour of Aer Lingus prevented the development of Dublin airport as an international hub and delayed the construction of an airport at Cork until 1961. The establishment of an Irish transatlantic air service was crucial in terms of national prestige and the acceptance of the Republic as a modern and outward-looking state as the 1960s approached, and it was to prove a critical factor in the development of the industry as that decade passed. Horgan speaks of Lemass' general difficulties in the post-war period as being 'a shortage of capital funds, a lack of enthusiasm on the part of colleagues and the electoral unpredictability that marked the years between 1949 and 1957, combined with the obstacles placed in his path by the Department of Finance'.[97] The tourism industry was no exception to the rule, and suffered by these constraints to an advanced degree. It is fair to say that tourism in Ireland in the 1950s was in a learning curve, and it would take the general upturn of the economy in the 1960s to apply a psychological boost and make the industry respectable. However, with the emphasis on attracting and developing manufacturing industry in the 1960s, and the disastrous consequences of the Northern Ireland conflict in the 1970s, it was only in the late 1980s that tourism's contribution to the balance of payments was recognised for what it was and substantial state investment, aided by European Community funding, was provided. Now, 80 years after the foundation of the state and in a global context, where recreation and leisure are growth industries on an unparalleled scale, the Irish state is finally prepared to capitalise on the vision and determination of those who fostered the positive exploitation of its natural resources in the early decades of its existence.

Ireland and the US in the Post-war Period

MAURICE FITZGERALD

This essay deals with certain features of the relationship between Ireland and the US in the first two decades after the Second World War. Drawn from a larger piece of research entitled 'Symbolism Versus Reality: Irish-American Diplomatic Relations, 1945–1963', its scope is not necessarily limited to bilateral diplomatic relations. It avails of other tenets in illustrating their long-standing ties, and small power–superpower relations within the transatlantic context, encompassing some of the main findings revealed by documentary evidence based in the National Archives in Dublin and, perhaps more significantly, presidential libraries across the United States of America. And it deals with a period that has, to a large degree, been ignored in the secondary literature.[1]

In many respects, the essential question addressed here boils down to whether the US perceived Ireland and Irish-American relations in the same way as the Irish did. As with all aspects of international relations (in truth, with all history) different phases of Irish-American relations were marked by both controversy and banality. Subjects dealt with in this essay vary from the questionable US practice of getting rid of troublemakers in their establishment by appointing them as American ambassador to Ireland, to the relatively maverick foreign policy of the latter, especially the idealistic tack the Irish pursued at the United Nations. In addition, it addresses the problem of partition, especially the US approach, and closes by dealing with visits by dignitaries, concentrating on the trip by President Seán T. O'Kelly to the US in 1959 and John F. Kennedy's reciprocal visit to Ireland four years later. It is with the personification of relations that this essay begins, however. By dealing with the issue of diplomatic representatives, it seeks to establish whether Ireland's perceptions of its relative importance are valid vis-à-vis the people Washington appointed. And it concentrates on US diplomats, the reason becoming clearer as this next section progresses.

MINISTERS AND AMBASSADORS

Ireland's official diplomatic representation in the United States dates back to October 1924, when Saorstát Éireann (the Irish Free State) sent its first diplomatic representative outside of the British Commonwealth. This event alone encapsulates the importance of the US to Ireland. However, the same criteria have not necessarily always applied the other way round. In truth, for Washington, Ireland is essentially another western European state, though one with a large and relatively influential ethnic population in the US.

Throughout the war years, the American minister to Ireland was David Gray. He was not a success. He continuously clashed with the policy of neutrality pursued by the Taoiseach, Eamon de Valera. Indeed, his efforts to isolate Ireland did little for his credibility or his professional integrity. Harry S. Truman had an enormous impact upon Irish-American diplomatic relations when he withdrew Gray in 1947, replacing him with George Garrett. Gray had been Franklin D. Roosevelt's appointee, but did not have much influence upon Truman. Garrett, on the other hand, was a relative success, although it has to be said that, for de Valera, anybody would have been a distinct improvement. For instance, Garrett made a valuable contribution to Ireland's case for access to Marshall Aid, the European Recovery Programme. In fact, he was so benevolent towards Ireland that he attracted the wrath of the chief of mission at the Economic Cooperation Administration in London, W. John Kenney. The latter spoke disparagingly of Garrett's 'impassioned plea to Mr Truman to get more [grant] money for Ireland' at a time when the US was not particularly well disposed towards Ireland.

The feeling in Dublin was that the Americans had begun to establish a disturbing practice of getting rid of troublemakers in their establishment – or as historian Dermot Keogh calls them, 'loose cannons' – by appointing them as United States ambassador to Ireland. Thus, it is the calibre of representatives that is particularly worth examining. When US Navy Secretary Francis P. Matthews made an impassioned, though injudicious, speech about the handling of the Korean War, he wound up at the American ambassador's residence in Dublin's Phoenix Park. As Dean Acheson wrote, Matthews had 'called for preventive war. He was made ambassador to Ireland'. Matthews wanted to come to Ireland at the conclusion of his career. The opportunity came a little earlier than he had anticipated. However, the reality of Ireland in the early 1950s did not quite match his expectations. One commentator has declared that 'nothing ... not even literature, has captured the dead, grey misery of Ireland in the 1950s, which was awful for almost everybody'.[2] This included the American ambassador. Nonetheless, Matthews made a relatively favourable impression. He also had the consolation of being a neighbour and friend of Papal Nuncio Gerald O'Hara, and wrote:

> ... I attend Mass every morning in his chapel. The American flavour of its devotional atmosphere does much as an antidote for some things existing in Ireland which might otherwise be quite depressing.

Matthews died of a heart attack before he had completed his term of office, the first American minister to pass away in office since William McDowell, who had died in 1934 at the banquet held to celebrate the presentation of his credentials. Despite the brevity of his tenure, the latter was still very important to bilateral relations simply because he presented his credentials to de Valera and not to the governor general, the British monarch's representative in Ireland.[3]

With regard to the calibre of American representatives, Scott McLeod is another case in point. Officially US State Department chief of security, McLeod was a 'witch hunter' during the early years of Dwight D. Eisenhower's first administration. Of course, this was the period in which the demagogue Joe McCarthy was at the height of his powers. McLeod's targets for elimination from the US State Department included Communist agents, 'fellow-travellers' (socialists and liberals), homosexuals and moral deviants. He managed to contrive one controversy too many though. US Secretary of State John Foster Dulles was asked to dig up a job for him, but McLeod turned down the post of US secretary to Guam. Finally, he was forced to take the ambassador's job in Ireland.

Whether it was a Democrat or Republican president, it did not matter. The Irish post was neither crucial nor terribly taxing. When Kennedy spoke to Irish ambassador John Hearne in 1961 on the topic of diplomatic representation, the US president promised to send a really good ambassador. But Hearne was dismissive. He understood that the Americans did not have enough 'good men' to go around. It is worth noting that Dublin was not prepared to accept a woman in the post at that time. Indeed, one of Hearne's predecessors as Irish ambassador in Washington, Seán Nunan, expressed the view that 'we are not desirous of having a woman in the post'.[4]

There are, however, other examples of the relatively poor standard of American representatives sent to Ireland. This assertion is not just limited to the appointment of ambassadors. Essentially operating as second in command in the embassy, US counsellors changed posts very regularly. Between 1947 and 1954, seven different people held this position, prompting the US ambassador in Ireland to comment that there had been too much 'chopping and changing'.[5]

This is not to say that Irish representatives accredited to the US always acted with complete propriety. Their fascination with partition – at the behest of Dublin – gained little except State Department antagonism. At other times, the activities of Irish diplomats attracted the ire of superiors and colleagues alike; for instance, highly narrative reports on subjects ranging from Teamsters' corruption to the Suez crisis often lacked substantive analysis. Still, the general standard of Ireland's representatives contrasts favourably with the rather poor calibre of their American contemporaries. US administrations apparently saw the Irish job either as a reward for services rendered to a political party, rather than to the country, or as a way to offload a liability. On the other hand, Irish governments viewed the US post as the pinnacle of a diplomatic career – as with Hearne – or as a platform to better things – as with Seán Nunan, who became the senior civil servant in Ireland's Department of External Affairs after his tenure in the US.

From this brief overview of diplomatic representatives, and the contrast between the approach of a small power and a superpower, this essay next moves on to investigate Irish-American relations within the context of the UN. Indeed, the multilateral platform afforded by this forum offers plenty of examples of bilateral relations at work.

THE MULTILATERAL ARENA

Ireland has always been a strong advocate of multilateral activity, dating back to its time at the League of Nations. The Dublin government believed that such a globally interactive institution should act as a bulwark for world peace through a policy of collective security, but had been disappointed by that organisation, just as it would be by the UN. However, the UN still offered a platform for a small nation to air its views on world peace and justice.

The Potsdam Conference of 1945 had dealt with the issue of neutrals. The US, United Kingdom, and Union of Soviet Socialist Republics (USSR) agreed to 'support UN membership for states which remained neutral during the war and which fulfil the qualifications for UN membership'. This policy was not fully implemented. Following Potsdam, five neutral unoccupied non-belligerents applied for UN membership: Ireland, Portugal, Afghanistan, Sweden and Yemen; of these, only the last three were admitted. Ireland's early application for membership showed a certain keenness to participate in international affairs after the suffocating and self-imposed alienation of its 'Emergency' – the Second World War. Despite American support, the USSR vetoed the Irish and Portuguese applications for admission.[6] Ireland's 'isolation, psychologically and intellectually' was acute, as 'Irish people found themselves strangers, and not very popular ones, in a strange post-war world'.[7] Irish applications were consistently vetoed by the Soviets until 1955, perhaps understandably, especially when it is considered that Dublin only opened bilateral diplomatic relations with the USSR in 1972.

The dawning of a new era of multilateral relations began for Ireland when it was finally allowed to join the UN in the mid-1950s. As it had proved in the League of Nations, Ireland had the potential to become a very active member upon the new global stage it had been given. The early years of its UN membership – especially between 1957 and 1961 – have been described by commentator and former diplomat Conor Cruise O'Brien as possibly Ireland's most exciting time, in purely diplomatic terms. Ireland's Minister for External Affairs, Frank Aiken, 'pursued an independent line at the United Nations, aimed at the reduction of cold war tensions … [especially] the non-dissemination of nuclear weapons'.[8] At the same time, the US continuously tried to massage the Irish vote, but failed.[9] And though its voting patterns coincided with the US more often than not, Ireland still voted independently as a small but neutral western European power, deviating from the expected path on numerous occasions, causing consternation in the process.

Although the 1956 Hungarian uprising and subsequent invasion signalled that the US was in no position to take any affirmative action regarding Soviet satellites in eastern Europe, this episode was roundly condemned, with Ireland and the United States in full agreement. The Suez crisis came as rather a shock and demonstrated the need for strong and tested leadership to run international affairs effectively. Charles Bohlen believed that the US acted responsibly during the crisis: 'I think he [Eisenhower] was quite right on that. It caused a great deal of trouble with our allies'.[10] Ireland's position in the UN was generally supportive of American handling of the affair.[11] It no doubt helped that this policy position went against British interests.

It is with regard to China that Irish-American relations reached one of their lowest ebbs. Dulles 'was perpetually arguing for a vigorous and even more vigorous form of containment of Communism' and was more dogmatic in his approach to the China question than Eisenhower might ordinarily have been.[12] The Americans strictly adhered to a policy of opposition, even to discussions about discussing the entry of Communist China into the UN, never mind debating actual entry. It was a political position and the question of fairness did not enter into the equation. Washington was lobbied hard to continue its policy, Irish-American politicians prominent among those promoting it. Sherman Adams reaffirmed:

> [the continued] firm opposition of this government and the American people to the seating of representatives of the Chinese Communist regime in United Nations bodies ... the United States does not intend to recognise the China Communist regime.[13]

Eisenhower's stated position remained that:

> ... existing international facts ... preclude the seating of the Chinese Communist regime to represent China in the UN ... We have every reason to fear that the Chinese Communist regime in fact now seeks representation in the UN in order to promote the objectives of international Communism by creating dissension among the nations of the world, rather than to become a partner in seeking just and peaceful solutions for the world's problems.[14]

The American executive and legislature were both strongly against Communist China's admission to the UN. The US stuck to its wartime policy of recognising administrations in exile, rather than 'puppet governments', when it suited its purposes. After all, the UN was still at war with China over Korea, and obviously 'an armistice is not peace'.[15] The Republican Platform of 1956 validated the government's position on 'Red China', opposing its seating in the United Nations and continuing the support afforded to the Republic of China on Formosa.

The Swedish government's position regarding China is interesting in this regard. They saw the problem of China simply as being 'which government should be recognised as the government of China'; in other words, which government should have China's membership of the United Nations and its permanent seat on the Security Council? Britain, Denmark, India, the Netherlands, Norway, Sweden and Switzerland all recognised the Peking government as having this legitimacy. The United States and a majority of the UN recognised the Formosa government in this respect. It is worth noting that back in 1950 Dulles had said:

> I have now come to believe that the United Nations will best serve the cause of peace if its Assembly is representative of what the world actually is, and not merely representative of the parts which we like. Therefore, we ought to be willing that all nations should be members without attempting to appraise closely those which are 'good' and those which are 'bad'. Already that distinction is obliterated by the present membership of the United Nations ... Some of the present member nations and others that might become members have governments that are not representative of the people. But if in fact they are governments – that is, if they govern – then they have a power which should be represented in any organisation that purports to mirror world reality.[16]

The Swedes held their ground in direct opposition to the US government's position on the China question. This was also to be the path that Ireland would courageously follow.

Frank Aiken – who was effectively based in New York – believed that both the Peking and Formosan governments should be represented at the United Nations as a matter of principle. He was not naive enough to believe, for instance, that a UN resolution could force the Chinese out of Tibet, but it would certainly have made the Chinese more accountable. At that stage, little more than an admonition of China could ever be expected from the UN due to the power of the veto. Aiken did not uphold the notion that the Peking government should take Formosan representation over. He did however believe that Formosa should co-exist with mainland China under the UN's aegis. The Irish foreign minister praised US patronage of Formosa, but he believed that China should be allowed to take a seat at the UN and, more importantly, on the Security Council. Aiken felt that the time to discuss the question in an adult fashion had come at last.[17]

On 23 September 1957, the US ambassador to the UN, Henry Cabot Lodge, sent a telegram to Dulles stating that 'the F[oreign] M[inister] of Ireland is going nuts – he is going to support the Red China item despite what we were told'. This decision obviously came as a huge surprise to the Americans. Because of protocol and diplomatic niceties, Lodge realised that in public he could only 'express regret' to Aiken over this decision; at the time though, Lodge wondered aloud if Dulles could not do something more useful.[18] US bitterness did not escape Aiken.[19] As Dulles was not on particularly good terms with him, this left the Americans in a quandary. Dulles and Lodge appeared to agree during their conversation that taking this position on China was 'a bad thing for a Catholic to do'. It was perhaps at this stage that the Americans thought to use Aiken's religion against him in order to force Ireland's hand.[20]

A telephone call followed to the Irish delegation at the UN and was received by the most senior member available, Máire MacEntee. At Eisenhower's behest, an eminent member of the American hierarchy, Cardinal Francis Spellman of New York, 'suggested' to MacEntee that the position taken by Aiken was inappropriate for a member of the Catholic church. He 'requested' that the Irish position on the China question be 'reviewed'. Such intimidatory tactics are interesting, not so much because a senior member of the American clergy was interfering in the affairs of a sovereign state, but because the United States government should use such an innovative stratagem. It was prepared to go to great lengths to keep the Chinese Communists out of the United Nations; indeed, China was not recognised by the US until Richard Nixon's presidency.

Despite such intimidation, the Irish foreign minister made a statement the following day, 24 September 1957, in which he said:

> Like many others here, we have no sympathy whatever with the ideology of the Peking government. We condemn its aggressive policies in China itself and its conduct in North Korea ... If merely by refusing to discuss the question of the representation of China in the United Nations we could do anything to improve the situation in China and Korea we would vote without hesitation in favour of that course. We are not, however, convinced that refusal to discuss the question can now serve such a purpose ... Our aims should be to win acceptance for the principles of the Charter in China and to secure self-determination for the people of Korea. The belief of my delegation is that in present circumstances progress can best be made to these ends by having a full and open discussion of the question of the representation of China in this Assembly. We are voting, therefore, in favour of the amendment proposed ...[21]

Not surprisingly, the reaction was tremendous. Newspapers and radio broadcasts delivered an instant sense of astonishment, while demonstrating a complete lack of understanding of the Irish government's reasoning. The stance of the Catholic church's hierarchy showed exactly where it stood; the *Irish Independent* quoted Archbishop Richard J. Cushing as saying:

> The encouragement given this diabolical regime by the Irish delegation at the UN shocked and saddened me and all the clergy and faithful of the Archdiocese of Boston. How could Ireland in the light of her own history do such a thing?

The archbishop of Armagh and Irish primate, Cardinal John D'Alton, said that all of Catholic Ireland was against the recognition of Communist China 'which is still guilty of cruel and persistent persecution'.[22] One Catholic newspaper talked of people of Irish descent being 'shocked ... stunned and saddened' at the Dublin government's stand.[23]

Aiken met the US Secretary of State on a couple of occasions to discuss the matter. The former remained adamantly in favour of discussing China's entry into the UN in the presence of a resolute and equally determined Dulles.[24] After all this trouble, it is worth remembering that, when it came to the time to vote, Ireland came out against Communist China's application for UN membership, having earlier supported a resolution condemning its invasion of Tibet. The whole approach to the China question altered under Kennedy, though not dramatically. US policy towards China did not radically change either – certainly not on the surface. The Kennedy administration nevertheless challenged the atmosphere around – rather than the substance of – its foreign policy. Thus, Aiken thought that he could discuss this issue without feeling intimidated. In fact, he felt that this administration was much more approachable and that his opinions received a much more sympathetic hearing. Aiken mentions discussing the issue with Kennedy's Secretary of State, Dean Rusk, and felt that at least his words were not falling on totally deaf ears.[25] Under Rusk, the US State Department showed more tact on the issue than was ever the case under Dulles.

It must be said that in Aiken, Ireland's UN delegation found an attentive leader and patron. He came to see the UN as the appropriate forum for him as Irish foreign minister, enjoying a large degree of freedom in formulating foreign policy, especially under Taoiseach Seán Lemass. Aiken led the Irish delegation in the UN from 1957.

> With a firm belief that the UN gives the smaller countries an opportunity to reduce East-West tensions, Aiken is largely responsible for Ireland's occasionally independent actions at the UN ...[26]

Multilateral organisations, such as the UN, thus offered Ireland a chance to raise matters about which it felt particularly strongly. But, while it made some progress regarding certain multilateral issues, even if Irish-American relations suffered, this was not to be the experience in relation to partition. In this regard, Dublin made little progress through Washington.

THE US APPROACH TO PARTITION

Until recent years, the central domestic and foreign policy ambition of the Irish government has been to abolish partition. The main development in the era under review was the growing mood in Dublin to resolve the crisis peacefully. In 1948, while out of government, de Valera paid an extensive visit to the US, along with Aiken. The main thrust of this American tour was to explain the link between partition and Irish neutrality, especially within the context of the Second World War. They had many interested listeners, including a young Congressman Kennedy, who is supposed to have made quite an impression upon them. De Valera met Truman on 10 March 1948. Having paid his respects, de Valera spoke against partition, but was stonewalled.[27] In truth, the whole visit was an irritant to the State Department, as it only aroused Irish-American pressure from various quarters:

> Mr de Valera's recent trip to this country has resulted in increased agitation for US intervention in this dispute, which this Department continues to consider as one to be settled between Ireland and Britain.

Much of the agitation centred on raising American interest so that Washington would have to bring pressure to bear on the London government. One suggested form included halting economic aid to the British as long as they 'occupied' Northern Ireland. In reality, de Valera's trip was ill timed. The State Department consensus was that the administration should not be seen to intervene or to take sides on the issue:

> It has long been the view of this Department that the subject of the boundary which partitions Ireland and Northern Ireland is one for discussion between the Irish and British governments and one in which this country should not intrude.[28]

De Valera's trip was a failure, just as a previous visit by Aiken had been in 1941, and as Irish foreign minister Seán MacBride's trip to the US would be in 1951. The hint was not taken.

Ireland and Irish-American votes were considerably more important around election time in the US, but other than that, the main western European countries the US focused on remained the UK, France, Germany and Italy. The Irish government's refusal to join the

North Atlantic Treaty Organisation (NATO), because such an action would reflect *de jure* recognition of partition, was a major development with long-lasting implications. The UK government's Ireland Act of 1949 proved to be the central thinking behind not only London's policy on partition, but the US position, because, although not stated overtly, it was mirrored closely in documents such as NSC 83/1, a policy the Eisenhower administrations followed rigidly. It would be a mistake to under-estimate the importance of NSC 83/1. Indeed, its central prognosis would still be valid a decade later in November 1960, outlining as it did the operational basis of US foreign policy towards Ireland. As Richard Finnegan has argued, 'Ireland's relationship with America hardly commanded the constant and diligent attention of the United States National Security Council'.[29] Such vigilance was not required.

Throughout the post-war period the United States took a markedly consistent approach to partition. Pressure from the Irish-American lobby remained persistent, but with little reward. Their activities were not going to force the US to take action favouring Dublin's view – certainly not in the face of the contribution Northern Ireland made in the Second World War or at the risk of endangering Anglo-American relations at the beginning of the Cold War. The White House referred all matters appertaining to partition to the State Department, where the issue was discreetly buried. Irish correspondence continuously tried to raise the issue, only ever meeting a similar sort of refrain from the State Department:

> The administration is well aware of the questions arising from the political status of Northern Ireland and has given the most careful consideration to the bearing of these questions on the relations of the United States with the Republic of Ireland and the United Kingdom, two of this country's closest friends. It is believed that this is not a matter in which the United States could properly or usefully intervene.[30]

One such letter from the Irish foreign minister in 1958 strongly reiterated Ireland's position on partition. Although Aiken accepted that the UK's position was causing resentment in Ireland and with Irish people abroad, he felt that the Dublin government was not in a position to force the issue; quite the opposite in fact. Ireland's policy, though invidious, was, he maintained, correct, and would be rewarded in time.[31] Under the premiership of Lemass, the Irish government's position on partition began to change noticeably. It had become increasingly obvious that active diplomacy and creative propaganda were never going to change the situation. Thus, Dublin's position transformed into a more conciliatory line towards the *de facto* state of Northern Ireland.

So, what happened to the US approach to partition when an Irish-American became president? The answer was not what the Irish might have wanted to hear. Kennedy's ancestry affected his position on partition, but not in a way that might have been expected. His relationship with UK Prime Minister Harold Macmillan was very strong. And, when he came to office, he was not about to antagonise one of America's major allies. This was in complete contrast to the position he took both in the House of Representatives and in the Senate. In 1956, for instance, Kennedy co-sponsored an unsuccessful resolution in favour of the whole of Ireland achieving self-determination, unless a plebiscite declared otherwise. In a subsequent conversation about partition, Irish ambassador Thomas J. Kiernan mentioned this to President Kennedy, but the latter had clearly been cultivating the Irish vote in 1956.[32] He held onto these views through to 1960, primarily because the issue was a vote-winner.[33] But when Kennedy became president, the issue stayed with the State Department. The Irish-American US president reverted to the official position, one of non-interference in a dispute between two states close to the United States. Kennedy understood the sentiment attached, but in a world facing far greater problems, partition held a certain lack of importance. During his presidency, as Irish hopes of partition being resolved rose to their zenith, the reality was the complete opposite; the chances of partition ending swiftly reached their nadir. Kennedy looked at partition as coldly and with as much detachment as he would any other foreign policy issue. The Irish ambassador in Washington maintained that:

> ... Kennedy was [Irish] in his blood reactions ... in his speed of communication, in his wit, in his ... self-debunking ... Behind that was something that wasn't Irish; the cold summing-up, the logical follow-up. And in the matter of issues between Ireland and England the reaction might come in a sentimental way. I don't know, but when it came to any kind of practical business, the other man behind, the cold man would take control, which is understandable. And the line I'd draw all the time was one of great understanding, of never any kind of intrusion on him in Irish affairs.[34]

Aiken discussed partition with Kennedy, but understood the reality of Washington's position:

> ... an American president has a long list of problems and over the years, the relations between Great Britain and the United States have been very close, and they felt a great need to keep together so, in these circumstances great powers don't take any public action that might upset that relationship.[35]

Interestingly, it was through the Irish ambassador that most of the politically significant Irish-American interaction on the partition question appears to have taken place. Under Robert Brennan, the Irish ambassador to the US during the Second World War, and throughout the subsequent tenures of Nunan and Hearne, the Irish embassy diligently followed the instructions emanating from the Department of External Affairs. In essence, they cultivated Irish-American politicians and groups in an effort to put pressure on successive Truman and Eisenhower administrations. Under Kennedy, the matter of partition was raised, but made little headway. The Irish ambassador to the US, T. J. Kiernan, describes once broaching the question by saying that he never asked the US president 'to take any line or make any intervention with Mr Macmillan'. In reply, Kennedy assured the Irish ambassador that he understood Ireland's position, but that it could prove very embarrassing to change policy or to be seen to intervene, thereby running the risk of adversely affecting the 'special relationship' between the United States and the UK.

On one particular occasion, Kiernan did not raise the question as such, but just wanted to assure Kennedy that the Irish government and people were not expecting the US president to raise the matter in Dáil Éireann (the Irish lower parliamentary house) when he visited in the summer of 1963. It was felt that Kennedy might find such pressure disconcerting. The Irish ambassador presumed that the subject would still be discussed privately in Ireland.[36] True to his reputation, Kennedy did briefly raise the matter in Dáil Éireann, but not as the Irish would perhaps have wished. In fact, he publicly called on the Irish people to look to the future rather than to the past on the partition question. No major declarations or moves favouring Ireland's interpretation of partition were taken by Kennedy during his presidency, though he would doubtlessly have discussed it privately, even if only in passing, with the British. The official US position remained the same. Kennedy's outlook was very European in many respects and, on the partition question, the son of the wartime US ambassador to the Court of St James was not prepared to court controversy for the sake of it. Kiernan described him thus: 'apart from his Americanism which was 100%, [he] was more British than Irish'.[37]

The State Department's official answer to enquiries on partition – which were limited to around three letters a month, mostly from the general public and sometimes from members of Congress on behalf of organisations urging US intervention – remained consistent:

> The Department of State has long been aware of the questions arising from the partition of Ireland. We believe, however, that this is a matter for determination by the United Kingdom and the Republic of Ireland, both of whom are friendly to the US, and is, therefore not one in which we can properly or usefully intervene.[38]

By 1962, the Irish government's policy demonstrated some change.

The Taoiseach established a personal 'preference for functional co-operation with Northern Ireland where possible', instead of pursuing a dogmatic and idealist line on partition.[39] Under the Lemass government, the IRA steadily lost support, indeed to such a degree that it quickly posed a decreased threat to the political status quo. Irish legislation passed during the Second World War enabled the government to keep this paramilitary organisation weak and relatively ineffective, as well as illegal. Dublin did not condone any of the IRA's activities at home or abroad; indeed, it was actively trying to curtail them. The main interest of the State Department regarding the IRA was to keep it from exerting pressure on Washington through Irish-American citizens and organisations. Indeed, the view of the US government appears to have been in favour of British and Irish actions at this time, and they seem to have privately held the view that IRA convicts were not political prisoners but terrorists.

The reality of the US government's position on partition was finally revealed under President Lyndon B. Johnson when he met the Northern Ireland Prime Minister, Terence O'Neill, on 17 March 1964. The reaction of the *Belfast Telegraph* was reported as being joyous, because theretofore politics rather than protocol had dominated relations between the United States and Northern Ireland. It was indeed a significant 'diplomatic victory'. The *Irish Times* editorial of 23 March 1964 speculated – probably correctly – that Kennedy would also have taken this step, as it was the general direction in which he was heading. The political reality of US government views on partition meant that it was never going to put undue pressure on London to solve this delicate problem.[40] By the mid-1960s, relations between Northern Ireland and the Republic had been improving for some considerable time. O'Neill's meeting with Johnson was a relative success from the perspective that it signalled to a large extent the removal of the Irish question from the American political agenda. It also helped to change the course of history.[41] Ireland's strong relationship with the US did not provide an 'open door' to American decision-making processes, as successive Dublin governments may have hoped regarding partition. Ever since the early 1960s, Ireland has had to face up to realpolitik at work.

Face-to-face meetings engineered by the Irish were not effective when aimed at specific policy areas that went against the national interests of their transatlantic cousins. They had more success when the target was stimulating better relations, especially when examined in terms of the relative weights of small power–superpower relations.

VISITS BY HEADS OF STATE
One of the primary symbols used to engender good relations between two countries is state visits. This article investigates two such trips, Pre-

sident Seán T. O'Kelly's visit to the US in 1959 and President John F. Kennedy's visit to Ireland in 1963. It is perhaps the lead-up to the O'Kelly trip, rather than the visit itself, that is most noteworthy, while the reciprocated journey four years later by the US president remains one of the historical highlights of Irish-American relations.

By the mid-1950s, the State Department was being persistently if unofficially asked to invite the Irish president to the United States, but 'had discouraged it just as much as [t]he[y] could within the framework of ... friendly relations with Ireland'. Although the State Department could see 'no foreign policy advantage', it was becoming increasingly obvious that the White House was beginning to recognise the political merits of such a trip. They 'noted that the Irish Embassy is particularly active in American political circles and is no doubt promoting the visit behind the scenes'.[42] Their assessment was that there were:

> ... no particular advantages and some disadvantages. His visit would be used to accentuate the partition of Ireland and to urge US support for its termination, and thus embarrass our relations with the British.

The State Department tried to keep the idea at bay despite informal approaches and furtive promotion of the idea by the Irish diplomatic corps in the US.[43] Pressure from the Irish lobby to invite O'Kelly was pretty standard fare for the State Department to deal with, and a reason could always be found to signify that this was not a 'propitious time' for such an invitation.[44] It was noted however that the main merit of such a visit would be to make inroads into the 'Irish Catholic vote'.[45] Such a trip, it was felt, 'if properly thought out, might have very healthy repercussions in favor of the administration'.[46]

The US ambassador to Ireland at that time, William H. Taft, held the view that 'no essential Ireland-United States benefits ... would accrue from ... [such a] visit', although it would strengthen relations. Nonetheless, Taft thought O'Kelly would jump at the chance to go to the US. However, it was clearly recognised that one of the controversies that could arise during such a visit was partition, although O'Kelly would be expected to be 'decorous' and diplomatic on the issue.[47] The chances were that newsmen and lobbyists would not be so circumspect. Throughout the debate over the merits (or not) of such a visit, State Department opinion held that it would have far more of a domestic impact than a foreign political one. Even so, the Irish desire to instigate official visits to the United States was remarkable. Unfortunately however, as Taft commented in early 1956:

> ... it would appear that the government is ... more interested in going to the United States themselves than making the more important gesture of using the president as a spokesman for Ireland.

Indeed, he described the earlier affair surrounding the suggested visit in 1956 as a 'three-ring circus', and remained concerned about the amateurish Irish approach.[48]

Finally, by early 1959, the US State Department and the Irish government found themselves in a position to sanction a visit by the Irish president. St Patrick's Day that year was thus very auspicious for Irish-American diplomatic relations, with O'Kelly visiting the United States at last. Eisenhower made the Irish president welcome with a brief speech of jocular and typical Americana, the US president telling him that:

> ... as I welcome you ... I find myself in a rather difficult situation, and I am sure that the protocol officers of our two governments wouldn't know exactly how to solve the problem ... It is this: today everybody in the United States is Irish ... So, I would say that for this day at least, though you come as the official president of Ireland, in our hearts you are president of all of us.[49]

After such a schmaltzy start, O'Kelly responded in kind, remarking that the hospitality he was receiving reflected the 'close friendship and mutual understanding which have always so happily existed between Ireland and the United States of America'.[50]

The incident meriting most attention during the visit came later that day at a White House state dinner, the US president introducing a slight barb into his welcome by saying:

> I pay again a tribute to this wonderful feeling of warm friendship that has never been broken between Ireland and ourselves – and incidentally, Mr President, I have always wondered how you people can call yourselves neutral, you are in every fight there is – and maybe that's another reason we like you – but in any event ... I ... express that feeling of warm friendship that we know exists between your people and ours, and which we know shall never be broken.[51]

The Irish president was not going to allow an opportunity of replying to pass without making some reference to Eisenhower's mention of Irish neutrality and he did so in a diplomatically coded, but easily understandable, way. O'Kelly remarked:

> The Irish nation, which as you have so kindly said more than once, Mr President, is among the oldest on the earth – is one of these that has won its freedom in recent times. I thank God that it should have been given to me to witness, though still unfortunately for less than the entirety of our ancient land, the realisation of the dreams and the endeavours of many generations of Irishmen, and to have the privilege of playing some part myself ... in that realisation.[52]

This low-key clash over the question of neutrality and partition did little to detract from a successful public relations exercise all round. Two days later, as O'Kelly departed, and in a reminder of longstanding affiliations, Eisenhower said:

> In the years that stretch out ahead of us, we must be friendly among our-selves. We must be close to our good friends – and Ireland is among the front rank of our good friends. We must have faith in ourselves. We must have faith in each other – and faith in our God.[53]

The visit was returned when Kennedy's last major trip abroad, in the summer of 1963, included Ireland. His election had of course caught the imagination of all Irish people, prelates included.[54] His visit to Ber-lin on 26 June was a political triumph, but his next destination was Dub-lin. Having made a tremendous impact in Germany, and with that re-action fresh in the world's mind, Kennedy came to Ireland. The Irish am-bassador to the US, T. J. Kiernan, disparagingly referred to the Berlin reception as a 'fearful affair, like a ritual of handkerchiefs all prepared, and the little white handkerchiefs waving. In Ireland it was entirely different. It was very much a grass-roots reception and he realised that'.[55] There was certainly warmth and a feeling of homecoming to the Irish visit, rather than the nervous tension in Berlin. And right from the rapturous arrival to the sad departure, it befitted an emigrant. This state trip would seem even more significant before the year was out.

Historian Ian McCabe has asserted that the US president's visit was not solely on emotional grounds.[56] However, the fact that Rusk did not accompany Kennedy to Ireland, but proceeded straight to the UK, clearly demonstrated Ireland's lack of international importance.[57] That Kennedy had a legitimate interest in, and love of, Ireland there is no doubt. The fact that this feeling did not influence him on partition or the appointment of particularly suitable ambassadors is neither here nor there. Kennedy was US president, and as such primarily served Ameri-can national interests. The visit itself was of tremendous political sig-nificance in Ireland. It was also being looked upon as an 'indication that Ireland is in the mainstream of international affairs', and the Irish clearly appreciated being informed directly of the world situation from the US perspective.[58]

The visit to Dunganstown, the Kennedy family ancestral home-stead, provided some of the most memorable images of the visit. It saw the US president greeted there by his Irish relatives. The president pictured outside in the yard, drinking tea and eating salmon sandwiches, made the trip come alive across the globe for television viewers, pro-viding a famous photo opportunity. The most important event of Ken-nedy's visit came after he laid a wreath upon the graves of the executed leaders of the 1916 Easter Rising at Arbour Hill, which itself was noted as being of 'great emotional significance' for Ireland. Kennedy was the first visiting head of state to make this gesture. In Leinster House, the home of the Irish parliament, Kennedy delivered the keynote speech of his visit and became the first foreign statesman since the foundation of the Irish state to address a joint session of the Oireachtas (the Irish houses of parliament). It was also the first time that the proceedings of Dáil Éireann were televised by Radio Telefís Éireann, the new Irish television network. In his address, the US president cited the growing relationship between Ireland and the UK as one epitomising the dictum that 'there are no permanent enemies'. While holding that history can teach us vital lessons, Kennedy added that people should not be dominated by or governed under that pretext. But, although he recognised the bitterness, he felt that Ireland had to live in the present, for the future, rather than the past. Using a quotation to emphasise his point, he said: 'The world is large when its weary leagues two loving hearts divide, but the world is small when your enemy is loose on the other side'. In response to the obvious question – what can Ireland do? – Kennedy again used a quotation, as he was apt to do: 'All the world owes much to the little "five feet high" nations'. In his view, all that could hold a nation back, no matter whether it was a small power or a superpower, was a lack of imagination.[59]

Citing Ireland's position as unique, Kennedy called for even greater efforts towards world peace and justice. Ireland was a mixture of the old and new, he said, a former colony and part of a growing Europe. It thus had 'the confidence of both sides and an opportunity to act where the actions of greater powers might be looked upon with suspicion'. However, Kennedy was also interested in another global conflict – the Cold War between east and west – with a 'harsh and oppressive Communist system' railing against freedom and self-determination. Ireland, he understood, was not neutral on this issue although it did obviously pursue an independent foreign policy. He knew that Ireland could never again tolerate foreign domination and would fight against it wherever it was seen; Ireland had helped censure the suppression of the Hungarian uprising, he said. He encouraged Ireland to continue using the stage afforded by the UN, his speech in Dáil Éireann making reference to its active and responsible participation in multilateral affairs. Indeed, he said: 'The major forum for your nation's greater role in world affairs is that of protector of the weak and voice of the small, the United Nations'.[60] Not surprisingly, Kennedy received a standing ovation. Nevertheless, despite his sentiments, there was some controversy. In his address, he jokingly used a phrase that originated in a letter by Lord Edward Fitzgerald, stating that 'Leinster House does not inspire the brightest ideas'. When it was written, it referred to the Fitzgerald residence, subsequently that of Dáil Éireann. After the speech, he went to Áras an Uachta-ráin (the Irish president's residence) and was rebuffed by de Valera, who told him that he 'had done no service to Irish politicians by this quotation'. The reference itself was historical in basis, but might have been put in context.[61] The rest of the trip passed without a hint of controversy.

The State Department's frank evaluation of the economic and political situation in Ireland formed an impressive part of the background information for Kennedy's trip. His pragmatic approach to Ireland has already been expanded upon and, once he became president, he did not need much convincing of where the US stood. This evaluation made some interesting points. The Irish decision to seek membership of the European Economic Community (EEC) was seen as an attempt to break with 'insularity' – the Irish government seeking to detach itself from its 'nationalistic and protectionist' roots. Despite the EEC's rebuff of the UK in 1963, and Ireland's inability to join on its own, Dublin correctly perceived that the time would come when Ireland would indeed be part of the EEC and thus prepared itself accordingly. Irish economic growth was seen as encouraging and progressive, enabling the government to proceed with its aim of rejuvenating the state. Politically, Ireland was seen as relatively stable. Its policy remained the economic development of the country so that Ireland could compete at a European level, if not globally. Ireland's yearning to join the EEC was not accompanied, however, by a parallel desire to join NATO, much to the chagrin of the Americans. Additionally, Ireland continued to display 'an independent attitude at the United Nations on such issues as disarmament and the rivalry between the Afro-Asians and the former colonial powers'.[62] The Central Intelligence Agency (CIA) security papers for Kennedy's trip also make interesting reading in that context. The main difficulty in Ireland, as perceived by the CIA, was going to be limited to the friendly exuberance of the crowds rather than any negative agitation or upheaval. Indeed, Robert Kennedy was to state his belief that the European trip was 'the happiest time of his administration, particularly his trip to Ireland'.[63] Nonetheless, despite events such as visits by heads of state, the reality of Irish-American relations meant that this small power was never unduly influential when it came to its transatlantic neighbour and superpower.

By dealing with four areas within the Irish-American relationship, rather than just giving an overview, this essay has raised some questions regarding bilateral relations in the two decades following the Second World War. The significance of diplomatic appointments should not be under-estimated, but whether it was in the multilateral arena or in bilateral relations, the reality of relations was grounded more in symbolism than reality. In the case of Ireland and the US, bilateral ties are characterised by networks and relationships that are both deep and wide. Throughout the period under examination, indeed to the present day, Irish-American links remained strong, whether in terms of Ireland's basic western orientation or via emigration. As recently as 1991, the US State Department asserted:

> US relations with Ireland are based on common ancestral ties and on similar values and political views. The United States seeks to maintain and strengthen the traditionally cordial relations between the people of the United States and Ireland.[64]

The appointment of businessman Dick Egan as US ambassador to Ireland in September 2001 under the George W. Bush administration is, however, a further illustration of Dublin's relative position in the diplomatic scheme of things.[65] The reality of this bilateral relationship remains some distance from fulfilling the aspirations of successive Irish governments or, indeed, of the Irish-American diaspora. But this is surely to be expected, even if the history of the first two decades after the war indicates that a greater degree of consideration by both sides would have been helpful in order to develop positive bilateral relations. At the same time, they amply demonstrate the relative strengths of a superpower and small power within the context of transatlantic relations.

A Great Time to Be in America: The Irish in Post-Second World War New York City

Linda Dowling Almeida

The migration of the Irish to New York City – indeed to the United States – in the years following the Second World War is a relatively under-researched topic of American social history. Most research on Irish immigration to America focuses on the nineteenth-century famine and post-famine movement. While the Irish have been leaving their homeland for North America virtually without interruption since the 1600s, late nineteenth-century immigration was the most dramatic population movement and arguably the most significant in terms of the Irish presence in the United States. But the migration of thousands of young Irish men and women across the Atlantic between 1945 and 1960 has its own significance in understanding the dynamics of new migration to mature ethnic neighbourhoods in cities like New York and for life in Ireland in the post-war period. Of more lasting importance how-ever is the observation that the post-war migrants were the last emigrants to leave Ireland before the great social and economic change of the 1960s opened up Ireland to the rest of the world. Those young men and women left a primarily rural and agrarian country dominated by Roman Catholic dogma culturally and Eamon de Valera politically and eco-nomically. Life in Ireland propelled almost one in six young people out of the republic after the Second World War. But the post-war way of life ended with T. K. Whitaker's *Economic Development* programme of 1958, which changed Ireland forever and arguably paved the way for the so-called Celtic Tiger economic boom of the 1990s and the first years of the twenty-first century. For many Irish-Americans and immigrants of the post-war generation the enormity of that change would not be fully apparent until the next generation of immigrants entered the United States and New York City neighbourhoods in the 1980s.

In terms of overall migration to the United States in the twentieth century, the 1950s marked one of three major waves of migration. The other two occurred in the 1920s and the 1980s. Small in comparison to the nineteenth-century Irish migration and to the numbers of other im-migrant groups entering the United States after the Second World War, it is significant in terms of the continuity of Irish migration over three centuries and the perpetuation of Irish and ethnic community life in the United States. Between 1951 and 1960 the Irish totalled about 50,000 out of 2.5 million immigrants.[1] It is important to note here that since the 1930s more Irish migrants entered Great Britain than the

United States, in a reversal of nineteenth-century trends, and that pattern continued through the twentieth century. Also, for the purposes of this essay, the focus is on New York City as a destination. New York proved to be a popular port for the Irish heading to America in the 1950s. Between 1958 and 1961 more than a third of all Irish immigrants admitted to the United States went to New York City, and of those migrants admitted to major cities, at least half chose New York.[2]

Why consider this group of migrants from among the hundreds of other nationalities represented in those dynamic years after the Second World War? They did not come in the same numbers as the three million Irish who entered the United States between 1850 and 1920. And they certainly did not face the same trauma as the famine migrants. But the fact of their migration raises several unanswered questions. Why did the Irish continue to leave even after they ceased to be a part of the United Kingdom? Who were these people and why had they been overlooked in the continuum of Irish-American history? The 1950s Irish and their community in New York stood out for me from work conducted among the subsequent generation of Irish immigrants who arrived in New York City in the 1980s. As the established predecessors to the 'New Irish', the 1950s population employed, housed and often advised the younger immigrants. But it was clear that the relationship was uneasy between the groups, and what became quickly apparent was that the differences between them went deeper than age.

These two groups of immigrants left two entirely different countries. Ireland in the 1950s was a small, isolated agrarian country with a primarily rural population. Still in the throes of post-colonial transition, its political, religious and cultural leaders were fixated on keeping the Irish socially and culturally pure – free from the corruption of outside forces, particularly those emanating from capitalist and Protestant powers such as the United States and Great Britain. The immigrants who left Ireland in this period were the first generation to emerge from a truly independent country, but a country still very much aware of its colonial past and one led by the hero of its struggle for independence – Eamon de Valera. The 1980s generation also left an independent Ireland, but the new migrants were free of the cultural, political and social baggage of the past. They were raised to focus on the future, not the past, and so possessed an outlook on the world that was less parochial, more international and less humble than their predecessors. About the only experience that these two generations shared as children of Ireland was the fact that they left.

Let's go back to the 1950s in Ireland. In the post-war world, the Irish struggled economically. Life had been hard in Ireland since the 1930s and the international depression. A poor economy in the United States, followed by the outbreak of war in 1939, slowed overseas migration. However thousands, particularly men, left for Great Britain in the late 1930s and into the 1940s to join the army or work in the factories activated to support the war effort. After the war, emigration increased and the number of women leaving Ireland soon out-paced the number of men, many going to join husbands, lovers and fiancés already abroad. Ireland stagnated economically in the years after the war. Between 1949 and 1957 income grew at only one-fifth the rate of western Europe and between 1955 and 1957 Ireland was the only country in the western world in which the consumption of goods and services actually fell.[3] Young Irish men and women watched the rest of the world surge forward economically as Ireland stayed in place committed to a pastoral idyll envisioned by Eamon de Valera and his Fianna Fáil party. In 1943 de Valera delivered his famous 'frugal comfort' speech on St Patrick's Day in which he described an Ireland of self-sufficient strong farmers and small industry serving a primarily domestic market, warding off the intrusion of foreign manufacturers and products that might 'contaminate the unique culture of the nation'. Unfortunately for de Valera, not all of the residents of the countryside shared his vision and many demonstrated their disagreement by departing.

Between 1946 and 1961, 531,255 people, almost 17% of the population of Ireland, left the country. Forty per cent of Irish people between the ages of ten and nineteen who were counted in the 1951 Irish census were gone by 1961. Most of the migrants went to Great Britain, but 68,151 left for America in the period during and after the Second World War, from 1941 to 1961.[4] They were mostly young men and women in their twenties, more women than men by a small margin, and most were probably single. United States Immigration and Naturalization Service (INS) figures for 1956 show that 79% of men and 77% of women emigrating from Ireland to the United States were unmarried.

These young people wanted to begin living their lives as independent adults. An emigration report commissioned by the Irish government and delivered in 1954 states, somewhat derisively, that the Irish left for material goods and comfort, specifically 'cigarettes and cinema'.[5] But emigrant testimony offers a more complex picture. 'Kevin Morrissey had a job with the post office in Galway, as he described it, a government position that was the envy of most people in his community. When he announced he was going to emigrate, he was told he was crazy to leave such a secure job. But, according to Morrissey, the pay was so poor that his income had to be supplemented by his parents, who could ill afford the contribution. He lived too far away from the job to commute, and needed help to meet living expenses. Beyond the low pay, he found his situation very unchallenging, with little future or prospects for change. As he saw it, his only choice was to move'.[6] Another woman from Clare explained that she had to 'make a living. Being the second eldest of eleven gave little choice and to get educated took money'.[7]

For the immigrants who entered New York in this period, the city was a place of wonder, abundance and opportunity. The United States was recognised around the world as the great victor of the Second World War. Thousands of war refugees, war brides and other immigrants clamoured to migrate to America. Congress passed several pieces of legislation loosening the restrictions on immigration to accommodate the demand from around the world.[8] To the Irish the United States was a familiar destination. It is safe to speculate that most Irish had friends or family who had emigrated to America at one time or another. Many Irish tell stories of the letters and care packages that arrived from Queens, New York or Dorchester, Massachusetts, filled with clothes and messages from American relatives. The gifts and hand-me-downs suggested a land of great wealth and opportunity. Immigrants tell of childhood visits from well-dressed American aunts and uncles with jobs so good they could afford to travel and visit Ireland. For people who rarely left their village and farm communities or for those who did not often handle money, the comforts and colour of a consumer economy were quite attractive. One immigrant wrote home in the 1950s describing the quantity and variety of food in New York: 'We had to sample Chinese food – we had chicken chow mein – so much of it we couldn't get through half'.[9] The irony is that most of these 'wealthy' Irish cousins and immigrants in the United States were more than likely working-class or middle-class people who were not considered wealthy at all by American standards.

Another point to remember about emigration in the 1950s is the finality of the trip abroad. Despite improvement in sea travel (from the low point of coffin ships in the 1840s) and the increasing popularity of air travel by the end of the decade, the move to America was expensive and it was permanent. Few who left in those years could afford to return to Ireland immediately, even if the move was not successful. One woman recalls that the flight to Idlewild airport in Queens, New York (now Kennedy International airport), in 1947 took seventeen hours in the air, with one stop to refuel in Canada. Upon arriving in New York, she had neither the money nor the desire to return to Ireland.[10] For most, there was nothing to return to. As a result the trip to America, just as in the nineteenth century, was considered a final one.[11] What this means for Irish-American communities is that the immigrants worked very hard to make their stay in the United States successful. And this was no less true in the 1950s.

By the middle of the twentieth century, the Irish-American community in New York City was an ethnic power group on the wane. From about the 1880s forward, the Irish controlled politics and the Catholic church in the city. They relied on large voting blocs of Irish immigrants and Irish-Americans to carry their Democratic Party candidates into office at least until the 1930s. The community's most famous politician was Al Smith, who worked his way up through the party system to become governor of New York State in the 1920s and the first Catholic candidate for president of the United States in 1928.[12] Smith, of course, was unsuccessful in his bid for president, and back in New York, the Irish Democrats lost the mayor's office to the Republicans and Fiorella La Guardia in the 1930s. The last Irish-born mayor elected in the city was William O'Dwyer (1945 and 1949). And although the Irish remained a significant presence in city politics for a decade or more after O'Dwyer left office, their political dominance was over.

In the Catholic church, the Irish wrested control of church hierarchy in the archdiocese of New York from the Germans in the middle of the nineteenth century, centralised power in the hands of the archbishop and provided thousands of vocations for the convent and the priesthood. Every archbishop of New York since John Hughes in the 1860s has been Irish-born or of Irish descent. In the 1950s Cardinal Francis Spellman ruled from St Patrick's cathedral in Manhattan and though many Catholic immigrants of different nationalities followed the Irish into New York, the Irish still dominated church hierarchy and accounted for a substantial proportion of the faithful and the religious communities after the Second World War.

Irish neighbourhoods after the war were composed primarily of blue-collar and middle-class Irish immigrants from the 1920s, their children and grandchildren. In 1950, 40% of the Irish-born population living in the New York-Northeastern New Jersey metropolitan area were between 40 and 54 years old. They numbered three times the population of the 20- to 39-year-old group. It was an ageing immigrant community. In New York, through the 1930s at least, the Irish were still well represented among the working-classes. They made up 33% of workers at Consolidated Edison Co., 60% of the International Longshoreman's Union, 70% of the fire department and 25% of the New York Telephone Company.[13] Historian Rob Snyder describes the Washington Heights neighbourhood of northern Manhattan in the 1930s and 1940s as a stable working-class community where married couples centred their lives around their children, their church, the local bar, family gatherings, the activities of the Ancient Order of Hibernians, Division 3, and impromptu music sessions in neighbourhood kitchens. 'Single adults attended Irish dances at the Innisfail Hall or Leitrim House, frequented neighbourhood bars, and watched Irish football games in Gaelic Park until they formed their own families'.[14]

It is safe to say that a neighbourhood like Washington Heights is typical of the kind of community the Irish entered after the war. United States census data suggests that by 1960 the largest number of first- and second-generation Irish were living in the Bronx and Queens. The Woodside, Queens, neighbourhood that Kevin Morrissey moved into in the late 1950s is typical of its time: a multi-ethnic community made up of Irish, Italians and Germans of middle-class income where most of the elementary-school children attended private school and half the secondary-school students attended private high school. Given the ethnic mix of the families, chances are the private schools were Catholic. Anecdotally two immigrant families in the Bronx bear witness to the data: both had children who attended parochial school and had lived in different parishes in the Bronx and Manhattan. 'One man who emigrated in 1956 said that he and his wife left Ireland to get work in New York. They were both the children of farmers. He worked as a carpenter in the city and his wife was a housewife. In the second family, both spouses had also left Ireland to find work, the woman in 1961, the man in 1956. Like the former family, both husband and wife had been raised on farms in Ireland. However, in New York, the wife had a job with Guardian Life Insurance as a filing clerk, while her husband worked as a carpenter'.[15]

These two couples typify many of those who left Ireland in the 1950s. Take a closer look at who these immigrants were. Most were single. In 1956 the INS data show that 79% of men and 77% of women coming from Ireland were unmarried, compared to 75% of women and 71% of men between the ages of 25 and 44 in the New York City metropolitan area who were married. Probably they completed about 11 years of school, but it is unclear if that education was completed in Ireland or in New York. Eleven years is about two years longer than the average time spent in school by most Irish students at the time, suggesting either that the better educated were leaving for America or that the immigrants pursued more schooling in the US High School Equivalency programmes. The GI Bill for service men and women offered advanced education opportunities for many immigrants. In his memoir, 'Tis, Frank McCourt writes about completing his education in New York and going to New York University on the GI Bill. As regards skills or work experience, it appears that most migrants had jobs when they left Ireland, based on entry interviews with the INS. But immigrant testimony from the period suggests that they were unsatisfied with the prospects of their employment.[16]

What did they do in New York? These young people entered established ethnic neighbourhoods, moved in with families or friends, found jobs, joined the army, went to school, married, raised children and built communities. Their neighbourhoods were anchored by the parish church. Typically Irish New Yorkers identified where they lived by their parish. When asked where home was, the reply was St Simon Stock, not Valentine Avenue. John Grimes, general manager of the *Irish Echo* newspaper in 1957 and publisher from 1978 to 1987, wrote about growing up in New York City:

We didn't live in New York City, or even the Bronx – we lived in 'Visitation [parish]'. That geographical definition lingered for years. Some time later, at the Friday Good Shepherd [another Bronx parish] dances, after my opening gambit, 'Do you come here often?' – tossed off suavely with each and every partner – I'd move in with, 'Where do you live?' which was invariably answered by, 'in St Raymond's' or 'in St Philip Neri's' or the like.[17]

Like the rest of the city, the Catholic church enjoyed tremendous growth through the 1950s. Cardinal Spellman administered an aggressive building campaign that included St Vincent's Hospital as well as church-run orphanages and the addition of eighty-one new elementary schools. The number of high schools rose from 87 to 99. (Note that Cardinal Spellman's charge was the archdiocese of New York which encompassed only three boroughs of the city – Manhattan, Staten Island and the Bronx – plus seven counties outside the city. Brooklyn and Queens were part of the Diocese of Brooklyn.) The number of students enrolled in Catholic schools in the archdiocese rose from 119,429 in 1939–40 to 216,013 in 1960–61. And by 1968, the number of students enrolled in non-public schools from kindergarten to twelfth grade in New York City (including the Diocese of Brooklyn) was 448,778.[18] So in the postwar period the church was still a very powerful presence in the city and the Irish were part of it.

The strength of the Catholic church and its institutions was enhanced in many ways by its visibility, starting at the top with Cardinal Spellman. He was a prominent figure in the city and the nation. The leader of the archdiocese of New York typically holds a national pulpit. But this leader was a particularly political animal who was quite comfortable as nominal leader of the American Catholic church. The cardinal began his career in Rome and learned early on the importance of connections. He carefully cultivated influential friendships. One of his mentors in Rome, Eugenio Pacelli, later became Pope Pius XII. Spellman also counted the Kennedy family among his friends, including John, the future president of the United States. In 1945 the cardinal inaugurated the Al Smith foundation dinners as a fundraiser for St Vincent's Hospital. The event grew in prestige to the point where every major party presidential candidate has attended the dinner in an election year since the end of the Second World War. But Spellman was not the only cleric seen around town. The actual number of priests and nuns was so much greater in the 1950s than in the twenty-first century or even the 1980s that it was common to see clergy or nuns on the street. And in the years before the Second Vatican Council they were easily spotted by the traditional habits and collars that they wore. A poem published in the hundreth anniversary edition of a popular Queens beach resort (the Rockaways) newspaper recalls a typical summer in the 1940s:

In the middle 1940s
Beach 116th Street
The penny arcade
The movie (forgot the name)
And Curley's Atlas Hotel.
Hamburgers on a bun with onions made by
a nice little old lady, Mrs Cronin, and only a quarter.
My Mom, Molly being a waitress in the dining room.
It was mostly frequented by priests and sisters.
I was a locker girl in the back.
Busy place on the weekend.[19]

Literally and figuratively in the years before the Second Vatican Council and the *Humanae Vitae* encyclical, the church loomed large in the lives of New York's Catholics. Irish-American writers – among them, Elizabeth Cullinan, Mary Gordon and Alice McDermott – write of the impact the church had on the everyday lives of its parishioners in the post-war period. Cullinan's book of short stories, *Yellow Roses*, describes Irish women who 'basked in the [parish] church's reflected glory' or the woman who looked from her front porch at the services across the street at Holy Family church: 'In winter the images lasted only as long as the opening and closing of the door … On clear nights, after Benediction, she always joined the voices, floating across the warm air …'[20] Classified ads in the *Irish Echo* for housing boasted apartments near churches and schools. And ads for summer vacation rentals offered 'home-cooked meals, churches and Irish-American music'.[21] An elderly woman living in St Nicholas of Tollantine parish in the Bronx remembered when school children paraded through the street to the church for May crownings in the spring. In 1995 the park was covered with litter, and she and another woman complained of the petty crime and purse-snatching that dominated current street life.[22] The son of an immigrant whose father belonged to the Holy Name Society of the fire department, a Catholic fraternal group, recalled the annual Communion breakfast. Held the Sunday after Easter, Holy Name members attended mass said by the cardinal, then marched out of St Patrick's cathedral and down Fifth Avenue to the Commodore Hotel on 42nd Street for breakfast.[23] An immigrant in the Bronx remembers the '11 o'clock Mass was always the High Mass and before that Mass, the Hibernians assembled at Fordham Road and with the Cork Pipers Band leading them they marched down the concourse to 181st Street where they turned left into the church. At their head in habit and white cloak marched Fr Donald O'Callaghan'.[24] The rituals and pageantry of the church displayed during the holidays and for its sacraments are virtually gone from city streets today, with occasional exceptions.

The absence of these traditions speaks as much to the lower profile of the church in certain neighbourhoods as it does to the changing demographics of the city. Irish Catholic children and grandchildren departed their neighbourhoods in the 1960s and the 1970s to the suburbs as they accumulated greater education and wealth but the immigrants who replaced them were not coming from Ireland. A priest who took over St Luke's parish on East 138th Street in the Bronx remarked in 1995 that 'within a few months [of my arrival in 1966] there were no Irish families left. We are an Afro-Hispanic community at present. St Luke's was an Irish parish up to 1966'.[25]

The strength and vitality of the 1950s ethnic community can also be measured in its fraternal organisations and social gatherings. By far the most significant organisations for the Irish during the post-war period were the county organisations. These groups functioned as important networking centres for new immigrants to secure jobs, housing and a social footing in a new world. Regular meetings throughout the year allowed recent arrivals to make contacts that facilitated their first months and years in New York and made America a less foreign place. Annual dinner dances attracted hundreds of patrons and raised money for the organisations' coffers. By the end of the 1950s many of the county groups met in the headquarters of the Irish Institute on West 48th Street. The institute was founded by Paul O'Dwyer, an immigrant who landed in New York in the 1920s and whose brother, Bill, was the last Irish-born major of the city. O'Dwyer was a lawyer, social activist and occasional political candidate who was well known in the city for his support for liberal causes and for a united Ireland. With a few friends he founded the institute to maintain and preserve the culture of Ireland in Ireland and America. The institute purchased a building on the West Side, reasoning that a physical establishment lent weight and legitimacy to their cultural agenda. O'Dwyer rented meeting space in the building to the county groups to defray costs and to reinforce the impression that the address was the place where the Irish met.[26]

In addition to the county meetings, the new immigrants gathered at the weekends to dance in venues like the City Centre Ballroom on Broadway in midtown or the Jaeger House on the Upper East Side of Manhattan. Young immigrants and Irish-Americans travelled from all the boroughs, the suburbs and beyond – some anecdotes claim from as far away as Ohio – to dance to the big band sounds of orchestras led by Brendan Ward at City Centre, featuring music made popular by Glenn Miller and the Dorsey Brothers. Between sets, smaller Irish bands played traditional céilí music or ballads. The musicians alternated through the night. Immigrants recall that the dances were big events for which the young people dressed up. Rebecca Miller, a music historian, argues that the popularity of contemporary big band music can be tracked to the immigrants' desire to be modern in the new world. The traditional music of home seisiúns recalled the poverty and stark social scene of the peasant Ireland which they had left behind. They did not want to appear backward in America.[27]

The desire to separate from the old world way of life was not entirely universal, but the reticence is echoed in the apparent lack of interest in organisations like Irish-language societies. Hoping that the renewed immigration after the war would boost membership, the leader of a language society was disappointed in the poor enrolment numbers.[28] However, anecdotal evidence from around the city suggests that traditional Irish culture was alive and well. Kilkenny-born Carmelite priest Seán Reid, who was elected Grand Marshall of the St Patrick's Day Parade in 1964, claims to have been the first Grand Marshall to begin his acceptance speech in Irish and continue in English. He was also known to give his sermons at St Simon Stock in the Bronx in Irish.[29] Traditional Irish music remained popular, if not mainstream. Immigrant interviews recall impromptu music sessions erupting in kitchens all around the city on Saturday and Sunday nights.[30] Mary Ford, in a short essay entitled 'To Monahan's', writes of the great social activity in her Aunt Monahan's house, where the parish priest played cards with her family and their immigrant friends and where every Friday and Saturday night they all gathered to party. Guests filled the house for dancing and singing long into the night. Years later, as a cautious and conservative mother who runs a quiet home, Ford still wishes for her children 'a place like Monahan's where there were stories told and stories made and the backyard was paved over so that everyone could dance'.

Despite the desire of many immigrants to raise their children as Americans in America, a core group of cultural societies as well as individuals kept Irish music, dance and language alive. Three branches of the Gaelic League most active in this period were the Bronx Gaelic League, the Philo-Celtic Society, which met on the Upper East Side of Manhattan, and the Gaelic Society of New York, known as the Westside Gaelic Society, which met at St Matthew's school hall on West 68th Street, in Manhattan. What some of the activists discovered as one generation passed to the next was that the grandchildren of the 1950s immigrants sought out the language lessons, dance instructors and music tutors that the first generation had neither the time, money nor interest to pursue. Parents, like Mary Ford, recognised the value of traditional culture to the family and the community.

Irish sports enjoyed popular participation during the 1950s when young athletes could be drawn from the pool of arriving immigrants. For example, Fr Reid and a friend formed the Kilkenny Hurling Club in the late 1940s, often recruiting potential players on return trips to Ireland.[31] It was not unusual for good athletes, even in the 1980s when migration resumed, to be offered jobs or help with housing if they agreed to play with a particular club. The popularity of Irish sports ebbed through the 1970s, along with the Irish ballroom dance scene, as the community aged and had greater family obligations and as the numbers of new immigrants dwindled. The American-born children of the Irish left for the suburbs or developed interest in American sports like baseball, basketball and American football, leaving behind immigrant parents and grandparents who could not sustain the community or its activities alone.

The young Irish who immigrated to New York City through the 1950s built families and communities that revolved around their church, their job and their neighbourhood. At work, at play and at worship, they belonged to overlapping populations of Irish and Irish-Americans that reinforced their sense of identity and belonging. The neighbourhoods they lived in functioned as ethnic nurseries, reinforcing their positions as American Irish. They were not self-consciously ethnic; they were ethnic by their everyday actions, by their address, by their job and by their parish. Pete Hamill grew up in Brooklyn in the 1940s and 1950s. His parents were immigrants who left Belfast in the 1930s, but his observation of the community holds true: 'There were no great pronouncements about who we were, we were Irish because our parents were Irish and all their friends were Irish'.[32] The transmission of culture and identity occurred naturally because children were surrounded by it every day. They heard the Irish language – or at least the English language with an Irish accent – at home, in school, at church. They heard the music in the apartment next door, or at the county dances or the parish hall. They watched their fathers play Gaelic football or hurling. They met their Irish cousins when they arrived on the doorstep looking for a place to stay while they sought jobs and housing. In so tight a community, it takes very little effort to understand who you are. But as Irish in America, they pursued the American dream. The 1950s generation leapfrogged up the socio-economic ladder in America, in large part due to the GI Bill and the prosperity of the 1950s, seeking advanced education for themselves and sending their own children to college. Andrew Greeley, a priest and sociologist with the National Opinion Research Centre, argues that by the 1970s the Irish were the most prosperous and best educated white ethnic group in the country, second only to the Jews in their level of achievement.[33] One consequence of that achievement was migration out of the city. The children of the 1950s left the urban neighbourhoods of their families for the space and prestige of the suburbs, seeking to provide even better opportunities for their own children.

The transition was not without its own issues of loss and nostalgia. Alice McDermott writes most movingly of this bitter-sweet migration in her fiction. At *Weddings and Wakes* is perhaps her most symbolic work, examining the inability of the daughter of a Brooklyn Irish family to sever ties completely with her family and the old neighbourhood. She travels back into the borough from the promised land of Long Island on a regular basis to visit with her stepmother and three sisters, dragging her bewildered young children with her. The ritual of the visits form the anchor of the youngsters' memory of their mother's family, but they will not carry the traditions or the need to return to the family base with them into adulthood. And while the mother tries desperately to find what she needs in the past, her husband, the children's father, works hard to create a specific history for his own nuclear family to remember. So for them and for many young Irish the connection to the neighbourhood and that time in the Irish-American community is often torn by virtue of their lives in the suburbs and the absence of those tight neighbourhood and family bonds forged in daily contact.

Edwin O'Connor also deals with the losses associated with Irish-American success. In *The Edge of Sadness*, the reader is introduced to two Irish-American priests dealing with crises of faith, in part due to their work amongst their childhood families and parishes. O'Connor follows two or three generations of Irish-American families, suggesting that success and time in America drain the ethnicity and therefore the colour and character from the community. With each new generation, the Irish become more polished, more educated, and somehow less Irish. It is only the more observant who recognise the loss with 'an edge of sadness' for what is compromised by life in America.

It is probably safe to argue that communities like the Irish neighbourhoods of the 1950s are not likely to emerge again, for a variety of legal, social, economic and political reasons. The introduction of the New Irish generation of immigrants in the 1980s demonstrated just how much Ireland had changed since the post-war period and just how much of an impact that change had on the Irish-American community. The young Irish of the 1950s wanted to make a change. While not always happy to leave Ireland, they understood their futures to be in America. They were grateful to the new country for the opportunity it afforded them and for the most part worked hard to become Irish-American. They joined the army, they got jobs, they married, bought homes, sent their children to Catholic school and eventually college: they participated in the American dream of the 1950s. As members of an Irish-American community they also possessed the traits that have marked the Irish in America for decades – religion, Irish nationalism and loyalty to the Democratic Party. Changes on both sides of the Atlantic in the 1960s and 1970s led to changes in the Irish and Irish-American sense of identity.

New leadership in Ireland in the 1960s brought the country into the twentieth century economically, socially and culturally. Government investment in social programmes for education and health care as well as economic programmes to encourage foreign business to locate in Ireland produced jobs and opportunity for the Irish in their own country. In the late 1950s the Industrial Development Authority began courting capital and industry from around the world and Ireland joined the European Economic Community in 1973. As the 1960s progressed, marriage and birth rates rose and for the first time in recorded history more people were entering Ireland than leaving it in the 1970s. Young people raised in this period described their youth as 'heady' days and remember promises that they would not have to emigrate.[34]

The social and cultural bleakness of rural Ireland lifted as well. Television made its way into Irish homes. The country's first television network, Radio Telefís Éireann, received approval in 1960 after nearly a decade of debate that at one time involved the Vatican, because of the fear that the medium would corrupt the purity of the Irish culture. By 1980, 92% of Irish households owned a television set, introducing international news and popular culture into living-rooms throughout the country and exposing Ireland to the rest of the world as never before.[35] At the same time the Catholic church's influence on the Irish population diminished. The Second Vatican Council loosened church regulations, and the 1960s marked the start of a long period of decreased vocations in the United States and Ireland from which the church has not recovered. In Ireland, recognition of the 'special position' of the Catholic church in the Irish constitution ceased in 1972, and in later years a series of sexual misconduct and child abuse scandals further eroded the once-dominant place of the clergy in Ireland. People reared in Ireland in the 1960s and 1970s did not share the same religious strength as earlier generations. A survey taken among 1980s Irish immigrants in New York showed that 45% attended mass as often as they did at home, while 49% attended less often.[36] Another survey, taken by the *Sunday Independent* in 1995, seemed to confirm the drift away from the church: 'In 1974, 91% of respondents said they attended mass once a week, in 1989 the number was 85% and today, it is just 64%'.[37] The strength of the Catholic church and the practice of Catholicism in Ireland weakened considerably in the last decades of the twentieth century to the point that it was no longer accurate to include religion – at least, Catholicism – as a mark of Irish immigrant identity.

In a post-de Valera era, nationalism in the Irish Republic took a back seat to economic and social progress. Most of the activism concerning independence and the unification of the thirty-two counties of Ireland originated in Northern Ireland. In the United States, however, Irish nationalism and interest in the political developments in the north remained solid among a core segment of the immigrant and ethnic community. In the 1950s the *Irish Echo* followed the debate weekly, and the border campaign, waged by the Irish Republican Army (IRA) between 1956 and 1962, received front-page coverage. Interest peaked again when conflict erupted in Northern Ireland in the late 1960s, touched off by Catholic civil-rights campaigns. Sympathetic immigrants and Irish-Americans in New York organised in a variety of groups to raise awareness and money in support of Catholics and the republican agenda. The activity was not without controversy, because headlines in the mainstream press in America focused on the violence in the north and the activities of the IRA. Few Americans, even Irish-Americans, understood the complex political, social and religious history of the troubles, so many were repulsed by the violence and killing reported in Belfast and Derry. But a strong core of support for reform in Northern Ireland remained within the Irish-American community, sustained by immigrants from the 1920s and 1950s. Many Irish-Americans, then, were disturbed by the apparent apathy of the 1980s immigrants regarding the question of the north.

The following examples demonstrate the divergent views of the two generations. First consider this exchange of letters in the *Irish Voice*:

> Are [the New Irish] so selfish and uncaring as to not be concerned about the British oppression and terror in the six counties? ... The Young Irish of today are complacent and apathetic, both in Ireland and when they emigrate here. Why should I, an American, be concerned about their status, when they will not take a few hours of their time to demonstrate in support of their brothers and sisters in the six counties? Why should I care about them and about Ireland, when they seem not to care themselves?

> The majority of young immigrants came here to work, not to become political activists. We were forced to emigrate because the Irish government failed to provide jobs. Stone [first letter writer] might think it some golden rule that once [in the United States] we are all obliged to turn into raving Provos [supporters of the Provisional IRA].[38]

Fr Martin Keveny, an Irish priest sent to live among the New Irish in New York in the 1980s, noted that the people in Ireland were more preoccupied by the economy than by the troubles. He cited the visit of Cardinal John O'Connor to Ireland in 1988 as an example. The Irish honoured the cardinal for the work he did on behalf of the young Irish immigrants in the New York; Irish-Americans, on the other hand, praised the trip, according to Fr Keveny, for the attention it brought to problems in Northern Ireland.[39] So while there is current interest in the peace process in the north and the aftermath of the Good Friday Agreement of 1998, Irish nationalism does not mark the Irish immigrant or carry the significance it did for the post-war generation. Eamon de Valera died in 1975; the current generation of Irish immigrants have no memory of him, the Civil War or the Anglo-Irish War. He and his fight are part of their history. Their focus is on the present and the future, not the past.[40]

The character of the 1980s immigrant is different from that of the 1950s immigrant – not as devoted to the Catholic church, post-colonial and international in outlook, more ambivalent about settling in New York, and less in awe of the United States. So upon contact in New York these two groups of Irish immigrants did not recognise one another. What this means for Ireland and the United States is that the relationship between the two countries will have to evolve with the changes in the population. The neighbourhood communities of the 1950s – with their overlap at work, at school, at church, at sporting events and social occasions – will probably not be seen again. Those nurseries of Irish ethnic identity are not likely to emerge in the twenty-first century, with its transience and technology. The Irish immigrant no longer has to put down roots. He or she has more choices, including the option to return home. The birth of the Celtic Tiger and its vigorous economy means that once again more people are entering Ireland than leaving it. So for the present, the Irish immigrant is a more mobile being than his or her post-war predecessor. The apparent temporary nature of Irish immigration among the current generation raises intriguing questions regarding the evolution of Irish-American identity and the relationship between Ireland and America. The constant flow and settlement of the Irish in New York City neighbourhoods in past generations lent vitality and strength to the ethnic community and its identity over time. The absence of these communities – and the changing nature of the Irish character itself – removes the immigrant and ethnic community in New York and other cities from what is going on in Ireland and could weaken or distance the bonds that are built in living and working together. The lapse of immigration in the 1970s and the consequent misunderstanding and confusion that occurred when the New Irish entered Irish-American neighbourhoods in the 1980s demonstrate the significance of steady contact. But this contact is complicated by the collapse of institutions like the Catholic church and nationalism, so that they no longer cement the relationship between the immigrant and ethnic community and guide a mutual sense of identity. The 1950s generation was the last of its kind to emigrate from Ireland and settle in New York and other American cities. Theirs will be the example against which to compare the future of Irish immigrant and Irish-American relations.

Inadmissible Departures:
Why Did the Emigrant Experience Feature so Infrequently in the Fiction of the Mid-Twentieth Century?

JAMES RYAN

In *Ireland 1912–1985: Politics and Society* J. J. Lee states that 'the imprint left by emigration will feature prominently as the archaeology of the modern Irish mind comes to be excavated',[1] asserting further on that 'it is to the writers the historian must turn, as usual, for the larger truth'.[2] Quite an accolade for the writers, but as far as the issue in question is concerned, it may not be deserved. The generation of writers who might have been expected to produce the larger truth about emigration from the war years to the early 1960s did not make a conspicuous attempt to do so.

This perception is shared by a number of writers and critics. George O'Brien, writing about the current wave of emigration literature in an essay titled 'The Aesthetics of Exile', tells us that 'although earlier generations of Irish writers expounded themes of departure and return, representations of emigration and exile in their work – especially in their novels – are few and far between'.[3]

Joe O'Connor, in his often-quoted introduction to *Ireland in Exile*, observes that 'At the heart of the Irish emigrant experience, there is a caution, a refusal to speak, a fear of the word',[4] then goes on to claim that 'The silence of the Irish exile is over now'.[5] Dermot Bolger, writing about his own family's experience of emigration in *Ireland in Exile*, makes a similar claim:

> My father is from a family of seven, my mother is from one of eleven. Apart from the uncle who kept the farm in Monaghan, on one side, and the uncle who kept the house in Wexford on the other, every other member of those two families emigrated to, and remained in, Britain. The only exceptions (apart from two early deaths) were for my father and one other uncle. Both of these managed to make homes for their families in Finglas, my uncle by spending a decade of his working life sending money home from car plants in the English Midlands, and my father by leaving Ireland every working week for over 40 years as a sailor. The rest of my family vanished into a glass wall of silence which is only now finally beginning to be broken.[6]

This notion, a glasnost of sorts, is also taken up by George O'Brien in 'The Aesthetics of Exile'. 'There is now the beginning of an end of silence,'[7] he writes, but goes on to point out that methodological and

theoretical models appropriate to an appraisal of the historical, sociological and cultural significance of the exile's formal return have yet to
be devised. This is the first difficulty in tackling the issue of silence.
And, since it is not one which is likely to be resolved here, the perceptions which may emerge must necessarily remain speculative.

I would like, insofar as it is possible, to distinguish between the
experience of emigration and the broader theme of exile. This theme,
exile, has received considerable attention from literary critics, not least
because it has been seen to encompass the predicament of inner exile.
In an essay titled 'Exilic Returns: Self and History outside Ireland in
Recent Irish Fiction', Roberta Gefter Wondrich observes that 'the Irish
literary imagination is still very receptive to the appeal of metaphorical
uses of exile',[8] further asserting that 'a great number of authors and texts
may be selected in fiction to testify to this enduring fascination ...'[9] It
is intended, insofar as is possible, to confine this essay to the experience
of emigration, to ask why an experience so central to Irish life in the
middle decades of the twentieth century figured so infrequently in the
fiction of the time.

There are, of course, difficulties involved in treating the experience of emigration as separate from the broad metaphorical use of exile.
A separate treatment assumes a static relationship between the two,
which is not necessarily the case. It is conceivable, for instance, that
the political climate in which some Irish writers worked in the middle
decades of the twentieth century, being overtly hostile to a literal
treatment of many of the ills which afflicted the infant state – including emigration – may, as a consequence, have inadvertently fostered a
metaphorical treatment of the experience. It is tempting to draw an
analogy here, to point to the hostile political climate which gave rise
to the widespread use of metaphorical representations of Irish grievance
in the seventeenth and eighteenth centuries. It is an irony, surely, that
a similar state of affairs could prevail in post-independence Ireland. At
any rate, the appeal of metaphorical uses of exile to the literary imagination must surely rest, first and foremost, in the imaginative scope
they offer.

There is, of course, no obligation whatsoever on writers to address
the social or political concerns of their day. They may, like Yeats, choose
to do so often and directly, or like Heaney, not so often and not so directly.
They may include or exclude socio-political concerns, or indeed thwart
them to suit their artistic purpose. However, a reluctance to speak, as
observed by the authors mentioned above, is in itself deserving of
attention.

The notion of a 'lost' decade is somewhat problematic here. If the
perceived silence about emigration is to be allocated a time-span, a number of years when the experience *per se* is not treated, or is only very

peripherally treated in fiction, then focusing exclusively on the 1950s is unsatisfactory. In expanding the time-span to include the previous decade, as I propose to do, it is relevant to point out that some of the writers featured most frequently here had, by the early 1940s, appropriated the term 'lost' to describe their generation. In May 1943, in the context of a discussion about exile, the following question was posed in *The Bell*: 'We who remain in Ireland and sometimes grow bitter and warped and silent – are we also a lost generation?'[10] So the period appropriate to this essay can be seen to stretch more or less from the early 1940s to the early 1960s – from the publication of Seán Ó Faoláin's *Come Back to Erin* in 1940 to the early work of Edna O'Brien, though for a more identifiable end to this perceived silence, it might be safer to turn to theatre, to the first performance of Brian Friel's *Philadelphia Here I Come* in 1963. From then on there was an increasing if intermittent acknowledgement of the experience as a facet of Irish life: background for the most part, but there all the same. It features in the work of Des Hogan and, to turn to theatre again, that of Tom Murphy, writers who paved the way for a younger generation for whom the experience became something of a vocational rite of passage – Colum McCann, Joe O'Connor, Michael Collins and so forth.

In the course of this now considerably extended period, the experience of emigration does make a very occasional literary appearance, a lone swallow like Dónall Mac Amhlaigh, whose *Dialann Deoraí* was at least in progress at the time, though it was not published until 1960 and not published in translation until 1963. Meanwhile it is pertinent to ask if, during the period in question, there were factors at work – cultural, economic, social or political – which forced writers into some sort of collective denial about the experience. The answer is not an unequivocal yes, but some theories can be put forward to account for that silence.

Was there some sort of crisis of the imagination for writers? Gaelic Revival archetypes, arguably necessary icons for a body politic in the complex process of asserting a right to nationhood, had provided considerable imaginative scope for writers working in the latter part of the nineteenth century. By the opening decades of the twentieth century, however, the imaginative limitations of these archetypes had become apparent. Joyce was critical of the creators of those archetypes from the outset. In 'The Holy Office' (1904) he declares his intention to debunk the folksy writers of his day. 'I carry off their filthy streams/ that they may dream their dreamy dreams'.[11]

Of more immediate relevance here are the specific attributes accredited to these archetypes by their creators and their handlers. In describing the ideal Gaelic Athletic Association (GAA) member the 1907 *Gaelic Athletic Annual* presents, without a grain of irony, a memorable archetype: '… a matchless athlete, sober, pure in mind, speech and deed, self-possessed and self-reliant, self-respecting, loving his religion and his country with a deep resistless love, earnest in thought and effective in action'.[12]

In 1907, this character, in one or other of his guises, was an important player in the quest for sovereignty. And, with that quest about to enter a new and more urgent phase, he was destined to become an even more important player. It is conceivable that with a less urgent socio-political part to play, he and those who shared the stage with him might have given way to more complex, more engaging versions of themselves. But the drive for greater independence went on and on, so these would-be inhabitants of the mythical republic continued to have an important socio-political role to fill.

Yeats, who had played a leading role in the shaping of these archetypes, had become wholly disillusioned with his creations by 1916. 'The Fisherman', which first appeared in February of that year, is an unequivocal testament to that disillusionment. That 'wise and simple fisherman'[13] had turned out to be 'a man who does not exist, a man who is but a dream'.[14] O'Casey, with his formidable nationalist credentials, a member of the GAA, the Gaelic League, the Irish Republican Brotherhood and Irish Citizen Army, might have been expected to lend credence to this notion of Irishness. But not so. No writer was as persistent as he was in giving this mythical figure feet of clay. *The Shadow of a Gunman* was completed in 1923, *Juno and the Paycock* in 1924 and *The Plough and the Stars* in 1926: all works which succeed on a wide range of levels, not least in their capacity to demythologise. The now legendary riots, particularly at performances of *The Plough and the Stars* in 1926, can be seen as public resistance to that demythologising process.

From the perspective of those who continued to cherish the long-serving icons of the nationalist cause, the work of these writers was not merely a challenge: it was something of an attempt – albeit indirect – to subvert the quest to achieve that larger measure of independence to which nationalist Ireland was committed. But while those who cherished and protected the icons might have found ways of explaining away lack of cooperation on the part of Joyce and Yeats, there were other writers coming on stream, writers whose backgrounds conferred considerable – if not unquestionable – authority to celebrate the simple life. O'Flaherty, Ó Faoláin, O'Connor. And they did celebrate it, but it wasn't quite simple enough.

By the late 1920s the need to protect that life had become a political imperative. The result was the 1929 Censorship of Publications Act. And, as has often been noted about state censorship, an assessment of its impact must not be confined to the work it subverts or seeks to subvert; it must include the effect it has on the creative process. The climate of caution which censorship creates frustrates that process; it marginalises writers – often making exiles of them in their own country. In trying to account for the perceived silence on the part of writers about emigration in the period in question, it would be difficult to overestimate the impact of the 1929 Censorship of Publications Act. Writers were not, of course, forbidden to portray the 'matchless athlete ... self-possessed and self-reliant' skulking off to industrial England with a cardboard suitcase, but they were implicitly forbidden to compromise him, which this lamentable fate surely would have done.[15]

Gerry Smyth in *The Novel and the Nation* makes this point very succinctly when he asserts that 'Irish cultural nationalism ... constructed Irish identity in terms of a specific temporal and spiritual matrix, investing in notions of homeland, geographical community, observable borders between nations, as well as the idea of the present as part of the narrative linking national past and national future. Emigration, however, upsets this matrix, fatally displacing the subject from received concepts of national space and time'.[16]

The emigrant was not seen to have a place in Irish life as it was officially imagined, so those who sought to investigate or chronicle Irish experience – writers, historians, sociologists and so on – frequently did not see fit to include him or her in the tableau for consideration.

If there were degrees of exclusion, then emigration to England can be seen to be further outside the net, more compromising than emigration to the US. Emigrants to England had crossed over to the other camp, as it were – engaged with the very culture from which the Irish nation was seeking to disentangle itself. In *Pleasant the Scholar's Life*, Maurice Goldring makes the point that emigration to Britain was considered to be ignoble: 'Britain was the oppressing country, while America had freed itself from England; Britain was a Protestant country, America a land of religious tolerance; Britain was harsh on its immigrant workers while America was a land of opportunity'.[17]

For many who grew up in rural Ireland during the time in question, the phrase 'gone to England' carried a resonance of defeat: a resonance which I, for one, found puzzling. It was an aspect of the experience of emigration which I attempted to capture several times in the opening section of *Home from England*. The following is one such attempt. The narrator here is about twelve. He calls his mother by her Christian name, Brid. His father is home from England for his annual two-week holiday:

> I love the inside of the church. It is full of importance. Even the one lost glove lying on the high sill above where I am kneeling has a sort of sacredness about it. After the prayers we stand about outside and several people nod and smile in our direction. My father is more than pleased

with it all and when we get home he starts naming the people we saw at the church. He asks Brid lots of questions about them and others, people who live miles away, people I didn't think he knew. She gives yes and no answers in a pleasant way, all the time moving about the room picking things up and folding clothes. Then he asks a question about the family who used to live up beyond the church, the Farrells. After a very long time Brid says she is not sure and the conversation trickles to a close. I want to say England, but I can't. During the silence which follows, I look out the kitchen window and across the green at the light spindling out from the big tree, drawing in the day.[18]

As stated, the treatment of the emigration experience in fiction was inhibited by state censorship. That censorship, a concerted attempt to halt the process of dismantling mythical Ireland, remained in place for almost 40 years. Interestingly, the 1929 Censorship Act had made the archetype more identifiable than ever. Defined as he was by the aspirations inherent in the act, he became a highly visible target. But he was, at the same time, a protected species. This produced a kind of stasis, a predicament for writers, which vindicated the decision made by those who had already emigrated, notably Joyce and O'Casey, while prompting those who stayed here to see themselves as growing 'bitter and warped and silent'.[19]

Viewed from a broader perspective, it might seem that too much is being made here of the oppressive role of the revival archetype. Compared with other states who were at the time actively legislating for their own archetypes, the Irish version appears positively harmless. Germany might be appositely cited; the USSR too, with the sinister cult of Stakhanov in full swing at the time.

Perhaps it is not entirely a coincidence that the two works which are frequently cited in explorations of the literature of emigration in post-independent Ireland appeared prior to the 1929 Censorship Act. These are two short stories by Liam O'Flaherty: 'Going into Exile', which was first published in the *Dublin Magazine* in April 1924, and 'The Letter', which was first published in *The Criterion* in April 1928.

In 'Going into Exile', O'Flaherty presents the 21-year-old Michael Feeney, due to leave for the US the following day, as locked into an impossible bond with his father, a bond which grudgingly recognises the necessity of emigration but which will not allow either to give voice to the profound sadness he feels:

They stood in silence fully five minutes. Each hungered to embrace the other, to cry, to beat the air, to scream with excess of sorrow. But they stood silent and sombre, like nature about them, hugging their woe.[20]

This unquiet silence follows an exchange in which Michael's father,

Patrick Feeney, says:

> It's a cruel world that takes you away from the land that God made for you.[21]

To which Michael replies:

> 'Oh, what are you talking about, father? … Sure what did anybody ever get out of the land but poverty and hard work and potatoes and salt?'
> 'Ah, yes,' said the father with a sigh, 'but it's your own, the land, and over there' – he waved his hand at the western sky – 'you'll be giving your sweat to some other man's land, or what's equal to it'.
> 'Indeed,' muttered Michael, looking at the ground with a melancholy expression in his eyes …[22]

To a body politic, many of whom were still in the process of 'repossessing' the land in the 1920s, Michael Feeney's words are decidedly unsettling. To others, they are downright seditious. He is not merely questioning the capacity of the land to provide a decent living but is challenging those who choose to present the very kind of poverty he describes as the price of nationhood. Crucially, his departure calls the economic viability of the state into question. But the moderate economic success of the Cumann na nGaedheal government of the period, coupled with high-profile projects such as the hydro-electrical plant at Ardnacrusha, went a long way towards keeping the uncomfortable question of economic viability at bay.

It was a different matter altogether in the 1930s, 1940s and 1950s. Fianna Fáil, in adopting an economic strategy in the drive for full sovereignty – the Economic War – linked notions of material sacrifice to the realisation of nationalist goals. In the light of this development, the stance adopted by Michael Feeney, the character in the story, takes on a somewhat different hue. He was not prepared to make that sacrifice, so his decision to leave for America to better his material circumstances becomes something of a selfish act, a rejection of the values of the fledgling state. Emigration had, in the changed political and economic circumstances of the 1930s, become surreptitiously tainted with disloyalty. This had the effect of further removing the emigrant from the widely held beliefs of the nation, placing his experience outside that encompassed by the term 'Irish'. And this may, at least in some part, be seen as a further reason for the apparent silence surrounding the experience of emigration.

In the second of the stories, 'The Letter', O'Flaherty probes another element of this experience. Here the tragic lot of a young woman, a recent emigrant to America, is revealed in the reaction her mother, father, brothers and sisters at home have to a letter from her containing a cheque for twenty pounds. As the tear-stained letter is read, their jubilation at receiving so much money gives way initially to unease, then to wild despair as the possibility that the money was ill-gotten comes into their minds. 'Why did I ever come to this awful place?'[23] the girl asks in the letter – and in doing so calls into question the popularly held notion of America as a land of opportunity. But more to the point, perhaps, her supposed fate – that of a fallen woman – confirms what those on the increasingly crowded moral high ground at home believed was lying in wait for the young female emigrant.

A concern for the purity of young women, linked as it is to a concern, among other things, for the promulgation of the archetype, became more conspicuous as the Catholic church's involvement in the legislative process increased. It is interesting to note that this concern featured very prominently in what little public discussion did take place about emigration. In the immediate post-war period there was a dramatic increase in the number of young women emigrating to England. The concern for their purity is noted by J. J. Lee in *Ireland 1912–1985: Politics and Society*. He points out that 'the threat, real or imagined, to the sexual morality of female emigrants resurfaced with the huge increase in the number of girls leaving after the Second World War'.[24] Bids to safeguard these young women by compelling them to stay in Ireland came to nothing. 'Of every 100 girls in Connaught in 1946, forty-two had left by 1951'.[25] This was an astonishing statistic by any reckoning.

But if they were not leaving out of economic necessity alone, as is asserted in more than one source quoted by Lee, then why were they leaving? It is beyond the scope of an *a priori* study to compile a conclusive list of reasons, but not beyond the scope of reasonable conjecture to fix on the prevailing moral climate in Ireland as being among those reasons. Recalled as absurdly restrictive by a number of Irish women emigrants, whose experience of emigration from Ireland to Britain is recorded in a publication entitled *Across the Water,* this code of sexual morality can, in some instances, be assumed to have contributed to the decision to emigrate.[26] Voicing dissatisfaction with the prevailing moral climate would necessarily have involved criticising the Catholic church. Unacceptable from any quarter, such criticism was altogether intolerable from young, uneducated women from lower socio-economic backgrounds. The 'larger truth' about their experience of emigration was arguably the least likely of all emigration experiences to surface in any form, fiction included.[27]

A notion of Ireland as morally superior, particularly in the sphere of sexual morality, was frequently employed in the bid to assert separateness from England. If not literally presented, it was implicit in age-old representations of Ireland as a much put-upon female and England as an opportunistic and callous male. That sense of moral superiority, partly conferred by victimhood, continued to feature in the battle for total separation waged throughout the 1920s, 1930s and 1940s. Indeed, there are grounds for suggesting that it played a more prominent part in these decades than it ever had before. Widespread public tribute paid to the Blessed Virgin, particularly during the Marian Year, might be seen as highlighting the extent to which sexual purity was acclaimed. Considered in this context, there was a sense in which going to England was seen as morally retrograde. It was a suitable place for young women who had already fallen, those for instance who had conceived a child outside marriage – the corollary being that it was not an admirable life-choice for a woman who wished to be considered Irish in the then most wholesome sense of the term.

Some departures were, of course, admissible. Emigration to the missions in Africa, China and South America, unlike other forms of emigration, was widely celebrated throughout the 1950s and 1960s. Publications which chronicled the work of the missionaries were very popular. *The Far East,* for instance, had a circulation rivalling that of all the major periodicals at the time. The character in its comic slot, Pudsy Ryan, was something of a national celebrity. In the light of the widespread public tribute paid to missionary emigration, it would seem reasonable to conclude that emigration which confirmed our notion of ourselves as morally superior was laudable, while forms of emigration seen as a bid for a more tolerant moral climate were not, and therefore could not be acknowledged. One way or another the lot of the individual emigrant was to a large extent obfuscated by political and cultural imperatives.

O'Flaherty's treatment of the experience of emigration, though significant, is relatively peripheral in his work as a whole, and can be confined in the main to the two short stories considered earlier. Seán Ó Faoláin's attempts to incorporate the experience of emigration into his work are equally few and far between. His most sustained attempt can be found in a novel referred to earlier, *Come Back to Erin.* It is, in his own words, 'unmitigated bilge … all melodrama and romantic escapism …'[28] This self-confessed failure is of interest here. It raises the possibility that emigration was not amenable to the type of treatment which Ó Faoláin considered apposite. The difficulty and frustration he experienced in writing *Come Back to Erin* is documented by Maurice Harmon in his biography of Ó Faoláin. Given the socio-political climate of the time it may well be that this difficulty and frustration stemmed from the fact that he was unable to incorporate his actual views about emigration into his fiction, at least not in a way which might readily reach his reading public. This serves as a good case in point of the predicament referred to earlier on, that stasis in which some writers found themselves in the middle decades of the last century. Ó Faoláin's actual views on emigration found frequent and unequivocal expression in his journalism. He had this to say in June 1945:

Surely it is not to let the country down but to try to raise it up, to reveal the drab poverty level of life which has sent our youth stampeding to the wartime cities of Britain and now threatens another exodus of their wives and children. Surely it is the duty of our writers to keep hammering at such facts as that our children today are as hopeless putty in the hands of morons ...[29]

This hard-hitting view of emigration is in stark contrast to the one which emerges in Ó Faoláin's fiction. The view which emerges in *Come Back to Erin* is not far removed from that found in sentimental ballads or Hollywood treatments like *The Quiet Man*.

One might well ask if there was a casual socio-political interest in preserving such sentimental treatments of emigration. They were, after all, unthreatening, too cliché-ridden to spark off serious debate. It was not unusual for the government of the day to evade contentious issues by tacitly encouraging a sentimental perception of them. John A. Murphy notes this tendency in de Valera's approach to the Ulster question:

> The Republican leader deplored the 'cutting off of our fairest province': Significantly he did not dwell on the separation of Protestant from Catholic, unionist from nationalist, but rather raised a sentimental lament for the loss of a fourth green field. Regrettably, this was to be the impoverished and sterile tone of anti-partitionism for the next 40 years. De Valera and the anti-Treaty deputies could with justice be accused of taking refuge from the painful realities of the problem in a self-righteous dream world of a mystically 'indivisible' republic.[30]

That same dream world provided refuge from the painful realities of emigration. Ironically it was one which Ó Faoláin endorsed, though by no means unequivocally, in *Come Back to Erin*. But of more importance is the absence of the experience in his fiction from this point, 1940, onwards. This takes on an added significance when it is considered that no other writer of his era successfully incorporated the experience into their work either. That is not to say that they didn't want to or didn't try.

A case in point is Mary Lavin. She frequently voiced an ambition to write about the experience of emigration and made a number of attempts to do so. One attempt failed her final, critical inspection and remained unpublished. Her difficulty with the theme becomes all the more interesting when it is considered that she herself had first-hand experience of emigration. Her father had left Frenchpark, Co. Roscommon, for the US at the end of the nineteenth century. Her mother emigrated from Athenry in Co. Galway in the early part of the twentieth century. She herself was born in East Walpole, Massachusetts, living there until she was eleven, when she and her family returned to Ireland.

Interestingly, the title of the story in which she tried to deal with the experience of emigration was 'Going into Exile', the same as that used by Liam O'Flaherty. This may have been a gesture of acknowledgement, a public statement of a belief, frequently aired in conversation, that the O'Flaherty story was in every sense a classic. In later life, her frustration at her inability to produce a satisfactory fictional treatment of the experience took the form of fine-combing the O'Flaherty story in search of flaws. One of her many collections of his short stories in which 'Going into Exile' appears has a number of observations in the margins. Many of these are indecipherable, but very clearly ringed beside the title of the story is the word 'homespun'.[31] Pejorative, but presumably consoling. She seems to have been equally consoled by the fact that in the opening paragraph, O'Flaherty wrote that there was 'a deep, calm silence outside the cabin'.[32] The basis of her quibble with this would seem to hinge on the fact that the Feeney family lived close to the sea, thereby precluding the possibility of 'a deep calm silence'. She also found fault with the notion that their kitchen was 'large'.[33] But the most revealing statement of all is made in response to an image which appears at the end of the fifth paragraph. Describing how Michael Feeney felt in the clothes he bought 'for going to America', O'Flaherty writes 'they appeared as strange to him and as uncomfortable as a dress suit worn by a man working in a sewer'.[34]

'Not a good image, wonderful as the story is,' Lavin wrote in the margin, but then added 'Take heart me!' acknowledging, with characteristic forthrightness, her motivation for searching for faults.

One writer who did chronicle the experience of emigration during the period in question was Dónall Mac Amhlaigh. As observed earlier, *Dialann Deoraí* was in progress in the 1950s and provides a valuable insight into the experience of emigration to England during that time.

In the process of reimagining emigration, currently under way, Mac Amhlaigh's voice may well grow faint. Curiously, he does not appear in Tim Pat Coogan's recently published *Wherever Green is Worn: The Story of the Irish Diaspora*. New and revived myths about Ireland and Irishness contained in the quasi-heroic notion of an Irish diaspora may force Mac Amhlaigh into the margins, or out of the picture altogether. There is little or nothing in his work which might contribute to a triumphalist notion of emigration: nothing to support the view that it was – in the long run – a glorious fate.

The fact that *Dialann Deoraí* appeared first in Irish is of interest here. The concept of Irish as a language of admissibility is a well-established one, and not just in admirably realised literary works such as *Cré na Cille*, but in popular culture too. Indeed, in the film *The Quiet Man*, referred to earlier, there is a pertinent example of Irish being used in this way. The scene in question portrays a distraught Maureen O'Hara trying to disclose to a priest the fact that she has refused to allow her marriage to John Wayne to be consummated. Her failure to convey this in English prompts her to use Irish, which she does to immediate effect. Perhaps it is fanciful to draw a parallel here, but it is possible that in choosing to chronicle his experience of emigration in Irish, Mac Amhlaigh was imaginatively free in a way his fellow writers working in English were not. At any rate, the reader of *Dialann Deoraí* is left with few illusions about the lot of the post-war emigrant to England.

The English translation, titled *An Irish Navvy*, appeared in 1963. This was also the year in which *Philadelphia Here I Come* was first performed. It was the year John F. Kennedy visited Ireland, an event which, among other things, re-enforced perceptions of emigration as heroic. It was also the year in which Patrick MacGill, the most celebrated chronicler of the emigration experience during the early part of the century, died. Curiously, he died on the same day John F. Kennedy was assassinated – a fitting end to an era in which emigration rarely featured in fiction. J. J. Lee's belief that the historian must turn to writers for the larger truth may be a lot sounder than implied at the outset. It may well be that their silence is a more eloquent, a more enduring testament to the 'lost decade' than anything they might have written.

'You want to be a British Paddy?': The Anxiety of Identity in Post-war Irish Migrant Writing

Liam Harte

Introduction: The Performing Migrant

In the twenty-first chapter of Pádraig Ó Conaire's novel *Deoraíocht* (*Exile*; 1910) the rootless protagonist, Micheál Ó Maoláin, evokes the social milieu of the 'Little Ireland' quarter of London. It is an area inhabited mostly by Munster people, one of whom is a druidic labourer 'savant', a self-appointed custodian of inviolable truths who brooks no rivals:

> [I]f somebody were to disagree with anything the savant said, he would just go to the big trunk he had brought with him from Ireland and take out a parcel wrapped in linen. He would open the parcel and take out a large book in manuscript. And how careful he was of that book! He would then show you in black and white where you had been wrong. And when he closed the book to put it away he would look at you as if to say 'Now what have you to say for yourself?' But he never said a word.[1]

This cameo forcefully lampoons the traditional Irish emigrant's fierce protection of his received historical memories from the destabilising effects of migrancy and the challenges of acculturation. Although uprooted himself, the co-ordinates of this purist's cultural and national identity remain rigidly rooted in a tradition which is no less immutable for being portable. His sacred ur-text immures and immunises; his speechless refutation of dissent leaves nothing to be said. In the words of Fintan O'Toole, '[t]he struggle to survive in England is occluded by the struggle to hang on to a fixed, finished identity'.[2] Or rather, the struggle to survive is enabled – and, in its purest form, ennobled – by adherence to an unchanging version of personal and national identity.

Eighty years on, another young fictional migrant, Eddie Virago, the self-consciously postmodern anti-hero of Joseph O'Connor's *Cowboys and Indians* (1991), arrives in London clutching an altogether more subversive text: F. S. L. Lyons' revisionist classic, *Ireland Since the Famine*. Whereas the savant's weighty tome underwrites the approved ideologies of cultural nationalism, Eddie's problematises and interrogates them. As such, it is an appropriate textual analogue of this postnational migrant's blithe dismissal of the social and symbolic archetypes inscribed by the act of migration. Eddie knows the emigrant pose, but seems impervious to the associated historical pain of displacement:

> Eddie tried to feel the way an emigrant is supposed to feel. Sentimental songs and snatches of poetry drifted like remembered smells into his consciousness and then eluded him. And although he was vaguely aware of the thousands of petulant Paddies who had crossed the same stretch of sea over the decades, and over the centuries too, he couldn't actually feel anything ... His awareness was all intellectual. Pain, loneliness, isolation, they were just words, and you could have used any other words to describe the same things but it wouldn't have made any difference to Eddie.[3]

Although Eddie's intellectualism is heavily satirised here (not least because it masks the very feelings he purports to disavow), the revisionary import of his thoroughly ironic renegotiation of what it means to be a late twentieth-century Irish migrant is unmistakable.

The juxtaposition of these two bookish migrations from opposite ends of the twentieth century foregrounds one of the central tropes in literary representations of the Irish in England: the dialectical tension between adherence to a fixed originary identity and the evolution of a flexible, contingent migrant identity. This tension is played out across different literary generations and genres, assuming fresh inflections and new accents in each text. Each representation of this theme, moreover, is inscribed by the particular circumstances of its composition, and by prevailing discourses about emigration. Thus, Ó Conaire's novel engages with early twentieth-century Gaelic revivalist propaganda which stereotyped rural Irish emigration to urban England as morally corrupting,[4] whereas *Cowboys and Indians* articulates the interior world of a voluntary, middle-class 1980s migrant, a member of what O'Connor himself dubbed 'the Ryanair generation'.[5] O'Connor's text also knowingly engages with colonialist discourse which, as Suresht Renjen Bald points out, has particular resonance for postcolonial migrants:

> When the migrant is a member of formerly colonised people and the border s/he crosses marks the land of the former coloniser ... the narrative of immigration comes to include not only the loss of 'continuity' and the search for 'belonging', but also the experience and negotiation of racism and colonialism.[6]

In postcolonial Irish migration narratives, therefore, England is more than a phenomenologically constituted material world; it is also a symbolic site of identity negotiation, where the migrant subject must forge a new imaginative relationship with his or her world in order to exist fully.

In many contemporary literary representations of Irish migrancy in England, this process of identity negotiation tends to polarise around the tropes of self-effacement and self-transformation. In Anne Devlin's *After Easter* (1994), for example, Greta Flynn finds her own experience of emigration as self-erasure – 'I left Ireland in 1979, but I never arrived in England. I don't know where I went' – echoed in the lives of the fellow immigrants she meets through her work as a teacher:

> Funny how people who leave their own country stop living, in some part of themselves, in the same year in which they left. A man came to see me the other day. He left Mayo in '56, this man – and his clock stopped.[7]

A similar sense of emigration as self-negation is invoked by the elderly female protagonists in Moy McCrory's short story 'Aer Lingus' (1985), who imagine the diasporic Irish plunging into a 'darkness' which obliterates all traces of their individual and cultural identity: 'The Irish, and generations of the once Irish [...] vanished absolutely, leaving nothing of themselves but holes in the ground where they had torn up clumps of soil to take with them and plant in foreign fields'.[8] Jap Kavanagh, one of the wretched London exiles in Jimmy Murphy's *The Kings of the Kilburn High Road* (2000), bears witness to the truth of this grim intuition: 'I'm vanishin' over here, the invisible fuckin' man. I was someone at home, know that?'[9] His ultimate fate may be read in that of the Mundy sisters in *Dancing at Lughnasa* (1990), for whom Brian Friel fashions an archetypally abject emigrant death following their flight from 1930s Donegal:

> They had moved about a lot. They had worked as cleaning-women in public toilets, in factories, in the Underground. Then, when Rose could no longer get work, Agnes tried to support them both – but couldn't. From then on ... they gave up. They took to drink; slept in parks, in doorways, on the Thames Embankment. Then Agnes died of exposure. And two days after I found Rose in that grim hospice ... she died in her sleep.[10]

This trope of migrant effacement is also evident in the early novels of John McGahern, where emigration to England functions as an index of the failure of post-colonial nationalism and the politics of economic autarky. Mahoney's despondent suggestion to his son in *The Dark* (1965) – 'You can go to England if all fails. You'll work in Dagenham and they'll call you Pat' – implies that the only kind of visibility available to the Irish in England is one which objectifies them as targets of racism and discrimination.[11] The milder effects of such racial 'othering' are registered in *The Barracks* (1963), where nurse Elizabeth Reegan is regularly assailed by cries of '"So you're Irish, are you!" in the tone that it's a miracle you seem civilised'.[12] In its most extreme form, however, such visibility can have pathological consequences, as the troubled heroine of William Trevor's *Felicia's Journey* (1994) discovers at the hands of the psychotically racist Joseph Hilditch.

One obvious and much-favoured alternative to such vulnerable visibility is strategic invisibility. Defined as subordinate others by the power structures of the dominant host culture, many Irish fictional migrants respond by reinventing themselves, often taking on as much protective coloration as they require to mask their ethnic difference. This means that their identity assumes a strategically performative dimension; they seek to 'pass' as non-Irish in order to avoid the negative consequences of identification.[13] Luke Moran, the dissenting eldest son in *Amongst Women* (1990), is one such immigrant impersonator. Having renounced the patriarchal order of the fortress-like Great Meadow, his father's dominion, we learn that he is busy 'turning himself into a sort of Englishman' in London.[14] Likewise, Helen Flynn, Greta's sister in *After Easter*, knows that her commercial career in England depends on the effective creation of a marketable self. As a northern Irishwoman, however, her self-dramatisation is complicated by issues of gender and nationality. Hence, her audacious decision to adopt an American accent, which she rationalises in ruthlessly pragmatic terms:

> London isn't a good place to have an Irish accent right now. I find when I'm buying or selling an American accent gets me through the door. Whereas an Irish accent gets me followed round the store by a plainclothes security man.[15]

Similar transgressive roles are performed by the intrepid Caithleen Brady in Edna O'Brien's *The Country Girls* trilogy (1960–64) and by Kate Quinn in Deirdre Madden's *One by One in the Darkness* (1996), both of whom rename and refashion themselves on moving to London. What all such migrant protagonists recognise is that they must become the active agents and not merely the passive subjects of transformation. Moreover, since their future depends upon the effective performance of a translated self, they must be prepared for the losses and gains which the act of translation brings.

As this brief overview suggests, the themes of identity articulation and negotiation occupy a dominant place in twentieth-century representations of the Irish migrant experience in England. The point needs to be repeated, however, that each literary expression of these themes is coloured by the prevailing cultural and ideological discourses of its time, so that there are many individual variations within the overall pattern. In this essay I want to examine the thematic variations disclosed in two post-war migrant texts: Walter Macken's *I Am Alone* (1949), which focuses on a young migrant's struggle to forge a new identity amidst the burgeoning modernity of late 1930s London, and Tom Murphy's *A Whistle in the Dark* (1961), which dramatises an Irishman's doomed attempt to extricate himself from the oppressive forces of family and community in order to advance himself socially and materially in

1950s Coventry. My argument is that these texts rehearse one of the central tensions permeating mid-twentieth-century Irish society – namely the tension between the values of rural fundamentalism and urban modernity – through their dramatisation of the theme of migrant self-fashioning. Both works feature migrant protagonists whose identities are in a state of transition, shifting between the polarities of their original and surrogate worlds. Their liminality means that they inhabit an intermediate zone which Homi Bhabha has described as the 'third space', a zone 'where the negotiation of incommensurable differences creates a tension peculiar to borderline existences'.[16] Now while these characters' 'borderline negotiations of cultural translation' are fully realised as singular experiences, I believe they can also be read allegorically in relation to unresolved tensions in Irish society at large.[17] It is my contention, therefore, that both texts are characterised by a double focus: their realistic portrayals of the travails of migrant protagonists in England are also emblematic of the challenges and stresses which attended the course of Irish modernisation in the latter half of the twentieth century.

The historical circumstances of the production of these texts, which form an important part of their shared thematic structure, can be briefly summarised. The period between the dates of their composition saw the newly established Republic move from an adherence to the policies of economic autarky to the implementation of a programme of rapid industrial expansion and economic modernisation. This ideological *volte-face*, the so-called Lemass/Whitaker 'revolution', exposed deep anxieties within Irish society about the far-reaching consequences of modernisation and its impact on traditional practices, values and beliefs. As Conor McCarthy points out, post-war American modernisation theory was the intellectual analogue of this socio-economic realignment. This theory was founded on a dichotomy between traditional societies, characterised by 'face-to-face social relationships, identities defined in local terms, the extended family [and] clientelist relations with political authority', and modern societies, which were defined as 'meritocratic, centred around the nuclear family, having a much more diffuse set of social relationships and a principally bureaucratic relationship with political authority'. As McCarthy makes clear, the underlying assumption was that 'this move from tradition to modernity is socially, economically and politically positive and progressive'.[18] Both works under discussion here bear the imprint of this thinking insofar as their narratives are subtended by a view of post-war Ireland as a society blighted by the regressive values of provincialism and nationalism, whereas England is associated with the progressive values of secular industrial modernity.

Such a view of emigration, of course, was profoundly at odds with the one voiced by many members of the Irish political and religious establishment in the 1950s. To them, English modernity was synonymous with moral and spiritual corruption and the attenuation of Irish character and identity. These concerns grew as the number of people out of work soared to new heights, and the 'second-wave' of Irish migration to Britain, which had begun in the mid-1930s, reached its zenith.[19] The majority of these migrants came from rural agricultural backgrounds and many ended up in British cities, much to the dismay of commentators such as the writer Bryan MacMahon, who in 1954 complained: 'The pattern of Irish life in the shoddy towns of industrial England is yet to reveal itself; it seems rather a pity that the rural Irish did not emigrate to rural England'.[20] However, as Fintan O'Toole has observed, it was in these industrial towns that rural migrants encountered an advanced form of capitalist modernity and as such were forced to inhabit an Ireland of the future long before their stay-at-home counterparts.[21] While migrant writers of the 1950s such as Dónall Mac Amhlaigh and John B. Keane are primarily concerned with chronicling the loneliness and alienation of the Irish in post-war England, Walter Macken and Tom Murphy focus on the dilemmas faced by migrant protagonists who wish to evolve new narratives of belonging.[22] By exploring whether it is possible for such displaced subjects to construct a viable subjectivity which reconciles the values of a traditional, rural society with those of a modern, industrialised one, *I Am Alone* and *A Whistle in the Dark* register several of the tensions and contradictions upon which post-1950s Irish society was built.

MAKING A HOME IN THE MODERN MAELSTROM: *I AM ALONE* (1949)

I Am Alone, Walter Macken's second novel, opens with an evocation of one of the most quintessential of Irish emigrant experiences: the boat journey from Dun Laoghaire to Holyhead. Our first impression of the protagonist, Pat Moore, is filtered through the penetrating gaze of an officious Dublin customs officer, who mentally categorises him as '[o]ne of the lower middle-class, poor but honest'.[23] However, Pat's atypicality among economic migrants of his class and generation is immediately signified by a volume of Shakespearean plays in his suitcase, an emblem of his aspirations to self-betterment, his burgeoning intellectualism and his affinity for English culture. His atypicality is further underlined by his striking autonomy of mind and contempt for the pieties of nostalgic emigrant nationalism, which anticipates Eddie Virago's irreverence by a full four decades:

> So what, he thought, am I expected to feel? Sorrow, tenderness, a lump in the throat, a knot of jumbled Irish emotions in the guts? Listen, he said, inside, you can stuff it up your jersey and if you have room in the same place you can squeeze Caitlin Ni hOulichaun along with it. He felt a great excitement in him that he was leaving … He … gathered a spit between his teeth and threw it at the water. The wind took it and whipped it away

so that it might have landed on the distant hills. Well, they can have it, he thought (p. 9).

Pat's iconoclastic leave-taking – is there a submerged trace of Joyce's 'snotgreen sea' here? – is that of a disaffected internal exile chafing under the constraints of cultural as well as economic deprivation. Emigration promises the freedom to forget the force-fed orthodoxies of cultural nationalism and re-create himself in a new nation.[24] Eager to embrace the modernity that England represents, he takes a subversive delight in seeing the myths of Irish pastoral life dissolve before his eyes: 'Why, he thought, slightly shocked, the fields are green! Then he laughed. Another illusion gone' (p. 14).[25] Feelings of homesickness are promptly rationalised and the first stirrings of nostalgia defused by a clear-eyed pragmatism born of a critical awareness of the gap between myth and reality:

> He had been in very small boats on rough seas before when they were out fishing for pollack and mackerel, and for a second his mind flashed back to the other [Galway] bay, with the seas sweeping into it and the glitter of sun on silver sands. Yeh, he thought, and the glitter of sun on stale margarine and bread, because you couldn't afford to buy anything else … (p. 11)

This opening chapter clearly establishes the protagonist as a migrant in flight from the conservative forces of a moribund, tradition-bound society. How ironic, therefore, that his flight from tradition should initially take him closer to it. His London lodgings turn out to be a miniature version of Catholic Ireland, its '[w]indows and door painted a pale green, like Mother Eire's cloak', its owner a man 'living his life out of the penny catechism' (pp. 21, 27). This zealot's fundamentalist outlook leads him to denounce England in archetypally moralistic terms as a pagan land of decadence where Catholic Irishmen lose their religion and bring shame on their nation. However, Seamus, the Connemara man he meets on his first labouring job, offers Pat an altogether more positive reading of the migrant experience, in which he contrasts the drudgery and factionalism of Irish working life with the meritocratic respect available to workers in England:

> Here there's a bitta dignity being a workman. They don't give a damn who yeh are or where yeh kem from or what way yeh talk. Can yeh work? they ask. And if yeh can work you're as good as the next man and better than most (pp. 43–4).[26]

Pat concurs with this optimistic, liberatory version of emigration and later expresses a similar admiration for English egalitarianism as opposed to 'the silly, petty, frightful snobbery of the small Irish town' (p. 47). However, he is antipathetic towards many aspects of immigrant Irish culture in London, particularly the nostalgic allegiance to local origins, which he regards as a barrier to integration and assimilation:

> Funny, he reflected, how they always called one another by the counties or towns they had come from. He was Pat from Galway. Why, he wondered? It would be better if they didn't hang on to their counties but tried to become part of the land they were living in. Naming you from your own place sometimes gave rise to nostalgia (p. 50).

He is also critical of the transplanted provincial rivalries and macho posturing that characterise the social inter-action of London Irishmen. When a fight breaks out between rival groups of Galway and Kerry migrants in a dance-hall, for example, he admits to feeling ashamed to be Irish. The 'return of the primitive' (p. 56) is how he describes it to his English girlfriend Maureen, a phrase which recalls the classic colonial binary of civility and barbarity and signals his own assimilative aspirations.

Unlike Seamus, therefore, Pat's desire for social status and acceptance means that he is not content to be a 'déclassé' labourer (p. 47). His infatuation with the snobbishly English middle-class Lelia Manning heightens his sense of social inferiority and outsiderness, while simultaneously strengthening his resolve 'to work the head and wear a white collar'. Confident in his conception of England as a land of meritocratic opportunity – the great promise of post-1945 welfare socialism – he secures a job as an insurance agent and begins to see himself as 'one of the great middle class' (pp. 111–12). Lelia remains unimpressed, however, having already accepted a marriage proposal from the affluent George. Still reeling from the shock of rejection, Pat proposes to the staid, respectable Maureen and sublimates his desire for social advancement in a modest dream of suburban ordinariness.

As this summary suggests, *I Am Alone* broadly conforms to the dominant thematic of Irish migrant writing outlined in my introduction. Macken's protagonist equates upward social mobility with assimilation and so deliberately seeks to refashion himself in order to gain entry to the club of bourgeois, white-collar Englishness. Changing his appearance and accent are the most obvious expressions of his desire for a new belonging. Buying a pinstripe suit, for example, 'made him feel much better, as if with this new suit bought in England he was at last becoming part of the place, getting rid of his former identity' (p. 49). But this process of self-reinvention is not an untroubled one. Rather, several layers of ambivalence accumulate around the protagonist's attempted apostasy, giving rise to feelings of self-division and contradiction. He finds that his identity and history cannot be erased by a simple change of location, clothes and accent. The forces of 'tradition', which the novel identifies as being socially conservative and politically nationalistic, persist at the heart of industrial modernity in the shape of his fellow Irish migrants, many of whom are defiantly resistant to English assimilation. Their presence serves as a permanent reminder of the indelibility of origins and a rebuke to his bourgeois ambitions of self-betterment. His desire for social acceptance is further complicated by his personal allegiance to friends from home, despite his antipathy to their behaviour and beliefs, and by his experience of anti-Irish hostility. For all his efforts to fit in, Pat is powerless to prevent the dominant imperialist discourse from stigmatising him as one of the 'filthy Irish that kyme over in a savage style' (p. 149), thereby reminding him of the deeply entrenched barriers to Irish assimilation in English society. Moreover, his admiration for the English entrepreneurial spirit is tempered by reservations about the ethical values of commercial culture, reservations which eventually cause him to resign from his insurance job because he believes customers are being financially exploited.

What purports to be a narrative of immigrant inclusion, therefore, is actually a mapping of one migrant Irishman's negotiation of the space of transitional identity, within which he must confront difficult choices and dilemmas. These anxieties are thrown into sudden relief when he discovers that Seamus is not the unassuming labourer he appears to be but an active IRA volunteer engaged in a London bombing campaign. Furthermore, his comrade in arms turns out to be an old schoolfriend of Pat's, Jojo Keaveney, whom he meets by chance in Piccadilly Circus. One could hardly imagine a more forceful embodiment of the past from which he is trying to escape or the difference he is trying to downplay than these two republican militants. Their radical divergence threatens his desire to become an invisible insider and jeopardises his relationship with his now pregnant wife. Although he remains outwardly calm in the face of police surveillance and questioning, inwardly Pat struggles to come to terms with this abrupt collision of his original and surrogate worlds, and in particular its effects on his quest for a new identity.

The eruption of republican militancy at the heart of Pat's metropolitan existence presents him with a stark test of his commitment to transcend tradition and make himself 'at home in the maelstrom', which Marshall Berman suggests is the hallmark of the modern consciousness.[27] There is no doubt that he is opposed to the politics of purblind republican nationalism. The clearest expression of this occurs in chapter twelve during a set-piece debate between Pat and Jojo. The latter's espousal of an uncompromising irredentism – he explains, confusingly, that he is on a political mission to 'restore' the 'castrated corpse' of the Irish Free State to 'full virility' – prompts Pat to defend ordinary English people who 'have never been to blame for anything that happened in Ireland', and to voice a hitherto concealed, and somewhat unconvincing, socialist conviction: 'What I care about is the number of poor people there are in the country, with empty bellies' (pp. 183–4). Opposition to republican militancy does not lead to axiomatic condemnation, however. In fact, Pat harbours a kind of anguished empathy for his fellow countrymen. While he connives in civilised outrage with his English neighbours, he privately understands Seamus and Jojo's motives and sees a certain honour – even nobility – in their purposeful idealism. Moreover, he believes that both are essentially good men, their violent deeds notwithstanding, and is prepared to lie to the police to protect Jojo's true identity.

The most disconcerting outcome of this interaction between past and present, however, is the extent to which these men, as embodiments of tradition and continuity, activate an archaic longing in Pat for a lost paradise of organic community sanctioned by the natural order. He first experiences the atavistic pull of this sentimental pastoralism when Seamus, his cover blown, abruptly leaves London for Connemara:

> For a few seconds then he [Pat] stood there on the street and he felt lost … Seamus had been a tenuous link that had bound him with home. To look at him was to see men trundling turf barrows on a bog with a great mountain rising behind them. Or men in a currach struggling with their cork on a scornful sea. Or the smell of hay newly cut by a swishing scythe, and bulging brown muscles raising forkfuls of it to the top of a cock of hay … All so far away, and so different to this carefully worked out civilisation of which he was now a part, with his flat in suburbia and his tiddly job, and the warmest part of it was Maureen and the English limpid eyes. For her it was worth all of it, but he felt that Seamus going had taken away a part of something. It didn't matter about why Seamus went. He put that out of his mind, the wrongs and the rights of it. It was Seamus as a person and what he had meant (pp. 156–7).

Here we see Pat in the grip of the very structure of feeling he deplores in other migrants: nostalgia for a utopian past or, in Salman Rushdie's terms, a fabulated 'imaginary homeland'.[28] The image of all that appears to have been lost in transit suddenly threatens to overwhelm him and the narcotic appeal of an idyllic west, which stands as a microcosm of the nation as a whole, proves almost irresistible. The past is fetishised as the embodiment of a unique cultural essence and then filtered through a redeemingly benign lens so that the impoverished, claustrophobic society he fled from is transformed into a peasant arcadia. This nostalgic lens also filters out politics: Pat's primitivist vision is predicated upon a separation of the human and the political realms which disavows the co-existence of republican militancy and western pastoral. In effect, nostalgia blinds him to the ways in which a relentless sentimentalisation of the past can fuel a political ideology of violence.

Although one critic has recently claimed that 'the critique of nostalgia and various forms of nationalism' is the dominant note of Irish migrant writing, a significant number of post-war texts register the power of nostalgia over the deracinated imagination nonetheless.[29] The process by which memory and desire manufacture idealised images of home is memorably rendered in Brian Moore's *The Lonely Passion of Judith Hearne* (1955) through the character of James Madden, whose migrant imagination transforms the monochrome reality of rural Donegal into a hyper-real landscape with all the lurid allure of a John Hinde postcard: 'The little place went Hollywood in the mind. The fields grew green, the cottage was always milk-white, the techni-coloured corn was forever stooked, ready for harvest'.[30] If this is nostalgia of the full-blown, stereotypical variety, then Friel's *Philadelphia, Here I Come!* (1964) dramatises its converse, nostalgia *avant la lettre*. Gar O'Donnell prepares for nostalgia *before* emigrating by transforming the recent past into a sentimentalised version of itself, so that 'even now, even so soon, it is being distilled of all its coarseness; and what's left is going to be precious, precious gold ...' By the end of the play the present is being subjected to the same prospective process, as Gar's heightened vision fetishises even the most mundane household rituals: 'Watch her carefully, every movement, every gesture, every private little peculiarity: keep the camera whirring; for this is a film you'll run over and over again – Madge Going to Bed on My Last Night at Home'.[31] Both of these examples bear out Fred Davis' observation that 'in the clash of continuities and discontinuities with which life confronts us, nostalgia attends more to the pleas for continuity and to the comforts of sameness'.[32]

In Pat Moore's case, however, nostalgia signifies more than a despairing rejection of an uncomfortable, fractured present in favour of a secure and certain past. It also betokens a crisis of his faith in the modernising impulse and a weakening of his resolve to transcend the constraints of tradition. Through Seamus and Jojo he feels the regressive tug of attachment to an authentic cultural homeland and an identity based on the values of rural fundamentalism. This essentialist, anti-modern version of identity runs counter to his attempt to evolve a more flexible, cosmopolitan subjectivity and exposes the instability of his migrant quest for a new belonging. Indeed there is a recurrent emphasis on the fearful loneliness of Pat's struggle with the competing claims of tradition and modernity, right up until the final chapter, where his inner paralysis is suddenly relieved by two momentous events: Jojo's capture by the police and the birth of his son. This symbolic coincidence rescues Pat from the perils of nostalgia and decisively reinvigorates his commitment to a future forged from a robust engagement with urban modernity. The ideal of a culturally authentic, territorially based nationality for which Jojo is fighting dissolves into a flexible concept of belonging symbolised by Pat's newborn baby who, Macken suggests, may evolve a genuinely modern identity, which will simultaneously encompass and transcend the antithesis between tradition and modernity. Pat now sees Jojo in a new light, as a man whose uncompromising political idealism and dangerous nostalgia place him outside the pale of modernity. In a pivotal moment of introspection he resists the renascent appeal of nostalgic traditionalism and resolves to continue his struggle for self-fashioning at the metropolitan centre:

> For a few moments he felt a terrible hunger in him to be at home again. People around him he knew. To whom you could talk ... And the smell of the sea and the touch of it ... All that. But it was nostalgia. It wasn't living. His fight was here. Something that was worth fighting for too. A chance for your own happiness and a something carved from adversity (p. 247).[33]

As I have already indicated, the really significant thing about this shift in perspective is that the nostalgic old-style nationalism which Jojo represents is replaced by a modern version of multiple belonging, the blueprint for which is embodied by the protagonist's '[h]alf English and half Irish' son (p. 250). Macken's affirmation of such non-traditional forms of identification based on notions of plurality and hybridity clearly anticipates current formulations of diasporic identification and imbues the conclusion with a distinctly contemporary feel. Here is a child for whom Bhabha's concept of the 'third space' may well become a lived reality, whose future may be an interstitial one 'that emerges *in between* the claims of the past and the needs of the present'.[34] Indeed he may well become one of those radically modern migrants whom Rushdie defines as being 'free of the shackles of nationalism', who 'root themselves in ideas rather than places, in memories as much as in material things; ... people in whose deepest selves strange fusions occur, unprecedented unions between what they were and where they find themselves'.[35] Despite the imminence of world war, the closing image leaves us in no doubt about the inevitability and desirability of modernisation. The migrant protagonist is shown advancing towards a 'determined and hopeful dawn' (p. 252), relieved of his burden of fear and loneliness and the weight of historical fixity.

DYING FOR RESPECTABILITY: A WHISTLE IN THE DARK (1961)

One of the most dramatic moments in *I Am Alone* occurs at the beginning of the penultimate chapter when IRA gunman Jojo Keaveney bursts into the suburban home of Pat Moore and his wife in a desperate bid to evade police capture. This sudden visitation brings the polarities of Pat's migrant world into intimate juxtaposition. The sanctuary of the home, symbol of ordered English modernity, is finally breached by the embodiment of militant Irish nationalism, making further equivocation impossible. Whereas this emblematic event occurs near the end of

Macken's novel, the opening scene of Tom Murphy's *A Whistle in the Dark* reveals that the domestic order created by the play's modernising agent, Michael Carney, has already been thoroughly violated by the recalcitrant forces of tradition in the form of his 'mad brothers'. The fact that the action never extends beyond the claustrophobic front room of a Coventry council house further underlines the key difference between these texts: Murphy's dramatisation of the quarrel between tradition and modernity is altogether more darkly intimate than Macken's and proceeds towards a much bleaker denouement in which the agents of tradition are shown to be mutinous, tyrannical and ultimately lethal.

Like Pat Moore, Michael Carney is a migrant in flight from the disabling effects of a society governed by the values of rural fundamentalism. His move to Coventry and marriage to Betty, his English wife, represents a determined attempt to leave behind a culture of nepotism, discrimination and social exclusion and embrace the opportunities available in what he perceives to be a modern industrial meritocracy. Emigration is also crucial in that it offers him an opportunity to break away from his sociopathic, tribalistic family and so shed an identity based on fealty to blood and soil. His past and future identities cannot be easily partitioned, however, since like Macken's protagonist, Michael is shadowed by the spectres of the past he wishes to exorcise. Three of his four brothers – Harry, Hugo and Iggy – have followed him to Coventry and have taken up residence in his home. As the action begins, this trio of disruptive lodgers are preparing for the arrival – or, more accurately, the invasion – from Ireland of their youngest sibling, Des, and father, Dada. With Michael at work, Betty has to endure his brothers' racist and misogynistic taunts, as well as the domestic chaos they cause. On his return, she poses a question which frames the clear choice her husband faces: 'Which comes first, which is more important to you, me or your brothers?'[36] This question is literally and metaphorically restated at various points in the narrative until Michael is eventually forced to choose between an anachronistic identity rooted in tribalism and tradition and a modern subjectivity based on a rational adaptation to the mores and manners of industrialised society.

Fintan O'Toole's description of Michael as 'the new Ireland labouring to be born' accurately characterises the transitional stage of his identity evolution.[37] He is, in Anthony Roche's words, 'the character in the play most obviously torn between the life into which he was born and the life he is trying to make, between the past and the present'.[38] In the opening act, he appears sufficiently distanced from the life into which he was born to be able to satirise patronising English expectations of Ireland's primitive quaintness in an accent borrowed from the life he is trying to make. But his mocking suggestion that the family sup tea from saucers and adopt a pig as a pet suddenly mutates into a parody

of modernisation Irish-style: 'And we'll be progressive, and grow sham-
rocks instead of geraniums. And turn that little shed at the end of the
garden into a hotel for the fairies and leprechauns' (p. 7). Michael evi-
dently regards Irish modernisation as little more than the commercial-
isation of folklore masquerading as progress, a strategy which seems hopelessly inadequate compared to the advanced industrialism of Coventry.
While his ironic humour suggests he is confident of having made the
successful transition from fairyland to factoryland, he has yet to experience the full force of 'the return of the repressed' and its radical potential to upset his assumptions and aspirations.

Michael's brothers' belligerent assertion of their racial otherness
problematises his desire to assimilate himself into English society through
self-discipline and hard work. Whereas he has firmly aligned himself
with the value systems of an industrial capitalist society, they are im-
placably committed to 'a way of life that believes it can elude urban industrial civilisation in the name of a warped, sentimentalised romance
of the past'.[39] Unlike him, they have no faith in the benign order of bourgeois society, whether it be English or Irish. On the contrary, they are
shunned outsiders in both societies, excluded from structures of power
and influence. In Ireland they are stigmatised as 'tinkers'; in England
they are 'thick Paddies'. Wherever they go they are rogue warriors, ready
to take on all comers, united by the belief that 'a man must fight back'
(p. 28). They regard Irish culture as being inherently nepotistic, populated by pious opportunists – 'Holy Marys pulling strings, and talking
about merit' (p. 14) – who hypocritically ingratiate themselves with those
in positions of civic and clerical power in order to gain preferential treatment.[40] The humiliation they endured at the hands of such authority
figures – the memory of which almost moves Harry to tears in Act Three
– has displaced itself to Coventry where, as thuggish pimps and racke-
teers, they exact remote revenge for the real and imagined injustices of
their youth.

O'Toole's claim that A Whistle in the Dark 'is not a play about emigration, even though it is set in England' seems to me to overlook the
extent to which Murphy's portrayal of the Carney brothers' corrupt and
criminal activities illuminates the darker recesses of working-class Irish
immigrant culture in 1950s Britain.[41] Several unpalatable truths are laid
bare here in a way that still has the power to disturb, 40 years on from
the play's original production. While it was the physical and verbal
violence which attracted most comment in the early 1960s, the sight
of Irish migrants in England being openly and belligerently racist is arguably more disconcerting for contemporary audiences. Far from being
the perpetual whipping boys of English racism, Murphy suggests that
many Irish immigrants were themselves racist and as such colluded in
the exploitation of other ethnic-minority groups whose numbers were

swollen by the influx of commonwealth immigrants in the 1950s. Thus we learn that Iggy Carney abuses his position as foreman on a building site to exploit the mainly black workers, who avail of the sexual services peddled by Harry, who is a pimp. Harry himself discloses a particularly malign racist streak when he voices a wholly disingenuous respect for black and Asian immigrants based on a devious recognition of their more vulnerable position in the racial pecking order:

> But I still like them. Respect them. Black, Muslims. They stick together, their families and all. And if they weren't here, like, our Irish blue blood would turn a shade darker, wouldn't it? … And then some people'd want our cocks chopped off too (p. 10).

His rancour is not confined to blacks and Asians, however. Harry knows that there are 'a lot of lousy Irishmen too' (p. 12), and later in the play turns his vitriol on the patronising attitudes of the cossetted Irish middle-classes who '[p]ray for the poor dirty pigs over here, now and at the hour of our death' (p. 80).

Michael displays no such bigotry or intolerance. When asked if he shares his brothers' hatred of the 'fly shams' of his youth, his reply underlines the psychological distance he has travelled: 'I know them. But they don't eat me' (p. 13). Predictably, it is Harry, the voice of recalcitrant tradition, who immediately punctures his presumption of immunity from prejudice: 'Your big mistake is thinking they don't do it to you'. He goes on to deny the possibility of transcending one's original identity and, in a highly charged scene, pours scorn on his brother's assimilationist aspirations by insisting on the rigidity of ethnic divisions:

HARRY: You're not a Paddy?
MICHAEL: We're all Paddies and the British boys know it.
HARRY: So we can't disappoint them if that's what they think. Person'lly, I wouldn't disappoint them.
MICHAEL: You won't fit into a place that way.
HARRY: Who wants to?
MICHAEL: I do.
HARRY: You want to be a British Paddy?
MICHAEL: No. But a lot of it is up to a man himself to fit into a place. Otherwise he might as well stay at home (p. 14).

There is clearly no space for hybridity or transgression in Harry's deterministic scheme of things. His disparagement of Michael's self-betterment ambitions and obeisance to 'them with the lovely white collars' (p. 79) is predicated on the belief that he will never escape his primary identification as one of the 'tinker' Carneys from Mayo. Though Michael believes otherwise, the gravitational force of his atavistic identity becomes increasingly hard to resist as the play unfolds.

Michael's crisis of identity and belonging is deepened by the arrival of Dada and Des, in each of whom he sees elements of his own character and choices reflected back at him. Dada embodies the past he longs to be rid of; Des, the future he might once have had. Dada enters trailing a hurricane of failure, self-delusion and angry remorse behind him. Like McGahern's Michael Moran, he is a manipulative fallen patriarch who has submerged his inadequacies in a compensatory myth of family supremacy (the 'World Champ Carneys'), which mesmerises all but his disaffected eldest son, who is Luke Moran in all but name. Whereas his father and brothers live by the light of their violent impulses, Michael has chosen the path of reason and self-discipline. The dialectic is starkly drawn: they are compelled to fight, he to talk. Thus he insists on countering Dada's sententious rhetoric with 'plain talking', only to be intimidated into silence by violent threats and reduced to the status of a child by his father, who taunts him with the truth: 'You can talk a bit, but you can't act. Actions speak louder than words. The man of words fails the man of action' (p. 31). Yet despite the simmering antagonisms between them, father and son have much in common. Both are driven by a desperate desire to transcend their lowly origins and gain social respectability, yet neither can reconcile themselves to their abject failure to achieve this. Consequently, a profound self-loathing is at the core of their tortured, conflicted selves. They also share similar behavioural patterns – Michael's harsh treatment of Betty replicates Dada's neglect of Mama – and linguistic affinities, as when Michael's speech patterns converge with those of his father in Act Two to create a brusque, elliptical dialogue. It is precisely because Michael recognises the insidious psychological repercussions of his bitter patrimony that he is driven to challenge his father's sovereignty at every turn.

Des, on the other hand, emerges as a much more benign doppelgänger. Young, impressionable and still relatively innocent, he brings out a Holden Caulfield-like paternalism in his older brother, who sees him as the last chance for achieving the holy grail of family respectability. But first he must be saved from the corrupting influences of the tribe, something which Michael believes can only happen in Ireland. This view, tellingly, causes him to revise his earlier characterisation of Ireland as a defectively modern society and posit instead a version of Irish modernisation in which merit prevails over nepotism and where industry and entrepreneurialism will be rewarded. Ireland is now imagined as a country where Des might prosper by getting 'something decent, a good job' (p. 16) and so avoid the socially indecent fate of his brothers. To exemplify his point, Michael cites the case of the Flanagan family, former neighbours of the Carneys, who rose 'from the dirt of the roads' – their father was a road sweeper – to socially respectable professions (p. 40). Michael's point is that there is no necessary contradiction between Irishness and progress, that it is possible both to be from Mayo *and* to be modern. But Des himself is the first to puncture such optimism by rejecting the suggestion that he might find work in the new factory at home: 'There's too many bosses in that factory job. Slave-drivers. You don't have to lick no one's shoes over here' (p. 27). Later, Harry savagely traduces Michael's modernising vision in a caustic parody of family *embourgeoisement*:

> We just want you to know we just turned over a new leaf. And we come to the conclusion that Des is going back to Mary Horan's country. And Hugo is going to the university, and I'm going paying for his fees. And Iggy is going joining the Foreign Legion of Mary. And Dada is going off, with his old one-two, killing Communists. And I'm going joining the nuns (p. 73).

By the end of Act Two, Michael's identity conflict has reached crisis point. As the fateful fight with the Mulryans looms, he loses Des to the blood instincts of the tribe and is left behind to agonise over his plight with Betty. Exasperated by her husband's impotent talk of self-transcendence – 'I want to get out of this kind of life … I don't want to be what I am' – she goads him into action, at which point he capitulates to the atavistic forces which have been newly unleashed: 'I'm Carney too, another Carney' (pp. 57–8). From this moment on, Michael's self-fashioning energies dissipate into an off-stage binge of self-destructive behaviour which is counter-pointed by the on-stage revelry of his brothers, crowned 'Champions of England!' by their deceitful father. This orgy of self-congratulation culminates in Dada's rendition of 'The Boys from the County Mayo', a classic ballad of sentimental emigrant nationalism which celebrates the fortitude, bravery and solidarity of dispossessed exiles. As a song which eulogises loyalty to a fixed, unchanging identity in the face of enforced migration, it resonates with the family's fierce pride and traditionalism. But the lyrics also arouse darker emotions in the Carney psyche, which become the catalyst for the play's bloody climax.

The role of sentiment and nostalgia seems to me to be central to the violent implosion of the family at the end of the play. There is something about the song's evocation of a brutal nostalgia for 'the land where we once had a home' that awakens a primal self-hatred in the Carneys which makes them turn their violence inwards, upon themselves. The stage directions tell us that 'they listen with considerable reverence' (p. 69) to the song, as if spellbound by its maudlin romanticism. As the internecine chaos begins, both Harry and Iggy try to reprise the ballad by invoking the line which urges brothers to 'stick together in all kinds of weather', but only succeed in accentuating its ironic appropriateness to the action. An interesting gloss on the play's conclusion may be found in recent provocative remarks by the playwright Declan Hughes on the relationship between nostalgia and violence in Irish culture. He claims that nostalgia is 'in many ways the Irish disease' which 'corrodes at every level: at its most extreme, it becomes the savagery of war'.[42] He goes on to cite Don DeLillo's assertion in *White Noise* (1985) that:

> Nostalgia is a product of dissatisfaction and rage. It's a settling of grievances between the present and the past. The more powerful the nostalgia, the closer you come to violence. War is the form nostalgia takes when men are hard-pressed to say something good about their country.[43]

These suggestive insights help us to understand the cultural dynamic which drives the Carneys' self-destructive urges. Theirs is indeed a nostalgia born of a furious disaffection for place and nation which emigration has done nothing to alleviate. Having long since ceased to have anything good to say about their country, they now find that they have nothing good to say about themselves – at least, nothing that they can believe in. Instead, a cacophany of internalised social insults from the family's past are ventriloquised in Dada's shouts of 'Scum! Tinkers! Filth!' as he orchestrates the final act of tragic fratricide. Whereas Pat Moore ultimately avoids the perils of nostalgia, the Carneys remain hopelessly in thrall to the tyranny of the past. There appears to be no redemption in modernity, least of all for Michael, whose psychological entrapment is mirrored in the choreography of the final tableau, which shows Dada marooned on a chair, isolated from his sons, who are gathered around Michael holding the body of Des. Murphy's scabrous vision allows little room for optimism, yet, as Anthony Roche has pointed out, '[t]his belated outward action suggests at least a partial acceptance by Michael of his own fragmented identity'.[44] Thus the 'determined and hopeful dawn' to which Macken's protagonist is seen advancing at the end of *I Am Alone* is here replaced by a more realistic, if sombre vision of a future shaped by the dialogical interactivity of the forces of tradition and modernity.

CONCLUSION: NEGOTIATING A THIRD SPACE
In his trenchant analysis of post-war Irish emigration to Britain, J. J. Lee asserts:

> It is to the writers the historian must turn, as usual, for the larger truth. It is they, some themselves emigrants, who best convey the fetid atmosphere of the forties and fifties, the sense of pervasive, brooding hopelessness at home, the emptiness, the uncomprehending remorse, the heartbreak and heroism of many caught in the web of the 'experience of abandonment' as families were sundered and communities withered.[45]

Lee is right, of course, but his comments are based on a reading of only one strand of Irish migrant writing, that which chronicles the socio-economic climate of the home society and the suffering of those left behind. As I have tried to show in this essay, literary representations of the Irish in post-war England contain equally valuable insights into the social and political changes taking place in post-war Irish society, as well as illuminating the material and psychological struggles of the migrants themselves. As we have seen, the migrant protagonists in *I Am Alone* and *A Whistle in the Dark* function as symbolic sites of cultural interrogation through which unresolved ideological tensions in the wider Irish socio-political sphere – in particular, the tension between the forces of tradition and modernity – are mediated. In my readings of these texts, I have sought to foreground the ways in which Walter Macken and Tom Murphy offer a vision of migrant characters seeking to negotiate a 'third space' between the claims of tradition and modernity, between a residual and an emergent Ireland. In this important respect, both works may be said to 'narrate' the nation by prefiguring and rehearsing one of the key tensions which under-pinned Irish society in the second half of the twentieth century, and which still resonates today.

'Making Aliya': Irish Jews, the Irish State and Israel[1]

DERMOT KEOGH

By the waters of Babylon, there we sat down and wept when we remembered Zion
(Psalm 137)

From the time of the Babylonian exile in the sixth century BC, before the common time, Mount Zion, one of the hills of Jerusalem, came to symbolise for Jews their longing to return to their homeland. Zionism, a term first used in the 1890s, was adopted by Theodor Herzal as the name for his political movement, which sought the return of the Jews from exile.[2] Zionists sought the establishment of a Jewish National Home in Palestine, which became the central idea in Zionism. The 'ingathering of the exiles' was the primary goal of what in the early twentieth century became a worldwide movement. The word 'aliya' in the title of this essay is derived from the word in Hebrew for 'ascent' or 'going up'.[3]

Immigration to Palestine between 1880 and the Second World War has been divided into five phases, or aliyot. The first aliya is dated between 1882 and 1903, when an estimated 20,000 to 30,000 Jews immigrated from Russia and the east to Palestine. That was the period in which Ireland experienced its largest immigration of Jews from Lithuania, who were fleeing the Russian pogroms.[4] The second aliya, 1904–14, brought another 40,000 mainly Russian Jews to Palestine. During the same period, eastern European Jews continued to arrive in Ireland, but in much smaller numbers than had been the case in the last two decades of the nineteenth century. The third (1919–23) and fourth (1924– 31) aliyas together brought over 120,000 Jews to Palestine, the fourth alone numbering nearly 90,000 Jews, coming mainly from Poland. The fifth aliya covered the years 1932 to 1938; during this, some 200,000 immigrants, mainly from Central Europe, came to Palestine. During the Second World War, about 80,000 Jews succeeded in entering Palestine legally and illegally. The same process continued after the war. Over 50,000 Jews succeeded in getting in, despite severe restrictions under the British mandate. After the declaration of the state of Israel in May 1948, the flow of Jewish immigrants grew dramatically. The new state allowed free immigration.[5]

This essay examines Irish-Jewish relations in the late 1940s and 1950s and Irish emigration to Israel during the same period. Dr David Birkhahn, who left Cork in the 1950s to 'make aliya', describes his own experiences in the final section of this essay.

Ireland has always had a relatively small Jewish population. Although there had been Jews in Ireland from the Middle Ages, the number remained quite small until the last decades of the nineteenth century, when pogroms in Russia forced tens of thousands of Jews to flee for their lives. The Jewish population of the twenty-six counties that were to become the Irish Free State in 1922 increased from 230 in 1871 to 394 in 1881; this population increased almost fourfold during the 1880s, to 1,506, and then doubled again in the 1890s, to 3,006. That figure rose to 3,805 in 1911 before reducing slightly to 3,686 in 1926. The Jewish community in the south increased to 3,749 in 1936 and grew again in the following decade, to stand at 3,907 in 1946, which was the highest number it ever achieved. Thereafter it declined to 3,255 in 1961, to 2,633 in 1971, to 2,127 in 1981 and to 1,581 in 1991.[6] By 1997, the Jewish population in the Republic of Ireland was estimated to be about 1,200, almost all of whom lived in Dublin, and the strength of the Irish Jewish community continued to decline in number in the early twenty-first century.

In Northern Ireland, the Jewish population had grown from 282 in 1891 to 1,342 in 1911, when 1,139 lived in Belfast. The figure rose to 1,352 in 1926 and 1,472 in 1937.[7] It reached its highest point in 1951, with a population of 1,474, of whom 1,140 were resident in Belfast. There were 1,191 in 1961, 959 in 1971, 517 in 1981 and 410 in 1991, with most of the community over 50 years of age.[8]

Emigration to Israel was one of the main reasons for the decline in the Jewish population, north and south, in the second half of the twentieth century. It was not the most important reason; the emigration of young Irish Jews to study abroad and to live in larger communities in Britain, Canada and the United States was much more significant. However, many Irish Jews made 'aliya' and went to Israel from the 1950s onwards. They followed others who had, since the 1920s, left to live in Palestine. This was done for both religious and political reasons. While the history of Zionism in Ireland has yet to be written, it is possible to sketch in broad outline the central significance of that movement throughout the twentieth century for many Irish Jews.

ZIONISM IN IRELAND

Russian immigrants to Ireland at the end of the nineteenth century founded the Hoveve Zion group. It met in Camden Street Synagogue. They were the first supporters in Dublin of the Jewish National Fund. The first local branch was founded in 1901 by Jacob Elliman, a Lithuanian immigrant described as being a 'staunch supporter of traditional Judaism and an ardent Zionist'.[9] Simon Cornick was the first chairman, but he retired after a few months and was replaced by Elliman. The latter held that post until 1937, when he was named life president.[10] J. Z. Gilbert, in the *Encyclopedia of Zionism and Israel*, adds the following:

> In 1907 the Dublin branch of the Order of Ancient Maccabeans, the Mount Carmel Beacon, was founded. In the 1920s the Dublin Jewish Debating Society was formed. It became affiliated with the Federation of Zionist Youth of Great Britain and Ireland. Later, it became the Tel Hai Beacon, a junior branch of the Order of Ancient Maccabeans ... In 1941 the Dublin Younger Commission of the [Jewish National Fund] was organised. The Children's and Youth Aliya Group was formed in 1946, and its Younger Committee in 1961. A Society of Friends of the Hebrew University of Jerusalem was established in 1948. The Joint Palestine Appeal was launched in Ireland in 1951.[11]

Esther Barron founded the Dublin Daughters of Zion in 1900. Rose Leventhal was chairperson of that group for over 40 years and was succeeded by Ethel Freedman. She held office for 11 years and was replaced by Annie Glass. The latter held that position in 1966, a year in which there were six Zionist women's groups in Dublin, one in Cork and three in Belfast. A Regional Council of Women Zionists, with headquarters in Dublin, co-ordinated their activities. They were affiliated to the Women Zionists of Great Britain and Ireland and to the Women's International Zionist Organisation.[12] The autonomous Zionist Council of Ireland was represented independently at the Zionist Congress in 1951, but the Irish organisation continued to maintain links with the London-based Zionist Federation of Great Britain and Ireland.[13]

Much more research requires to be done to trace the emigration of Irish Jews to Palestine in the early decades of the twentieth century. The case of Max Nurock is hardly typical but it is worth recalling here. The son of two Lithuanian immigrants, William and Rachel Nurock, he had a distinguished academic career in Trinity College Dublin where he was awarded a number of distinctions. He served in the British army during the First World War. He spent most of his working life in Palestine, where he served as junior chief secretary to the high commissioner, Sir Herbert Samuel. Later he served in the Israeli diplomatic service.[14] Chaim and Jacob Herzog, the sons of the chief rabbi of Ireland, Isaac Herzog, went to complete their education in Palestine in the mid-1930s. Their father became the chief rabbi of Palestine in 1937. Chaim served as an officer in the army and later went on to become president of Israel. His brother, Jacob, had a distinguished career in the Israeli diplomatic service. He was offered but turned down the position of chief rabbi of Great Britain and the Commonwealth.[15] The Nurocks and Herzogs are but two examples of Irish Jewish families who went to Palestine in the 1920s and 1930s. Further research will reveal other cases of Irish Jews who exchanged Ireland for a life in Palestine.

The Zionist activities of Irish Jews attracted the hostile attention of many polemical Irish Catholic writers in the 1930s. Prominent among these were two clergymen, the Holy Ghost priest, Denis Fahey, and the Jesuit, Edward Cahill, while hostile articles also appeared in Catholic journals such as the *Cross*, the *Catholic Bulletin* and the *Irish Rosary*. These attacks took the form of various accusations: that many Jews in Europe were involved in revolutionary left-wing politics; that Jews were part of a global conspiracy made up of Freemasons and Communists; that Jews had a double and conflicting allegiance to the country in which they resided and to Israel. The Catholic polemicists were usually of the view that Jews would always choose the interests of Zionism over the national interests of the country in which they lived. In this climate of suspicion and fear in the 1930s in Ireland, it is not surprising that Jews who were active supporters of Zionism did not seek nation-wide publicity for that cause.

Eamon de Valera came to power at the head of a Fianna Fáil government in 1932. He served as Taoiseach for 16 years and lost office in early 1948, a few months before the foundation of Israel. In the intervening years, he took a strong personal interest in the future of Palestine. He was a friend of the chief rabbi, Isaac Herzog. As Minister for External Affairs throughout the period from 1932 to 1948, he was in a good position to follow developments in the Middle East. His regular attendance at the League of Nations in Geneva brought him further knowledge of the politics of the region. According to his party colleague, Robert Briscoe, he showed himself to be interested in Zionism. De Valera, who was to visit Israel with Briscoe when he was out of office in 1951, sent the secretary of the Department of External Affairs, Joseph Walshe, to Palestine in the 1930s to report first-hand on what was happening there.[16]

A split in the Zionist Organisation in 1935 constituted a potentially serious source of disunity for the Jewish community in Ireland (this remains to be determined by further research). The original Zionist movement covered a broad spectrum 'from the right-wing, religious-orientated Mizrahi through the General Zionists in the centre to the left-wing Zionist socialists'.[17] Each of those general groupings was in turn divided into other groupings. Irish Jews gave their allegiance overwhelmingly to the Zionist Organisation. But a small number, led by Robert Briscoe, supported the New Zionist Organisation (NZO). Its founder, Vladimir (Ze'en) Jabotinsky,[18] was accused by David Ben-Gurion, who became the first prime minister of Israel in 1948, of espousing the cause of extreme nationalism and of imitating fascist methods.[19] Jabotinsky, in opposition to other Zionist positions, favoured the mass migration of Jews to Palestine. He attempted to persuade the British government to 'evacuate' the masses of Polish Jews to Palestine where, in 1935, 24,300 of the 30,703 people who entered the country were from Poland.[20]

Jabotinsky further disagreed with the leaders of Zionism, Chaim Weizmann and David Ben-Gurion, over the proposal to partition Palestine contained in a British Royal Commission report published in July 1937.[21] This was a proposal for which de Valera had no sympathy and made his opposition known at the League of Nations.[22] Within two years, however, the British – with an estimated 40% of its entire field force tied down in Palestine – reversed its policy on partition, and imposed a strict quota on the number of Jews allowed to enter the area.

An NZO delegation, led by A. Abrahems, was sent to Dublin on 6 December 1937. The visit lasted until 12 December. Hardly an impartial source, the London-based *Zion News* reported that they had found among the Jewish community in Dublin 'an eagerness to become acquainted with the problems of Partition' and the policies of the NZO. A number of members of the Zionist Organisation, according to the report, decided to secede and join the NZO. It was decided not to make that news public until a further visit took place in the near future.[23] The *Zion News* also wrote on page one of the same issue:

> Ireland, in particular, must be regarded as of special importance to the future of the Movement. That country has been exposed to problems and experiences not dissimilar, in many ways, to those of the Jewish people; and that of the Zionist Movement. Its own nationalist Movement has been split from top to bottom on ideological and political grounds, remarkably like the differences within the Zionist movement ... Zionist roots struck in Ireland at the present time may, in the future, produce fruits which few can, at the present moment, foreshadow or even approximately estimate.

Jabotinsky visited Dublin in December 1938. Accompanied by Robert Briscoe, who was then a TD, he met de Valera and returned to see the Taoiseach again after he had paid a visit to the Papal Nuncio, Paschal Robinson. No official minutes for these meetings have been located, but according to Briscoe's memoirs, Jabotinsky was cross-examined by de Valera; they discussed the Jewish rights to Palestine, and Jabotinsky drew certain parallels with the Irish famine and with the dispersal of the Irish after that great tragedy.[24] Jabotinsky also had a meeting with Joseph Walshe at the Department of External Affairs. Afterwards, Jabotinsky said: 'My immediate impression [on twice meeting de Valera] was of that broad-minded humanity, that chivalrous consideration for a neighbour's sorrows and ideals, and that innate simple courtesy one almost instinctively associated with the very atmosphere of Éire'.[25] During the course of the visit, he established a Dublin committee of the NZO.[26] The presence of a branch of the NZO in Dublin did not add to Robert Briscoe's popularity among the majority of his co-religionists.

Irish army intelligence, during the war years, reported on Briscoe's Zionist activities. They believed him to be a member of the supreme body of the NZO.[27] Shortly before the war, Briscoe had gone on missions for that organisation to South Africa and to Poland.[28]

Despite the divisions in Irish Zionism, the Jewish community remained active members of the respective organisations. The Jewish Representative Council, founded shortly before the Second World War, acted as a liaison between the community and government. However, the minutes of that body for the war years – an important source – have been lost.

During the post-war years, the Irish government under de Valera responded positively to appeals for support for Jewish relief. Although his government had pursued a very illiberal policy towards Jewish refugees during the war, de Valera actively sought to reverse that line in 1945. In 1946, he provided for the sending of kosher meat to Europe. This involved providing work permits for a number of Jewish butchers to travel from the continent to conduct the slaughter of the animals. All the correct procedures were adhered to in the abattoirs. The meat was tinned and sent abroad for use for relief purposes.

IRELAND AND THE RECOGNITION OF ISRAEL

Ireland was denied access to the United Nations in the immediate post-war period, and so the Dublin government was very much a spectator as events in Palestine unfolded between 1945 and 1948. In 1945, the British government refused to allow the emigration to Palestine of thousands of Jews who had survived the Holocaust. A report by the UN Special Committee on Palestine, dated 31 August 1947, was adopted as General Assembly Resolution 181(II) on 29 November 1947. It proposed the partitioning of Palestine into Jewish and Arab states with Jerusalem and the holy places under the direct supervision of the UN. Article 81 of the UN Charter was to be used as the basis for such an international agreement. It was further recommended that Jerusalem – a holy city for three faiths – should be a *corpus separatum* to include the existing municipality of Jerusalem plus a specified surrounding district.[29] The map of the city was drawn to include many outlying areas.

As the interested parties were unable to find a negotiated solution, the armed conflict in the region intensified in 1947 and 1948. Jewish volunteers found their way to Palestine to fight for the cause of an independent state. A number of Irish Jews (the exact number remains to be determined by further research) went to Palestine in those years to participate in the fight to defeat the British forces deployed there under mandate. On the eve of the expiry of the mandate, the state of Israel was proclaimed on 14 May 1948 and a provisional government was established. It fell to David Ben-Gurion to make that proclamation.

An Arab-Israeli war followed and lasted until the beginning of 1949. On 11 May 1949, Israel was admitted to the United Nations. An armistice was signed between Israel and the Arab countries in the summer of 1949. Jerusalem was proclaimed the capital of Israel in 1950. That remained a matter of international dispute.[30] Irish Jews, together with other Jewish communities around the world, received the news of the declaration of a state of Israel with great enthusiasm.

It fell to the inter-party government to handle Irish-Israeli relations in the first two years of the existence of the new state. The Minister for External Affairs, Seán MacBride, was a member of Clann na Poblachta. That party had been set up in the post-war period to challenge Fianna Fáil and provide the electorate with a 'republican' alternative. A barrister who specialised in the defence of 'republicans' and a former chief of staff of the IRA, MacBride had no previous ministerial or parliamentary experience when he took office in early 1948. Apart from speaking French, his awareness of matters foreign and his understanding of the complexities of international politics remained an unknown quantity. His relative inexperience showed in the indecisive manner in which he handled the question of Irish recognition of the state of Israel. MacBride's temporising must be examined in the light of two factors – Irish partition and, more significantly, Irish popular sensitivities, specifically the concerns of the Catholic hierarchy over international control of Jerusalem and the holy places. The former issue, partition, ought to have been a major factor in contemporary Irish deliberations about the partitioning of Palestine. That was not the case. The issue of control of the holy places took precedence over all other considerations. The Irish government sought to remain close to the position of the Holy See on this matter and monitored all policy developments in that light. That position was sustained until the late 1950s. Support among Irish Jews for the recognition of the state of Israel remained constant from 1948, but their voice was not powerful enough to change Irish policy.

Many of the major international powers, including the United States and the Soviet Union, were swift in their response to recognise the state of Israel. Britain, burdened by a painful recent history of involvement in the region, granted *de facto* recognition on 29 January 1949 and *de jure* recognition on 27 April 1950. Dublin quickly followed London's lead in the matter of *de facto* recognition but not that of *de jure* recognition. MacBride sent a telegram on 15 February 1949 to the Israeli Minister for Foreign Affairs, Mose Shertok, giving *de facto* recognition to that state. A reply was received the following day acknowledging the decision and conveying the deep appreciation of the Israeli government and the hope for the early establishment of formal relations between the two countries.[31] That hope was to go unfulfilled for many years. *De jure* recognition – much to the disappointment of Irish Jews – did not come until 1963 and the formal exchange of diplomatic relations did not come until 1974. The story of that procrastination was bound up for nearly a decade with Irish government sensitivities over control of the holy places.

ARCHBISHOP MCQUAID, IRISH JEWS AND THE HOLY PLACES

As with anxieties in Dublin over the bombing of Rome during the war years, there were grave concerns in Ireland about damage to the holy places in 1948. There was also a continuous if not growing risk of greater damage to the holy places in a region where protracted peace was unlikely to be established for some time. Irish Catholic concern about the holy places was expressed in its most extreme form in the pages of *Fiat*, a publication issued by Maria Duce. Founded in 1945 by a number of lay Catholics, it had Fr Denis Fahey as its father-figure and chief ideologue. A member of the Holy Ghost order, he published widely in the 1930s and 1940s on topics relating to the international power of Freemasons and the financial and political power of Jews. The subject of Jerusalem and the holy places surfaced frequently in a most strident fashion in the columns of *Fiat*.[32] Maria Duce may have been behind a campaign to get different county councils to submit to government an identical resolution on putting the holy places under international control. During the summer of 1949 the Department of the Taoiseach received resolutions passed by county councils in Limerick, Clare and other counties.[33] The activities of Maria Duce came to the attention of the World Jewish Congress, which appealed on 14 February 1950 to the Jewish Representative Council in Dublin to try to check its influence.[34] The behaviour of Maria Duce was well known to Jewish leaders in Dublin. So strident were its activities to become in the early 1950s – actions that included placing pickets on a theatre in Dublin where Danny Kaye was performing – that the archbishop of Dublin, John Charles McQuaid, used his power to curb its growth. Maria Duce tended to lose momentum from the mid-1950s onwards.

Archbishop McQuaid enjoyed ease of access to Irish government departments. He appears to have had a very good informal relationship with the Minister for External Affairs, Seán MacBride. Irish-Israeli policy and the question of the future of the holy places was an unresolved issue on the desk of the minister at that time. It was also an issue of growing importance in domestic Irish politics. There was evidence that Irish public opinion was becoming agitated about the safety of the holy places. The newly-arrived chief rabbi of Ireland, Immanuel Jakobovits, was disturbed by what he found. Because of what the chief rabbi described as 'some mild anti-Jewish demonstrations sparked off by the worldwide agitation on the holy places', he sought a meeting with the archbishop in May 1949. He went to see McQuaid 'in an effort to prevent any serious outbreaks' of hostility to Irish Jews in Dublin or in other parts of the country. He was accompanied by the chairman of the Jewish Representative Council, Edwin Solomons. Jakobovits explained in his memoirs that he had gone to 'reassure him [the archbishop] of the protection of Catholic rights and property in Israel and to request his assistance in preserving the happy relations between Jews and Catholics in Ireland'.[35]

On 26 May, McQuaid wrote a letter to Jakobovits outlining the content of the exchanges. The text of this letter, albeit in draft form with the archbishop's own hand-written changes, is on file in the records of the Department of External Affairs.[36] McQuaid spoke of the 'sentiment of apprehension among our people', to which he had drawn attention during the meeting:

> [It] still persists, and, in my belief, is about to develop. That sentiment, as Mr Solomons – because of his having lived all his life in Dublin – at once appreciated, is very deep and is more widespread than I had first calculated. The apprehension of our people, which is shared by Catholics all over the world, concerns the international status of Jerusalem, the immunity of the Holy Places, not merely of Jerusalem but of Palestine, the rights which, throughout many centuries we have acquired in respect of the Holy Places, and the opportunity of peaceful access to all the Holy Places.[37]

McQuaid felt that if the chief rabbi could secure – as he had ventured to suggest – any adequate, firm and authentic guarantees concerning those matters from the Israeli government, this 'would avail much to allay our fears'. The archbishop did not feel that a declaration from the Israeli legation in London could have the same effect as a statement from the seat of the central government. An official declaration from the Israeli government would 'receive wide publicity in Ireland, but, what is equally important, will be carefully noted wherever Irishmen are found, that is, throughout the universe, and especially, in the United States of America'.[38] The archbishop continued:

> Such a declaration would greatly assist, too, in preventing unfortunate repercussions, such as you stated you fear may arise in Dublin.
> During the war, it was happily possible for me, with the very alert sagacity of Mr Edwin Solomons, to help to forestall incidents which could have provoked retaliation or roused unjust antipathy.
> *It would indeed be a grievous* [sic] *pity, if after having safely traversed a period of world-wide and unexampled crisis, innocent people of your community should now suffer hurt, by reason of the attitude and actions of irreligious members of Israeli people, whose merely political or commercial aims would never be countenanced by the peaceful members of your community in Dublin.*[39]

McQuaid regarded it as of cardinal importance that Israel should not be seen to be speaking with two voices: on the one hand, giving guarantees in respect of the holy places, and on the other, being 'the voice of a group which seems to have regard only to the seizure and control, for its own ends, of the territory that is for us the Holy Land'.[40] In his journal, published in 1967, Jakobovits quoted the section in italics above and commented:

> In other words, Irish Jews were warned that they would be treated as hostages, be subjected to 'unfortunate repercussions' and would 'suffer hurt' if Catholics were not satisfied with the protection of their interests in Israel. This represents an unprecedented situation in our history. Here is a Jewish community being held accountable and threatened with reprisals for the actions of an independent country, thousands of miles away, for whose policies this community is not responsible and in whose affairs it has no say.[41]

That may have reflected the chief rabbi's immediate reaction to the letter. There is evidence that he wished to go public with the issue; but he was persuaded from doing so by wiser and more prudent counsel in the Jewish Representative Council, whose chairman, Edwin Solomons, had wide experience in the handling of Jewish-Catholic relations.

The sequel to the meeting – details of which may be found in the archbishop's personal papers – is of interest. Following the meeting, Edwin Solomons intervened with the chief rabbi, expressing his concerns in a letter to McQuaid dated 25 May about the attitude of the Israeli government in reference to the holy places. There had been reports in the national press about a meeting in Galway, where it was held that the Israeli government were not giving freedom of religion, particularly to Catholics. 'As you know, I have many Catholic friends and they were definitely disturbed about these reports', he wrote, adding:

> If these statements are correct it would lead to most serious repercussions in every country, including Ireland. I feel so strongly about the whole matter that some statement should be made without delay; if necessary, someone – you, if it is possible – should go to London. Regarding the appointment of a representative here, the person so appointed must be 'persona grata' to the Irish government and the Catholic Church. It must not be forgotten, about 93% of the population are Catholics.[42]

McQuaid replied on 26 May:

> I am grateful for your note, in which you so kindly let me know your further intervention with the Chief Rabbi concerning the Holy Places.
> I wish to thank you particularly for your immediate and sympathetic understanding of the whole position. That understanding was very evident on Monday at our meeting.

The Chief Rabbi is anxious to help to avoid trouble but, if I may say it, he is very young and, as a new appointment in our country, scarcely appreciates the force of the sentiment that is developing. For instance, you could never have countenanced the publication of his proposed letter. He was a shrewd editor who just said nothing.

I have written to the Chief Rabbi and, as it is he who should reveal my letter, I would be glad if you would kindly ask him to let you see it. I have but set down my remarks on Monday. Only this may I add: that the feeling of apprehension is not being allayed; on the contrary, it is likely to develop.

You know that I will do all in my power to see to it that the repercussions be not unjust towards your community. It would be a grievous wrong, if the actions of a group of irreligious Israeli people, with mere political and commercial aims to pursue, should cause hurt to innocent people in Dublin, who would never countenance their methods.[43]

Solomons replied to McQuaid three days later:

I am grateful for your friendly, kindly and helpful letter – definite steps are being taken to make what I regard as the most important point, viz. to have a very clear announcement regarding the Holy Places – Lord Samuel, a distant cousin of mine, gave a broadcast on Friday night – *Palestine Today* – in which he definitely stated that there would be no change regarding free access to the Holy Places. He has just returned from Palestine. I am writing asking for a copy of the broadcast. I don't know whether he will send same. I will tell him the anxiety we feel here and hope his broadcast is the view of the Israeli government. I saw your letter addressed to the Chief Rabbi today – I have the impression the Chief Rabbi realises the urgency of the matter, and will do his utmost. I understand the outlook of my fellow countrymen on this important issue and other matters. It may interest you to know my grandfather, Elias Solomons, came to Dublin from London in 1824. You may rest assured: when I have anything to report, you will have same without delay.[44]

Jakobovits wrote to McQuaid on 31 May:

Whilst the Irish Jewish Community has no means to influence the policy of the state of Israel and cannot, therefore, assume any responsibility for that policy, we shall – as the community which appreciates, and sympathises with, Catholic sentiments probably more than any other – use our best endeavours to elicit from the central government at Tel Aviv a reiteration of its policy for widespread publication – which, I am very glad, you assure me such an official declaration would receive in Ireland – and thus to assist in your efforts at solving the present issue. May I also express my profound gratitude for your generous assurance that the Jewish citizens here can continue to count upon the gracious goodwill of your distinguished self.[45]

McQuaid sent the secretary of the Department of External Affairs, Frederick Boland, a copy of his correspondence with the Chief Rabbi. The latter replied on 3 June: 'I heard, purely by accident, that the chief rabbi put the letter before his council, and that the question dealt with in it is now receiving the solemn and anxious consideration of the leaders of Dublin's Jewry'. Boland asked whether or not he should send a copy of the letter to Joseph Walshe, who was by this time Irish ambassador to the Holy See.[46] It is not clear whether that was done or not. But it is likely, at the very least, that Walshe was made aware in broad outline of the details of the controversy. On 4 June, the archbishop wrote to the chief rabbi acknowledging receipt of a statement made by the Israeli representative to the United Nations: 'Further, I thank you for your efforts to elicit from the Tel-Aviv government a statement concerning the due guarantees of protection for the Holy Places'. This sequence of letters concluded on 12 June when Edwin Solomons sent McQuaid a report on the holy places by his kinsman Lord Samuel. But the archbishop did write on 13 June to Mgr Gino Paro at the papal nunciature. He explained that on the day he had received a letter from Paro he had discussed the issue of the holy places with the Lord Mayor of Dublin and with the Minister for Finance, Patrick McGilligan, who had served in the 1920s as Minister for External Affairs. He also had had a meeting with a Professor O'Brien, described as a goodwill ambassador from New York.

The professor was of the view that mass demonstration of Catholics on the issue of the holy places would not be effective in the United States but he did think that Cardinal Spellman 'could affect much in private with Mr Truman'. The archbishop wrote: 'I fear I cannot agree with the former point: every manifestation makes for some good, where Jews are concerned'. McQuaid told Paro that he would raise the matter with the government, and added: 'I cannot see *de jure* recognition being accorded to Israel, without definite guarantees being given concerning the Holy Places. In this context, I am constantly in touch with the government'.[47] McQuaid then went on to relate his exchanges with the chief rabbi:

It is interesting to record an interview sought by the Chief Rabbi and the lay head of the Jewish community, Mr Solomons. The latter is a very honourable man, having for acquaintances and friends all his life Dublin Catholics. The Chief Rabbi is very young.

The Chief Rabbi was greatly worried by a *Fides* statement on Zionism and saw the repercussion when the Mansion House was picketed during a Jewish celebration for the foundation of Israel. He had prepared an answer for the *Irish Press*, which the *Press* would not fortunately publish. I advised him to refrain from any such replies and Mr Solomons completely agreed.

During the interview, I made very clear the intense feeling of our people in regard to the Holy Places and warned the Chief Rabbi that, if trouble started in Dublin, it would be hard to curtail it. I urged that he use his good offices with the [Israeli] government to give adequate and clear guarantees. He agreed to do what he could to secure guarantees.

The enclosed letter represents my statement to the Chief Rabbi on the interview we had. The enclosed answer of the Chief Rabbi is, to a certain extent, satisfactory. The documents which he enclosed are of little value, in my opinion, because they are concerned chiefly with proving the aggression of the Arabs. What is much more valuable is the enclosed copy of a letter sent me by Mr Solomons, with an excerpt from a letter written by his kinsman, Lord Samuel. This much would seem to have been gained: the Jews are realising that a worldwide feeling concerning the Holy Places is being manifested. And to quote the Chief Rabbi, when I urged importance of world opinion: 'We Jews,' he declared, 'to put the matter on its lowest basis, have too many hostages in the Christian countries to wish to have trouble in the Holy Places'. In speaking thus, he put his finger on that which most worries a Jew: the fear of reprisals.[48]

McQuaid repeated at the end of his letter to Paro that he had kept the Irish government informed of these interviews in view of the interest that the government was taking in the holy places.[49]

On 13 July 1949, Seán MacBride outlined in Dáil Éireann Irish policy on Israel and the holy places. He made a special appeal to the government of Israel on the placing of the holy places under an international regime. He felt such an act of generosity would do more than anything else to bridge the gulf between Christian and Jew. That gulf had been responsible down the ages for so much hatred and suffering, and people in Ireland could justly claim to have been more successful in closing the gulf than in most other Christian countries:

> We know how cruelly and unjustly the Jewish people have suffered from intolerance and persecution throughout the centuries. I, personally, am glad that the pages of our history have never been stained with anything of the kind. On the contrary, I think we can claim that our common suffering from persecution and certain similarities in the history of the two races create a special bond of sympathy and understanding between the Irish and Jewish peoples.[50]

The leadership of the Jewish community in Ireland continued to be anxious to help find a way forward on the issue of the holy places. MacBride wrote to Joseph Walshe in Rome on 22 August and told him that he had been approached by 'a number of prominent Jewish people here who are anxious to know if they could assist in any way'. He had also recently been approached with a view to granting *de jure* recognition to Israel.[51] The issue of *de jure* recognition, as has been mentioned, was not to be resolved until the 1960s. In the interim, the Irish government faced a range of problems arising out of its *de facto* relationship with Israel.

The death of the president of Israel, Chaim Weizmann, on 9 November 1952 presented an unnecessary protocol problem for the Irish government. An External Affairs memorandum noted that on 11 November the minister, Frank Aiken, had addressed a message to his Israeli counterpart conveying sympathy with him, his colleagues and the relatives of Dr Weizmann on the death of their 'great leader and statesman'. The memorandum emphasised that the message had deliberately used the phrase 'your colleagues' instead of 'the Government of Israel'. Neither did the statement refer to Weizmann as 'President of Israel' but only as 'great leader and statesman'. The writer raised the question as to whether there should be official representation at a service in the Adelaide Road synagogue in Dublin on 16 November. The protocol was that on such an occasion the president, the government or the Minister for External Affairs – or all three – could be represented.[52] Iveagh House had advised against the president attending the service: 'It would not seem desirable that the president, who, when he sends a message of sympathy on the occasion of the death of the head of state or other distinguished person, usually conveys not alone his own sympathy but also the sympathy of the people of Ireland, should be represented at this service'.[53] But on the general question of representation, the advice was not so clear-cut:

> We have in this country a Jewish community, all or nearly all of whom are Irish citizens and whose relations with their fellow citizens are extremely harmonious. Moreover, a member of the Jewish community, Deputy Briscoe, is a member of Dáil Éireann. Though the Jewish community are nearly all Irish citizens, they, no doubt, feel sympathetically disposed towards the state of Israel and its government, and all of them almost certainly regard the late Dr Weizmann as President of that state and an outstanding leader of the Jewish people everywhere in the world. Doubtless, they would not be displeased if there was some official representation at the Service.[54]

But there was an alternative view: 'We must not overlook the possibility that any official representation at the Service might be unfavourably viewed by a not inconsiderable body of opinion in this country. Indeed, such representation might be liable to be misconstrued and imply a degree of recognition of the state of Israel which we do not accord'.[55] There was also a query about whether flags would be flown at half-mast on the day of the funeral. 'The question does not now arise since funeral is over', minuted another official. The memorandum also carried a minute, dated 11 November 1952: 'Minister will be represented by Deputy Briscoe'.[56] This pedantic approach merely illustrated the silliness of the Irish position of refusing to grant *de jure* recognition to the state of Israel.

Ireland was admitted to the United Nations in 1956 and took up its position in the General Assembly. The Irish delegation was seated beside that of Israel. However, Irish policy on the recognition of Israel remained something of a backwater in the post-Suez period.

Noël Browne raised the question of establishing diplomatic relations with Israel in Dáil Éireann in late 1958. Con Cremin, now secretary of the Department of External Affairs, commented on the deputy's question. He recalled the remark made by Joseph Walshe that the attitude of Pope Pius XII was not entirely shared by other senior Curia officials. 'There may thus be some change in Vatican thinking on the subject', he wrote. On the other hand, Tardini, who had expressed a hard-line position in 1955 to Cremin, had since become secretary of state 'and such greater influence as this position gives him is hardly calculated to render the Vatican position less rigid'. Cremin did not recommend changing Irish policy towards Israel, and gave Aiken the following argument in favour of retaining existing Irish policy: 'I think that such a step [establishing diplomatic relations] in respect of Israel at the present moment might lead to wrong interpretations on the part of the Arab States and might thus compromise whatever beneficial action we may be able to take in the United Nations towards solving the Arab-Israeli problem'.[57] Frank Aiken took Cremin's advice. The minister told the Dáil on 26 November 1958 that while he appreciated the desirability of developing cultural, trade and other associations with a number of other countries, he did not think that Dublin would be justified at present in undertaking the additional cost involved in establishing further diplomatic missions.[58]

However, the election of Pope John XXIII helped change the policy of the Holy See towards Israel. Con Cremin changed his own position in the early 1960s on the question of Israeli recognition. Frank Aiken was also persuaded to change Irish policy. On 10 July 1962, Cremin wrote to the ambassador to the Holy See, T. V. Commins. The secretary referred to the disadvantages of not having given de jure recognition to a number of states, mentioning Jordan and Israel by name. Cremin told Commins that the minister proposed to approach the government shortly to accord de jure recognition to Israel and Jordan. He was anxious that the Vatican should be made aware of this intention. It was also to be pointed out to the Holy See that it was not Aiken's intention to establish a mission at the present time in either country. The Irish approach was to be made informally.[59]

Commins reported to Dublin on 24 July that he had been assured by a Vatican official that the economic factor involved for the Irish was perfectly understandable and valid and that Dublin needed to have no fear that Irish action in according de jure recognition to Israel would be misinterpreted by the Holy See. Indeed, the Vatican official said, it probably could be argued with some force that the Holy See itself had indirectly given such recognition to Israel by the acceptance of a special ambassador from that country on two occasions – the obsequies of Pope Pius XII and the coronation of his successor, Pope John XXIII – and by the exchange of telegrams between the latter and the president of Israel on the last-mentioned occasion.[60] Neither, he added, would the Holy See have any adverse reaction to the exchange of diplomatic or consular missions if it were so decided. But the Holy See would ask Dublin to ensure that any future diplomatic or consular representative would not reside in Jerusalem or act in any way likely to imply recognition of Jerusalem as the capital of Israel.[61] The anomaly of Ireland's relationship with Israel was at last laid to rest when *de jure* recognition was accorded to that state in 1963.[62] In December 1974, Ireland and Israel agreed to an exchange of diplomatic representatives. This was to be initially on a non-residential basis. At first, Ireland's representative in Switzerland, William Warnock, was accredited to Israel. As a matter of convenience, that was changed in 1979 when it was decided to accredit the Irish ambassador to Greece to Israel. The Irish government gave approval for the establishment of an Israeli embassy in Dublin in 1993. Zvi Gabay presented his credentials on 22 July 1995. Brendan Scannell was appointed as the first resident Irish ambassador to Israel, setting up an Irish embassy in Tel Aviv in 1996.[63]

IRELAND, ISRAEL AND THE SUEZ CRISIS

It is not clear just how many Irish Jews had emigrated to Israel by the middle of the 1950s. This figure will only be computed accurately by examining the files in the relevant Israeli government ministries. But the crises in the Middle East in 1956 – Suez in particular – obliged the Irish government to set in place contingency plans for the evacuation of Irish citizens from Israel. That was complicated greatly by the fact that the country did not have any formal representation in Tel Aviv. But the Irish files reveal a number of very interesting facts about both the Irish in Israel and the ability of a government to think pragmatically. The background is as follows. The plight of Irish Jews in Israel was brought to the attention of the Irish authorities in Dublin by a letter from J. S. Steinberg, 500 Perdes Hanna, Israel. Writing on 31 March 1956, he addressed his letter to the Secretary, Department of External Affairs:

> A chara,
> As the political situation in this part of the world grows more tense, the question of protection of Irish nationals has arisen. On enquiring at the British Embassy in Tel Aviv, I was informed that they were not authorised to act on behalf of the Irish government and that they are accepting regis-

trations of British subjects only. I wonder, therefore, whether it would be possible for some arrangements to be made by which Irish nationals could feel more secure in the event of the situation worsening. I think there are quite a number, especially Irish university graduates, who, while participating in educational and humanitarian work, never forget their loyalty to, and affection for, Ireland.

Mise le meas[64]

Steinberg had already been in contact with the leadership of the Irish Jewish community in Dublin. His initiative, possibly on behalf of other Irish citizens in Israel, had prompted action by the Department of External Affairs. The secretary of the department, Seán Murphy, had phoned the chief rabbi, Immanuel Jakobovits, to get from him the names of Irish Jews living in Israel. Replying on 26 March, Jakobovits told Murphy that he did not have a complete list, nor was he in possession of all addresses. He suggested putting an advertisement in the *Jerusalem Post* requesting Irish citizens to register at a given address. The names supplied by the chief rabbi were as follows:

Mr and Mrs Sol Cantor (and one child)
Mr and Mrs M. Copperman (and two children)
Mr and Mrs H. Finegold
Mr and Mrs J. Jaswon (and one child)
Mr and Mrs N. Jaswon
Mr and Mrs D. Silverstein (and two children)
Mr and Mrs S. Yodaiken (and two children)
Mr and Mrs J. S. Steinberg (and three children)

The chief rabbi felt that the list, though incomplete, included the majority of Irish nationals in Israel. Jakobovits was anxious that arrangements should be made to ensure that in an emergency Irish citizens had the same protection and privileges as were enjoyed by other non-Israeli nationals.[65]

According to a later list on departmental files, the names of Irish citizens in Israel were as follows:

Mr H. Orgel, Kiriat Bialik, Haifa
Mr J. Copperman MA, Pagi, Jerusalem
Mrs Levine (*nee* Esther Baker), Rehavia, Jerusalem
Miss Annie Baker, Rehavia, Jerusalem
Mr R. D. Lev, B.Sc., Bnei Brak
Mr M. Browne, Tel Aviv
Mrs Schwarzman, Talpiot, N. Jerusalem
Dr J. Jaswon, Kfar Hanasi
Mr L. Hyman MA, 15 Peysner St, Haifa
Mr P. Rifkin, Lavee, near Tiberias
Mr C. Kaye

Dr F[?] Zuriel (alias Finegold), Tivon
Mr G. Cohen
Rabbi Copperman, 13 Gaza Road, Jerusalem.[66]

In a minute to the secretary of the Department of Finance on 7 September 1956, Murphy in External Affairs wrote:

> It is not at present possible to give a firm figure for the total number of the persons in these categories [adult Irish citizens in Israel; wives of Irish citizens in Israel; children of Irish citizens in Israel] but such information as the Department has been able to obtain suggests that the figure should not exceed about fifty, comprising about twenty adult males, about fifteen adult females and about fifteen dependent children. The cost of repatriating these persons to Ireland by air, which is the most expensive mode and which might prove necessary, is estimated at approximately 3,400 pounds. The cost of repatriation by land and sea, including a small amount for subsistence, would at the lowest amount to approximately 2,000 pounds.[67]

But that is to jump forward in the process. It would appear that Steinberg acted as a spokesperson in Dublin for the Irish community in Israel. He travelled to Dublin and was interviewed on 12 July 1956 by an official in the Department of External Affairs. His case was very simple. Other countries had long before registered their respective nationals and, he assumed, also prepared the necessary travel and transfer arrangements in the event of an emergency. Steinberg stressed that, in the event of war, there was no neighbouring country in which Irish citizens in Israel could hope to find refuge. All the surrounding countries, he pointed out, were hostile to Israel. If Irish citizens were obliged to leave Israel 'they would have to face starting back to Ireland'. He was asked particulars about his own position under Jewish citizenship law:

> He said he was not an Israeli citizen. He was an alien under the law and would have to get a visa for his return to Israel in September. I told him I thought there was some form of easy access to Israeli citizenship made available to returning Jews. Mr Steinberg said there was such a scheme but it had now expired. All returning Jews had to declare themselves as opting for Israeli citizenship before a certain date; after which, to gain Israeli citizenship, they had to naturalise in the normal fashion and spend a qualifying residence of five years.[68]

Obviously, something had to be done to provide for the contingency of an emergency. But any direct overture to the Israelis would risk the almost certain raising of the question of *de jure* recognition. There was an obvious course of action but it did not recommend itself immediately to the Irish government: Dublin might ask the British government to take care of the interests of Irish citizens in Israel in the event of an emergency. This was discussed at length by the Irish ambassador in London, Frederick Boland, and the secretary of the Department of External

Affairs, Seán Murphy. In the end, sensitivities and practical difficulties were overcome.

The Suez Crisis concentrated minds in Dublin. On 26 July 1956, Gamal Abdul Nasser announced the nationalisation of the Suez Canal. There was a heightened fear of war in the region. Seán Murphy instructed the London embassy to raise the issue of the protection of Irish citizens in Israel with the relevant British department. An Irish official went to see the assistant under-secretary of the Commonwealth Relations Office, MacLennan, on 21 August 1956. The response was favourable: in principle, the British government were always prepared to take on the protection of Irish citizens whenever Dublin requested it. He saw no reason why there should be any objection in the case of Irish citizens in Israel. MacLennan said he would start the machinery moving immediately. But, in the meantime, his government would require a note formally making the request and indicating the nature and scope of services that might be required.

In order to proceed with arrangements, permission had to be obtained from the Minister for Finance. Seán Murphy explained in a memorandum dated 7 September 1956 the reason for that course of action. In the light of the international situation, it was proposed that 'subject to the agreement of the Israeli and British authorities, British consular officers in Israel should be authorised to act on behalf of Irish citizens and their dependants there in regard to the provision of consular facilities of an emergency nature, if the necessity arises'. Those facilities were to include the 'transmission to this Department by British Consular officers of requests for passports and passport renewals and endorsements and the subsequent delivery of the passports to applicants; the repatriation of Irish citizens and their dependants from Israel if this proves imperative'.[69] Oral sanction was received from Finance and the formal written permission was sent to Iveagh House on 26 September. It would appear that the contingency arrangements were put in place.

Happily, it seems no Irish citizen in Israel found it necessary to avail of the contingency arrangements.

MAKING ALIYA: A PERSONAL ACCOUNT
David Birkhahn is from Cork. He emigrated to Israel in 1959. He kindly wrote an account of how his brother, sister and himself made aliya.[70]

> The Birkhahns are a third-generation Irish-Jewish family. Solomon Bernard, my grandfather, emigrated from Latvia in 1888 and settled in Cork. His marriage to Rebecca Levin (from Lithuania) was one of the first Jewish weddings in Cork in 1891. While many Jewish immigrants to Ireland in the nineteenth century from the Baltic countries earned their living as peddlers and small-time traders, Solomon Bernard was a herring-exporter who operated with his two brothers in Riga and Stockholm.

The family name may have reference to a bird indigenous to the Black Forest in Germany. The name is comprised of two words – 'Birk', which means birch tree in English, and 'Hahn', which is the German for cock.

My father's name was Isaac Joseph. He received his licence as a dentist in 1913 having served his apprenticeship in Cork city with Dr George Goldfoot. He started a practice with his brother Ben in the same city. Later he opened a practice in Bantry and, within a few years, he had opened branch practices at Skibbereen, Ballydehob, Schull, Goleen, Castletown, Adrigole and Kenmare. Depending on demand, he attended in those areas once a week, a fortnight or monthly.

I qualified in 1951 at University College Cork and went into my father's practice. I made aliya in 1959. What follows is my general account of the reasons for Irish emigration to Israel in the 1950s.

While the non-Jewish emigration from Ireland in the 1950s and 1960s was due to the depressed economic situation in the country, a prime factor in Jewish emigration to Israel was the appeal of the Zionist ideology, encouraging resettlement in the historic homeland. The establishment of the state of Israel encouraged large numbers of Jews to emigrate there in the late 1940s and early 1950s. Irish Jews went to Israel in large numbers, relative to the size of the local population.

That is not to say, however, that the economic factor was not also a consideration in many cases. There was a dearth of good job opportunities in business and among different professions in Ireland in the 1950s. Moreover, many young Irish Jews wished to live in larger communities of their co-religionists. Israel offered both economic opportunities and the fulfilment of Zionist goals.

The continuing emigration both to Israel and to other countries drained the Irish Jewish communities of leading professional and business people. In the medical profession, approximately twenty physicians and eight dental surgeons settled in Israel in the 1950s and 1960s.

Emigration to Israel was composed mainly of second- and third-generation Jews who settled mainly in the coastal plain from Tel Aviv to Netanya. The professional classes tended to settle in the large cities, while others opted to reside in kibbutzim and moshavim.

Another generation of emigrants followed the Six-Day War in 1967. That event had a profound effect on Jewish communities throughout the world, including Ireland.

Irish Jews who arrived in Israel in the 1950s came to a country where several Irish Jews had already reached positions of prominence in the professions and in public life. Max Nurock was the doyen of Irish Jewry in Israel; he emigrated in the early 1920s. Upon the establishment of the state of Israel in 1948, he joined the Foreign Office and became the Israeli ambassador to Australia.

Bernard Cherrick was vice-president of Hebrew University and was an influential fundraiser for the university. The late Professor Mervyn 'Muff' Abrahamson was the head of internal medicine at the Rebecca Sieff Hospital in Safed. He was also the honorary president of the Israel-Ireland Friendship League.

My brother, Professor Jesmond (Sandy) Birkhahn, was head of anaesthesiology at the Ramban Hospital in Haifa for over 40 years.

Louis Hyman, born in Dublin in 1912, was a member of the Senate of Trinity College. He settled in Haifa in 1935 and was head of the English Department of Hugim Secondary School. Hyman's *The Jews of Ireland*, which traced in great detail the immigration of Jews to Ireland from earliest times, immortalised his name and is thus intertwined with the annals of Irish Jewry.

The Herzog family was one of the best known to emigrate to Israel. Chief Rabbi Isaac Herzog was the first chief rabbi of Ireland. In 1936, he received a call to become the first chief rabbi of Palestine.

His two sons, Chaim (Vivian) and Jacob, were notable personalities in Israel. Chaim, who was a lawyer in a prestigious law office, reached the rank of general in the Israeli army and was also Israel's ambassador to the United Nations; his career was subsequently crowned by his election as president of the state of Israel.

Jacob was appointed to many important government positions: deputy director general of the Foreign Office, director general of the president's office and advisor to four prime ministers; as well, he paved the way to the Vatican's recognition of Israel. His debate at McGill University in 1961 with the internationally known historian Arnold Toynbee was one of the highlights in a brilliant career which was cut short by his demise in 1972.

All Jewish emigrants from Ireland had influence on other family members. The Coperman family takes pride in the number of emigrants from their family – six. Moshe, an engineer, came on aliya in 1950, followed over the years by Rabbi Yehuda, who founded the Jerusalem College for Women; Isaac, a doctor; Gershon and sister Leila. Mrs Sara Coperman also joined her children.

Cork, although it was the home of a small community of about sixty families in the 1950s, boasts of at least two separate (and related) families of six members – the Birkhahns – and four members of the Jackson family. Professor Jesmond (Sandy) Birkhahn, and his wife Dorothy, emigrated to Israel in 1955; I followed in 1959, and my sister, Claire, in 1959. She was in charge of the Geriatric Division of Public Health in Jerusalem. Our parents, Isaac Joseph and Sophie, emigrated to Israel in 1983.

Additional emigrants included David Jackson, barrister, who emigrated in 1954, followed by his sister Susan, mother Rachel (Ray), and by his brother Rabbi Edward, who emigrated to Israel upon his retirement as rabbi of Hampstead Garden Suburb Synagogue in London.

The Irish Jewish emigrants have a strong emotional attachment to the country of their birth, and the existence of the Israel-Ireland Friendship League was the outcome of hundreds of Irish Jews settling in Israel. The league was founded in 1969. I was elected founder chairman and held office until 1998. This organisation holds regular meetings and seeks to maintain strong intellectual and cultural ties between Ireland and Israel.

Notes

Introduction: The Vanishing Irish

1 Heinrich Böll, *Irish Journal – A traveller's Portrait of Ireland* (London: Vintage, 2000), p. 4

2 *Ibid.*, pp. 3–6

3 *Ibid.*, p. 94

4 *Ibid.*, pp. 94–5

5 Dónall MacAmhlaigh, *An Irish Navvy –The Diary of an Exile*, trans. Valentin Iremonger (London: Routledge and Kegan Paul, 1964). See pp. 1–69.

6 Tony O'Malley, 'Inscape – Extracts from Life and Landscape in Callan and County Kilkenny', in *Martello* (Dublin: Royal Hibernian Academy of Arts, 1991), [Special Issue], pp. 149–150.

7 John A. O'Brien (ed.), *The Vanishing Irish* (London: W. H. Allen, 1955), 2nd Edition, pp. 7–14 and pp. 220–40.

8 *Ibid.*, p. 227.

9 Bryan MacMahon, 'Getting on the High Road Again', in John A. O'Brien (ed.), *The Vanishing Irish*, pp. 209–15.

10 Response to request for submission on the reform of Seanad Éireann from the Disability Federation of Ireland (DFI), June 2003. The editors are grateful to John Dolan for forwarding Professor Dermot Keogh a copy of this submission and a copy of his enlightening paper 'Building a more Civilised Society in Ireland', Presentation by John Dolan, Disability Federation of Ireland to the Patrick MacGill Summer School (July) 2003.

11 St Mary's (Dominicans) 1848. St Josephs (Christian Brothers) 1856 with the Vincentians providing chaplaincy services to both schools. The Daughters of Charity of St Vincent de Paul were also active in this area. The schools, St Marys and St Josephs, were not owned by the religious orders but by the Catholic Institute for the Deaf which was established by the Catholic Archbishop of Dublin. NAD was established in 1963 by parents and others and it is significant in that it was a lay organisation. See DFI 'Submission', p. 10.

12 *Ibid.* The Irish Sisters of Charity founded St Mary's School in Donnybrook 1857 and the Carmelite Brothers (the order no longer exists) established a school in Clondalkin in 1851. The latter had moved to Drumcondra (St Joseph's) by 1856. The Rosminian Order was invited to take over its operation in 1955.

13 *Ibid.*, p. 10. See also the engaging survey of structures and conditions in Joe Robbins outstanding study, *Fools and mad: a history of the insane in Ireland* (Dublin: IPA 1986).

Memory and Forgetting: The Ireland of de Valera and Ó Faoláin

* This is the text of a talk commissioned by Professor Dermot Keogh and given by John Banville at a symposium of the same name at University College, Cork, in April 1995. The symposium was organised by Prof. Keogh on behalf of the History Department, UCC.

1 Julia Carlson, *Banned in Ireland: Censorship and the Irish Writer* (London: Routledge, 1989), p. 149

2 *Ibid.*, pp. 31–2.

Reflecting on Ireland in the 1950s

1 Popular fantasies about the Masonic bias of the newspaper were not wholly without foundation. Many members of the board, and most of the executives, were in fact Freemasons, as I soon found out when I joined. However, the policy followed by Smyllie was essentially liberal, and this presumably had the approval of the board. Dublin Freemasonry, in any case, had no strong political 'line' to follow and was

generally live-and-let-live in matters of religion. Broadly speaking, it represented Protestant business and professional interests.

2 *An Age of Innocence: Irish Culture 1930–1960* (Dublin: Gill and Macmillan, 1998).

3 Salvador de Madariaga, *Victors Beware* (London: Jonathan Cape, 1946).

4 Aiken, in my opinion, is one of the unsung heroes of Irish twentieth-century history. His somewhat close-mouthed approach misled superficial observers into considering him inarticulate and limited in outlook; his record, however, suggests the reverse. I once asked a leading Irish diplomat, the late Tadgh O'Sullivan, what his impressions were of Aiken. He answered that he found his judgement on foreign affairs usually shrewd and informed – 'he always seemed to know just what was happening, even in out-of-the-way places'.

5 See Maurice Harmon, *Ó Faoláin: A Life* (London: Constable, 1994).

6 For a study of Irish censorship, see Michael Adams, *Censorship: The Irish Experience* (Dublin: Scepter Books, 1968).

7 Clann na Poblachta was a neo-republican party founded by Seán MacBride in the mid-1940s. It performed reasonably well in the general election of 1948 and as a result MacBride became Minister for External Affairs in the first inter-party government, while Browne took over the Health portfolio. During the 1950s, however, the party's decline was rapid and MacBride – a leading lawyer – eventually abandoned party politics for good.

8 A sometimes-critical view of Browne as Minister for Health is given in *To Cure and to Care: Memoirs of a Chief Medical Officer* (Dublin: Glendale Press, 1989) by the late Dr James Deeny, who had helped to implement Browne's measures against TB in Ireland and was himself a greatly respected medical man and administrator. See also recent biographies of Browne and McQuaid: John Horgan, *Noël Browne: Passionate Outsider* (Dublin: Gill and Macmillan, 2000); John Cooney, *John Charles McQuaid: Ruler of Catholic Ireland* (Dublin: O'Brien Press, 1999).

9 The Dawson Gallery, as its name suggests, was in Dawson Street, while the Ritchie Hendriks Gallery was on St Stephen's Green. The latter was run by David Hendriks, a Jamaican who had the support of his wealthy uncle, Ritchie.

10 For writings on modern or recent Irish art, see Bruce Arnold, *A Concise History of Irish Art*, rev. ed. (London: Thames and Hudson, 1977), my own book *Irish Art 1830 to 1960* (Belfast: Appletree Press, 1994), Brian S. Kennedy, *Irish Art and Modernism* (Belfast: Queen's University, 1991), and Dorothy Walker, *Modern Art in Ireland* (Dublin: Lilliput Press, 1997).

11 The essential Irishness of MacNeice has been stressed recently by poet-critics such as Derek Mahon, Michael Longley and Eamon Grennan.

12 For the variety of musical events in Dublin see G. Cox (ed.), *Acton's Music: Reviews of Dublin's Musical Life 1955–1985* (Bray: Kilbride Books, 1996). Acton was for many years the respected music critic of the *Irish Times*.

13 This celebrated court case, which received widespread media coverage in 1954–5, was the result of an unsigned article in the *Leader* magazine that probably was intended to be merely provocative and satirical, but was in fact tasteless and ultra-personal. Its authorship has never been authenticated, though informed suspicion points to the poet Valentin Iremonger and the historian Desmond Williams, two members of an ambitious and talented group of young university intellectuals who had hoped to give the magazine a new tone and topicality. This attempt backfired, however, since the legal costs ruined it. Kavanagh was at first unsuccessful in his suit, but appealed and was awarded damages. (According to one eye-witness account Kavanagh had been rude and even insulting to Iremonger – a high-spirited, sensitive man – shortly before in McDaid's pub, his usual stamping-ground.)

14 Patrick MacDonogh, *Poems*, ed. Derek Mahon (Dublin: Gallery Press, 2001). See also article by Mahon, 'Forgotten poet is our loss', *Irish Times*, 14 July 2001.

15 Seán Ó Tuama (ed.), *Nuabhéarsaíocht 1939–1949* (Dublin: Sairseal agus Dill, 1950). This anthology was a landmark for the time, and after half a century it remains one.

16 The behaviour of various young people who attended the fleánna ceoil at the beginning of the 1960s marked the start of sexual libertarianism in Ireland. A printer
of my acquaintance who went to one in a Midlands town remarked to me afterwards: 'I'm telling you, there wasn't a blade of grass to be seen!'

Leaving the Blaskets 1953: Willing or Enforced Departures?

1 Published by Clarendon Press (Oxford 1944; New York: Doubleday), with illustrations
by Ida M. Flower.

2 George Thomson, *Island Home: The Blasket Heritage* (Dingle: Brandon, 1987).

3 Peig Sayers, *An Old Woman's Reflections* (Dublin: Government Publications, 1939).

4 Muiris Ó Súilleabháin [Maurice O'Sullivan], *Fiche Bliain ag Fás* [Twenty Years A-Grow-
ing] (London: Chatto and Windus, 1933).

5 Tomás Ó Criomhthain [Thomas O'Crohan], *An tOileánach* [The Islandman] (Dublin:
Talbot Press, 1929).

6 Muiris Mac Conghail, *The Blaskets: A Kerry Island Library* (Dublin: Town House, 1987).

7 Cole Morton, *Hungry for Home: Leaving the Blaskets – A Journey from the Edge of Ireland*
(London: Viking, 2000).
Official documents reproduced with permission from the National Archives of
Ireland, Department of the Taoiseach (D/T) S14122, A–D, NAI.

The Vanishing Irish? The Exodus from Ireland in the 1950s

1 Liam Kennedy, *The Modern Industrialization of Ireland, 1940–1988* (Dublin: Economic
and Social History Society of Ireland, 1989), p. 15.

2 Anne Lynch, *The Irish in Exile: Stories of Emigration* (London: Ethnic Communities Oral
Project 1988), p. 2.

3 *Ibid.*, pp. 3–4.

4 *Ibid.*, pp. 5–6.

5 W. E. Vaughan and A. J. Fitzpatrick (eds.), *Irish Historical Statistics: Population, 1821–
1971* (Dublin: Royal Irish Academy, 1978), tab. 56, p. 266.

6 Brendan M. Walsh, 'Expectations, Information, and Human Migration: Specifying an
Econometric Model of Irish Migration to Britain', *Journal of Human Science*, 14, no.
1 (1974), p. 108.

7 Donal Garvey, 'The History of Migration Flows in the Republic of Ireland', *Population
Trends*, 39 (1985), p. 25.

8 Enda Delaney, 'Placing Post-war Irish Migration to Britain in a Comparative European
Perspective, 1945–1981', in Andy Bielenberg (ed.), *The Irish Diaspora* (London: Long-
mans, 2000), pp. 331–56.

9 John A. O'Brien, 'The Irish Enigma', in *idem* (ed.), *The Vanishing Irish: The Enigma of the
Modern World* (New York: McGraw-Hill, 1953), p. 3.

10 O'Brien and company received a stern rebuke in 1954 from R. C. Geary, the distinguished statistician and Director of the Central Statistics Office, for these misinterpretations of statistics; see R. C. Geary, 'Are the Irish Vanishing?', *Éire–Ireland: Weekly
Bulletin of the Department of External Affairs*, no. 227 (March 1954), pp. 5–9.

11 Enda Delaney, *Demography, State and Society: Irish Migration to Britain, 1921–1971* (Liverpool and Kingston/Montreal: Liverpool University Press, 2000), p. 161.

12 *Ibid.*, pp. 205–6.

13 Brian Girvin, 'Political Culture, Political Independence and Economic Success in Ireland', *Irish Political Studies*, 12 (1997), p. 61.

14 Delaney, *Demography, State and Society*, p. 203.

15 Commission on Emigration and Other Population Problems, 1948–1954, *Reports* (Dublin, 1955), para. 290.

16 This paragraph draws heavily on detailed evidence presented in Delaney, *Demography, State and Society*, chapters 4–5.

17 For more details on the 'affluent worker', see Ross McKibbin, *Classes and Cultures:
England, 1918–1951* (Oxford: Oxford University Press 1998), pp. 132–33.

18 Commission on Emigration, *Reports*, para. 425.

19 Brendan M. Walsh, 'Influences on Mobility and Employment in Irish Family Farming', *Irish Journal of Agricultural Economics and Rural Sociology*, 2, no. 1 (1969), p. 17.

20 Douglas Massey, et al., *Return to Aztlan: The Social Process of International Migration from Western Mexico* (Berkeley: University of California Press, 1987).

21 See Enda Delaney, 'State, Politics and Demography: The Case of Irish Emigration, 1921–1971', *Irish Political Studies*, 13 (1998), pp. 25–49; Pauric Travers, '"The dream gone bust": Irish Responses to Emigration, 1922–60', in Oliver MacDonagh (ed.), *Irish–Australian Studies* (Canberra: Australian National University 1989), pp. 318–42.

22 For more details, see Delaney, *Demography, State and Society*, pp. 203 ff.

23 J. J. Lee, *Ireland, 1912–1985: Politics and Society* (Cambridge: Cambridge University Press, 1989), pp. 371 ff.

24 Quoted in Delaney, *Demography, State and Society*, p. 194.

25 Quoted in Lee, *Ireland, 1912–1985*, p. 386.

26 Delaney, *Demography, State and Society*, pp. 179–86, 234–48.

27 See Lee, *Ireland, 1912–1985*, p. 374.

28 *Ibid*. For a brilliant analysis of this issue, see J. J. Lee, 'Continuity and Change in Ireland, 1945–70', in *idem* (ed.), *Ireland, 1945–70* (Dublin: Gill & Macmillan, 1979), pp. 166–77.

The Commission on Emigration, 1948–1954

1 Commission on Emigration and Other Population Problems, 1948–1954 (hereafter CEOP) (Dublin, 1954) p. 1.

2 *Irish Independent*, 27 March 1948.

3 *Irish Independent*, 24 March 1948.

4 *Ibid*.

5 *Irish Times*, 23 April 1948.

6 *Irish Press*, 25 March 1948.

7 *Irish Press*, 22 April 1948.

8 *Ibid*.

9 *Irish Press*, 26 April 1948, Letters to the Editor.

10 CEOP, p. 25.

11 *Ibid*., p. 123.

12 *Ibid*., p. 130.

13 *Ibid*., p. 30.

14 TCD, Marsh Papers MS 8301, Surveys of Leitrim and Donegal by Dr Geary and Mr O'Leary.

15 TCD, Marsh Papers MS 8301, Survey of Killarney and Tralee by Mr Honohan.

16 TCD, Marsh Papers MS 8301, Congested Districts Summaries. Memoranda – submitted from Co. Galway.

17 *Ibid*.

18 *Ibid*.

19 CEOP, p. 143.

20 *Ibid*., p. 85.

21 *Irish Times*, 1 February 1949.

22 CEOP, p. 79.

23 TCD, Marsh Papers MS 8301, Summaries of Evidence.

24 CEOP, p. 79.

25 *Ibid*.

26 *Ibid*., p. 134.

27 *Ibid*.

28 *Ibid*., p. 135.

29 *Ibid*.

30 *Ibid*.

31 *Ibid.*, p. 139.
32 TCD, Marsh Papers MS 8300/1–31, Memorandum submitted by Bórd Cuartaíochta na hÉireann (Irish Tourist Board), 25/8/1948.
33 *Ibid.*
34 *Ibid.*
35 CEOP, p. 135.
36 TCD, Marsh Papers MS 8306, Rural Survey of Co. Cork by Rev. Dr Lucey and Prof. McCarthy.
37 CEOP, p. 136.
38 *Ibid.*
39 *Ibid.*
40 *Ibid.*, p. 137.
41 *Ibid.*
42 Cited in *Irish Press*, 26 May 1954.
43 CEOP, p. 138.
44 *Ibid.*, p. 137.
45 *Ibid.*
46 TCD, Marsh Papers MS 8301, Summaries of Evidence.
47 *Ibid.*, Memorandum submitted by Coisde Oideachais Ghairme Beatha, Conndae Liathdroma, 28 June 1948.
48 *Ibid.*
49 *Ibid.*
50 *Ibid.*
51 TCD, March Papers MS 8305, Memorandum submitted by Dr P. Moran, Ardee, Co. Louth, June 1948.
52 *Ibid.*
53 *Ibid.*
54 *Ibid.*, Memorandum submitted by the Irish Housewives Association, June 1948.
55 TCD, Marsh Papers MS 8306, Rural survey, Kilkenny. Conducted by Mr Byrne and Mr O'Leary.
56 CEOP, p. 138.
57 *Ibid.*
58 TCD, Marsh Papers MS 8307–8, Transcripts of Evidence.
59 CEOP, p. 138.
60 *Ibid.*
61 *Irish Times*, 1 February 1949.
62 TCD, March Papers MS 8301, Summaries of Evidence.
63 CEOP, p. 102.
64 *Ibid.*
65 TCD, Marsh Papers MS 8305, Memorandum from Mr Michael J. Molloy, Milltown, Co. Galway.
66 TCD, Marsh Papers MS 8300, Department of Social Welfare Employment Branch to the Secretary, CEOP, 5/11/1948.
67 TCD, Marsh Papers MS 8305, Memorandum from Mr Michael J. Molloy, Milltown, Co. Galway.
68 TCD, Marsh Papers MS 8305, Memorandum submitted by Coisde Oideachais Ghairme Beatha, Conndae Liathdroma, 28 June 1948.
69 TCD, Marsh Papers MS 8305, Memorandum submitted by the Irish Housewives Association, June 1948.
70 *Ibid.*
71 TCD, Marsh Papers MS 8306, *Rural Survey, Galway City* by Mr McElhinney.
72 TCD, Marsh Papers MS 8300, Department of Social Welfare Employment Branch to the Secretary, CEOP, 5/11/1948.
73 *Ibid.*
74 CEOP, p. 122.

75 TCD, Marsh Papers MS 8301, Summaries of Evidence.
76 *Ibid.*
77 TCD, Marsh Papers MS 8306, Rural Surveys.
78 CEOP, Addendum No. 2 by Dr R. C. Geary and Dr M. D. McCarthy, p. 203.
79 *Ibid.*
80 *Ibid.*, p. 180.
81 *Ibid.*, p. 139.
82 TCD, Marsh Papers MS 8301, Dr Beddy's survey of Co. Mayo and Co. Sligo.
83 CEOP, p. 140.
84 *Ibid.*, p. 138.
85 *Ibid.*, p. 139.
86 *Ibid.*, p. 141.
87 *Ibid.*, p. 140.
88 *Ibid.*, Reservation No. 6 by Rev. A. A. Luce, p. 230.
89 *Ibid.*
90 *Ibid.*, p. 140.
91 *Ibid.*
92 *Ibid.*, p. 180.
93 *Ibid.*
94 *Ibid.*
95 *Ibid.*, p. 141.
96 *Ibid.*, p. 139.
97 *Ibid.*, p. 140.
98 *Ibid.*, Reservation No. 2 by A. Fitzgerald, p. 222.
99 *Ibid.*, p. 140.
100 *Ibid.*
101 *Ibid.*
102 *Ibid.*
103 *Ibid.*, p. 118.
104 *Ibid.*, p. 168.
105 *Ibid.*
106 *Ibid.*
107 *Ibid.*, p. 166.
108 *Ibid.*
109 *Ibid.*
110 *Ibid.*, p. 167.
111 *Ibid.*, p. 155.
112 *Ibid.*, p. 156.
113 *Ibid.*, p. 172.
114 *Ibid.*
115 *Ibid.*, p. 174.
116 *Ibid.*
117 *Ibid.*
118 *Ibid.*
119 *Ibid.*, p. 175.
120 *Ibid.*
121 *Ibid.*
122 *Ibid.*
123 *Ibid.*, p. 176.
124 *Ibid.*, p. 143.
125 *Ibid.*
126 *Ibid.*, p. 178.
127 *Ibid.*, Addendum No. 1 by Rev. Thomas Counihan, p. 192.
128 *Ibid.*, p. 1.
129 *Ibid.*, p. 180.

130 *Ibid.*

131 *Dáil Debates* (4 December 1952), Vol. 135, Col. 763.

132 *Irish Independent*, 10 May 1954.

Aspects of Local Health in Ireland in the 1950s

* In the preparation of this paper, I am grateful for the efforts of the staff of the National Archives in retrieving obscure files, and indeed Mary O'Doherty, archivist at the Royal College of Surgeons, for similar assistance in relation to the James Deeny papers. Professor Dermot F. Keogh read a draft of this paper, providing probing and stimulating comment.

1 Cf. J. H. Whyte, *Church and State in Modern Ireland, 1923–70* (Dublin: Gill & Macmillan, 1971); N. Browne, *Against The Tide* (Dublin: Gill & Macmillan, 1986); R. Barrington, *Health, Medicine and Politics in Ireland 1900–70* (Dublin: Institute of Public Administration, 1987); E. McKee, 'Church–State relations and the development of Irish health policy: the Mother and Child scheme 1944–53', *Irish Historical Studies*, vol. XXV, No. 98, 1986; J. Deeny, *To Cure and To Care: Memoirs of a Chief Medical Officer* (Dublin: Glendale, 1989).

2 J. Deeny, 'The Health Bill of 1947' undated (1948) lecture delivered at medical conference in Cork, Deeny Papers, RCSI.

3 Whyte, *Church and State*, p. 123.

4 Department of Health Survey of Dispensary Districts 1960, M100/50, D/H, NAI.

5 See B. Hensey, *The Health Services of Ireland* (Dublin: Institute of Public Administration, 1959), p. 35 and *passim* for further discussion of roles. See Barrington, *Health*, for excellent background on difficulties establishing the CMOs across the country from the 1920s.

6 Memorandum on Annual Reports of County Medical Officers, by Mr Grimes, attached to Minute of 3 December 1951, M100/160, D/H, NAI.

7 Minute by J. Darby, 1 February 1952, M100/160, D/H, NAI.

8 Minute by P. R. F. Fanning for J. D. MacCormack, 2 April 1952, M100/160, D/H, NAI.

9 Summary of replies to memorandum on Annual Reports of CMOs, 23 September 1957, M100/160, D/H, NAI. This summarises contributions since 1951 and some contributors may have left the department at this stage.

10 Minute for Mr Herlihy, 31 August 1960, M100/160, D/H, NAI. The complacency is captured in a late reply on 31 August 1960: 'As B Section have reminded us periodically about this, I think we should send a reply now'!

11 Memorandum by Chief Medical Adviser for J. Garvin, 30 January 1947, Deeny Papers, RCSI.

12 General observations of County Council and Department on remedying defects etc., of Dispensary Premises, September–October 1950, A25/114, D/H, NAI.

13 *Ibid.*

14 *Ibid.*

15 Report by Michael F. Daly, 10 October 1949, A21/150 vol. 1a, D/H, NAI.

16 *Ibid.*

17 P Kennedy to Secretary, Leitrim County Council, 22 July 1949; Secretary, Leitrim County Council, to Secretary, Department of Health, 1 May 1950; Note dated 12 February 1960, A16/65, D/H, NAI.

18 Department of Health, *Health Progress 1947–53*, Pr 2086 (Dublin: Stationery Office, 1953), p. 6.

19 See B. Hensey, *The Health Services of Ireland*, fourth edn (Dublin: Institute of Public Administration, 1988), p. 37.

20 Department of Health minute, 19 June 1958, A21/238, D/H, NAI.

21 Guidelines for Dispensary Residences, 1947, Deeny Papers, RCSI.

22 Draft of Galway County Medical Officer of Health Annual Report, 1954, M11/33, D/H, NAI.

23 Department of Health, Annual Report 1959, draft section on Maternity and Child

Health Services, M107/17, D/H, NAI. To be fair, one should also acknowledge Hensey's contemporary comment: 'While the obligation to organise this service is placed on all health authorities, it will be some time before the service operates throughout the country'. See Hensey, *Health Services*, p. 84.

24 County returns and extract reports on operation of Child Welfare Clinic Services, 1957–8, M107/ 14, D/H, NAI.

25 Clare CMO to Chief Officer, Clare Public Health and Public Assistance Department, 9 February 1954, D3/72, D/H, NAI.

26 Mayo CMO to Secretary, Mayo County Council, 25 February 1954, D21/112, D/H, NAI.

27 See copy of circular of 13 December 1944 on file D119/4, D/H, NAI. Workers from Northern Ireland were covered up to 1940, but no arrangements were made for their repatriation.

28 Minute by J. Deeny, 16 January 1945, D119/4, D/H, NAI.

29 See Minutes and Notes for 1945 on file D119/4, D/H, NAI.

30 Memorandum to Secretary of each County Council and County and City Manager, 4 Feb 1952, D119/4, D/H, NAI.

31 J. Deeny, BCG Memorandum, 19 August 1946; T. Brady, Memorandum, 26 August 1946; S. MacEntee to Medical Research Council, 31 August 1946, D113/1, D/H, NAI.

32 Extract from National BCG Committee Report for 1952, cited in National BCG Committee Report, 1954; National BCG Committee Report BCG, 1953.

33 *Irish Press*, 8 May 1953.

34 *Irish Press*, 19 May 1953.

35 *Irish Press*, 26 May 1953.

36 *Manchester Guardian*, 7 May 1954.

37 *Manchester Guardian*, 16 July 1954, *Irish Times*, 17 July 1954, *Irish Press*, 19 July 1954.

38 *Irish Times*, 26 July 1955.

39 Department of Health Press Release, 26 July 1955, D119/1, D/H, NAI.

40 *Westmeath Examiner*, 13 August 1955.

41 J. A. Charles to J. Deeny, 8 November 1957, D119/20, D/H, NAI.

42 *Ibid.*

43 Minute for Secretary, 9 January 1959, D119/21, D/H, NAI.

44 Return of patients from Great Britain for treatment for TB, 18 May 1959, D119/23, D/H, NAI.

45 Deeny memorandum on BCG programme, November 1958, BD112/697, D/H, NAI.

46 T. O'Sullivan to Mayo/Clare County Managers, 28 January 1959; Mayo CMO to Secretary, Mayo County Council, 17 February 1959; Clare CMO to Clare County Manager, 31 March 1959, BD112/697, D/H, NAI.

'Too Fond of Going': Female Emigration and Change for Women in Ireland 1946–1961

1 John Healy, *No One Shouted Stop!* (formerly *Death of an Irish Town*). First published 1968 (Achill: House of Healy 1988), pp. 38–9.

2 Bryan MacMahon, 'Getting on the High Road Again' in John A. O'Brien (ed.), *The Vanishing Irish* (London: W. H. Allen, 1954), p. 207.

3 The classic sociological accounts, which spurred (and were spurred by) the women's movements of the 1970s and 1980s, are Catherine Rose, *The Female Experience: The Story of the Woman Movement in Ireland* (Galway: Arlen House, 1975) and Jenny Beale, *Women in Ireland: Voices of Change* (Dublin: Gill and Macmillan 1986). Other classic accounts of women in the Free State and Republic are Mary Clancy, 'Aspects of Women's Contribution to Oireachtas Debate in Ireland 1922–37' in M. Luddy and C. Murphy (eds.), *Women Surviving* (Dublin: Poolbeg Press, 1990), pp. 206–32; Mary E. Daly, *Industrial Development and Irish National Identity 1922–39* (Syracuse: Syracuse University Press, 1992), and Yvonne Scannell, 'The Con-

stitution and the Role of Women' in Brian Farrell (ed.), *De Valera's Constitution and Ours* (Dublin: Gill and Macmillan, 1988), pp. 123–36. Margaret Ward's classic *Unmanageable Revolutionaries* (Dingle: Brandon Press, 1983) also gives an account of women in the Free State, pp. 199–263. See also Amy Wieners, 'Rural Irishwomen, their Changing Role, Status and Condition' in *Eire– Ireland*, Earrach/Spring 1994, pp. 76–91; the *Journal of Women's History* (Bloomingdale: Indiana University Press) Vols 6/7, Winter/Spring 1994–5, Nos 1 and 2, special issue on Irish women; Mary O'Dowd and Maryann Valiulis (eds.) *Women and Irish History* (Dublin: Wolfhound Press, 1997), Introduction, p. 13; a useful summary of contemporary feminist perceptions of all the disabilities suffered by Irish women is provided in Frances Gardiner, 'The Unfinished Revolution' in *The Canadian Journal of Irish Studies*, Vol. 18, No. 1 (1992), pp. 15–39. J. J. Lee's authoritative *Ireland 1912–1985: Politics and Society* (Cambridge: Cambridge University Press, 1989), p. 335 and *passim*, suggests that the women who stayed were those who settled for less.

4 The classic account of women's emigration after the Famine remains Robert E. Kennedy Jr, *The Irish: Emigration, Marriage and Fertility* (Berkeley: University Of California Press, 1973). See also P. O'Sullivan (ed.), *Irish Women and Irish Migration* (London: Leicester University Press, 1995), P. O'Sullivan (ed.), *Patterns of migration* (London: Leicester University Press, 1997). On women's emigration in the twentieth century in particular, see Pauric Travers, 'Emigration and Gender: The Case of Ireland 1922–1960' in M. O'Dowd and S. Wichert (eds.), *Chattel, Servant or Citizen? Women's Status in Church, State and Society* (Belfast: Institute of Irish Studies, QUB, 1995), pp. 187–199, and his '"There Was Nothing for Me There": Irish Female Emigration 1922–1971' in P. O'Sullivan (ed.), *Irish Women and Irish Migration*. See also Kate Kelly and Triona Nic Giolla Choille, *Emigration Matters for Women* (Dublin: Attic Press, 1990).

5 See, for example, Hasia R. Diner, *Erin's Daughters in America* (Baltimore: Johns Hopkins University Press, 1983).

6 For a fuller discussion see C. Clear, *Women of the House: Women's Household Work in Ireland 1922–1961: Discourses, Experiences, Memories* (Dublin, 2000), pp. 13–26.

7 *Ibid, passim* but especially pp. 68–95.

8 Dorothy Macardle, 'Irishwomen in Industry', *Irish Press*, 5 September 1931.

9 Mary Daly, 'Women in the Irish Free State 1922–1939: The Interaction between Economics and Ideology' in *Journal of Women's History*, *loc.cit.*, pp. 99–116.

10 See Clear, *Women of the House, passim*.

11 Bryan MacMahon, 'Getting on the High Road Again', *loc.cit.*, pp. 206–7.

12 See Clear, *Women of the House*, pp. 143–215.

13 John D. Sheridan, 'The Day Before Yesterday' in *Bright Intervals* (Dublin: Talbot Press 1958), pp. 54–8.

14 Pauline Bracken, *Light of Other Days: A Dublin Childhood* (Cork: Mercier Press1992), pp. 116–18.

15 Mona Hearn, *Below Stairs: Domestic Service Remembered in Dublin and Beyond 1880–1922* (Dublin: Lilliput Press, 1993), *passim*.

16 Mary Healy, *For the Poor and for the Gentry: Mary Healy Remembers her Life* (Dublin: Geography Publications, 1989), pp. 76–7.

17 Elizabeth Boyle, 'A Plan for the Northern Houseworkers' [meant also to have application in the south], *The Irish Housewife*, Vol. 1 (1946), pp. 31–3. Louie Bennett, 'The Domestic Problem', *ibid.*, pp. 29–30. Peter Moser, 'Rural Economy and Female Emigration in the West of Ireland 1936–1956', *UCG Women's Studies Review*, Vol. 2 (1993), pp. 41–52.

18 E.g., Evelyn Mahon, 'Women's Rights and Catholicism in Ireland', *New Left Review*, No. 166, Nov–Dec 1978, pp. 53–78; Rose, *The Female Experience*; Beale, *Women in Ireland, passim*.

19 See Clear, *Women of the House*, pp. 46–67, and pp. 143–215, for a discussion of these comments and observations.

20 See Rose, *The Female Experience*, and Beale, *Women in Ireland, passim.*

21 Clear, *Women of the House*.

22 Travers, 'Gender and Emigration', p. 191, but more particularly, 'There Was Nothing for Me There', pp. 163–5.

23 Department of Education, *Annual Reports and Results of Examinations*, 1925–1961.

24 The classic demographic–social account is K. H. Connell, *Irish Peasant Society* (Oxford: Clarendon Press, New York: Doubleday, 1968); more recent works include Robert E. Kennedy, *The Irish*, and Timothy Guinnane, *The Vanishing Irish: Households, Migration and the Rural Economy in Ireland 1850–1914* (Princeton: Princton University Press, 1997).

25 For a summary, see the sources in notes 3 and 4. I must confess that my own research, at one stage, also led me to this conclusion: see C. Clear, *Nuns in Nineteenth-century Ireland* (Dublin: Gill and Macmillan, 1987), pp. 1–35.

26 Edmund J. Murray, 'The Key to the Problem', in O'Brien (ed.), *The Vanishing Irish*, p. 72.

27 Patrick B. Noonan, CSSp, 'Why Few Irish Marry', in O'Brien (ed.), *The Vanishing Irish*, p. 51.

28 John D. Sheridan, 'We're Not Dead Yet', in O'Brien (ed.), *The Vanishing Irish*, p. 186.

29 Mary Frances Keating, 'Marriage-shy Irishmen', in O'Brien (ed.), *The Vanishing Irish*, p. 170.

30 Miriam Rooney, 'Our Block', in O'Brien (ed.), *The Vanishing Irish*, p. 197.

31 Sean Ó Faoláin, 'Love Among the Irish', in O'Brien (ed.), *The Vanishing Irish*, p. 113.

32 John M. Hayes, 'Stemming the Flight from the Land', in O'Brien (ed.), *The Vanishing Irish*, pp. 127–42.

33 *Report of the Commission on Emigration and Other Population Problems 1948–54* (1956), R. 84, Reservation No. 1, W. R. F. Collis and Arnold Marsh, pp. 220–1. Moser, 'Female Emigration', p. 47.

34 Cited and discussed in Clear, *Women of the House*, p. 201.

35 For a fuller discussion of single women, see Clear, *Women of the House*, chapter 1. Report of the Interdepartmental Committee on the Question of Making Available a Second Dwelling-house on Farms (1943), NAI S13413/1. This committee is discussed in Travers, 'Gender and Emigration', and in Clear, *Women of the House*, pp. 44, 171–2, 177, 212, and referred to by almost all of the contributors to O'Brien (ed.), *The Vanishing Irish*.

36 Clear, *Women of the House*, pp. 171–216.

37 See, e.g., Kevin Devlin, 'Single and Selfish', *Christus Rex*, Vol. 6 (1952), pp. 223–32, and Seán de Cléir, SJ, 'Marriage and Family in Irish Life', *ibid.*, pp. 303–13. John D. Sheridan, 'We're Not Dead Yet', in O'Brien (ed.), *The Vanishing Irish*, also deplores the selfishness of some young men. Moser, 'Female Emigration', p. 46.

38 Anna Kelly, 'What's Wrong With Marriage?' reprinted in the *Irish Digest*, Vol. XIV, No. 2, December 1942, pp. 9–11.

39 Reprinted in the *Irish Digest*, Vol. XIV, No. 2, December 1942, p. 70.

40 See Maryann Valiulis, 'Neither Feminist nor Flapper: The Ecclesiastical Construction of the Ideal Irish Woman' in O'Dowd and Wichert (eds.) *Chattel, Servant or Citizen?*, pp. 168–78; John D. Sheridan, 'We're Not Dead Yet' in O'Brien (ed.), *The Vanishing Irish* (1954) and *Emigration Commission Report*, Minority Report by Most Rev. Dr Lucey, pp. 335–63.

41 See, for example, G. Duby, M. Perrot and F. Thebaud (eds.), *A History of Women in the West V: Toward a Cultural Identity in the Twentieth Century* (Cambridge: Harvard University Press, 1996).

42 Clear, *Women of the House*, p. 201; also for numbers of hairdressers, pp. 204, 217.

43 Travers, 'There Was Nothing for Me There'.

44 Moser, 'Female Emigration', p. 45.

Before Cadden: Abortion in Mid-Twentieth-Century Ireland

1 Memorandum on the Cadden case: NAI, Department of the Taoiseach file S 16116. The English trip is noted on p. 7.

2 The trial and Appeal Court judges were unwilling to accept a manslaughter plea as they considered that, given her maternity-nurse qualifications, Mamie Cadden must have been aware of the possible consequences of her actions.

3 Kenneth E. L. Deale, *Beyond Any Reasonable Doubt? A Book of Irish Murder Trials* (Dublin: Gill and Macmillan, 1990), p. 152.

4 Section 58 of the Offences Against the Person Act reads:
'Every woman, being with child, who, with intent to procure her own miscarriage, shall unlawfully administer to herself any poison or other noxious thing, or shall unlawfully use any instrument or other means whatsoever with the like intent; and whosoever, with intent to procure the miscarriage of any woman, whether she be or be not with child, shall unlawfully administer to her or cause to be taken by her any poison or other noxious thing, or shall unlawfully use any instrument or other means whatsoever with the like intent, shall be guilty of a felony, and being convicted thereof shall be liable ... to be kept in penal servitude for life ...'

Section 59 made it a misdemeanour to supply 'any poison or other noxious thing, or any instrument or thing whatsoever' knowing that it was to be used to procure an unlawful miscarriage.

5 The controversy was multi-layered and developed in the context of ongoing conflict between central government and the Co. Mayo local authorities – and local Catholic hierarchy – over the Mayo librarianship case and local government appointments. For discussion of some of the issues involved in the Mayo case see: Dermot Keogh, *The Vatican, the Bishops and Irish Politics 1919–39* (Cambridge: Cambridge University Press, 1986), pp. 166–77; J. J. Lee, *Ireland 1912–1985: Politics and Society* (Cambridge: Cambridge University Press, 1989), pp. 161–67.

6 See NAI, Department of the Taoiseach file, S2547A for translation of the statutes by the secretary of the archbishop of Tuam. For details of the Harty meeting see Keogh, *The Vatican, the Bishops and Irish Politics*, p. 169.

7 Undated memo in Department of Justice file, S2547B. A note on the memo reads 'Returned by Professor O'Sullivan 24/3/31'. John Marcus O'Sullivan was Minister for Education. Dermot Keogh suggested that O'Sullivan might have written the memo.

8 Rev. David Barry, 'Medical Ethics', *Irish Ecclesiastical Record*, vol. XX, August 1922, pp. 168–80. The reference to 'embryotomy', implying intervention at an early stage in pregnancy, is interesting.

9 Barry, 'Medical Ethics', p. 170.

10 *Irish Times*, 11 February 1929.

11 Lambeth Conference Report, 1930: *Encyclical Letter from the Bishops with Resolutions and Reports* (SPCK, Macmillan, 1930), pp. 89–90.

12 Lambeth Conference Report, p. 91.

13 The annual reports of the Dublin maternity hospitals – published in each subsequent year in the *Irish Journal of Medical Science (IJMSc)* – provide statistics on obstetric practices and some patient details. They list cases of craniotomy. Most suggest that there was no discernible foetal heartbeat when the operation was performed, but a few do appear to have been performed on live foetuses. Taking examples of circumstances in which craniotomy was used from the Coombe and Rotunda Hospital reports for 1928, the Coombe report refers to a case in which 'craniotomy was necessary owing to the contracted pelvis and hydrocephalic head in the baby' (*IJMSc*, 1929, p. 519). An entry under 'decapitation and craniotomy' in the Rotunda report gives details of a woman referred to the hospital from 'the country' having already been in labour for three days with the foetus in the breech position. It notes that, late on the fourth day, 'Extraction was thought to be the only chance for the child, but aftercoming head was caught on the contraction ring, necessitating decapi-

tation' (*IJMSc*, 1929, pp. 142–43).

14 26 February 1931, memorandum of conversation between Gilmartin and Sir Joseph Glynn (negotiating on behalf of the government): Department of the Taoiseach file S2547A.

15 The 1935 ban on contraceptives was introduced with all-party agreement. A committee of Dáil deputies who drew up headings for the bill (based on the recommendations in the unpublished August 1931 Carrigan Report) recommended that doctors should be permitted to prescribe contraceptives. The decision to prohibit their import and sale was taken within the Fianna Fáil cabinet but accepted by opposition parties.

16 Tony Farmar, *Holles Street 1894–1994: The National Maternity Hospital: A Centenary History* (Dublin: A. and A. Farmar, 1994), pp. 86–87 and p. 100. For examples of attacks on non-Catholic medical practices see: 'Molula', 'A Call for Catholic Action. The Medical School of Trinity College' in *The Catholic Bulletin*, vol. XXI, no. 2, February 1931, pp. 139–43, and Rev. M. P. Cleary, 'The Church of Ireland and Birth Control', *Irish Ecclesiastical Record*, fifth series, vol. 38, December 1931, pp. 622–29. (Delivered as the annual charity sermon at the National Maternity Hospital.)

17 State file: Court of Criminal Appeal, no. 18 of 1945, evidence of A. W. Quinine, in the form of vaginal pessaries, was used as a spermicide. In this essay I have used initials when referring to women who gave evidence of having abortions, as it is possible that some may still be alive. I use full names in referring to those who faced abortion charges, as these names are already in the public domain.

18 State files: Dublin Circuit Criminal Court, 1 June 1944, indictment no. 157 and 10 October 1944, indictment no. 52.

19 State file: Circuit Criminal Court, 10 October 1944, indictment no. 52, statement by James Ashe.

20 See Barbara Brookes, *Abortion in England, 1900–1967* (London: Croom Helm, 1988), 'The Medical Profession 1900–1939', pp. 51–78 and 'Women and Abortion Law Reform', pp. 79–104. The 1938 Bourne case clarified British law on the 'life' and 'health' issue when the judge, Mr Justice Macnaghten, held that a doctor operating to prevent a woman becoming a 'physical or mental wreck' was operating to preserve her life. (The Bourne case is briefly referred to below.)

21 State file: Circuit Criminal Court, 10 October 1944, indictment no. 52, statements by Ashe and Flynn. A fictional examination of the abortion issue in Ireland demonstrated one constraint on medical practitioners who did not accept Roman Catholic medical teaching and were employed in hospitals: the personnel they worked with. In Signe Toksvig's novel *Eve's Doctor* (London: Faber and Faber, 1937) (quickly banned in Ireland), the central figure, Master of a fictional Irish maternity hospital, perforates the head of a hydrocephalic infant during childbirth. He claims that he can hear no foetal heartbeat, but has aborted a full term pregnancy for social (the woman involved was the sole provider for six small children and a sick, unemployed husband) and eugenic reasons. An assistant, who had listened to the foetal heart and knows that it had not stopped, reports the case to the parish priest and the doctor's career is ruined.

22 R. S. Rose, *An Outline of Fertility Control, Focusing on the Element of Abortion, in the Republic of Ireland to 1976*, PhD. Thesis (Institute of Sociology, University of Stockholm, Sweden, 1976), p. 122.

23 Barbara Brookes, *Abortion in England, 1900–1967*, p. 40.

24 *Report of the Inter-Departmental Committee on Abortion, 1939* (London: Stationery Office, 1939), Birkett Report, pp. 9–11. Evidence of some witnesses suggested that the percentage of criminal abortions was considerably higher.

25 National Archives, state books at the Circuit Criminal Court: Donegal 1932, indictment 1 and Monaghan 1935, p. 27. Evidence in the latter case suggests that when the woman was four months pregnant she bought menstrual regulators in a local chemist's shop. They came with a leaflet recommending a more effective product, available by post from London, which she sent for. The abortifacient effects of drugs are further discussed below. These and the 1949 Capaldi case are the only cases I have found in which proceedings were taken against the woman seeking an abortion. The state abandoned the 1935 Monaghan trial after nine days.

26 Quote and information on substances used taken from the state file on the case: Dublin Circuit Criminal Court, 1 June, 1944, indictment no. 93. The disqualified maternity nurse died before the case came to court. The man responsible for the pregnancy was sentenced to six months' imprisonment on charges of administering noxious substances with intent to cause abortion but an unlawful carnal knowledge charge failed because, as the young woman's birth had never been registered, satisfactory proof of age could not be produced.

27 Copy of submission dated 27.2.26: NAI, Department of Justice file 7/1/5. Kerr's submission carried the stamp of approval of the local bishop, Most Reverend Dr McKenna.

28 Evil Literature Committee papers, NAI, Department of Justice file 7/2/17. (The reference to 'steel' may imply either iron chloride or iron filings. 'Bitter apple' is colocynth. See John M. Riddle, *Eve's Herbs* [Harvard: Harvard University Press, 1997], pp. 195 and 229, for reference to the uses of both). The Birkett Report, p. 42, also expressed concern that "' ... female pills" sold ostensibly for the cure of menstrual irregularities' contained abortifacient drugs. Whether such pills were effective was a matter of dispute. Barbara Brookes, *Abortion in England*, pp. 117–19.

29 *Report of the Committee on Evil Literature* (Dublin: Stationery Office, 1927), pp. 16 and 19.

30 For example, see *The Irish Chemist and Druggist* (official journal of the Pharmaceutical Society of Northern Ireland), August 1931, p. 228; September 1931, p. 250; November 1931, p. 322; and *The Chemist and Druggist*, 19 December 1931, p. 722. This activity may also have been related to the Lambeth conference decision and publication of *Casti Connubii* noted above.

31 *The Irish Chemist and Druggist*, September 1931, p. 250. A copy of this warning is also filed in NAI, Department of Justice file 8/20/1.

32 As discussed with reference to prosecutions below.

33 Dr John McGrath, second statement: NAI, state file at the Central Criminal Court, Laois, 1 June, 1948, indictment no. 3.

34 The evidence in abortion cases, some of which are discussed below, suggests that a number of the methods referred to were used in Ireland. John M. Riddle's *Eve's Herbs* is the best recent source for the history of abortifacient drugs. Useful contemporary sources on drug uses include: W. Hale White, *Materia Medica: Pharmacy, Pharmacology and Therapeutics*, twenty-fourth edition (London: J. & A. Churchill, 1939). Alternative uses of ergot of rye are described on pp. 395–402; those of quinine on pp. 349–351; and of apiol on p. 63. For discussion of the use of apiol and other drugs as abortifacients, see: 'Production of Abortion by Drugs', in Keith Simpson (ed.), *Taylor's Principles and Practice of Medical Jurisprudence*, vol. II, twelfth edition, 1965, pp. 105–11. This refers to a 1937 study suggesting that apiol caused abortion in 16 out of 20 cases, p. 107.

35 Rev. John McCarthy, 'Incurring of Censure Attached to Crime of Abortion', *Irish Ecclesiastical Record*, fifth series, vol. 69, Jan–December, 1947, pp. 1007–10. (Notes and Queries.) The theme of the article was whether the taking of drugs or using other means, 'while sinful because of intention', might not lead to the censure of excommunication. Quotations from pp. 1008 and 1009.

36 Statement by E.H.: NAI, state files at the Central Criminal Court, Laois, 1 June 1948, indictment nos. 2 and 3.

37 British *Report of the Inter-departmental Committee on Abortion* (the Birkett Report), p. 41. The 1930 Lambeth Conference Report, quoted above, taking account of the views of Anglicans world wide, acknowledged (p. 89) that 'the sale of drugs designed to procure abortion is large'.

38 *Irish Times*, 30 May 1940.

39 References to the Anthony case are based on *Irish Times* and *Cork Examiner* accounts from 28–31 May 1940.

40 Details of case based on material in NAI, state file at the Circuit Criminal Court, 4 October 1943, indictment nos. 106–108 and at the Court of Criminal Appeal, no. 53 of 1943.

41 Statement by Dr John McGrath: NAI, state file at the Circuit Criminal Court, 4 October 1943, indictment nos. 106–108.

42 I have not found a reference to more serious charges arising from the death of Mrs B.

43 Details of case based on material in NAI, state files at the Central Criminal Court, Laois, 1 June 1948, indictment nos. 2 and 3.

44 Evidence of Dr Frank Creedon: *Irish Times*, 29 May 1940.

45 Evidence of E. R. and M. R.: NAI, state file, Dublin Circuit Criminal Court, 10 October 1944, indictment no. 46.

46 Detective Inspector Martin O'Neill quoted in case summary, p. 4: NAI state file, Court of Criminal Appeal, no. 53 of 1943.

47 *Irish Times*, 7 June 1944.

48 It is not possible here to consider fully the shortcomings of maternal death and criminal statistics as sources of information on abortion rates, but I examined aspects of this issue in my thesis: Sandra Larmour, *Aspects of the State and Female Sexuality in the Irish Free State, 1922–1949*, PhD Thesis (NUI, History Department, University College Cork, 1998).

49 Rose, *An Outline of Fertility Control*, pp. 121–23.

50 NAI, state file at the Dublin Circuit Criminal Court, 4 October 1943, indictment nos. 106–108.

51 *Irish Times*, 22 July 1944 and *The Irish Reports*, 1945, pp. 237–52.

52 NAI: state file, Dublin Circuit Criminal Court, 17 April 1945, indictment no. 36.

53 Capaldi: NAI, state file, Dublin Circuit Criminal Court, 2 June 1949, indictment no. 45; Moscow: *Irish Times*, 21 April 1950; Thornton: *The Irish Reports*, 1952, pp. 91–97.

54 *Irish Independent*, 29 April 1974. Quoted in Rose, *An Outline of Fertility Control*, p. 73. When Rose discussed the issue with him a few weeks later, Professor Browne suggested that the sepsis cases resulted from illegal abortions carried out in England rather than Ireland, although the press report quoted him as stating that criminal abortions 'are taking place in Dublin. They always have taken place and always will take place …'

55 The figure from Hansard, Parliamentary Debates, House of Commons, 28 June 1974, cols. 544–545, quoted in Rose, *An Outline of Fertility Control*, p. 75.

56 Caitriona Clear, *Women of the House: Women's Household Work in Ireland 1922–1961* (Dublin: Irish Academic Press, 2000), p. 123, quoting from A. P. Barry, D. Meagher and E. O'Dwyer, 'Heart Disease in Pregnancy', *Journal of the Irish Medical Association*, vol. 38 (1956), pp. 82–83.

Tourism and the Irish State in the 1950s

1 The *Continental Daily Mail*, 'Special Survey of Ireland', 30 June 1951.

2 Department of External Affairs, *Ireland – An Introduction* (Dublin: Dept of External Affairs, 1950).

3 C. S. Andrews, *Man of No Property* (Dublin: Lilliput Press, 1982), p. 22.

4 Troy D. Davis, *Dublin's American Policy – Irish-American Diplomatic Relations 1945–1952* (Washington DC: Catholic University of America, 1998), p. 108.

5 NAI, Department of the Taoiseach, S13087B, Department of Finance Memorandum to government on the inter-departmental Working Party on Dollar Earnings, first Interim Report, 18 November 1949.

6 *Ibid.*

7 NA, Department of the Taoiseach, S14270, letter from John A. Costello, 15 June 1948.

8 NA, Department of the Taoiseach, S13087B, extract from budget speech by Minister for Finance, p. 5.

9 *Irish Independent*, 29 October 1948.

10 *An Bord Cuartaíochta Annual General Report* for year ending 31 March 1949.

11 NA, Department of the Taoiseach, S13087B, Department of Finance Memorandum for the Government 'The tourism industry', 16 February 1950.

12 *Ibid.*

13 *Ibid.*, Memorandum for the Government, Report of the Committee on Tourism, 13 June 1950.

14 *Ibid.*, Copy of memorandum from Theodore J. Pozzy to Joseph E. Carrigan, 30 January 1950.

15 *Ibid.*, Department of Industry and Commerce Memorandum 'Proposal by Hilton Hotels Incorporated for Hotel in Dublin', March 1950.

16 *Ibid.*, Department of Industry and Commerce Memorandum 'Reports Submitted by the Irish Delegation on the Study of American Hotel Methods', May 1950.

17 *Ibid.*, Department of Industry and Commerce note, March 1950, 'Dispatch of Party of Practical Hoteliers to the United States of America'.

18 *Ibid.*

19 *Ibid.*

20 *Synthesis of Reports on Tourism 1950–1951* (Dublin: Stationery Office, 1951).

21 *Ibid.*, p. 1.

22 *Ibid.*, pp. 9, 10.

23 NA, Department of the Taoiseach, S13087B, Preliminary Report of the Irish Hotels Commission for American Tourism, 30 September 1950.

24 *Ibid.*, ECA, *Technical Assistance Programme in Travel, Hotel and Allied Activities, Report* by Brendan O'Regan and Patrick F. Dornan, 29 April 1950, p. 7.

25 *Ibid.*, Department of Industry and Commerce memorandum 'Reports Submitted by Irish Delegation', May 1950.

26 *Ibid.*, Department of External Affairs, Memorandum for the Government, 'Dollar Earnings', 4 May 1950.

27 *Ibid.*, Department of the Taoiseach note 'Tourist industry', 30 May 1950.

28 *The Caterer and Hotel Keeper*, 18 March 1950, p. 5.

29 *Irish Independent*, 'Tourism a major asset of nation', 27 October 1950, p. 7.

30 *Irish Independent*, 'Travel as inspiration to peace', 18 October 1950.

31 Tourist Traffic Act (Dublin: Stationery Office, 1952).

32 *Dáil Debates*, Vol. 129, Col. 1118, 27 February 1952.

33 *Ibid.*, Col. 1119.

34 *Ibid.*, Col. 1123.

35 *Bord Fáilte Annual Report* for year ending 31 March 1952.

36 *Ibid.*

37 *Dáil Debates*, Vol. 129, Col. 1124, 27 February 1952.

38 *Dáil Debates*, Vol. 129, Col. 1342, 28 February 1952.

39 *Ibid.*, Col. 1384.

40 NA, Department of the Taoiseach, S11356C, Department of theTaoiseach Note, 17 July 1951.

41 *Dáil Debates*, Tourist Traffic Bill, 1954, Vol. 148, Col. 130, 9 February 1955.

42 *Ibid.*, Col. 133.

43 *Ibid.*, Col. 135.

44 *Dáil Debates*, Tourist Traffic Bill, 1954, Vol. 148, Col. 44, 16 February 1955.

45 Interview with Kevin O'Doherty, 8 March 2002.

46 *Bord Fáilte Éireann Annual Report* for year ending 31 March 1956.

47 *Ibid.*

48 *Irish Times*, 13 December 1954, p. 5.

49 *Ibid.*, p. 7.

50 *Dáil Debates*, Vol. 148, Col. 142, 9 February 1955.

51 Garret FitzGerald, 'Irish Economic Problems' in *Studies*, Autumn 1957, p. 271.

52 James Deegan and Donal A. Dineen, *Tourism Policy and Performance – The Irish Experience* (London: International Thomson Business Press, 1997), p. 24.

53 Tourist Traffic Act (Dublin: Stationery Office, 1957).

54 *Bord Fáilte Annual Report* for year ending 31 March 1958.

55 Quoted in Ronan Fanning, *Independent Ireland* (Dublin: Helicon, 1983), p. 192.

56 Deegan & Dineen, *Tourism Policy and Performance*, p. 25.

57 *Ibid.*, p. 26.

58 NA, Department of the Taoiseach, S13087E, Speech by Seán Lemass at closing banquet of Congress of International Hotel Associations, 2 April 1960.

59 NA, Department of the Taoiseach, S13087D. Department of Industry and Commerce, letter from John Leydon to Maurice Moynihan, 29 April 1952.

60 *Irish Times*, 26 February 1952.

61 *Irish Press*, 8 March 1952.

62 *Irish Press*, 7 April 1952.

63 NA, Department of the Taoiseach, S15297A, letter from Patrick Little to Eamon de Valera, 12 April 1952.

64 *Bord Fáilte Annual Report* for year ended 31 March 1954, p. 12.

65 *Irish Press*, 16 March 1953.

66 *Evening Herald*, 20 April 1953.

67 *Daily Mirror*, 7 April and 9 April 1953.

68 *Bord Fáilte Annual Report* for year ending 31 March 1954, p. 12.

69 *Irish Press*, 27 March 1953.

70 *Irish Times*, 12 February 1958.

71 *Irish Press*, 31 February 1958.

72 *Irish Times*, 17 February 1958.

73 *Sunday Press*, 27 April 1958.

74 *Irish Times*, 15 February 1958.

75 NA, Department of the Taoiseach, S13087D, Report of An Bord Fáilte board meeting, 29 May 1958.

76 *Ibid.*

77 *Evening Herald*, 24 July 1958.

78 *Irish Times*, 2 September 1958.

79 NA, Department of the Taoiseach, S13090A, Department of Industry and Commerce Memorandum for the Government – Report on civil aviation for 1948, 28 April 1949.

80 *Ibid.*, Department of Industry and Commerce Memorandum for the Government on suggested discussions with the United States government regarding the bilateral air transport agreement, 27 January 1947.

81 NA, Department of the Taoiseach, S13090B, Department of Industry and Commerce Memorandum for the Government – report on civil aviation for 1948, 28 April 1949.

82 NA, Department of the Taoiseach, S10325C, Department of Industry and Commerce, Statement by United States delegation on first day of discussions, 14 September 1949.

83 *Ibid.* Note no. 321 from American Minister, 21 September 1949.

84 NA, Department of the Taoiseach S13090A, Department of Industry and Commerce Memorandum for the Government – Request by the United States Government for revision of the Air Agreement of 3 February 1945, Appendix C, 17 September 1949.

85 NA, Department of the Taoiseach, S10325C, Minister of External Affairs, Memorandum to Government – Air agreement with United States, 13 July 1950.

86 *Ibid.*, Department of Finance Memorandum for Government – Air agreement with United States, 17 July 1950, and Department of Industry and Commerce, 17 July 1950.

87 NA, 2000/13/8, Department of Industry and Commerce Conference No. 313, 3 September 1953.

88 *Ibid.*

89 NA, 2000/13/10, Department of Industry and Commerce Conference No. 358, 29 July 1954.

90 John Horgan, *Séan Lemass – The Enigmatic Patriot* (Dublin: Gill & Macmillan, 1996), p. 89.

91 NA, Department of the Taoiseach, S13090B/C, Department of Finance Memorandum for the Government – Aer Rianta Teoranta, Aer Lingus Teoranta and Aerlínte Teoranta, Accounts for the year ended 31 March 1953, 21 July 1953.

92 NA, GISI/215, Speech to Irish Airline Pilots Association, 11 November 1958.

93 Bernard Share, *The Flight of the Iolar* (Dublin: Gill and Macmillan 1986), p. 90.

94 *Ibid.*, p. 92.

95 *Ibid.*

96 *Ibid.*, p. 93.

97 Horgan, *Lemass*, p. 108.

Ireland and the US in the Post-war Period

1 For instance, Seán Cronin basically ignores the whole period in question, while Troy Davis is interested only in the Truman administrations. Seán Cronin, *Washington's Irish Policy, 1916–1986: Independence, Partition and Neutrality* (Dublin: Anvil Books, 1986); Troy D. Davis, *Dublin's American Policy: Irish-American Diplomatic Relations, 1945–1952* (Washington: CUA Press, 1998). See Maurice Fitzgerald, 'Symbolism versus Reality: Irish- American Diplomatic Relations, 1948-1963' (University College Cork: M. Phil Thesis, 1997).

2 Nuala Ó Faoláin, 'Women want power and influence so as to change the world for the better', *Irish Times*, 19 April 1993.

3 T. Ryle Dwyer, *De Valera: The Man and the Myths* (Dublin: Poolbeg, 1991), p. 193.

4 Seán Nunan telegram (untransmitted draft), *circa* late May 1951, Department of External Affairs (D/FA) file P218, NAI.

5 Joseph Brennan to Conor Cruise O'Brien, 28 January 1953, D/FA-318/40/3, NAI.

6 'Agreements Reached at the Cairo, Tehran, Yalta, and Potsdam Conferences: Implementation and United States Policy' – Research Project #80 September 1948, Subject Series, Box #69, White House Central Files (Confidential File), Harry S. Truman Library, Independence, Missouri (HST).

7 Máire O'Brien & Conor Cruise O'Brien, *Ireland: A Concise History* (London: BCA, 1992), pp. 159–60.

8 O'Brien & O'Brien, *Ireland*, p. 165.

9 John W. Hanes to Henry Cabot Lodge, 6 February 1956, General Correspondence and Memoranda Series, Box #4, Dulles Papers, HST; Hanes to Horace Flanigan, 9 February 1956, General Correspondence and Memoranda Series, Box #4, Dulles Papers, HST; Flanigan to Hanes, 10 February 1956, General Correspondence and Memoranda Series, Box #4, Dulles Papers, HST; Flanigan to Hanes, 16 February 1956, General Correspondence and Memoranda Series, Box #4, Dulles Papers, HST.

10 Charles Bohlen oral history transcript, Dwight D. Eisenhower Library, Abilene, Kansas (DDE), p. 5.

11 Liam Cosgrave oral history transcript, John F. Kennedy Library, Boston, Massachusetts (JFK), p. 2.

12 James R. Shepley oral history transcript, DDE, pp. 13–16.

13 Sherman Adams to John W. McCormack, 6 July 1954, Official File 85-DD, Box #332, White House Central Files, DDE.

14 Dwight D. Eisenhower to Walter H. Judd, 24 October 1953, Subject Series, Box #99, Central Files, DDE.

15 *Evening Star*, 8 August 1953, A-4, Official File 85-DD, Box #332, Central Files, DDE.

16 Oster Unden to Matthew Woll, 28 October 1954, Official File 85-DD, Box #332, Central Files, DDE.

17 Frank Aiken oral history transcript, JFK, pp. 17–18.

18 Lodge to John Foster Dulles, 23 September 1957, Telephone Calls Series, Box #7, Dulles Papers, DDE.

19 Aiken oral history, p. 18.

20 Lodge to Dulles, 23 September 1957, Telephone Calls Series, Box #7, Dulles Papers, DDE.

21 Paper clippings, General File 122, Box #816, Central Files, DDE.

22 *Irish Independent*, 9 October 1957, General File 122, Box #816, Central Files, DDE.

23 *Tablet*, 28 September 1957, General File 122, Box #816, Central Files, DDE.

24 Aiken oral history, p. 19.

25 Aiken oral history, pp. 19–21.

26 Background paper, 'Vice-Presidential Security File', Box #3, Johnson Papers, Lyndon B. Johnson Library, Austin, Texas (LBJ).

27 'Presidential Appointments File', Box #88, President's Secretary's Files, Truman Papers, HST.

28 John D. Hickerson to Matthew J. Connelly, 28 May 1948, '218-Miscellaneous (1945–Oct. 1950)', Box #823, Official File, HST.

29 Richard B. Finnegan, 'Irish-American relations', in William Crotty & David E. Schmitt (eds.), *Ireland on the World Stage* (Harlow: Longman 2002), pp. 95–110.

30 Howard Pyle to P. J. Morrissey, 9 July 1956, General File 122, Box #816, Central Files, DDE.

31 Aiken speech to the Federation of American Societies for Irish Independence, 18 August 1958, General File 122, Box #816, Central Files, DDE.

32 Thomas J. Kiernan oral history transcript, JFK, pp. 11–12.

33 John F. Kennedy to Thomas McGuigan, *circa* 1960, cited in McGuigan to Lyndon B. Johnson, 22 January 1964, 'CO 125 Ireland', Box #42, Johnson Papers, LBJ.

34 Kiernan oral history, p. 9.

35 Aiken oral history, pp. 29–30.

36 Kiernan oral history, p. 8.

37 *Ibid.*, p. 9.

38 Benjamin H. Read to McGeorge Bundy, 30 September 1963, 'CO 125 Ireland', Box #60, Kennedy Papers, JFK.

39 John Bowman, 'Cabinet's decisions without comment', *Irish Times*, 1–2 January 1993.

40 *Irish Times* editorial, 23 March 1964, 'National Security File', Box #195, National Security File, Johnson Papers, LBJ.

41 Bundy to Johnson, 17 March 1964, 'National Security File', Box #195, National Security File, Johnson Papers, LBJ, Terence O'Neill to Bundy, 26 March 1964, 'National Security File', Box #195, National Security File, Johnson Papers, LBJ, O'Neill to Johnson, 26 March 1964, 'National Security File', Box #195, National Security File, Johnson Papers, LBJ.

42 Mr Merchant to Herbert Hoover, 15 September 1955, Official File 183-J(2), Box #870, Central Files, DDE.

43 Hoover to Wilton B. Persons, 16 September 1955, Official File 183-J(2), Box #870, Central Files, DDE.

44 Adams to Charles J. Horan, 2 April 1954, Official File 183-J(2), Box #870, Central Files, DDE; Horan to Eisenhower, 22 May 1954, Official File 183-J(2), Box #870, Central Files, DDE.

45 Maxwell M. Rabb to Roderick O'Connor, 24 May 1955, Official File 183-J(2), Box #870, Central Files, DDE.

46 Rabb to O'Connor, 13 July 1955, Official File 183-J(2), Box #870, Central Files, DDE.

47 Taft to Hanes, 22 July 1955, General Correspondence and Memoranda Series, Box #4, Dulles Papers, DDE.

48 Taft to Hanes, 6 January 1956, General Correspondence and Memoranda Series, Box #4, Dulles Papers, DDE.

49 Eisenhower speech, 17 March 1959, *Public Papers of the Presidents of the United States:*

Dwight D. Eisenhower (Washington: Government Printing Office, 1960), pp. 282–83.

50 Seán T. O'Kelly speech, 17 March 1959, *Public Papers*, p. 283.

51 Eisenhower speech, 17 March 1959, *Public Papers*, pp. 284–85.

52 O'Kelly speech, 17 March 1959, *Public Papers*, p. 285.

53 Eisenhower speech, 19 March 1959, *Public Papers*, p. 289.

54 Brendan Behan to Kennedy, 15 July 1961, Special Correspondence, Box #28, President's Office Files, Kennedy Papers, JFK.

55 Kiernan oral history, p. 3.

56 Ian McCabe, *Irish Times*, 7 January 1993.

57 William R. Tyler oral history transcript, JFK, p. 23.

58 'Vice-Presidential Security File President Kennedy's Travel President's European Trip Briefing Book – June 1963', Box #3, Vice-Presidential Security File, Johnson Papers, LBJ.

59 Kennedy speech to Dáil Éireann, 28 June 1963, *Irish Visit: The Complete Text of President Kennedy's Speeches with Illustrations* (Dublin: Grafton, 1963), pp. 19–25.

60 Kennedy speech, *Irish Visit*, pp. 19–25.

61 Seán Lemass oral history transcript, JFK, p. 6.

62 'The President's European Trip', Vice-Presidential Security File, Box #3, Vice-Presidential Security File, Johnson Papers, LBJ.

63 Edwin O. Gutham & Jeffrey Shulman (eds.), *Robert Kennedy In His Own Words: The Unpublished Recollections of the Kennedy Years* (New York: Bantam Books, 1989), p. 384.

64 US Department of State publication #7974, 'Ireland: Background Notes' (Washington: Government Printing Office, 1991).

65 US Embassy homepages, http://www.usembassy.ie/ambassador/us_ ambassador.html, 25 June 2002.

'A Great Time to Be in America': The Irish in Post-Second World War New York City

1 Immigration and Naturalization Service, *1992 Yearbook of the Immigration and Naturalization Service* (Washington, DC: Government Printing Office, October 1993), table 2, p. 27.

2 See Immigration and Naturalisation Service Annual Reports, table 12B for 1958, p. 41; 1959, p. 38; 1960, p. 38; and 1961, p. 38. See also Linda Dowling Almeida, *Irish Immigrants in New York City, 1945–1995* (Indiana University Press, 2001), p. 23.

3 Fergal Tobin, *The Best of Decades: Ireland in the 1960s* (Dublin: Gill and Macmillan, 1984), p. 4–5. J. J. Lee, *Ireland 1912–1985: Politics and Society*, (Cambridge: Cambridge University Press, 1989), pp. 341–62. John A. Murphy, *Ireland in the Twentieth Century* (Dublin: Gill and Macmillan, 1975), p. 142. Almeida *Irish Immigrants in New York City*, p. 25.

4 Central Statistics Office, *Ireland Census 91, Vol. 1, Population Classified by Area* (Dublin: Stationery Office, June 1993), p. 24. National Economic and Social Council (NESC), *The Economic and Social Implication of Emigration* (Dublin: National Economic and Social Council, March 1991), p. 74; Immigration and Naturalization Service, *1992 Yearbook of the Immigration and Naturalization Service* (Washington, DC: Government Printing Office, October 1993), table 2, p. 27. See also Almeida, *Irish Immigrants in New York City*, p. 23.

5 See Almeida, *Irish Immigrants in New York City*, p. 24. Commission on Emigration and Other Problems, *Commission on Emigration and Other Problems 1948–1954, Reports*, Pr 2541 (Dublin: Stationery Office, 1956), p. 136, paragraph 295.

6 *Ibid.*, p. 34. Based on interview with Kevin Morrissey, 9 February, 1995.

7 *Ibid.*

8 The War Brides Act (1945) and the GI Fiancé(e) Act (1946) admitted the foreign-born wives and fiancé(e)s of members of the armed services. Leonard Dinnerstein and David Reimers, *Ethnic Americans: A History of Immigration*, third ed. (New York:

Harper and Row, 1988), pp. 85–90. Almeida, *Irish Immigrants in New York City*, p. 8.

9 Letter from Peggy Hegarty, New York, NY, to Mom and Den, County Kerry, Ireland, 14 March 1957. Courtesy Peggy Hegarty Tanner. See Almeida, *Irish Immigrants in New York City*, p. 35.

10 Interview with Rosaleen Fitzgibbon, 1 December, 1993.

11 Traditionally among immigrant groups, the Irish have had the lowest rate of return.

12 Andrew Jackson was the first president of Irish descent (1829–37).

13 WPA Historical Records survey, Federal Writers Project, Box 3579, 'Irish in New York', folder 5, 'Occupations and Location', A. Fitzpatrick, 'The Irish Race in Various Industries, Professions, etc.', 1938.

14 See Almeida, *Irish Immigrants in New York City*, pp. 36–37 and Robert Snyder, 'The Neighborhood Changed: The Irish of Washington Heights and Inwood since 1945,' in *The New York Irish*, ed. Ronald H. Bayor and Timothy Meagher (Baltimore: Johns Hopkins University Press, 1996), p. 442.

15 Almeida, *Irish Immigrants in New York City*, pp. 42–43.

16 *Ibid*, pp. 31–36.

17 John Grimes, *The Best of Times: Reminiscences*, Christmas 1989. Courtesy Claire Grimes. Almeida, *Irish Immigrants in New York City*, p. 89.

18 Robert I. Gannon, SJ, *The Cardinal Spellman Story* (New York: Doubleday and Company, 1962), pp. 302–03. *Survey of Non-public Schools, New York State, 1968–1969* (University of the State of New York, State Department of Education Department, Albany, July 1969), table 5.

19 Mary Hennessy Trotta, 'Memories of Rockaway Long Ago!' *The Wave*, Hundredth Anniversary Edition, 24 July 1993, p. 48. See also Almeida, *Irish Immigrants in New York City*, p. 98.

20 Elizabeth Cullinan, 'Estelle', pp. 5–6, and 'Voices of the Dead', p. 103, *Yellow Roses* (New York: Viking Press, 1977).

21 *Irish Echo*, 7 September 1957, p. 10 and 21 September 1957, p. 15.

22 Almeida, *Irish Immigrants in New York City*, p. 98.

23 *Ibid.*, p. 96.

24 *Ibid.*, p. 96 and p. 176.

25 Letter to Linda Dowling Almeida from Gerald Ryan, St Luke's Church, 623 East 138th Street, Bronx, NY, 24 March 1995.

26 Irish Institute, *A Brief History of the Irish Institute*. Courtesy of Kevin Morrissey. Almeida, *Irish Immigrants in New York City*, pp. 56, 112 and 120.

27 Rebecca Miller, 'All Roads Lead to City Centre Ballroom', *The New York Irish*, ed. Bayor and Meagher, pp. 492–94.

28 Almeida, *Irish Immigrants in New York City*, p. 117. J. H. '*Cuimhnicinn* [Remembrance]', *An Teanga Mharthanach* [Living Language], Spring 1993, p. 22.

29 Interview with J. D., 20 April 1995. See also, Almeida, *Irish Immigrants in New York City*, p. 176, n. 69 and p. 181, n. 43.

30 See *From Shore to Shore: Irish Traditional Music in New York City*, a video produced by Patrick Mullins and Rebecca Miller, Cherry Lane Productions, 1993.

31 Almeida, *Irish Immigrants in New York City*, p. 123.

32 Pete Hamill, 'Notes on the New Irish: A Guide for the Goyim', *New York Magazine*, 15 March 1972, pp. 33–39.

33 Andrew Greeley, *The American Catholic: A Social Portrait* (New York: Basic Books, 1977).

34 Almeida, *Irish Immigrants in New York City*, pp. 61–62.

35 Letter to Linda Almeida from Dermot O'Sullivan, chairman, EBU Statistics Group, Radio Telefís Éireann, Dublin 4, Ireland, 1 November 1994. Robert Joseph Savage, Jr, 'Irish Television: The Political and Social Genesis', PhD dissertation (Boston College, 1993), chapter 8 and pp. 492–94. Almeida, *Irish Immigrants in New York City*, pp. 54–55.

36 Almeida, *Irish Immigrants in New York City*, p. 100. Survey published in the *Irish Voice* (New York), 16 March 1991, p. 34.

37 *Irish Voice*, 8–14 November 1995, p. 4.

38 Paul Stone, Floral Park, NY, letter to the *Irish Voice*, 18 February 1989, p. 9. Rose Fitzgibbon, Brooklyn, NY, letter to the *Irish Voice*, 11 March 1989, p. 11.

39 Almeida, *Irish Immigrants in New York City*, p. 134. Interview with Fr Martin Keveny, March 1989.

40 *Ibid.*, pp. 130–37.

Inadmissible Departures: Why Did the Emigrant Experience Feature so Infrequently in the Fiction of the Mid-Twentieth Century?

1 J. J. Lee, *Ireland 1912–1985: Politics and Society* (Cambridge: Cambridge University Press, 1989), p. 375.

2 *Ibid.*, p. 384.

3 G. O'Brien, 'The Aesthetics of Exile', in Liam Harte and Michael Parker (eds), *Contemporary Irish Fiction: Themes, Tropes, Theories* (London: Macmillan, 2000), p. 35.

4 J. O'Connor, Introduction, in Dermot Bolger (ed.), *Ireland in Exile* (Dublin: New Island Books, 1993), p. 16.

5 *Ibid.*, p. 17.

6 D. Bolger, Foreword, in Bolger (ed.), *Ireland in Exile*, p. 10.

7 O'Brien, 'The Aesthetics of Exile', p. 36.

8 Roberta Gefter Wondrich, 'Exilic Returns: Self and History outside Ireland in Recent Irish Fiction', *Irish University Review*, Vol. 30, No. 1, 2000, p. 1.

9 *Ibid.*

10 *The Bell*, May 1943.

11 J. Joyce, 'The Holy Office' Broadside (late 1904–early 1905). Printed in Croatia (then part of Austro-Hungarian Empire) and possibly in Dublin also. Reprinted in *The Portable James Joyce* (New York: Viking Press, 1947) [with introduction and notes by Harry Levin].

12 *Gaelic Athletic Annual*, 1907.

13 W. B. Yeats, 'The Fisherman' (London: Everyman, 1992), pp. 197–8.

14 *Ibid.*

15 *Gaelic Athletic Annual*, 1907.

16 G. Smyth, *The Novel and the Nation: Studies in the New Irish Fiction* (London: Pluto Press, 1997), p. 148.

17 M. Goldring, *Pleasant the Scholar's Life: Irish Intellectuals and the Construction of the Nation State* (London: Serif, 1993), p. 110.

18 J. Ryan, *Home from England* (London: Phoenix, 1995), p. 14.

19 *The Bell*, May 1943.

20 L. O'Flaherty, *Going into Exile: Selected Short Stories of Liam O'Flaherty* (London: New English Library, abridged edition, 1970), p. 100.

21 *Ibid.*

22 *Ibid.*

23 L. O'Flaherty, *The Letter: More Short Stories of Liam O'Flaherty* (London: New English Library, abridged edition, 1971), p. 104.

24 Lee, *Ireland 1912–1985: Politics and Society*, p. 377.

25 *Ibid.*

26 Mary Lennon, Marie McAdam, Joanne O'Brien (eds.), *Across The Water: Irish Women's Lives in Britain* (London: Virago, 1988).

27 Lee, *Ireland 1912–1985: Politics and Society*, p. 384.

28 M. Harmon, *Sean Ó Faoláin* (London: Constable, 1994), p. 125.

29 *Ibid.*, p. 143.

30 John A. Murphy, *Ireland in the Twentieth Century* (Dublin: Gill & Macmillan, 1975), p. 61.

31 L. O'Flaherty, *Going into Exile: Selected Short Stories of Liam O'Flaherty* [Lavin Family

Archive Copy] (London: New English Library, abridged edition, 1970), p. 98.

32 *Ibid.*

33 *Ibid.*

34 *Ibid.*, p. 99.

'You want to be a British Paddy?': The Anxiety of Identity in Post-war Irish Migrant Writing

1 Pádraig Ó Conaire, *Exile*, trans. by Gearailt Mac Eoin (Conamara: Cló Iar-Chonnachta, 1994), p. 104.

2 Fintan O'Toole, 'The Ex-Isle of Erin: Emigration and Irish Culture' in Jim Mac Laughlin (ed.), *Location and Dislocation in Contemporary Irish Society* (Cork: Cork University Press, 1997), p. 162.

3 Joseph O'Connor, *Cowboys and Indians* (London: Flamingo, 1992), p. 6.

4 See Philip O'Leary, *The Prose Literature of the Gaelic Revival, 1881–1921* (Pennsylvania: Pennsylvania State University Press, 1994), chapter 7.

5 See O'Connor's introduction to *Ireland in Exile*, ed. Dermot Bolger (Dublin: New Island Books, 1993), pp. 11–18.

6 S. R. Bald, 'Negotiating Identity in the Metropolis: Generational Differences in South Asian British Fiction' in *Writing Across Worlds: Literature and Migration*, eds. R. King, J. Connell and P. White (London: Routledge, 1995), p. 70.

7 Anne Devlin, *After Easter* (London: Faber, 1994), pp. 16, 58.

8 Moy McCrory, 'Aer Lingus' in *The Water's Edge and Other Stories* (London: Sheba Feminist Publishers, 1985), p. 172.

9 Jimmy Murphy, *The Kings of the Kilburn High Road* in his *Two Plays* (London: Oberon Books, 2001), p. 65.

10 Brian Friel, *Dancing at Lughnasa* (London: Faber, 1990), p. 60.

11 John McGahern, *The Dark* (London: Faber, 1983), p. 137.

12 John McGahern, *The Barracks* (London: Faber, 1983), p. 86.

13 There is, of course, a long tradition of Irish identity being performed or staged in Britain. For an illuminating and entertaining historical analysis of dramatic expressions of stage Irishry, see Owen Dudley Edwards, 'The Stage Irish' in *The Creative Migrant*, volume 3 of Patrick O'Sullivan (ed.), *The Irish World Wide: History, Heritage, Identity* (Leicester: Leicester University Press, 1994), pp. 83–114.

14 John McGahern, *Amongst Women* (London: Faber, 1990), p. 148. Interestingly, on the one occasion when Luke returns to Ireland for a family wedding, he deliberately tries to seem invisible. See pp. 152, 155.

15 Devlin, *After Easter*, p. 9.

16 Homi K. Bhabha, 'How Newness Enters the World' in his *The Location of Culture* (London: Routledge, 1994), p. 218.

17 Bhabha, *The Location of Culture*, p. 223.

18 Conor McCarthy, *Modernisation, Crisis and Culture in Ireland, 1969–1992* (Dublin: Four Courts Press, 2000), pp. 14–15.

19 Enda Delaney, *Demography, State and Society: Irish Migration to Britain, 1921–1971* (Liverpool: Liverpool University Press, 2000), pp. 45, 151.

20 Bryan MacMahon, 'Getting on the High Road Again' in *The Vanishing Irish*, ed. J. A. O'Brien (London: W. H. Allen, 1954), p. 207.

21 See Fintan O'Toole, *The Ex-Isle of Erin* (Dublin: New Island Books, 1997), especially the essay 'No Place Like Home', pp. 129–42.

22 For evidence, see Mac Amhlaigh's *Dialann Deoraí* (1960) and Keane's *Self-Portrait* (1964).

23 Walter Macken, *I Am Alone* (London: Pan Books, 1977), p. 5. Subsequent page references will be incorporated into the text.

24 Pat's view of emigration as an exciting adventure – 'I think it's great. I love going to England' (p. 10) – contrasts sharply with his stay-at-home sister's anachronistic, stereotypical impression of it: 'She had never been out of their town in her life and

when she thought of a ship at all, she thought of the famine ships going to America
with the hundreds of Paddies crowded and dying in the holds and the steerage' (p.
8).

25 Conversely, he later finds that the English countryside seems to conform to romantic
artistic representations of it: 'It was too like the exact replica of what the English
novelists had written' (p. 102).

26 When pressed about his reasons for leaving Ireland, Seamus' disaffection from a culture of nepotism, gombeenism and inequality provoke him to become 'almost blas-
phemously lyrical about how his country had thrown him out, not given him the
ways of making a living' (p. 59).

27 Marshall Berman, *All That is Solid Melts into Air* (London: Verso, 1983), pp. 345–6.

28 Salman Rushdie, *Imaginary Homelands* (London: Granta, 1991), p. 10.

29 Aidan Arrowsmith, 'M/otherlands: Literature, Gender, Diasporic Identity' in *Ireland
in Proximity*, eds. Scott Brewster et al (London: Routledge, 1999), pp. 129–44.

30 Brian Moore, *The Lonely Passion of Judith Hearne* (London: Paladin, 1988), p. 47.

31 Brian Friel, *Philadelphia, Here I Come!* (1964) in his *Selected Plays*, ed. Seamus Deane
(London: Faber, 1984), pp. 77, 99.

32 Fred Davis, 'Nostalgia, Identity and the Current Nostalgia Wave', *Journal of Popular
Culture*, vol. 11, no. 2, Fall 1977, p. 420.

33 So great is the effect of the experience of fatherhood on Pat that his yearning for Irish
pastoral suddenly transmutes into a fetishistic liking for the English industrial sub-
lime: 'He liked the overhead cables of the trolley buses, so alien to him formerly, and
thought how he liked the silent shine of them and all the people in them, with the
strange accents' (p. 251).

34 Bhabha, *The Location of Culture*, p. 219. The emphasis is in the original.

35 Rushdie, *Imaginary Homelands*, pp. 124–5.

36 Tom Murphy, *A Whistle in the Dark* in his *Plays: 4* (London: Methuen, 1997), p. 9. Subsequent page references will be incorporated into the text.

37 Fintan O'Toole, introduction to *Plays: 4*, p. xii.

38 Anthony Roche, *Contemporary Irish Drama: From Beckett to McGuinness* (Dublin:
Gill & Macmillan, 1994), p. 143.

39 O'Toole, introduction to *Plays: 4*, p. xii.

40 A contemporaneous play about emigration, John B. Keane's *Many Young Men of
Twenty* (Dublin: Progress House, 1961), voices a similar critique of Irish nepotism.
The character Danger Mulally claims the 'short history of modern Ireland' can be
summarised 'in one word – PULL!' (p. 25).

41 Fintan O'Toole, *The Politics of Magic: The Work and Times of Tom Murphy* (Dublin:
Raven Arts Press, 1987), pp. 46–7. Roche's reading of the play is more attuned to
the thematic importance of its emigrant setting. See chapter four of his *Contemporary Irish Drama*.

42 Declan Hughes, 'Who The Hell Do We Think We Still Are? Reflections on Irish
Theatre and Identity' in *Theatre Stuff: Critical Essays on Contemporary Irish Theatre*,
ed. Eamonn Jordan (Dublin: Carysfort Press, 2000), p. 11.

43 Cited by Hughes in *Theatre Stuff*, p. 12.

44 Roche, *Contemporary Irish Drama*, p. 144. This reading tempers O'Toole's claim that
in killing Des, Michael kills his own future. See *The Politics of Magic*, p. 56.

45 J. J. Lee, *Ireland 1912–1985: Politics and Society* (Cambridge: Cambridge University
Press, 1989), p. 384.

'Making Aliya': Irish Jews, the Irish State and Israel

1 This article is based largely on a survey of the archives of the Department of Foreign
Affairs and the Department of the Taoiseach; Archbishop John Charles McQuaid's
papers in the Dublin Archdiocesan Archives; and interviews conducted in Israel in
June 2001. Dr Paula Wylie, a former doctoral student working under my direction,
completed a case study on Ireland's recognition of Israel as part of her work. I am very

grateful to her for having supplied me with a range of documents that she discovered on Ireland and Israel during the Suez crisis. She generously allowed me to publish them as part of this study.

2 For background, see Walter Laqueur, *A History of Zionism* (New York: Holt, Rinehart and Winston, 1972).

3 Bernard Reich and David H. Goldberg, *Political Dictionary of Israel* (Lanham, Maryland and London: Scarecrow Press, 2000); see entries for Aliya and Zionism, p. 11 and p. 429.

4 Dermot Keogh, *Jews in Twentieth-Century Ireland: Refugees, Anti-Semitism and the Holocaust* (Cork: Cork University Press, 1998), chapter 2.

5 Reich and Goldberg, *Political Dictionary of Israel*; see entry for Aliya, p. 11.

6 For population statistics, see Keogh, *Jews in Twentieth-Century Ireland*, pp. 9–11; Censuses of Population, Republic of Ireland.

7 Census of Ireland, Province of Ulster, 1891 and 1911; Census of Population of Northern Ireland, 1937. (Data kindly supplied by Dr Caroline Windrum.)

8 Censuses of Northern Ireland. (Data kindly supplied by Dr Caroline Windrum.)

9 J. Z. Gilbert, 'Zionism in Ireland', *Encyclopedia of Zionism and Israel* (New York: McGraw-Hill, 1971), p. 552.

10 *Ibid.*

11 *Ibid.*

12 *Ibid.*

13 *Ibid.*

14 Keogh, *Jews in Twentieth-Century Ireland*, pp. 67–8, 91 and 231–2.

15 *Ibid.*, pp. 78–82, 88, 124 and 162.

16 Robert Briscoe (with Alden Hatch), *For the Life of Me* (New York: Little Brown and Company, 1958), pp. 264–5.

17 Leni Yahil, *The Holocaust: The Fate of European Jewry* (Oxford and New York: Oxford University Press, 1991), pp. 188–9.

18 For a study of his early life, see Shmuel Katz, *Lone Wolf: A Biography of Vladimir (Ze'en) Jabotinsky* (Barricade, 1996), two vols.

19 Yahil, *The Holocaust*, p. 188.

20 *Ibid.*

21 Bernard Wasserstein, *Britain and the Jews of Europe 1939–1945* (Oxford and New York: Oxford University Press, 1988), p. 12.

22 Brian Kennedy, *Ireland and the League of Nations: International Relations, Diplomacy and Politics* (Dublin: Irish Academic Press, 1996), p. 254.

23 *Zion News*, 20 December 1937, p. 5.

24 Briscoe, *For the Life of Me*, pp. 267 ff.

25 *Ibid.*, pp. 264–5.

26 *Irish Press*, 12 December 1938. The members of the committee, under the chairmanship of Dr Abrahamson, were Robert Briscoe, Dr Baker and H. Good. See D/FA, 105/51, NAI.

27 Keogh, *Jews in Twentieth-Century Ireland*, p. 297.

28 Briscoe, *For the Life of Me*, pp. 267 ff.

29 Boland Memorandum, 9 February 1948, D/FA, 305/62/1, NAI.

30 Mordecai Naor, 'The Twentieth Century' in *Eretz Israel* (Bnei Brak, Israel: Steinmatzky), pp. 256–294.

31 MacBride telegram and reply, Embassy to the Holy See [Box 2], 14/68/1, D/FA, NAI.

32 Dermot Keogh, 'The Role of the Catholic Church in the Republic of Ireland 1922–1995', in *Building Trust in Ireland* (Belfast: Blackstaff Press, 1996).

33 Various resolutions from county councils and vocational education committees in D/FA 305/62/1, NAI.

34 Immanuel Jakobovits, *Journal of a Rabbi* (London: W. H. Allen, 1967), p. 56.

35 *Ibid.*, p. 126.

36 McQuaid to Jakobovits, 26 May 1949, D/FA 305/62/1, NAI; the letter on file is typed

but signed by the archbishop himself. The words 'the international status of Jerusalem' are written in his own hand. Why would a letter of this kind be sent in draft form to Iveagh House? Is it possible that Ambassador Walshe had privately advised the archbishop on the content of the reply to Rabbi Jakobovits?

37 *Ibid.*

38 *Ibid.*

39 *Ibid.*

40 *Ibid.* The archbishop ended: 'May I thank you again for the ready courtesy with which you have graciously accepted my suggestions in the present crisis, and may I assure you of my constant goodwill in assisting you to find a just and sympathetic solution to the difficulties of the situation'.

41 Jakobovits, *Journal of a Rabbi*, p. 126.

42 Department of Foreign Affairs File, Box 1, Holy Land Folder, John Charles McQuaid Papers, Dublin Archdiocesan Archives. DDA McQuaid papers, AB8/B/XVIII.

43 *Ibid.*

44 *Ibid.*

45 *Ibid.*

46 *Ibid.*

47 *Ibid.*

48 *Ibid.*

49 *Ibid.*

50 Dáil Éireann debates, Vol. 117, Cols. 866–7, 13 July 1949.

51 MacBride to Walshe, 22 August 1949, D/FA 305/62/1, NAI.

52 Memorandum by T. J. H., Department of External Affairs, 11 November 1952, D/FA, 305/62/1, NAI.

53 *Ibid.*

54 *Ibid.*

55 *Ibid.*

56 *Ibid.*

57 Embassy to the Holy See [Box 2], 14/68/1, D/FA, NAI.

58 *Ibid.*

59 *Ibid.*

60 *Ibid.*

61 *Ibid.*

62 Damien Cole, Middle East Section, Department of Foreign Affairs to me, 8 February 1996.

63 Israel and the Holy See made a joint declaration on 29 June 1992 announcing the establishment of a permanent bilateral working commission aimed at initiating diplomatic relations. The 'fundamental agreement' between Israel and the Holy See was signed on 29 December 1993. Sergio I. Minerbi, 'The Vatican and Israel', in Peter Kent and John Pollard (eds), *Papal Diplomacy in the Modern Age* (Westport and London: Prager, 1994), p. 189.

64 Steinberg to Seán Murphy, Secretary, Department of External Affairs, 31 March 1956, D/FA 319/25/9, NAI. (This and subsequent references on this issue were kindly supplied to me by Dr Paula Wylie.)

65 Jakobovits to Seán Murphy, Secretary, Department of External Affairs, 26 March 1956, D/FA 319/25/9, NAI.

66 Dublin to Biggar, London Embassy, 14 September 1956, D/FA 319/25/9, NAI.

67 Murphy to Secretary, Department of Finance, 7 September 1956, D/FA 319/25/9, NAI.

68 Departmental minutes by Woods, 12 July 1956, D/FA 319/25/9, NAI.

69 Murphy to Secretary, Department of Finance, 7 September 1956, D/FA 319/25/9, NAI.

70 I am grateful to Professor David Birkhahn for writing this piece for this volume.

Index

Abrahems, A. 256
Acheson, Dean 188
Aiken, Frank 32, 190, 192-197, 265-266
America/United States – Irish-American
    17-19, 21, 32, 38-39, 46, 48, 55, 69,
    71, 83, 91, 106, 110-112, 136, 141-
    142, 168-172, 178, 182-184, 187-
    193, 195-201, 204-210, 213-220, 225,
    227-228, 231, 253, 258, 260, 263
    Manhattan 12-13, 210-211, 214-215
    Boston 40, 71, 92, 183, 194
    Chicago 183
    New York 12-13, 19, 39, 183, 185,
    192-193, 206-207, 209-216, 218-220,
    263
Andrews, C. S. 164
Anthony, Ellen 156-158, 161
Ashe, James 152-153, 160
Auden, W. H. 38-39
Australia 18, 91, 136, 271
    Sydney 12-13

Barrett, Craig 113
Barron, Esther 254
Barry, Kevin 169
Barry, Rev. David 149
Beckett, Samuel 29, 42, 180
Beddy, J. P. 87, 96
Behan, Brendan 31, 33-34, 43, 47
Belfast 39, 107, 216, 219, 253-254
Belfast Telegraph 199
Bell, The 28, 42, 223
Ben-Gurion, David 255-257
Birkhahn, David 252, 270
Boland, Frederick 263, 269
Boland, Gerard 179
Bord Fáilte 172-175, 177, 179-181, 185
    (see Tourist)
Bottomley, Arthur 172
Böll, Heinrich 11-12, 18, 26
Briscoe, Robert 255-257, 265
Britain
    England 11-14, 17-18, 22, 25, 34, 36-
    37, 40, 45, 48, 55, 72, 76, 79-81, 83-
    87, 89, 91-96, 100-103, 108, 110,
    126-132, 135, 140, 147, 153-154,
    156-157, 159-161, 163, 170, 176-177,
    195, 197, 206-208, 221, 225-226, 228,
    230-240, 246, 249-251, 253-254, 258
    London 11-13, 22, 36, 39, 80-81, 127,
    153, 184, 188, 195-196, 199, 233,
    235-236, 239-242, 254, 256, 260-262,
    269-270, 272
    Leeds 12
    Liverpool 12-13, 22
    Luton 12
    Manchester 12
    Wales 117, 127, 153, 156, 161
    Fishguard 80
    Holyhead 14, 176 238
    Scotland 81, 89, 117
Brocklebank, Charles 152
Brocquy, Louis 36, 47
Browne, Alan 161
Browne, Bishop Michael 33, 143
Browne, Noël 34-36, 45, 130, 266
Byrne, Archbishop Edward 151

Cadden, Mary Anne (Mamie) 18, 147,
    155, 161
Cafferky, Dominick 173
Cahill, Edward 255
Campbell, George 36
Canada 18, 209, 253
Carrigan, Joseph 168
Catholic Standard 32
Censorship 26-28, 30-31, 33-34, 36, 38,
    41-42, 47, 155, 224-226
Charles, J. A. 131
Childers, Erskine 40
Christenberry, R. K. 169-170, 172-174
Clann na Poblachta 35, 173, 258
Clann na Talmhan 173
Clare 119, 125, 131-133, 208, 259
    Shannon 168, 171-172, 182-185
    Ennis 179
Clarke, Austin 34, 44
Coleman, William 161
Collins, Patrick 36, 47
Collis, Robert 142
Colum, Pádraic 31
Connemara 11-12, 92-93, 239
Connolly, Cyril 41
Coogan, Tim Pat 231
Cork 14-15, 19, 33, 39, 42, 66, 80-81, 91,
    118-119, 125, 131, 156, 158, 181,
    186, 213, 252, 254, 270-272
Cork Examiner 68, 157
Cornick, Simon 253
Cosgrave, Liam 172
Cosgrave, W. T. 151
Costello, J. A. 33, 35, 166

Cowell, Dr 128
Cremin, Con 266
Cullinan, Elizabeth 213
Cumann na nGaedheal 107, 148, 227
Cushing, Richard J. 194

D'Alton, Cardinal John 194
Dáil Éireann 84, 92, 103, 172, 182, 198,
    203-204, 264-266
Daly, John 156-158, 161
Daly, Michael 123
Darby, John 120-121, 124
de Valera, Eamon 17-18, 21, 23, 26-29,
    32, 35, 44-45, 48, 66, 71, 84, 95, 103,
    141, 144, 178-179, 182, 188-189, 195,
    204, 206-208, 218-219, 230, 255-257
Deale, Kenneth 147, 156-157
Deeney, James 118, 122, 127-128, 131-
    132
DeLillo, Don 250
Dempsey, J. F. 175, 182
Derry 22, 219
Devlin, Anne 234
Dillon, Gerard 36, 47
Donegal 51, 89, 119, 125, 131, 154, 170,
    235
Donoghue, Denis 38
Dornan, P. F. 169, 171
Dublin 11-14, 17, 19, 32-33, 35-42, 48,
    62, 70, 75, 82, 88, 92, 96, 108, 121-
    122, 127, 131, 135, 143, 147, 151-
    152, 154, 158, 160-161, 163, 168,
    170, 172, 174, 176, 178-181, 183-190,
    194-196, 199, 204-205, 238, 253-254,
    256-260, 262-270, 272
Dublin Magazine 41-42, 226
Dulles, John Foster 189, 191-194

Economic Development 45, 80, 86, 103,
    107, 111, 116, 177, 206
Eisenhower, Dwight D. 189, 191, 193,
    196, 201-202
Eliot, T. S. 38-39
Elliman, Jacob 253
Emigration 12-13, 17-19, 21, 31, 44-45,
    48, 54, 57, 68, 71-104, 129-132, 135-
    136, 140-142, 144, 146, 153, 164,
    166, 176-177, 202, 205, 208-209, 211,
    218-223, 225-235, 237-239, 243, 249-
    250, 252-254, 257, 267, 270-272
Envoy 34, 42
Europe 12, 17-18, 27-29, 36, 38, 81, 105,
    109-110, 112, 114-115, 117, 122, 136,
    166, 168, 171, 176, 184, 186-188,
    191, 195, 198, 203-204, 208, 218,
    252, 255, 257

Fahey, Denis 255, 259
Fallon, Pádraic 44
Fanning, Patrick 120
Fianna Fáil 22, 34, 45, 88, 103, 105, 107,
    109, 164, 172, 182, 208, 227, 255,
    258
Fianna Gael 45
Fiat 259
FitzGerald, Garret 110, 176
Flower, Robin 48, 69
Flynn, Cecil 152-153
Flynn, Dr Michael P. 131
Fógra Fáilte 172-176, 178
Ford, Mary 215
France 36, 112-113, 195
Freedman, Ethel 254
Friel, Brian 223, 235, 243
Frost, Robert 38

Gabay, Zvi 267
Gaeltacht 46, 49-52, 54, 56, 60, 67, 69,
    99-100
Gageby, Douglas 41
Galway 14, 33, 89-90, 94, 119, 124-125,
    131, 133, 143, 208, 230, 239-240, 261
Garret, George 184, 188
Germany 36, 108, 110, 112-113, 195,
    202, 226, 271
Gilbourne, Kathleen 158-159
Gilmartin, Archbishop Thomas 150
Glass, Annie 254
Goldring, Maurice 225
Gordon, Mary 213
Gray, David 188
Grimes, John 211

Hamill, Pete 216
Hanrahan, Dr 133
Haughey, Charles 45
Hayes, Fr John 142
Healy, John 135, 146
Hearne, John 189-190, 198
Heaney, Seamus 222
Hemingway, Ernest 26, 38
Hendriks, Ritchie 37
Herzog, Chaim 254
Herzog, Isaac 254-255, 272
Herzog, Jacob 254
Hess, Evelyn 130
Hillery, Patrick 45
Hughes, Declan 250
Hughes, John 210

IRA 22, 29, 176, 199, 219, 241, 244, 258
Irish Catholic 21, 23
Irish Echo 211, 213, 218
Irish Housewives Association 88, 92, 140
Irish Independent 23, 88, 194
Irish Press 21-23, 41, 43, 88, 129, 144, 263
Irish Times 23, 31, 35, 40-41, 88, 93, 157, 176, 178, 180-181, 199
Israel 19, 112, 252-255, 257-272
Italy 81, 171, 195

Jabotinsky, Aladimir 255-256
Johnson, Lyndon B. 199
Joyce, Dr 131, 133
Joyce, James 29, 33, 180, 223-224, 226, 239

Kavanagh, Patrick 31, 42-43
Keane, John B. 238
Keating, Mary Frances 142
Keating, Seán 37, 47
Kelly, Anna 47, 144-145
Kelly, Charles E. 140
Kelly, Oisín 36, 47
Kennedy, John F. 40, 187, 194-195, 197-200, 202-204, 212, 232
Kenney, W. John 188
Kerr, James J. 154-155
Kerry 15, 48, 53, 62-65, 68, 89, 96, 119, 125, 131, 139, 166, 169, 240
  Blaskets 17, 48-54, 57-58, 60-71
Keveny, Fr Martin 219
Keynes, John Maynard 106, 108-110
Kiely, Benedict 30, 34, 47
Kiernan, Thomas J. 197-198, 202
Kilkenny 13, 15, 93, 215
Kingsmill-Moore, T. C. 160
Kingston, Richard 38

Labour party 17, 22, 36, 45
Lavin, Mary 230-231
Lee, J. J. 84-85, 107, 221, 228, 232, 250-251
Leitrim 92, 119, 123
Lemass, Seán 17, 45, 80, 85-86, 114, 164, 166, 172-175, 177-179, 182-186, 194, 196, 199, 237
Leydon, John 164, 183, 185
Limerick 32, 259
Little, Patrick 178
Living Art movement 36-38
Lodge, Henry Cabot 193
Longley, Michael 39
Lucey, Cornelius 33, 91, 95, 145

Lyons, F. S. 233

MacAmhlaigh, Dónall 13-15, 18
Macardle, Dorothy 138
MacBride, Seán 35, 171, 184, 195, 258-259, 264
MacClelland, Alan 180
MacDonald, Norman 130
MacEntee, Seán 128
MacGonigal, Maurice 36
Macken, Walter 236, 238, 240, 243-245, 250
MacLeod, Iain 129-130
MacMahon, Bryan 16-18, 135, 139, 238
MacManus, Francis 44
Macmillan, Harold 197
MacNeice, Louis 38-39, 44
MacNeill, Major Gen. Hugh 179
MacPartlend, Dr 125
Madden, Deirdre 236
Mahon, Derek 39
Maria Duce 259
Marsh, Arnold 142
Marshall Aid 110, 166, 178, 188
Matthews, Francis P. 188
Maynooth 35, 106, 148
McCann, Colum 223
McCarthy, Conor 237
McCarthy, Joe 189
McCon, C. F. 124
McCrory, Moy 235
McDermott, Alice 213, 216
McDowell, William 188
McGahern, John 235, 248
McGilligan, Patrick 166-168, 263
McGrath, John 154
McGuinness, Jim 41
McGuinness, Norah 36
McGuire, Edward 38
McPolin, James 129
McQuaid, John Charles 26, 33-34, 259-264
McQuillan, Jack 35, 174
McWilliam, F. E. 36
Miller, Paul 172
Moloney, Mary 151-152, 158, 160-161
Monaghan 154, 221
Moore, Brian 243
Moore, George 42
Moore, Henry 37
Moore, Marianne 38
Morrissey, Daniel 167-168, 171-172, 183, 208
Moser, Peter 140, 143-145
Murphy, Jimmy 235

Murphy, Seán 268-270
Murphy, Tom 121, 223, 236, 238, 245-246, 250-251
Murray, Edmund 141-142, 144

National Gallery 37
New Yorker 38
Newman, W. A. 41
Northern Ireland 22, 39, 117, 170, 176, 186, 195-196, 199, 218-219, 236, 253
Norton, William 174-176
Nunan, Seán 189-190, 198
Nurock, Max 254, 271
Nurock, Rachel 254
Nurock, William 254

Ó Cadhain, Máirtín 46
Ó Conaire, Pádraig 233-234
Ó Criomhthain, Tomás 48, 68
Ó Direáin, Máirtín 46
Ó Faoláin, Seán 25, 28-30, 33-34, 42, 47, 142, 223-224, 229-230
Ó Fearacháin, Roibeárd 44
Ó Móráin, Dónall 46
Ó Riada, Seán 46-47
Ó Ríordáin, Seán 46-47
Ó Súilleabháin, Muiris 48
O'Brien, Conor Cruise 190
O'Brien, Edna 223, 236
O'Brien, Eldon 145
O'Brien, Flann/Brian O'Nolan/Myles na Goplaeen 31, 35, 43, 47
O'Brien, George 88, 221, 263
O'Brien, J. P. 164-166, 174
O'Brien, Kate 47
O'Callaghan, Fr Donald 213
O'Casey, Seán 180, 224, 226
O'Connor, Joe 221, 223, 233-234
O'Connor, Cardinal John 219
O'Connor, Edwin 217
O'Connor, Frank 28, 34, 44, 224
O'Doherty, M. K. 168-169
O'Donnell, Peadar 42
O'Driscoll, T. J. 175, 185
O'Dwyer, Paul 214
O'Dwyer, William 210, 214
O'Flaherty, Liam 224, 226-227, 229, 231
O'Hara, Gerald 188
O'Kelly, Seán T. 179, 187, 200-202
O'Malley, Donogh 45
O'Malley, Tony 15, 18
O'Meara, P. B. 126-127
O'Neill, Terence 199
O'Rahilly, Alfred 35
O'Regan, Brendan 169, 171, 181, 185

O'Reilly, Helen 147, 159
O'Sullivan Seamus 41-42
O'Sullivan, Seán 36, 47
O'Toole, Fintan 233, 238, 245-246

Palestine 252-258, 260, 262, 272
Plunkett, James 32, 44
Pound, Ezra 38-39
Pozzy, T. J. 168
Price, Dorothy 128
Programme for Economic Expansion 45, 80, 86, 177

Quinlan, W. F. 166

Radio Éireann 40, 44, 203, 218
Reid, Nano 36
Reid, Fr Seán 215
RHA 37, 179
Robinson, Paschal 256
Roche, Anthony 245, 250
Roosevelt, Franklin D. 188
Roscommon 119, 125, 131, 139
Rose Tattoo, The 180
Rose, R. S. 153, 160
Rusk, Dean 194, 202
Ryan, James 19, 103
Ryan, John 42

Salinger, J. D. 38
Samuel, Sir Herbert 254, 262-264
Saroyan, William 38
Sayers, Peig 48, 68
Scannell, Brendan 267
Scott, Patrick 36
Scott, William 36
Sheehy, T. J. 168
Sheridan, John D. 139, 142, 145
Shertock, Mose 258
Sligo 96, 119, 125, 135
Smith, Al 210, 212
Smith, Brendan 180
Smyllie, R. M. 31, 41, 47
Smyth, Gerry 225
Solomons, Edwin 260-264
Souter, Camille 38
Spellman, Cardinal Francis 193, 210, 212, 263
Steinberg, J. S. 267-269
Stevens, Wallace 38
Storey, Sam 129
Stross, Dr Barnett 130
Swanzy, Mary 36
Swift, Patrick 36

Taft, William H. 200
Thomas, Dylan 26, 44
Thomson, George 48
Tóstal, An 178-182, 186
Tourist Association 164, 167-168, 171-172, 174-175
Tourist Board 90, 165-170, 172-175, 178-181
Travers, Pauric 145
Treston, Dan 44
Trevor, William 235
Trippe, Juan 178
Truman, Harry S. 188, 195, 198, 263
Tuberculosis 15, 19, 125-134

Vanishing Irish 16, 81, 141, 144-145
Waddington, Victor 37
Wall, Mervyn 44

Ward, Con 127
Weizmann, Chaim 256, 265
Wexford 15, 17, 21-22, 24-25, 29, 44, 221
Whitaker, T. K. 45, 52, 80, 86, 107, 114, 206, 237
White, W. J. 40
Wicklow 15
Williams, Christopher 151-152, 158, 160-161

Yeats, W. B. 39, 42, 222, 224

Zion News 256

Also available from
Mercier Press

MICHAEL COLLINS AND THE MAKING OF THE IRISH STATE
edited by Gabriel Doherty and Dermot Keogh

Collins has generally been portrayed in writing and film as a revolutionary guerrilla leader, a military tactician and a figure of great personal charm, courage and ingenuity. This collection of essays challenges that over-simplified view. *Michael Collins and the Making of the Irish State* is a professional evaluation of Michael Collins and his contribution to the making of the Irish state, which brings to light his multifaceted and complex character.

With contributions from many leading historians working in the field, and written in an accessible style, the essays make full use of archival material and provide new findings and insights into the life and times of Michael Collins.

DE VALERA'S IRELANDS
edited by Gabriel Doherty and Dermot Keogh

The years of influence of de Valera are central to this interpretation of post-independence Ireland. De Valera has been made to shoulder personal responsibility for many of the defects in Irish society in that period. The essays in this book seek to re-examine and re-evaluate that charge.

Contributors include: Owen Dudley Edwards, Caitriona Clear, Brian P. Kennedy, John McGahern, Gearóid Ó Tuathaigh and Garret FitzGerald.

THE COURSE OF IRISH HISTORY
edited by T. W. Moody and F. X. Martin

A revised and enlarged version of this classic book provides a rapid short survey, with geographical introduction, of the whole course of Ireland's history. Based on a series of television programmes, it is designed to be both popular and authoritative, concise but comprehensive, highly selective but balanced and fair-minded, critical but constructive and sympathetic. A distinctive feature is its wealth of illustrations.